# THE GRAMMAR OF ROCK

# THE
# GRAMMAR
# OF ROCK

ART AND ARTLESSNESS IN
20TH CENTURY POP LYRICS

by Alexander Theroux

Fantagraphics Books
7563 Lake City Way NE
Seattle, Washington 98115

Editor: Gary Groth
Design: Emory Liu
Editorial Assistants: Kristy Valenti, Gavin Lees,
Kara Krewer, Anna Pederson
Associate Publisher: Eric Reynolds
Publishers: Gary Groth and Kim Thompson

To receive a free full-color catalog of comics, graphic novels, prose novels,
artist monographs, and other fine works of high artistry, call 1-800-657-1100,
or visit www.fantagraphics.com. You may order books at our web site or by phone.

ISBN: 978-1-60699-616-4

First Fantagraphics Books printing: February, 2013

for Sarah

always the song in my heart

"Here was Beauty and here was Nowhere."
— Dionne Brand

Rock 'n' roll music, any old way you choose it, is one of the things I know I will most miss when I'm on my way out. I love it, and have from the beginning, even its attractive imbecilities. Growing up, I had in my room a favorite clunky red plastic radio, which I always kept low, listening to pop music and rock 'n' roll while I also attended to less important matters like translating Latin and memorizing French vocabulary. I enjoyed the music but tended to concentrate on the lyrics, which I took more or less as a form of reading. It may have been a form of transferal. I did not mind all the nonsense really. There was no end to it, for one thing; deliberate lunacies often made a song what it was. Then, what could you do about it? I accepted pretty much everything. Nothing "country," of course, which to me, even in the 8th grade, seemed as sad and moronic as the stupid hats and loud shirts worn by the people who sang it. This is not a snobservation, only a personal confession of what I felt. What I particularly enjoyed — even found myself listening for over the years — were certain phrases and squibs in various songs, usually hip, that compiling in my mind, could be read as a documentary of slang's (and somehow paraliteracy's) progress, if not in modern America, then at least in my own school and among my just as passionate friends. Longfellow's *Evangeline* and Alfred Noyes's "The Highwayman" were poetry. This was real life.

I remember, for instance, deliberating what Chuck Berry meant us to understand in the song "School Days" when he sang:

> Back in the classroom, open your books,
> Cheat, but the teacher don't know I mean she looks.

Unfortunately, that is exactly how the line goes. But my young friends and I spent weeks debating other possibilities. I believed for the longest time it was, "Ah, but the teacher don't know how mean she looks," while a buddy insisted it went, "Even the teacher don't like her mangy looks." An article in *Goldmine* (Jan. 29, 1988) cites Chuck Berry's "powerful facility for letter-perfect encapsulation," which is generally true, although for reasons of rhyme he is often forced to throw in not only the odd semi-enclitical phrase, such as in the word-salad cited above or the line "watch her look at her run, boys" in "Sweet Little Sixteen," but as in the song "No Money Down" even to reverse them:

> I want power steering and power brakes,
> I want a powerful motor with a *jet-off take*,
> I want air conditioning, I want automatic heat,
> I want a full Murphy bed in my back seat.

Slang, thought Walt Whitman, was, creatively, "the lawless...element... behind all poetry," its beating heart, frankly, the outlaw spark of poetic wonder. The lawless germinal element of it thrilled him, for he saw it was the "wholesome fermentation or eructation of those processes eternally active in language, by which froth and specks are thrown up, mostly to pass away; though occasionally to settle and permanently chrystallize [sic]." In the wild, demotic use of "undocumented language" which Whitman was forever celebrating he found "an attempt of common humanity to escape from bald literalism and express itself illimitably, which in highest walks produces poets and poems, and doubtless in pre-historic times gave the start to, and perfected, the whole immense tangle of the old mythologies." It was in verbal fecundity that the Good Gray Poet found a renewing inclusiveness, and it became his delight to introduce into the national idiom the parlance of everyday life and labor, for, as he said, "around the markets, among the fish smacks, along the wharves, you hear a thousand words, never yet printed in the repertoire of any lexicon."

Creative illiteracy, of course, goes back even before 1945, to the very beginnings of rock 'n' roll — long before pop music became whitened and mechanized. Cootie Williams's "Juicehead Blues." Rufus Thomas's "Bear Cat." John Lee Hooker's "Crawling Kingsnake." "Rocket 88" by Jackie Brenston and his Delta Cats. Louis Jordan's "That Chick's Too Young To Fry." Elmore James's "Dust My Broom." The Clovers' "Your Cash Ain't Nothin' but Trash." Stick McGhee's "One Monkey Don't Stop No Show." Jelly Roll Morton's "If You Don't Shake, You Don't Get No Cake." Amos Milburn's "Chicken Shack Boogie." But this was all part of a deep and heartfelt soulfully and stylistically undiluted folk tradition, vocal harmonies and gentle wails and shouted blues, born of a slavery that prevented even a smidgen of education for 400 years. The dreamers, the romantics among us — or is it the romantic in each of us? — will perspicaciously add that such words and phrases can be properly turned only in a moment of true inspiration, when we have lost our self-conscious, calculating natures and can thereby express our authentic selves. (Although I am frankly still a bit doubtful about that conspicuously infralogical line from the so-called "Negro national anthem," composed in 1900 by J. Rosamond Johnson — his brother James wrote the words — "Lift Every Voice and Sing:" "Sing a song full of hope that the future has brought us.")

A whole vocabulary — in one sense, an entire language — has come from such music and the pioneering black radio stations (like WERD in Atlanta, WYLD in New Orleans, WLOU in Louisville, WDIA in Memphis, known throughout the South as the "Mother Station of the Negroes," etc.) that in the late '40s and '50s pushed and played it, and consequently we've been left a lovely great catalogue of finger-poppin' R&B words like "hincty," "zoo-zoos," "whuppin'," "juicehead," "poontang," "shag on down," "hamfat," "gleeby," "mogatin'," "grind," "motorvatin'," "lickin' stick," "jelly roll," "scronch," "poppa-stoppa, "ditty," "good booty," "spo-dee-o-dee," "3 x 7," "black cat bone," "cross-cut saw," "the Sip," "honey dripper," "gutbucket," "haints," "ash haulin'," "stavin' chain," "coon can," and, among many others,[1] the unique word "meekin" (cuckolding would be my guess).

Meekin. Other folks' girls. The slang and sass seems called for. Spice. *Sass*. We hear it in the Cadillacs' 1956 hit song, "Speedoo,"

> Well now they often call me Speedoo
> But my real name is Mister Earl
> Always meekin' brand new fellas
> And takin' other folks' girls.

Lyrics, charming and naïve, represent a certain primitivism — what Richard Goldstein in *The Poetry of Rock* calls "accidental art" — particularly in his innocent notion that poetry and verse should rhyme and that all rhythmic spaces should be filled, even if filling them necessitates juggling words or even the creation of new ones. His work is expressly functional, resulting in, because born of, simplicity. In "Too Much Monkey Business," for example, every verse rhymes, and when words cannot fill the existing spaces, the artist dexterously fills them with a flexible "aah," which concludes each verse-change each time one is verbalized. In one case they imply a sigh of disgust and in another a type of sullen indignation. The language of Berry's verses may be ordinary, but he employs it naturally and without phony attitudinizing, although if I had my druthers I'd still prefer those unexpected malaprops one suddenly hears in the shouted songs and soulful blues and mournful strumming pleas of greats like Waters, Little Walter, Howlin' Wolf, Son House, James Cotton. Blind Lemon Jefferson, Bukka White, Mississippi John Hurt, Charley Patton, Roosevelt Sykes, Mance Lipscomb, Memphis Minnie, Big Joe Williams, T. Bone Walker, and, especially, Sonny Boy Williamson, as, for instance, in his "It's Sad To Be Alone" ("...so sad to be lonesome too much *unconvinion* to be alone") or in "Let Your Conscience Be Your Guide" ("...you have a strong *consistution*") or in "Have You Ever Been in Love" ("heavy-*hipted* woman.") [My italics]

---

1    The evocative adjective, "funky" cannot legitimately be listed here as an original example of black hippitude, since Charles Dickens was the first to use the word in *The Posthumous Papers of the Pickwick Club* (1836).

One wants to consecrate the old Highway 61, the migratory road — 1,400 miles, paralleling the lazy Mississippi River — that stretched from the Mississippi delta to the Canadian border, carrying all those black singers to Chicago and points north in search of the promised land. Guys like blues legend Robert Johnson learned to play listening to other blues greats on the creaky old porches of sharecropper shacks. But with the advent of the mechanical cotton picker in 1944, plantations gave way to bigger business — a bale of cotton (500 pounds) cost planters $39.41 to pick by hand, and $5.26 by machine — and farm laborers, most of them black, began to stream north. Sharecropping became obsolete in an instant. Between 1910 and 1970 more than 12 million Southerners pulled up stakes to move and settle in the North, mainly in the industrial Northwest and Midwest. A running ribbon, old Highway 61 rolled on past the birthplaces and homes of such Southern music greats as Muddy Waters, Son House, Elvis Presley, and Charley Patton. It had long been sung about, dreamed of, ridden hard, even died on. Bessie Smith, the "Empress of the Blues," met her tragic death in a bad automobile accident on Highway 61, and one of its travelers, Robert Johnson, was even said to have sold his soul to the devil at the crossroads of US 61 and US 49, specifically in the town of Rosedale, just down from rustic Clarksdale where guitars on a highway grid now serve his memory as a historical marker. Johnson had been born in Hazlehurst, and his grave is supposedly in Quito (near Itta Bena), but the town of Rosedale figures in the lyrics for one of Johnson's most famous songs, "Traveling Riverside Blues": "Lord, I'm goin' to Rosedale," he wails, "gon' take my rider by my side." *My rider* — could that have been Old Scratch himself? Oooo-weee-ooo! It is amazing that that one blues song of Johnson's, "Traveling Riverside Blues," has had a major influence on rock-n-roll: Eric Clapton remade it as "Crossroads," but Led Zeppelin also covered it, notoriously — commemorially? — purloining a line from it for "Lemon Song:" "You can squeeze my lemon 'til the juice runs down my leg."

Rolf Potts on his blog *Vagabonding*, visiting Roseland and having lunch at Leo's Market, where the Crossroads Blues Society is headquartered sitting alongside Highway 1 where Highway 8 intersects, explains that a waitress there handed him a wrinkled, typewritten transcription of a "vision" about Johnson's fateful moment that had appeared to bluesman Henry Goodman as he was traveling the lonely road from Rosedale to Anguila. The hair-raising story, "Meeting with the Devil at the Crossroads"[2], is a gem of scary hoodoo giving a detailed account how in the moonlight on a dark October night, having been playing down in Yazoo City and over at Beulah and now trying to get back up to Helena, walking

2       http://www.vagablogging.net/robert-johnson-sold-his-soul-to-the-devil-in-rosedale-mississippi.html

along, Johnson suddenly encountered a tall, barrel-chested stranger, "black as the forever-closed eyes of Robert Johnson's stillborn baby," sitting by the way whose dog lets out "a low, long soulful moan, a howling like never heard before, rhythmic, syncopated grunts, yelps, and barks, seizing Robert Johnson like a Grand Mal and causing the strings on his guitar suddenly to vibrate, hum, and sing with a sound dark and blue, beautiful, soulful chords and notes possessing Robert Johnson, taking him over, spinning him around, losing him inside of his own self, wasting him, lifting him up into the sky... Johnson looks over in the ditch and sees the eyes of the dog reflecting the bright moonlight or, more likely so it seems to Robert Johnson, glowing on their own, a deep violet penetrating glow, and Robert Johnson knows and feels that he is staring into the eyes of a Hellhound as his body shudders from head to toe."

"I got to have that sound, Devil-Man. That sound is mine. Where do I sign?" The man says, "You ain't got a pencil, Robert Johnson. Your word is good enough. All you got to do is keep walking north. But you better be prepared. There are consequences." "Prepared for what, Devil-man?" "You know where you are, Robert Johnson? You are standing in the middle of the crossroads. At midnight, that full moon is right over your head. You take one more step, you'll be in Rosedale. You take this road to the east, you'll get back over to Highway 61 in Cleveland, or you can turn around and go back down to Beulah or just go to the west and sit up on the levee and look at the River. But if you take one more step in the direction you're headed, you going to be in Rosedale at midnight under this full October moon, and you are going to have the Blues like never known to this world. My left hand will be forever wrapped around your soul, and your music will possess all who hear it. That's what's going to happen. That's what you better be prepared for. Your soul will belong to me. This is not just any crossroads. I put this 'X' here for a reason, and I been waiting on you." Robert Johnson rolls his head around, his eyes upwards in their sockets to stare at the blinding light of the moon which has now completely filled tie pitch-black Delta night, piercing his right eye like a bolt of lightning as the midnight hour hits. He looks the big man squarely in the eyes and says, "Step back, Devil-Man, I'm going to Rosedale. I *am* the Blues." The man moves to one side and says, "Go on, Robert Johnson. You the King of the Delta Blues. Go on home to Rosedale. And when you get on up in town, you get you a plate of hot tamales because you going to be needing something on your stomach where you're headed."

Chuck Berry knew Johnson's "Come On In My Kitchen," "Kind Hearted Woman Blues," "I Believe I'll Dust My Broom," "Cross Road Blues," "Terraplane Blues," "Last Fair Deal Gone Down," and "Hellhound on my Trail," which became a moderate regional hit, selling about 5,000 copies. Berry, like the great bluesmen from Mississippi, had no education. Why would that matter? While still a high school student, he was serving a prison sentence for armed robbery between 1944 and 1947. On his release, he then settled into married life while working at an automobile assembly plant. But many great songwriters had no schooling. Hank Williams, who, according to the critic Tony Scherman, "might be the only country-music artist to whom the term genius fully applies," was also uneducated and, like ninety percent of the blues singers, read nothing more erudite than copies of *Billboard* and comic books. But Chuck wasn't lazy, never repeated pronouns, and in his lyrics always looked for the identifiable and, above all, concrete — splendidly concrete — detail. Rock rolled right off of his tongue. "The coolerator was crammed with TV dinners and ginger ale."

Curiously, as has often been pointed out, that there is very little *black* about Chuck Berry's songs. The closest he comes to any hipness on-stage is doing his famous duck walk — "scooting" is his word for it. His lyrics are heard to be comprehensible because in a strange way he is as much country as rock-and-roll. He knew where the money was and, wanting to break into the world, to capture the white listening-audience, was not averse to writing lyrics with references to cross-racial experience or to relying on the kind of crisp, understandable diction everyone could understand. "I wrote songs white people could buy," Chuck sagaciously declares, "because that's nine pennies out of every dime. That was my goal, see: to look at my bankbook and see a million dollars." His lyrics are frankly right out of *Archie* and *Jughead* comic books and deal broadly with fast cars, malt shops, high school hops, girls named Betty, autograph books, ice-cream sodas, mad teenage crushes, dogmatic parents, and Fabian faces. "School Days" and "Sweet Little Sixteen" have little to do with the idiosyncratic black experience — certainly not the world of Louis Jordan or Wynonie Harris, Phil Flowers or Little Hilton, Bessie Smith or Laverne Baker, whom when she was younger they used to call the "Yas Yas Girl," a phrase which had its scatological origins in a slang-song called "Duck's Yas Yas." It was a great jukebox race-song, real low down, and went in part, "Mama bought a chicken, mistook it for a duck, stuck it on the table with the legs straight up. Yonder comes sister with a spoon and a glass, catch the gravy drippin' from the yas yas yas." Shocking?

Are you aware that there was once a popular song in this country, "I Reach For You," written by Dana Suisse, in which the word "*as*" in the line, "I reach for you, as I reach for a star," had to be changed to the word "like" — I promise, I am not making this up — in order that the ambiguity, "I reach for your ass, I reach for a star," could be avoided and not offend the ears of any delicate listener?

But in certain songs there was indeed chicanery in lyrics, and a good deal of the wink-wink, nudge-nudge variety was certainly going on in the lyrics of those early so-called "race" songs. Most black hipsters back in the '20s and '30s pretty much knew what the word "jelly-roll" meant in the scatological department, understood the street meaning of "good booty," dug the significance of such lines as "I'm like a one-eyed cat peepin' in a seafood store" and "I'm a back-door man" and "Got my mojo workin'." When vaudeville and cabaret-singer, Mamie Smith, in "Going Crazy with the Blues" sang of her "applesauce" and "cookies," no one misguessed about that either. Neither were they particularly confounded by what Bessie Smith meant when she salaciously referred to her "lock and key" in the 1927 song with that same title, nor by what "tutti frutti" meant when ticklingly sung by "Little Richard" Penniman in that mid-1950s hit. I remember the thrill of seeing Little Richard looking utterly wild in *The Girl Can't Help It* (1956) wearing that loose grey silk suit with baggy trousers and banging on the piano, reminding me of the Consul Sulla's prescient warning to his aristocratic party, as recorded by Suetonius' *De Vita Caesaurum* — Caesar always, decadently, wore his toga *fluxiore cinctura* (with a loose binding) — "Beware of that boy with the loose clothes." Caesar was also mocked by Cicero for fastidiously wearing a belt over that very loose senatorial tunic — it sported a cocky broad stripe and fringed sleeves that reached down to his wrists — a style that, to many, seemed effeminate, prissy, and unique.

Sexuality played a significant role in blues music. Colorful metaphors of "jelly rolls," "peach trees," "handy men," and others were widely used to veil thinly frank talk of sexual desire and satisfaction. The emphasis on sexual satisfaction for women was itself radical in the 1920s. Do you recognize the name Bo Carter (born Armenter Chatmon) who was an active member of the Mississippi Sheiks, best remembered for their hit, "Sitting on Top of the World"? He did the original recording of "Corinna, Corrina" in 1928, the song which later hit big for Big Joe Turner. The titles of some of his bawdy songs — all from the 1930s — give a good idea of the double entendre: "Banana in Your Fruit Basket," "Please Warm my Wiener," "My Pencil Won't Write No More," "Don't Mash My Digger So Deep," "Let Me Roll Your Lemon," "Pussy Cat Blues," "Pig Meat Is What I Crave," "What Kind Of Scent Is This?" "The Ins and Outs of my Girl," "Mashing That Thing," "It's Too Wet Pin In Your Cushion," "Your Biscuits Are Big Enough for Me," and "Ram Rod Daddy." He was a Delta Blues legend whose instincts for poetry were as strong as they were for Robinson Jeffers. This was before white teenagers were tuning in. There was Barbara Carr's "Bone Me Like You Own Me," Dinah Washington's "Big Long Slidin' Thing," Todd Rhodes' "Rockett

69," Bullmoose Jackson's "Big Ten Inch," saucy songs right up there with the trademark remarks of Mae West's early-career vaudeville performances like "I'm the kinda girl who works for Paramount by day, and Fox all night" and "I feel like a million tonight—but only one at a time."

Language — brash private jive — was an African-American kick, served up with speed and brassy rectitude. Women singers were, if anything, even raunchier than the men. "Credit" for the filthiest blues ever recorded is in fact unanimously awarded to Lucille Bogan (a.k.a. Bessie Jackson) who was known for her extremely risqué material. Under the name of Jackson, Bogan recorded "B.D. [Bull Dyke] Women's Blues" in 1935. "Bulldaggers or Bull Dykes," she insisted, "can lay their jive just like a natural man/ B.D. women sure is rough/ they drink up many a whiskey/ and sure can strut their stuff." Her song "Shave 'Em Dry, Part II" was equaled for its forthrightness only by Derek and Clive in the '70s. Her record company issued a cleaned-up version of the song, but even this was too much for many listeners, and her career came to an end shortly after its release. It was not only black singers, either. Customers used to flock to Big Jim Colosimo's Café, a flashy joint at 2126 South Wabash St. in Chicago that was owned by the thug who reigned as lord of all the city's vice and gambling, simply to hear Sophie Tucker sing "Angle Worm Wiggle," a song that was so suggestive — and she helped to vivify it with gestures — that she once got arrested.

You have not lived until you have heard Tampa Red's "Let Me Play With Your Poodle," Blind Boy Fuller's "Sweet Honey Hole," Jimmie Gordon's "Bed Spring Blues," Big Bill Broonzy's "How You Want It Done," and songs like Texas-born Victoria ("Sweet Peas") Spivey's "Black Snake Blues,"

> I been savin' up since I doan' know when
> I ain't playin' Santy Claus to any men
> This little thing I ain't gonna abuse it
> If I ever get broke I certn'y can use it…

The incontestable fact remains that to know what the lyrics of those blues songs meant or to understand what a supercalifragilisticexpialidocious mojo was or to discern the hidden sexual meanings that could be found in almost all of them did not exactly require an advanced degree from Princeton. We poor unreconstructable honkies eventually had our own lyrical, if secret, embedments, I suppose. Billy Joel's song "Uptown Girl" is supposedly — can be — about anal sex. The old "Row, Row, Row" is about sex, they say. I have heard the same thing about "Tip Toe through the Tulips" and "I'm Forever Blowing Bubbles" and

"Bye Bye Blackbird," but who can honestly know? I am told that Bob Dylan's "I Want You" is about heroin. It was constantly blabbed about that the Beatles' "Lucy in the Sky with Diamonds" is about LSD. Do you find that so strange? Cole Porter's "Pilot Me" is about Charles Lindbergh and fucking, according to show-biz critic Rex Reed. And I am convinced that the old hobo ballad, "The Wabash Cannonball," a favorite of hillbilly singers in the 1930s, is smirkingly — in spite of the notorious gender-confusion of the lyrics, where the famous choo-choo is alternately referred to as "she" and "he" — is about the sexual athleticism of a big stud. How can anyone sing the third verse without catching its innuendo?

> She was coming from Atlanta
> on a cold December day.
> As she rolled into the station,
> I could hear a woman say,
> "He's mighty big and handsome
> and sure did make me fall,
> He's a-coming toward me
> on the Wabash Cannonball."

All the while we lucky whites had "Moon River" ("It all happened on the white keys," admitted composer Henry Mancini, who although his soul was small he sold it for cash to Hollywood) and the Fontane Sisters' old, arthritic "Hearts of Stone" with its hokey refrain, literally "Doo doo wah, doo doo wah," Rosemary Clooney's 1950s hit, "Botch-A-Me" — why tax lard-assed uninformed Americans with having to know the *actual* Italian word for kiss? — and Kay Starr's cheesy "Rock and Roll Waltz" ("One, two, and then rock; one, two, and then roll"). I remember certain old singers now more for their TV commercials than for their singing, sadly enough, Rosemary Clooney promoting Coronet paper towels ("They're from Geoooorgia-*Pacific!*") and Dinah Shore for Chevrolet ("Seeee the Yew Ess Ay in your Chevrolet"). Was Joni Mitchell correct when she observed, less than charitably, that "all 'whitey' knows is funeral and war marches and the polka"? Didn't any of those anti-musicological drabsters from the dull, primordial 1950s who in the 1980s were all sitting around waiting for Elvis to re-appear ever realize that even back in 1938 a song had already come and gone that was groovier than what they were singing — "Rock It For Me" (words and music by Kay and Sue Werner)? Just to make manifest that *some* coolness was available even then (and notice, the verb *rock* was used as it would be for the next eighty years), it began:

I used to spend my nights at op'ras
Listening to the arias of Pagliacci,
But now you couldn't get me to an opera
Since I've made this new discovery

Refrain:
I heard there came to town
A new rhythm thriller, Done up brown,
It really is a killer,
Now I'm all thru with symphonies,
Oh! ROCK IT FOR ME...?

What malediction specific to our age, on the other hand, gave us the memorable Pat Boone with his version of "Tutti Frutti," which Columbia Records appropriated from Little Richard and dopily sanitized to give Eisenhower's America the white-bread version they would not be put off or offended by? "I had to change the lyrics to several of Little Richard's songs...part of 'Tutti Frutti' went 'Boy, you don't know what she's doing to me.' I just couldn't sing that," the dauntless, ever-creative Boone manfully confessed years later, "so I sang, 'Pretty little Susie is the girl for me.' It worked just as well. The kids didn't care. I mean, they were not listening to the words much anyway." That was the 1950s.

That was back in the days when Sinatra, weighing in on the early music of Elvis, found it wanting. "His music is deplorable, a rancid-smelling aphrodisiac," said Frankie when the King hit it big. "It's the most brutal, ugly, degenerate, vicious form of expression it has been my displeasure to hear."

But it had attitude, it had drive, it had the beat.

Oh, and variety, we had that, too. Some of it even made sense. Creative stretch. Real reach. But some of that variety was of the sort that we could not quite identify. "Under the Boardwalk" is a tango, the Drifters' "Save the Last Dance for Me" a mambo. Does that come as a surprise to you? So is "Rumble" a mambo, that thumping song from the Bernstein and Sondheim musical, *West Side Story*. (The bad-ass 1958 instrumental of the same name by Link Wray and His Raymen, utilizing distortion and feedback — since described as the first song ever to use a power chord, the "major *modus operandi* of the modern rock guitarist" — is actually an overture, one long portentous announcement, but of what? A fistfight between gangs!) Helen O'Connell's "Green Eyes," way back in the '40s, was a rhumba, and the Andrews Sisters' hit, "Rum and Coca-Cola" pure calypso. Cole Porter's catchy "Well, Did You Evah!" from *High Society*, marked "Tempo di Polka" on the music sheet, turns out to be in fact a giddy gavotte. Tony Martin's "I Get Ideas" is a *tango-canción* (a tango with lyrics). I am still convinced that the Fleetwoods' "Tragedy" approximates a religious hymn — or comes very close to it. The Police's "Every Breath You Take" and Burt Bacharach's horrid lounge-core offering, "I Say A Little Prayer," two anemic efforts in music which never fail to remind me of the loss of taste and quality in pop music, seem to be sort of anthems for stalkers. Bacharach as a composer was artifice personified, at least to me. "In the song 'Alfie,' Bacharach, as usual, builds gorgeous vocal arches over a quagmire of verse," noted Ned Rorem in his *Pure Contraption*, "as also occurs to a lesser degree in Harvey Schmidt's 'Try to Remember,' Bobby Scott's 'A Taste of Honey,' [and] Jule Styne's 'People.'" Bacharach had anti-genius for writing — interminably — cheeseball music. He wrote a lot but far too much, obviously trying to make up in quantity — like poor, prolific Steve Allen, jack of all trades, master of none — what he lacked in quality. (On the other hand, Franz Schubert, who in one creative period of two years wrote 239 songs, composed rapidly, it seems, but did so remarkably well. But, hell, Fredrick Schiller Faust who wrote literary Westerns under the pen name Max Brand averaged a new book every four months for seventy-five years. I am also reminded in this matter of Rudolf Nureyev's answer to a reporter who asked the great dancer to assess out of the 250 performances he gave, how many he was happy with. Nureyev's answer? "Three.") Bacharach's "True Love Never Runs Smooth," accompanied as it is with hokey zither and accordion, is frankly a cha-cha. How different from Tommy Tucker's prelapsarian arrangements. Way back in high school I recall that at parties we used to dance the cha-cha — incongruously — to the brilliant wild-blue riffs of Tommy Tucker's "High Heel Sneakers" which offered the truly unforgettable line, "Put on yo' hah-heel sneakahs and yo' wig-hat on yo' haid."

But here, I do not want to appear a fanatical grammaticaster. Working on the presumption — I am assuming that you agree — that the proper use of grammar in any and all circumstances should involve the proper *construct*, its structure, its architecture, I would like to think that you also feel it should work toward comprehension on one level and the forces of moral necessity on another. I am convinced to some degree that writing about music is in a sort of flaccid sense like dancing about architecture. But it is surely important to try to consider some of the pitfalls of the craft, where it succeeds and where it does not — and to reach out a little bit further to try to find out why. The link between thought and language, reinforcing nothing less than the importance of connecting and communicating, operates in the name of right reason. It is pointed out by Henry Hitchings in his masterful *The Language Wars* that in the opening chapter of her famous novel *Uncle Tom's Cabin*, Harriet Beecher Stowe condemns on several levels the unscrupulous slave trader named Haley who wants to take Tom down river to sell him as chattel in the Deep South. Stowe is annoyed not only by that brute's would-be genteel "gaudy vest" and "flaunting tie" but also by what that garishness in cheap, loud, and immoderate terms seems vulgarly, dangerously, creepily to presage of his true villainous personality, rude manners, fractious behavior, and uncouth speech. Of Haley Mrs. Stowe, reporting from some height, notes "His conversation was in free and easy defiance of Murray's Grammar, and was garnished at convenient intervals with various profane expressions, which not even the desire to be graphic in our account shall induce us to transcribe."

Of all languages, music may be the most formidable. In music, above all, communication may find its most eloquent possibilities. "All art constantly aspires towards the condition of music," declared Walter Pater in *The Renaissance*. In other words, he puts forth the thesis that while all the arts seek to unify subject matter and form, music is the only art in which subject and form are seemingly one. Echoing that, Ezra Pound who was interested in music and once actually wrote an opera to the verse of François Villon — he liked to say that he learned his craft as a poet from Igor Stravinsky — remarked in his *ABC of Reading*, "Music rots when it gets too far from the dance. Poetry atrophies when it gets too far from music." It is the struggle to keep pure the power of words. Cognition is involved. We should care to know not only the nature of its language, its vocabulary, its grammar.

"The word grammar has a number of meanings," Hitchings goes on to say. "People speak of 'bad grammar' or 'correcting' someone's grammar as though there is agreement about what grammar itself is, but the word is elastic. One of the definitions provided in the single-volume *Oxford Dictionary of English* is 'a set of actual or presumed prescriptive notions about correct use of language,' and it is this aspect of grammar that excites most discussion and anxiety. 'Actual or presumed' gets to the heart of the matter: there are notions, and then there are the mere notions of notions. However theoretically pleasing they may be, the categories into which language is organized by grammarians are porous." One can speak or write grammatically without communicating in a pleasing or especially effective way, of course, and that is an ungainsayable fact. Variety in expression, moreover, can be defended, and feeling outrage may not be the same thing as being right in matters of grammatical correctness. Purism is often the mark of language in decline beyond that, Hitchings writes. He goes on to say, "Communicating on some level of agreed-upon speech cannot be denied as being important to, indeed crucial to, any nourishing, flourishing, flowering civilization. Language is mutable, in short. As American anthropologist Edward Sapir stated, 'All grammars leak.'" But traditions are crucial where the alternative is barbarism, and vincible ignorance should be abhorred. Elastic is fine. But spare me the chaos of any jabbering, maleducated Boeotian who feels the need to defend ignorance. What it is in our power to make better, we must so do. While grammar should — and must never — be rigid, language is democratic, not anarchic.

As I have already mentioned, song comes to us under many guises, forms, and faces. There is no end of aliases — or should I more properly say disguises? For example, the close-to-unbearable title-song Bacharach wrote for the film of the same name, "What's New Pussycat?" is a waltz. So is his painfully kitschy "What the World Needs Now (is Love, Sweet Love)." Upon consideration, one comes to find that many songs are waltzes. Irving Berlin's "The Girl That I Marry" — from *Roberta* — is a waltz. So is Hugh Martin and Ralph Blane's "The Boy Next Door" from *Meet Me in St. Louis*. "Some Day My Prince Will Come," the big hit from Walt Disney's *Snow White and the Seven Dwarfs* — music by Frank Churchill, words by Larry Morey — is a waltz, although it has since become a standard among jazz musicians, including Miles Davis, Dave Brubeck, and Bill Evans. Are you surprised to learn that Ross Bagdasarian's "The Chipmunk Song" from 1958 is a waltz? It has a merry-go-round quality to it, but the song which is cute has something saving in it of '60s irony, with none of that thin, ersatz, sort of canned breeziness we all painfully suffered with that incessant marvinhamlishization of music back in the '70s with songs like Burt Bacharach's "You'll Never Get To Heaven," "Hey, Little Girl," "Walk On By," and banal offerings like "Promises, Promises," a song with a manic drive, almost a *prestissimo* tempo, and changing rollover meters that, although it starts off in 3/4 time — which is, incidentally, at least to me, far too fast — is much too wayward to be called anything like a waltz. "Mexicali Rose" is a waltz. "The One Rose" is a waltz. "The Loveliest Night of the Year" is a waltz, as well. Elvis Presley's "Are You Lonesome Tonight" — one of the King's major hits — is also a waltz.

The title of "I Can't Tell a Waltz from a Tango," a popular song written by Bob Hoffman and Dick Manning and sung by Patti Page in 1954, always sort of amused me, since a tango is not two jumps from a Viennese waltz, and I believe it is still danced as a *vals* in the barrios of Rocha and Rio de la Plata.

What seems to be one thing, appears as another. E. Y. Harburg and Jay Gorney's "Brother, Can You Spare a Dime?" (1932), which as part of the 1932 musical, *New Americana,* and "Remember My Forgotten Man" (1933) by Al Dubin and Harry Warren, which is featured in *Gold Diggers of 1933*, are editorials. And Fred Astaire and Jane Powell's famous bickering duet in *Royal Wedding* (1951), "How Could You Believe Me When I Said I Love You When You Know I've Been a Liar All My Life" — considered to be the longest title of any song in MGM musical history — is an altercation. Kool & the Gang's banal "Celebration" is not even a song, but pure cheerleading, as is Queen's incantatory and frankly morbid — and unremittingly droning — "We are the Champions."

Ben E. King's "Stand by Me" is an exordium. Johnny Cash's "Ring of Fire" is a Mexican mariachi number. Roy Orbison's "Candy Man" is a harmonica riff where the rip of his metallic voice actually sounds like part of the instrument. The Tee Set's "Ma Belle Amie," most of which sounds like Ubangi twaddle, is 1969 reggae. If you should find yourself bewildered and unable to comprehend half of that song, understand that it is not American or English but rather Dutch pop, its lead singer Peter Tetteroo being whiter than the flakes of a snow globe. "Neat Neat Neat," the second single by the punk group, The Damned, is, more than anything, less a song than a brawl or rumble, with its bellicose opening riff, *doom-didda-doom-didda-doom.* Captain Sensible's purring snarl of a bass line kicks it off, with Dave Vanian the Transylvanian and his screaming Gothic face, and then the whole band cranks it and is gone. "It sounded like a fight," Craig Ferguson of CBS' the *Late Late Show* told *Playboy* (December 2011), "and at that time I enjoyed that kind of activity. Listening to that song was literally the turning point in my life." But if "Neat Neat Neat" is a fight, what is the Dead Kennedy's "Holiday in Cambodia" but pure armaggedon? It is as if Swift's Blefescu has become suddenly real, a world inhabited by chanting metal-voiced pygmies, a bunch of horn-mad little quilps spitting out lyrics from chewed barbed wire! "Pol Pot! Pol Pot! Pol Pot!"

The plangent song, "Tenderly," is subtextually a sexual confession of how gentle *intercourse* can be. ("The evening breeze/ caressed the trees/ tenderly/ The trembling trees/ embraced the breeze tenderly…Your arms opened wide/ and closed me inside/ You took my lips,/ you took my love/ so tenderly"). Petula Clark's "Downtown," to Glenn Gould — the classical pianist oddly having become, before he died, something of a water-carrier for the pop-singer and her songs (see his essay "The Search for Petula Clark") — is an "intoxicated adolescent's daydream," her song "Who Am I?" a "document of despair," and "My Love" a "vigorous essay in self-advertisement," with its

> My love is warmer than the warmest sunshine,
> Softer than a sigh;
> My love is deeper than the deepest ocean,
> Wider than the sky

standing in highest stead as "a proud, secure Methodist tract — preordained, devoid of doubt, admitting of no compromise, and as legions of Petulas gyrate, ensnared within its righteous euphony," Gould, on a roll, enthusiastically continues, "galleries of oval-framed ancestors peer down upon that deft deflation of the lyrics, and approve."

Elvis Presley's "Suspicious Minds" is, weirdly, a hymn. It is a song, inexplicably, in my opinion, also unanimously voted by fans around the world as their favorite Elvis song of all time, according to Sonny West, one of the Memphis Mafia. In the 1970s the King turned pretty much everything he sang into a hymn. (What was Elvis's own favorite song of all his recordings? He always said, "You'll Never Walk Alone.") Why not make hymns out of one's troubles and joys? Is it not all part of "penumbra" theory, gravitational pull? Pa Vernon and Ma Gladys from Tupelo and Memphis found little else to admire in their music. That old gospel chestnut, "Praise the Lord, I Saw the Light," for example, a particular song Hank Williams wrote alluding to his great delight and relief whenever, flying in over Alabama, he got his first glimpse of the saving run-way lights of the Montgomery Airport. Elvis's "If I Can Dream" — I consider this later song of his a masterpiece — is a Civil Rights march, at least to me. Listen to the militant force of that final wind-up, the drive. Picture Elvis singing that song at the top of his form from the steps of the Lincoln Memorial in Washington, D.C. on August 28, 1963 — it would have fully mesmerized that massive crowd to its very roots.

We cannot help but see, then, that pop music is, among other things, an extensive gallery of postures and is, as the Bard was to playwright Harold Pinter in his *A Note on Shakespeare*, a compendium of diverse attitudes and odd approaches, "fluid and hardened at the quick; gross and godlike, putrescent and copulative; raddled; attentive; crippled and gargantuan; crumbling with the dropsy; heavy with elephantiasis; broody with government; severe; fanatical; paralytic; voluptuous; impassive; muscle-bound; lissome; virginal; unwashed; bewildered; hump-backed; icy and statuesque. All are contained in the wound which Shakespeare does not attempt to sew up or re-shape, whose pain he does not attempt to eradicate." I think it worthwhile to look at the successes and failures of this music, bringing an intelligence to the legitimate and therefore compulsory facts to conclude what we will.

There is no formula offered, for no formula has made this music. It is various as it is vexing, as silly as it is sensational: no one thing, in short. Again, as Pinter points out of the Bard. "His tongue is guttural, Arabic, pepperish, composed, parsimonious, transparent, voluminous, rabid, diarrhoeic, laundered, dainty, mellifluous, consonantal, stammering, naked, scabrous, naked, blade-edged, one-legged, piercing, hushed, clinical, dumb, convulsed, lewd, vicious," and he goes on to list sixty more adjectives.

Songs can be subtle. They are not always what they seem. Lilt can hide a lyric. The seemingly innocuous "Jimmy Cracked Corn" — its correct name is "The Blue-Tail Fly" — is not the simple knees-hugging old American camp-fire song known to all of us who chanted it while roasting weenies, a lively, upbeat 1840s minstrel song handed down for a hundred and fifty years, but in point of fact a bitter revenge chant, an expression of hostile glee sung by blacks on the occasion of a slave-master's death ("Jimmy crack corn and I don't care/ My massa's gone away"). What seems to be (just as often) is not. At a party at Los Alamos, Robert Oppenheimer, father of the Atomic Bomb, once abruptly — eccentrically, if you will — quirkily declared that Mozart's brilliant "24th Piano Concerto in C minor" would make "a wonderful revolutionary song." Neil Sedaka's "Calendar Girl," notice, is also a march. So is Irving Berlin's "Alexander's Ragtime Band" — with its bizarre lyric about music being "so nat-u-ral that you want to go to war" — which, beyond that, is not really ragtime at all but rather a song about ragtime. (You have to listen closely, but there is even an internal quote of Stephen Foster's "Old Folks At Home" so subtly imbedded in the song — "If you want to hear the 'Swanee River' played in ragtime" — that one barely notices.)

Who can ever predict how a song will be heard or even in which queer direction a song is going to go? I mean, one particularly rousing Presbyterian hymn that I happen to love, "Redeemed, How I Love To Proclaim It" (Fanny Crosby, 1885) — you can almost hear the clop-clop-clop — is a cowboy song. The majestic and soulful hymn, "Jerusalem," with its heart-piercing lyrics about Christ appearing in England (words thanks to William Blake), my wife Sarah and I quite happily if incongruously chose to be sung at our wedding. Interestingly, I have always thought that the "*Veni Creator Spiritus*," that supreme Roman Catholic hymn often sung at ordinations as the ultimate lullaby, one that at the sacred hour of Compline the Trappist monks always chant in the dark at the end of the day as a kind of spiritual nightsong. Speaking of lullabies, I have always been convinced that the seemingly romantic song from *High Society*, the soothing "True Love," is actually a lullaby. In the film, in fact, the scene where an older Bing Crosby croons the song to a younger Grace Kelly — it quickly becomes a duet — seems to make that very point, as she lies on his lap in a twilight mood. "Didn't He Ramble," one of the oldest of New Orleans jazz tunes, is a march, a six-eight march just like John Philip Sousa's "Washington Post March." The wistful "Lili Marlene" is a waltz *and* a march, both. A nostalgic old favorite of soldiers on both sides of the European and African theaters, the Axis as well as the Allies, the music was written by Norbert Schultze and recorded in 1939 by Lale Anderson, a German cabaret singer herself, although it was later popularized soulfully by the German-American Marlene Dietrich who of course made the song world famous. Nazi Reich Minister of Public Enlightenment and Propaganda Josef Goebbels characteristically ordered Anderson to record the song, to sing it, to a drumbeat, which she obligingly did. A march. But anyone can see it is also a sweeping little waltz. I own a rare copy of "Lili Marleen" [sic] — the real *Schallplatte* on a 78 r.p.m. — recorded by Andersen in 1942.

The highly popular World War I signature song of Broadway's George M. Cohan's, "Over There" — three bold notes to the title — is little more than a bugle call. Who would deny that the song "Blue Skies," written in 1926 by Rodgers and Hart for the musical *Betsy* — the song was popularized by Al Jolson — is actually a Yiddish offering with its angled flats and sharps? Richard Rodgers and Lorenz Hart were both Jewish, of course. Speaking of transformative oddities, is not Cole Porter's plodding "I Love Paris" virtually a dirge? Quite so. A leaden, peculiarly arduous melancholic dirge. Listen to those cheerless and disconsolate opening blue notes — canted like a coffin being carried down a flight of stairs. Speaking of dirges, although "Chapel of Love," the 1964 hit by the Dixie Cups, addresses the alchemic moment of happiness and excitement that a girl feels on her wedding day

> Spring is here, the sky is blue, woe, woe, woe
> Birds all sing, as if they knew
> Today's the day we'll say, "I do"
> And we'll never be lonely anymore.

one rather wistfully hears a tone of sheer reluctance. When in the refrain the group dolefully chants, "Goin' to the chapel, and we're goin' to get married," it sounds to me like some kind of medieval Rogation Day lament, almost as if the group of girls were unwillingly moping along in a harrowing procession. The gravity which I gather we are to take for solemnity is all wrong. The song, which was written by Jeff Barry, Ellie Greenwich, and Phil Spector, is "narrated" from a girl's point of view, but in spite of the lyrics the musical mood conveys in its utter lack of joy and enthusiasm the very *opposite* of the words being sung and makes it sound, subtextually, as if she is going to her funeral. Curiously, Cole wrote another of his hit songs, "I Get A Kick Out of You," after having been being beaten up by a malicious and outraged truck-driver that he had picked up in a homosexual encounter. (Sinatra who does a marvelous rift with that final *you* loved Cole Porter, his ideal — urban, hip, ironic — composer.) To some degree, therefore, the song constitutes a diary entry or a confession or love letter — even a crime report! I have always got a kick out of Coward singing his own gaily-draped version of his splendid song, "I've Been to a Marvelous Party" which offers as many seductively stressed sibilants as Al Stewart's fey "Year of the Cat." ("She comes out of the sun/ in a silk dress/ running like a watercolor in the rain") One of Coward's comically decadent stanzas goes,

> I've been to a marvellous party.
> We played a wonderful game.
> Maureen disappeared and came back in a beard
> and we all had to guess at her name.
> Cecil arrived wearing armour,
> some shells, and a black feather boa.
> Poor Millicent wore a surrealist comb
> made of bits of mosaic from St. Peters in Rome
> but the weight was so great that she had to go home
> — well, I couldn't have liked it more.

Brilliant, but so gay, so deliciously, self-pamperedly precious. It never fails to recall for me in cherished reflection an anecdote from one of composer and diarist Ned Rorem's essays on his friend Truman Capote: "I remember also the first television production of a Capote oeuvre, 'A Christmas Memory,' and Frank O'Hara's guffaw when Geraldine Page appeared on the screen, looked mistily out at the country dawn, and uttered the script's first line, 'It's fruit-cake time.'" The late John Lennon, described in 1969 by the witty, epicene British comedian and actor Kenneth Williams as "that Beatle married to an Asiatic lady...that unprepossessing person with tin spectacles and this curious nasal Liverpudlian delivery," always somehow managed to jigger his songs to mean less or more than they at first seemed. For example, the song "In My Life," is nothing less than a short story, isn't it? "No. 9" is a Buddhist chant. Can a pop-song be nothing but just plain *nagging*, of the real pain-in-the-ass sort? What else is John and Yoko's "Give Peace a Chance"? It comes across like nothing but interminable wailing, a brutal ear-killing harangue I would add to any taxonomy of painful aural abuse, especially those abrasive lines which come across like the demented drone of a mentally-unstable couple or the mad rant of a bunty maiden aunt. "All we are *saaaaying* is give peace a *chaaance.*" You want to throw broken shoes at them. (Many novels of course never cease to nag. Look at the books of that squarely-built near-dwarf, Ayn Rand, a hysterical reactionary who affected a cape and cigarette holders whose didactic speeches went on for entire *chapters*. I distinctly recall once having helicoptered a copy of *Atlas Shrugged* clear across a room.)

While we are discussing John Lennon, look closely at his wistful, utopian ditty "Imagine" — is it not the Communist Manifesto in song, along with, by the way, offering some of the most forgivably inane lyrics in pop music? ("Imagine all the people, living for today... Imagine there's [sic] no countries, it isn't hard to do"). Crystal Gayle's solicitous "Don't Take Me Half the Way" is of course a sexual proposition, *hooking*, except it is put in song. Then tell me, Frank Sinatra's "The House That I Live In" is not a sermon? Tony Bennett's "I Wanna Be Around" is not a bitter threat of spiteful aggression? The jingle from the early Disney film, *Three Little Pigs* (1933), "Who's Afraid of the Big Bad Wolf," is not a Depression anthem? Wake up, people. Did not E.M. Cioran convince us that only inert things add nothing to what they are? Judy Garland's version of "Little Girl Blue" — listen closely to hear in its sad, muffled hysteria the singer's nagging self-doubt which is worse than wistful, that cold, jittery moaning low — is of course nothing less than a suicide note. Her stone version of "I Love Paris" is not sung — it is condoled! Neither lute nor nightingale is involved. I will always insist, moreover, that Garland's version of "Have Yourself A Merry Little Christmas," as she dolefully presents it, is in the end more lugubrious than the *"Dies Irae"* — in tone, in intent, in point of view, and in effect. A vocal cortège. "Next year all our troubles will be miles away." "Someday soon, we all will be together, if the Fates allow." "Until then, we'll have to muddle through somehow." It is nothing but dreary projection from a bleak present, a message of unconvincing expectation and longing — all about next year, deferred hope, trying to *recover.* In their longing, futility and insistent sense of regret, Judy Garland's songs equal in sum, to me at least, the melancholy of Dr. Samuel Johnson's *Rasselas,* his apologue of 1759 that was written to express his idea, one of his favorite themes, that human life is everywhere a state in which much is to be endured and little to be enjoyed. "The truth is that," he wrote, "no mind is much employed upon the present: recollection and anticipation fill up almost all our moments."

On the subject of Christmas and gloom, what is Irving Berlin's "White Christmas" but a gloomy wool-gathering reverie, a brooding and doleful castle-building pipe-dream written by a nostalgic Jew in a pensive moment looking for sleighs, sentiment, and snow? There is no Christ here, no angels, no faith. Jody Rosen in his book *White Christmas* writes, "The world's favorite Christmas song is not an ode to joy, or snowmen, or Santa. It is a downer, a lament for lost happiness – in spirit, if not in form, a blues."

What is ever what it seems? I mean, why do almost all the cartoon characters in the Dr. Seuss books look exactly like Heinrich Himmler? The second album of the White Stripes, *De Stijl*, got its title from the aesthetically austere philosophy of early 20th-century Dutch artists, among them Mondrian, and Jack White has said that he and Meg (his ex-wife) actually think of the band as an art project! Half the time, if not more, what we say in fact leaves out, omits — the vocal equivalent of "negative space" — a more important something which in a real sense the very omission more painfully confesses, which is why, I suppose people listen, very like paying attention to a detective story so that, once we find out who the killer is, we can relax.

But what can possibly surprise us, in the final analysis, after one learns that the lyrics to the religious hymn, "Amazing Grace," can be sung to the tune of TV's *Gilligan's Island*? ("Amazing grace! How sweet the sound / That saved a wretch like me!/ I once was lost, but now am found/ Was blind, but now can see...")

Distillation is all. We who are masters of indirection — and I daresay that includes every last soul in the human race — finally fool no one. Consciousness by definition interrogates itself. Has not the art of virtually every mass-market paperback cover in America been a version of "Slaughter on Tenth Avenue"? One could deconstruct the forms of pop music and every musical sub-genre all day, from greasy soul to subversive cock-rock to old '50s songs with their gooey centers to the punk phenomenon to hip-hop. I wonder how many of us have ever stopped to ponder the fact that our national anthem, "The Star-Spangled Banner," is actually a composition, almost wooing in its earnestness, in its pleading, of three questions. Consider the first line, for example:

> Oh, say can you see
> by the dawn's early light
> what so proudly we hailed
> at the twilight's last gleaming?

What singer in trying to manage the architectonics of this anthem, even if struggling to reach its several almost impossibly high notes, has ever vocally sought to stress the significance of the lyrics for the *questions* they pose? A more apposite question perhaps might be, how many singers ever get the lyrics right? For the Super Bowl in Dallas on February 2011, instead of properly singing, "O'er the ramparts we watched were so gallantly streaming," pop-tart Christina Aguilera belted out, "What so proudly we watched at the twilight's last reaming." Then Huey Lewis and the News sang the National Anthem at the divisional AFC playoff game between the New England Patriots and the Denver Broncos on

January 14, 2012 and with visible strain literally barked out, because they couldn't hit, the notes at "and the rockets' red glare" — in every assault of the song always the moment of *crise* — and, typical with all singers, also went flat as a flawn on the last word "Brave," for that is where the song without uplift comes to an abrupt and leaden stop. For just plain awful, it is hard to beat Aerosmith's Steven Tyler's grackle-like attempt to sing the anthem just a week later on January 23 which was cacophonous enough to strip off wallpaper. He almost expired at the "land of the free," when he had to throw his head back in a yowl to even approach that note!

I would have to say that the late Whitney Houston's dazzling rendition of the "Star-Spangled Banner," sung before the 1991 Super Bowl, was the nonpareil, certainly the authoritative pop example, heartfelt, soaring, regal.

Has anyone ever pointed out, by the way, that it was during the War of 1812 that American forces in a rather overreaching way were actually trying to conquer *Canada* with the fond imperialistic hope of trying to annex that country as our own? (One wonders if there is any lurid connection to that fact that on the Canadian ten dollar bill the flag flying over the Parliament building is, portentously, the American stars and stripes!) In any case, it was while watching Robert Goulet struggling to sing "The Star-Spangled Banner" — and he too was screwing up the lyrics — that Elvis Presley, briefly enjoying television with his daughter, Lisa Marie, as they were eating dinner, in a fit of pique, maniacally yanked out his handgun and furiously blew away the TV set. "That'll be enough of that shit," he said, returning to his meal. When his daughter wondered why he had "killed" their television, according to Sonny West, one of the Memphis Mafia, in *Elvis: Taking Care of Business*, Elvis replied, "Aw, daddy didn't like what was on, so I just turned it off from here."

"The Star-Spangled Banner" celebrates a single, parochial episode about a war we know little about, chronicling the failure of a British assault, and one that many historians feel should not have been fought. The lyrics come from "Defence of Fort McHenry," a poem written in 1814 by the 35-year-old lawyer and amateur poet, Francis Scott Key, after witnessing the bombardment of that fort by the British Royal Navy ships in Chesapeake Bay during a battle in the War of 1812, while the melody had previously been applied to at least 84 other sets of lyrics *in the U.S. alone!* "The verse of our national anthem was superimposed… onto an old drinking song — which is perhaps why everyone sounds drunk when intoning it," wrote Ned Rorem in *Critical Affairs: a Composer's Journal,* who goes on to say that is "is a narrow and vicious piece: bad poetry on bad music expressing bad sentiments. And its performance grows increasingly bad as our sense of whatever patriotism is broadened, along with our musical sophistication." The song, "Rule Britannia," embodies the outlines of the British Constitution, while "The Star-Spangled Banner," while puffing the values of victory, fixes mainly on the durability of our flag. In any case, who has ever sung it with any understanding of its emotional sense or shown anything like vocal commitment to its meaning?

The answer is no one. None. Nobody. So much for cognition. I might point out that Finns, on the other hand, have often become so aroused upon hearing Jean Sibelius' majestic "Finlandia" with its growing feeling of triumph and final cadences that rise to a climax of terrific power and eloquence that public performances have had to be prohibited — and that song is not even the Finnish national anthem ("*Maamme*," a.k.a."*Vårt Land*" is) — whereas when our own anthem is being played at sporting events obstreperous fans begin cheering and howling rudely at the line "our flag was still there" just to hasten play! It is a bitch to sing. Aside from the fact that singers, especially of such a gasping rollercoaster of an anthem, have to concentrate on remembering the highly archaic and oblique lyrics of the thing — and, incidentally, there is only one key in which the song can be sung as regards the melody — they soon realize, fatally, almost to a one, that the song is bracketed by the most extreme highs and lows in the history of vocal music. One waits for the screechy "and the rockets' red glare" as for the slashing fall of a guillotine blade. The menace in singing "The Star-Spangled Banner," the preposterous difficulty at the heart of it, the unavoidable fact, highly revealing in intent, that the theme of this anthem is ruinously, gloomily, about nothing less than pure *destruction*. The song is notoriously difficult for nonprofessionals to sing, because of its wide range — an octave and a half. Humorist Richard Armour cites the song's difficulty in *It All Started with Columbus*:

> In an attempt to take Baltimore, the British attacked Fort McHenry, which protected the harbor. Bombs were soon bursting in air, rockets were glaring, and all in all it was a moment of great historical interest. During the bombardment, a young lawyer named Francis Off Key [sic] wrote "The Star-Spangled Banner", and when, by the dawn's early light, the British heard it sung, they fled in terror

It is also leaden, weak in the uplift, demanding of breath-lift, a literal drag of subject matter, madly martial, arguably bellicose, the red burst of bombs elegantly giving the *argumentum ad auctoritatem* to our national profile. "Every time I hear it," a friend of mine used to say, "I want to go out and beat the shit out of a Russian!"

French chemists who over years of long practice developed that special olfactory gift for memorizing scents and scent-combinations were popularly known as "Noses" — "*Bouquins.*" They worked to be capable of recognizing and combining thousands of different fragrances in order to achieve perfect harmony. Why not dub people with comparative auditory talents "Ears" — *Manches* or *Poignées*, say? Without claiming to be in possession of anything like paranormal or preternatural gifts, I believe I do have something of a talent — or curse, if you will — for listening, a sort of intense aural alertness (not merely hearing) which is just another acute aspect of human cognition.

The ear *is* part of vision. In Marshall McLuhan's *The Medium is the Massage: An Inventory of Effects* (1967) that scholar and communication theorist, playing on the words "message" and "massage," argues that technologies — from clothing to the wheel to the book, and beyond — are the messages themselves, not the content of the medium. He examines how modern media are extensions of human senses. What is notable is that of the many ways we are now reachable half a century later, and total reachability seems to be a perverse fixation of ours today, what I call the anti-*Walden* phenomenon, all the phonations, discordant sounds, incidental music, mobile phones, etc. can often result in the *prevention* of a connected stream of conscious thought. We are implicated this way, now, more than ever. One of the Dadaist-like photographs in McLuhan's book shows an ear serving as an eye.

I cannot say if I can or should be legitimately numbered in that great group of "Ears" and whether it is actually an art or not, but I do believe I can say that I brought to the business more than an amateur's ardor listening on the second-hand GE 808C transistor radio I had when I got a bit older, one that sported tiny triangles at 640 and 1240 kHz on the dial, civil-defense symbols that highlighted the two frequencies indicating the emergency broadcast points if and when the Soviet Army invaded Massachusetts. It was a portable radio. I took it with me to the beach, plunked it down nearby when I was raking leaves, sat with it in my backyard.

It was around this time in what back then was called Junior High School that my neighborhood pals and I often debated about what was the first rock 'n' roll record. In 1947, blues singer Roy Brown recorded "Good Rockin' Tonight," a song that parodied church music by appropriating its references, including the word "rocking" and the old gospel call "Have you heard the news?" with the worldly lyrics about dancing, drinking and sex. With all sorts of inauthentic reasons we argued that the first rock 'n' roll record was either "Gee" by the Crows or "Earth Angel" by the Penguins. It is hard to say. Now I believe I would nominate "It's Too Soon to Know" by the Orioles, featuring the gifted Sonny Til (the stage name of Earlington Carl Tilghman) on lead vocals, which was recorded in July 1948 and played mainly on so-called "race" radio stations. The Orioles are acknowledged to be the first vocal group — they started the big trend in bird groups (The Crows, The Larks, The Penguins, etc.) — naming themselves after the state bird of Maryland, their home state.

Purists may fight for other songs for the honor of being the first. In May 1948, Savoy Records advertised "Robbie-Dobey Boogie" by Brownie McGhee with the tagline, "It jumps, it's made, it rocks, it rolls. If you are a real hairsplitter, "My Man Rocks Me (With One Steady Roll)" by Trixie Smith was issued back in 1922, which was actually the first record to refer to "rocking" and "rolling" in a secular context. Papa Charlie Jackson recorded the driving "Shake That Thing" in 1925. The rock 'n' roll beat, along with key phrases ("jivin'," "move it," "jump," "rock me," etc.) of that genre, picked up and put down everywhere, spread like foraging kudzu in the South. The melody line of Jim Jackson's "Kansas City Blues," recorded in 1927, was transmogrified by Charlie Patton in "Going To Move To Alabama" in 1929 and by Hank Williams in "Move It On Over" in 1947 before emerging in Bill Haley's "Rock Around The Clock" in 1954 when its lyric presaged Leiber and Stoller's own "Kansas City." Jackson's popular hit contains the line, "It takes a rocking chair to rock, a rubber ball to roll," which had previously been used in 1924 by Ma Rainey in "Jealous Hearted Blues" and which Bill Haley would later incorporate into his 1952 recording, "Sundown Boogie."

There was a kind of High Seriousness that took place in the early '60s where social intensity in the writing of — and interest in hearing — serious lyrics displaced the kind of witty '30s and jokey '40s and earnest '50s variations we tended to find in those perhaps less wired decades, for whatever reasons. My radio was to me more than a piece of vernacular architecture. It was a source of knowledge. I loved the music, the entertainment, the drama. But it was the words that came through the radio that plugged me into the world, words the showed me that language — as Karl Kraus put it — was the mother, not the maid of thought.

The famous Sapir-Whorf Hypothesis states that language determines, influences, thought. It is an illusion to imagine that one adjusts to reality essentially without the use of language or that language is merely an incidental means of solving specific problems of communication and reflection. It was Benjamin Lee Whorf's thesis in fact that language actually determines the way in which its speakers perceive the world. Hans-Georg Gadamer, the decisive figure in the development of twentieth century hermeneutics, went so far as to declare, "Nothing exists except through language." Ezra Pound went so far as to believe that bad writing destroyed civilizations and that good writing could save them.

It was to words that I gave patient end receptive attention. My delight was word-play, conundrums, and cryptic meanings. Codes fascinated me as a kid, and so did puppets. It developed into a determination to be a poet. I wrote and illustrated a small novel on small yellow pages in the seventh-grade that I typed on a schoolfriend's typewriter, which his older brother, for reasons I can no longer remember, ripped up. I do remember it was filled with, by God-only- knows what kind of xenoglossic effusions, a lot of odd, duck-faced characters speaking in crazy miratives and those cartoon swear words I loved called "maledicta" like **@#$!!**@#$ Is!** At night, listening to the radio, in the close dark, opened up the theater of the entire world for me, one great monody, a theater of the mind. I saw that words kept track of our history and culture, our triumphs and our troubles. I wonder what other mystifications the night held for me, what refuge or sanctuary it allowed me as a fugue from the real world, since I, a chronic bed-wetter for years, fixed on a place I could not, would not leave.

It is sometimes said that there are only two basic plots in fiction: someone goes on a journey, or a stranger comes to town. To me they are often — if not always — one and the same. A fellow who goes on a journey is inevitably a stranger who comes to town. It is the voyager who is traveling to discover what he needs to see. He is waiting for the coming of the Cocqcigrues, for the mystery to be cleared up. No one journeys to more distant or unknown places than a waking adolescent.

My dreams were paradoxically paramount in my waking life, but they came basically from books, and my mind was full of the hundreds of stories that had been read to me about Old Mother West Wind and the Merry Little Breezes; the Pied Piper of Hamelin — my favorite fable — Johnny Molasses who became a Christmas ornament; the strange children of Pie Country who wore their hair crinkled around the edges and whose suits were made of crisp, brown stuff woven to look like a pastry crust, a land where the High Pastry Cook ranked higher than the King; Old Doctor Wango Tango who lived on a biscuit a day, and Old Doctor Wango Tango who got quite light this way; and scrappy Brer Rabbit who, meeting a Preacher-Man who was on his way to have a delicious fried chicken dinner, had to be among the first bunnies in the animal kingdom to be harboring Marxist thoughts:

> Dat's de way de world go 'round,
> Dat's de way de world go 'round.
> All fer dat preacher!
> None for dis creature!

Was I a Communist? I ask only because I also recall I could not explain to myself the food misallotment in Helen Bannerman's *Little Black Sambo* where Black

Mumbo eats only twenty-seven pancakes while Black Jumbo ate fifty-five and Little Black Sambo ate one hundred and sixty-nine, "because he was no hungry."

I grew up listening to all sorts of music. My first true waking memory is of my mother walking through a room singing, in turn, "The Girl That I Marry" and "You Were Meant for Me." I developed a passionate love for certain pieces, even writing down their titles, like Gustav Holst's "Jupiter" from *The Planets* and George Whitefield Chadwick's "Jubilee" and Samuel Barber's "Adagio for Strings [Opus 11]."

I listened to hundreds of radio shows, which, back then, was actually a form of watching and created an interest, I'm sure, in my later becoming a writer. Mysteries, serial dramas, concerts, news, quiz shows, hit parades, a variety of formats and genres. *Inner Sanctum*; *The Great Gildersleeve*; *Sky King*; *Cavalcade of America*; *The Jack Benny Program*; *The Buster Brown Show*; *The Lone Ranger*; *Boston Blackie*; *Lux Radio Theater*; *Sergeant Preston of the Yukon*; *Straight Arrow*; *Truth or Consequences*; *Jack Armstrong, the All-American Boy*; and *The Whistler*. "In radio we can do anything the audience can imagine. In television we can do anything the carpenters can build," said Fred Allen. If predication is the process of bringing ideas together and coupling them, then the true test of sound predication, I feel, is that the ideas that are brought together belong together, and that for me was what validated the world of radio, in that voices were everything. I have often been struck watching Federico Fellini's *8 ½*, his unsurpassed autobiographical film, how important *voices* were to him — it is an omnibus of fantasy, folly, rambles, monologues, tender yearnings, and delirious lust — and framed so much of the past that he recollected with such wit.

It was particularly modish, especially in the latitudinarian '60s, to speak of the lyrics of rock music as "poetry." And to some degree a certain few lyrics — quixotic, hip, inventive, strange, careeningly or reflectively lyrical — came sufficiently close. There was a lot of earnestness about this back in that decade. Vain people love the idea of discovery. The 1960s was big for what can be called "recency illusion," the belief that something we have just noticed has only just started happening. Groovy young people seriously dressed like native Americans with headbands and face-paint, smoked spliffs and advocated free-love, as if poetry, sex, indeed freedom, had only just been discovered, ignorant of 19th Bohemia, Parisian "Apaches," Dadaists, beatniks, and wild iconoclasts from every generation past. '60s types in their most identifiable morph were desperately grave, arrogant, naïve, idealistic, and earnest all at once. Types like this — I will not number myself among them even for the sake of argument — tend to listen closely to song lyrics, to ponder the words, to heed and to hearken to lyrical advice and suggestion. In its worst and most extreme actualization it was a painful period of dewy-eyed and simplistic naturopaths, primitive wavy-gravyites who were suspicious of rules and laws and got married in meadows, half-naked, and wrote their own vows — being described as "plastic" was the worst of all insults — and loved communes. They were credulous beyond the telling and listened to the "truths" in rock as if it were coming from the Cumaean Sibyl. (I would have to select John Lennon's enthusiastic but potty, almost comical "Imagine," although released in 1971, as the definitive effluent — lyrics, title, melody, philosophy, faith, and code of dogma — coming from that murky pond.) "And rock is also educational," said Frank Zappa. "How to ask a girl for a date, what love is like." And oh the deep, spectral-wide, far-ranging questions one listened to with every expectation of an answer, from Jimmy Clanton's "What am I gonna do on Saturday night?" to the Shirrelles "Will you still love me tomorrow?" to Jimi Hendrix's ultra-woozy, grammatically-muddled "Have you ever been experienced?" Do you wanna dance? Am I blue? Where is love? Where or when? How much do I love you? Why baby, why? How can ya say that? What is love? ("Five feet of heaven in a ponytail.")

When I was a pre-teen, since I was already confused enough about subject matter — why, I wondered, was every song about *love?* — my concern for the lyrics of songs grew into epistemological worries. So central was love to people it seemed to animate every poet's waking hour, even — especially — the bitter ones. What a reductive subject, it seemed to me. There was all of life to be considered, thousands of emotions, an infinite variety of topics to address, to write about, but music had settled on this one like a girl over a valentine? It seemed to me in its desperation a kind of abruption, the cutting off of an opportunity in the same way that the policy nowadays is to lock the doors of a department store immediately when a lost child is not found in 15 minutes — that frantic, that critical, that irremediable. It came under my notice not without alarm doing a 7th-grade book report that Johnny Appleseed blamed his strange ways on an unhappy love affair. It would become a theme repeated in books that I read later. It became clearer of course as I reached adolescence, but not all that much. In high school I noticed that the poet Sylvia Plath, rejected by a man, committed suicide with a bitter heart. Henry David Thoreau's proposal to one Ellen Sewall early in November, 1840, after his brother, John, had proposed to her, was spurned. The letter no longer survives, but it is likely that his November 1, 1840, *Journal* entry was related to that letter. It reads:

> I thought that the sun of our love should have risen as noiselessly as the
> sun out of the sea, and we sailors have found ourselves steering between

the tropics as if the broad day had lasted forever. You know how the sun comes up from the sea when you stand on the cliff, and doesn't [sic] startle you, but every thing, and you too are helping it. (*Journal 1*, 193).

Many entries from Thoreau's daily *Journal* from July 1839 to November 1840 relate to his feelings of love for young Ellen. Following her father's wishes, Sewall turned down his proposal, yet he would carry her memory with him to the very end of his life. In 1862, shortly before he died, Thoreau is reported wistfully to have confided about this passion to his sister, Sophia: "I have always loved her." I was heartened many years on to read that Frau Alma Mahler shared my preoccupations about romance. She confided to her diary on November 9, 1901: "A new idea occurred to me: art is the outcome of love. While love for a man is a tool for creativity, for a woman it's the principal motive. I was never less productive than when I was in love...I can concentrate on nothing else."

At age 9 I was not interested in love — or collecting comic books or watching movies of googly-eyed aliens or mole-like humans or even watching television. I was a "library cormorant," as Samuel Taylor Coleridge described himself at the age of 20. I got decent grades, had bad handwriting (my only Cs), questioned everything, surveyed my small dreams, became an altar boy, loved syllogisms and deductive reasoning and was prone to try out logic on people as if I were using a fingerhold, feared girls, learned to write secret codes, had puppets and gave neighborhood puppet-shows, and always drew cartoons all over my notebooks. A boy named John Slupski and I shared an elaborate dream life in grammar school that was borrowed from *The Adventures of Tom Sawyer*, a novel I treasured. We memorized specific passages from that book and spoke them in dialect. We sneaked into a crawlspace under my front porch on Webster St. to smoke corn-silk in corncob pipes and talked about how "spunk water" cured warts, as Huck Finn sagely advised who also declared that it required a dead cat: "Why, you take your cat and go and get in the graveyard 'long about midnight when somebody wicked has been buried; and when it's midnight a devil will come, or maybe two or three...and when they're taking the feller away, you heave your cat after 'em and say, 'Devil follow corpse, cat follow devil, warts follow cat, I'm done with ye!' That'll fetch."

For no great reason that I can explain I came to view the world as a word puzzle and, with no special aptitude I can name, fixed on the whys and wherefores of language. I rolled the word "inauguration" over my tongue in 1948, the year that Truman was inaugurated, the day my 3rd grade class was escorted over to the Elks Club by Miss Cook where we were invited to watch the ceremony. I still remember the flickering TV screen and the sobriety of that national event.

Another teacher, another year, assured our class that General Eisenhower's dim pronouncement upon launching D-Day, "OK, we'll go," was momentous, but to me that sounded — rhetorically — truly mediocre. On a school day trip to a small dairy farm in Chelmsford, north of Boston, a farmer explained that a cow's sudden awkward assbackwards crash into a wooden stall indicated she was "presenting," a word that bewildered me until the next day in the library I lugged over to my table a huge reference study on primates and within seconds was absolutely disgusted. I always pronounced February 14 "Valen*time's* Day" and much preferred that word, even after being corrected, to the real one. Same with the word "chimbly." What was diphtheria, I wondered? Trespassers? Bra cups? Fielder's choice? I badgered a priest to explain to me what Jesus wrote on the ground in John 8:6. I loved the comic strip *Li'l Abner*, and walked around spouting, "Corn-grad-joo-lations!" and "amoozin but confoozin" and "natcherly." I heard a lady describe a man as a "heel" to my mother, bewildering me whose father was in the shoe business, and only much, much later when I saw a few Zachary Scott movies (*Cass Timberlane, Mildred Pierce, Born to be Bad*, etc.) did that coin correctly slot.

At 5 years old I saw my mother's brassieres on the clothesline and asked my mother why "eyeglasses" were hanging out to dry. At the age of 6, I noticed an old black man sitting on a crowded MTA train as we were traveling into Boston from Medford and, pointing to him, reassuringly shouted out to my Mother and Father, "HE IS JUST AS GOOD AS WE ARE." I once inadvisably glued my finger and thumb together at the Magoun Library in 4th grade, trying to amuse a pretty little girl on whom I had a crush, and when the librarian came over angrily to inquire what the problem was and I pointed with a shrug and replied, "Mucilage" — a word that always made me laugh — she very coldly stated, "You are more to be pitied than censured." In the fifth grade I memorized — and won $10 for naming — the Twelve Apostles. It is funny how certain words stick with you. Isn't that exactly what concerned Holden Caulfield in wanting to protect his sister, 10-year-old Phoebe?

I compartmentalized. I believe it is a Catholic thing, a way of understanding the chain of being as James Joyce explains it early in *A Portrait of the Artist as a Young Man*. I fear that I was addicted in a hidebound way to the kind of form, method, and system manifested by James Boswell in his *London Journal: 1762-63*, which was to become later, not surprisingly, one of my favorite books. I had categories in my head where subjects were kept as in a file, aware that the American Indian — another fascination of mine from earliest memories — always regarded each *month* as a separate season (the Oglala Sioux began the year with the "Moon of Frost in the Teepee," call the summer months the "Moon of Making Fat," etc.) and that even the Chinese always divided the year into 24 seasons ("Spring" starts on February 4, "Rainwater" on Feb. 19, the "Waking of Insects" on March 6th, etc.). I was enamored with Indian lore and thumbing through *Rabble in Arms* before I could fully understand it still managed to marvel at the rich and sympathetic depiction of Indian life in New England and elsewhere. My father's mother, Eva Brousseau, was part-Menominee, a woodland people who had been settled in what is now the state of Wisconsin for thousands of years. Many French soldiers in the New World took Menominee women as their wives or lovers. In the early 19th Century, however, the United States government, intimidating the Menominee, swindled them out of their land. Today, with only about 35 fluent speakers of the language, the culture of these Native Americans, aristocrats of this continent, faces extinction. It fit my view. I found much of the world in a frayed state, a burlap bag with loose ends, which it needed megalomaniacal me to bind up. Who appointed me didn't seem to matter. Oddly enough, I took my willingness to oblige as a sign of humility, not *folie de grandeur*.

Mine were nothing more than fledgling questions of cognition, perception, and awareness. When in his essay, "On Popular Music," Theodore W. Adorno castigates young people for appropriating a popular hit as their own. ("That's my song, the song, the song that was playing when I first kissed X"), while in fact the "apparently isolated, individual experience of a particular song" was known among and being shared with millions of other people, an innocent enough presumption, he was not addressing my problem. I was something of an anti-pluralist early in life and found myself resenting that the world was already in motion when we arrived, that much of history had already happened, where, say, "You're a Grand Old Flag" was already a hit, where we inherited so much of what had already *gone on*. We were not blank blackboards, in short. The writing was on the wall.

I remember as a kid asking my mother, in all innocence, why they sang, "When the m-m-moon shines over the cow *shed*" in the song "K-K-K-Katy," failing to divine anything like a scatological echo. My anxieties when growing up were invariably cognitive and, as I say, almost always concerned with words and their meanings. This is how I believe I headed my boat into the harbor of music and lyrics. Was it not a mistake to say "The Girl *That* I Marry"? What about the strangely missing definite article in "We Three Kings of Orient Are"? Or the line, "Walking with *your* baby *mine*" in "In the Good Ol' Summertime?" [My italics.] Confusing. All of it. In junior high school when we loudly sang in chorus, "I Shall Not Be Moved," for some civic or patriotic function or other, I had not the slightest doubt that the simile, "Just like a tree planted by the waters/ I shall not be moved" was lame, simply because — hello! — a tree, any tree, planted by water, for godsakes, is surely by any definition weak! Does one have to be John Muir or Luther Burbank, George Washington Carver or Joyce Kilmer, to access that fact with true certitude? One other quibble on this old song? Noah Webster in his *Dictionary* assures us that the word *shall* in the first person simply foretells, whereas only when used in the second and third persons does it promise, command, or threaten — therefore in the martial ballad, "I Shall Not be Moved," at least lexicographically, *shall* is used there — at least to a grammarian, and certainly to a pedant — in a comparatively weaker way than was intended. The words of "Why Couldn't Last Night Last Forever?" I recognized, even as a young pippin, was a lyric so temporally muddled, a confusion like a few out-of-focus noises, as to be paradoxical and wrong. When Judy Garland in "Over the Rainbow" sang the words, "When trouble melts like lemon drops," it seemed to me, even as a youngster — although youth is the age for spotting inconsistencies — to be an image so inexact and therefore so completely stupid for anyone to speak of melting while mentioning in the same breath one of the hardest teeth-breaking candies on the planet, that I wondered if I had suddenly dropped into cuckooland.

I do not mean to be hard on Garland. In a real sense, "Over the Rainbow" plagued the poor woman all her life. Many singers have found to their bafflement that they have been trapped by the popularity of their work. A. Conan Doyle, who had much larger ambitions for literature, tried to kill off his famous detective, Sherlock Holmes. Henry James was pestered all his life by importunate fans of what was to his mind a slight short story, *Daisy Miller*, which was one of his few works in print when he died in 1916. Bing Crosby grew completely weary of repeatedly having to sing, "White Christmas," and W.B. Yeats could become apoplectic at public readings when over and over again he was requested to recite, "The Lake Isle of Innisfree," one of his lesser lyrics, one that to his great grief he even had to record. It is the crisis of the theme song, I daresay. How saturnine a face was drawn every time Vaughan Monroe had to sing, "Racing with the Moon"? Or Bing Crosby, "When the Blue of the Night (Meets the Gold of the Day)"? Or Gene Autry, "Back in the Saddle Again"? Or Tony Bennett, "I Left My Heart in San Francisco"? Or Perry Como, "Dream Along With Me?" Did not all the words become so many empty echoes, heard once again only to disappear? The lyrics must sound after a while like the drone of crickets, heard (at least by the insects) solely in the knees.

Do I hear the opposition say words do not matter? That language does not make our world, not distinguish us from apes, not constitute the very means —

with intensity, by incantation, through intelligence — by which we communicate and express whatever ideas sit at the very heart of our being? "Meaning begins in the words, in the action, continues in your head and ends nowhere," Harold Pinter wrote in a letter back in 1958 to Peter Wood, director of *The Birthday Party*, warning him off any facile or reductive epistemologies. "Meaning which is resolved, parceled, labeled, and ready for export is dead, impertinent — and meaningless. I examine my own play and ask, what's going on here?" Pinter is correct in seeking to avoid a "packaged" response to complexity, for sure, but he was an atheist and had no faith in the Word as St. John deeply understood it. We may not come to anything like full meaning at times, but the finding is in the seeking. It was the schoolmaster John Yeomans who in his "philosophic comment on the old alphabet" in 1759 wrote,

> Words are not, as some gross ears interpret, only a grinding or chafing of sound of types and letters, striking the outer ear by the operation of the breath or spirit; but they are very man or mono, principle and very self, everlasting of infinite, dread-united meaning, the express disposition of his nature in the heart, and not in the inked and graven sign. They are spirit, and they are life; they are death, and they are destruction... The word is very God and very Devil, good and evil, virtue and vice; and letters are as shadows.

The Evangelist St. John, who is symbolized in art by the eagle to indicate the heights to which he rises in his Gospel as well as the acuity of his spiritual perception, assures mankind that "In the beginning was the Word, and the Word was with God, and the Word was God. He was with God in the beginning." (John 1:1-2) The Greeks used the term, the Word, not only of the spoken word, but also of the unspoken word, the word that is still in the mind — the idea of reason itself. "When they applied it to the universe, they meant the rational principle that governs all things," we read in the NIV Study Bible. *Reason.* It is the right use of language that constitutes a bulwark not only against ignorance and babble but irrationality itself, the pollution of madness and falsehood. What is more important than that language — rising above chop-logic, political demagoguery, lies, bullshit — make sense?

I have alluded above to Thoreau. Let me add I was also amazed while I was growing up to find that so many songs dealt not only with the subject of nature but that were also neo-religious, tree-worshipping, pantheistic eco-exaltations of the "Climb Every Mountain" variety. Mountains. Seas. Thoreau who was and is my hero meditated on trees, saw how cows created their own shade, and, having studied Linnaeus, loved among other things to demonstrate "how accurately flowers perform the service of a time-piece." Still, I was scandalized that he ignored Christmas in his cabin at Walden. Curiously, no one in the Gospels comes to God by way of nature. Nowhere does the New Testament record an instance of anyone coming to believe in Jesus Christ as the Messiah simply because his or her heart was gladdened or their spirit uplifted by the glories of nature — you can look it up — and yet in the musical world nature as such, in the classic songs of our most popular and best composers, quite suffices for love, faith, hope, even sex. ("People who meet/ in this romantic setting/ are so hypnotized by the lovely/ Evening summer breeze/ warbling of a meadowlark/ moonlight in Vermont")

Was it pantheism I had been warned about that kept me so fearful about equating God with nature and sinning against the First Commandment? To me exalting nature above God made a wound in the earth parallel to what is called in gardening a "clairvoyee" — a window-like hole cut in a hedge — and badly profaned it. So love should not be the subject of songs, nor should nature. And how about sex?

There was an unwholesome, because repressed, interest in sex in the 1950s. People were just as horny back then, probably more so, but everything marked by, or arousing, an immoderate or unwholesome interest or desire back in that decade, any lyric or reference in song to sexual desire, had to be addressed or approached by hints, euphemistic nudges, fake and fatuous purity, the fraud of ham-handed suggestion. It was all sham delicacy, circumlocution, pomposity, and pretense. What were the 1950s exactly like in that regard? Let one example stand for the many. In *A Summer Place* (1959), arguably one of the most prurient movies ever filmed, a distraught Sandra Dee, the love interest of tall, earnest Troy Donahue, meekly tells her severe mother, "We capsized [our boat], and we spent the night on the beach," when instantly comes from the soundtrack — portentously — an ominous musical thunderclap! Dee's vicious mother ingeniously played by an outrageously OTT Constance Ford, a bottle blond who is all jutting chin and icy sarcasm — throughout the movie and with great relish seems to be channeling the fiend, Nazi Ilse Koch, the Bitch of Buchenwald — and who demands that her innocent daughter immediately undergo a thorough medical examination. Nudge, nudge. Back in the 1950s, hints had to serve. "You give me a 'thrill.'" "I found my thrill/ on Blueberry Hill." Smitten lovers were "slaves" to love, whatever that meant. Addicted? Lost? A curvaceous young girl was a "bundle of charms." *Charms*, a protean word back then — a euphemism and a dysphemism, both — could mean anything. Lyrics about seduction, lust, temptation were transmuted into dumb euphemisms. The song "Temptation" is a good example: 1933

> You came, I was alone, I should have known
> You were temptation
> You smiled, luring me on, my heart was gone
> And you were temptation
> It would be thrilling, if you were willing
> And, if it can never be, pity me...

Any lyric with the word "ecstasy" back in the crew-cut-wearing, straight-arrow Eisenhower years spoke subtextually of orgasms. It was all of it a syntax of dodging and default, of escape and prevarication. Circumlocutions and passwords were employed for just about every lusty and lascivious idea there was. *Atmosphere* had to suffice. The archetypal song in this category is Tony Martin's "I Get Ideas" (1951):

> When we are dancing
> And you're dangerously near me
> I get ideas, I get ideas.
> I want to hold you
> So much closer than I dare do.
> I want to scold you
> 'Cause I care more than I care to.
> And when you touch me
> and there's fire in every finger
> I get ideas, yes I get ideas.
> And after we have kissed goodnight
> and still you linger
> I kinda think you get ideas too.

*I kinda think*!?

To one degree or another, this sort of thing never fully goes out of style. You can hear the same kind of low-brow euphemisms, for example, in Billy Paul's meretricious "Me and Mrs. Jones," a couple who had a "thang" goin' on: "Me and Mrs. Jones, we got a thing going on,/ We both know that it's wrong/ But it's much too strong to let it cool down " as well as in the Manhattans' tacky, trashy, tawdry "Kiss and Say Goodbye" (1980) who are singing about an adulterous assignation about to end, which comes with a fillip in the way of a deep-voiced — and reechy — spoken narrative:

> This has got to be the saddest day of my life
> I called you here today for a bit of bad news
> I won't be able to see you anymore
> Because of my *obligations*, and the ties that you have.
> We've been meeting here everyday
> And since this is our last day together
> I wanna hold you just one more time.
> [My italics.]

Of *course* Barry White did a cover of it. Regarding the tryst song, the definitive example is probably "Slip Away" by Alabama soul singer Clarence Carter's "Now I know it's wrong/ the things I ask you to do/ but can you slip away baby/ 'cause I got to see you/ I feel a deep burning inside/ Oh, I wish you could slip away..."

Mind you, regarding the point raised above about Christ and the power of nature, I never denied nor would, the glory of God in evidence, nor fail to acknowledge that all creation serves the Lord. "The heavens declare the glory of God; and the firmament shows his handiwork," we read in Psalm 19, and in Romans 1:20 ff. we read, "For the invisible things of him from the creation of the world are clearly seen, being understood by the things that are made, even his eternal power and Godhead."

As I say, I was a hopeless pedant, even as an intense, pertinacious, and fairly nosy youngster. It is a wonder that I did not end up a logical positivist. Why, I wistfully wondered in the wint'ry Christmas song, "Sleigh Ride," could there possibly exist a line, "There's a birthday party at the home of Farmer Gray,/ It'll be the perfect ending of a perfect day," when of all days of the year that particular day was quite obviously and exclusively the occasion of the birth of Christ, one not to be made redundant and/or blasphemed by the usurpation by some passing chawbacon-in-overalls with a mule or two as having a parallel party or celebration and that one — seriously — being called "perfect"?

It remained a serious annoyance to me that others seemed so casually to disregard what I considered weighty matters, as for example in the matter of Christmas songs. It was not, egregiously, "It Came Upon *A* Midnight Clear" as everyone somehow always sang it, but correctly "It Came Upon *The* Midnight Clear" [my italics]. In the venerable song "God Rest Ye Merry, Gentlemen," the comma, as almost never happened when it appeared in print, was meant to come after Merry. Then, it was "Joy to the World, The Lord *Is* Come" [my italics], not *Has* Come — a Christmas song to which people in pronouncing it, further irritating me, never gave the full title. Speaking of that season, I came to resent another fib that people commonly tried to fob off which only further contributed to my youthful cynicism: the muscular assertion, repeated as an article of faith, that no beautiful white snowflake of the many that fell from the beginning of time was ever the same. I felt I was being fobbed off with a lie. Whenever I heard that sing-song ditty, popular among children, "Jesus loves the little children,/ All the children of the world./ Red and yellow,/ black and white,/ All are precious in his sight,/ Jesus loves the little children of the world" I wondered why when I was walking around in my little shoes I had never managed to lay eyes on a person with such distinct hues — and if they existed, I mean, why no one green or blue, orange or purple?

I was a hidebound and compulsive literalist. It made life easy. I have no doubt that I was also a pain-in-the ass. Every question had an answer. Was not that the entire logic of things, the whole point of life? I was a peculiar child. Forming in me was also a belief that through art, in any shape or form, one got a second chance in life. I was devoted to radio dramas, which I listened to in the dark with something of a lonely thrill. It was at this age that I gave puppet shows for other kids in the neighborhood, devoured books on ventriloquism, went around proclaiming — to nobody in particular — "Off with their heads!" I drew Al Capp's Shmoos all over my notebooks in the fourth grade. A hero during one period of my pre-adolescence was the bank robber Willie ("The Actor") Sutton, master of disguises, and whenever my mother had to go to the post office I always asked to tag along so I could to look at the "wanted" posters on the wall there specifically to see that triangular small-faced man with the slick mustache. He robbed a hundred banks but allegedly never followed through when a woman screamed or a baby cried. He never carried a loaded gun, could assume any disguise, and was a master at breaking out of prison. On one level or another, I identified withhis cleverness, that and his raccoon efficiency. What other dream could an adolescent possibly have?

I could not figure out what "certained poor shepherds" meant in "The First Noel," nor how "My country 'tis of thee, sweet land of liberty" then correlated with "to thee I sing." (If one addressing the country was singing, "It is ['tis] of thee [I sing]," where on earth was the grammatical logic in repeating — and only a line away — "Of thee I sing"? I remember being at church with my father, where that kind and pious man thought it highly irreverent of me to be nudging him so, and, nodding directly ahead as a sign for me to be paying attention to the altar ("Eyes front," father would often have to repeat to his rubbernecking children, even at the dinner table), he would not acknowledge me, anxious in the pew, even though I had I thought quite precociously spotted a singular/ plural gaffe in the Gospels that I very badly wanted to point out to him and, even better, to have his beaming approval of my apologetical insight. When we were walking out together after the service, waiting for a suitable interval, to put paid to what I knew he took for my obstreperousness, I mentioned the curious Scriptural line in my missal: "If the salt *have* lost its flavor" [my italics] and announced to him with assured insistence that it was a big mistake. My father was not impressed with my scholarship, only with my pedantry and my jittery inattention at Mass, but he nodded in acceptance and we dropped the matter. I remember how my brothers and I would often exasperate my father when on Sundays he took us on local historical trips around Boston foolishly inquiring of him whenever we spotted printed on the train rails the dire MTA warnings, "Spitting Forbidden" (surely a sign invoking a different time), "Dad, shouldn't it be one or other, 'Spitting Forbidding' or 'Spidden Forbidden'?" A little of that went a long way with him, and he would tell us to stop horsing around. He was from the "Life with Father" school and while loving and fair brooked no nonsense and from our earliest years, whenever any of us were leaving the house he always said — as if we were scions of the Duke of Wellington and born in Blenheim Palace — "Remember who you are."

When I scan the cherished but often fluctuating landscape of my childhood, turning over toadstone after toadstone, I see that I was always looking for answers. In one sense, I was nothing *but* a question. I was known for that, to a degree. A question is as much an assault as a subversion in that it challenges authority but, equaling need, has a touch of hubris. It hates the clockwork condition and happily follows Walt Whitman's advice, "Resist much; obey little."

I was bothered by — failing to understand — paradox, as well. Take, for example, the rather odd title of Thornton Wilder's play, *The Skin of Our Teeth*, a non-visual, never mind impossible image. It bothered me to distraction, and in a sense still does. In the seventh grade, it was the same with *Macbeth* when he spoke of "murdering sleep," and then later when I ruminated unhappily over the title "Leaves of Grass," a mad inaccuracy that had me shaking my head over Walt Whitman: was he drunk? Miss Sullivan in the sixth grade on Friday afternoons, as a treat, read us long passages from Hamlin Garland's *A Son of the Middle Border*, and, sitting there, utterly bewildered, I would only be wondering over and over, how could there be a middle border when borders were, by definition, precisely *never* in the middle? When we were saying our prayers at night, even at the age of five or six, me and my brothers lay in our consecutive beds like dwarves, muttering,

> Now I lay me down to sleep
> I pray the lord my soul to keep;
> If I should die before I wake
> I pray the Lord my soul to take

my burden lying there in the dark was wondering anxiously what the rigorous difference was between "my soul to keep" and "my soul to take," and if so what exactly was it? Along with that was my added discombobulation in pondering whether death was so arbitrary that a person could be summarily snuffed out simply by going to *sleep*! I can say that I felt it profane to question authority, especially parental and/or divine authority. But what seemed to me to be a mistake also seemed to me to warrant correction. I felt it oafish to quibble, but wasn't it also oafish to state, as, for example in the commercial for the Negro College Fund, that "A mind is a terrible thing to waste"? A mind is not a "terrible thing," to be philosophically precise. The slogan should be: "It's a terrible thing to waste a mind," even if one must insist that anything — whatever that thing may be — *can* be wasted. The ad as it stands is a Wittgensteinian horror. If anything, a dumb advertisement was a terrible thing!

One tends to forget that children see things with fresh eyes, are ill-disposed to accept what to adults over a period of time accept as normal, habitual, acceptable. This is why lying to children is so shocking to them, a scandalous fault that in many instances is not forgotten over a lifetime. I remember being at the movies to see *The Babe Ruth Story* and seeing a "preview of coming attractions" for a movie where a thug, played by Richard Conte, I think, is trying to strangle a man with a crowbar. I was terrified, almost mute, for it was the first example of violence — *the very first* — I had ever seen. The image was printed on my retina, as it were, to last over the course of a lifetime.

When in the song "Those Faraway Places (With Strange Sounding Names)" I heard the lines, "We'll go to China or maybe Siam," I bafflingly questioned myself: *those* are strange-sounding names? When in our own country we had our own unusual names like the ones I daily came across in maps like Patchogue? Kokomo? Osceola? Apalachicola? Sheboygan? Oshkosh? Winnipesaukee? *Massachusetts*?

I was bothered by everything. As I look back, I was perplexed, whether justifiably or not, by the nursery rhyme, "The Man in the Moon," read to me by my instructive and literate mother, a former school-teacher, whose correct pronunciation of the English town, always to my consternation

> The Man in the Moon
> Came down too soon
> To inquire his way
> To Norwich

never included the W I saw there, an objection I never expressed for fear she might put the book down and make me sleep.

> He went by the south
> And burnt his mouth
> With eating cold
> plum-porridge.

I even worried apropos the "Star-Spangled Banner" that no normal person ever said, never mind sang, "Oh say, can you see." I was earnest. I thought the title "The Alms-Uncle," Chapter One of Joanna Spyri's *Heidi*, was a mistake for — a misspelling of — "The Aunt Uncle," although, not that I ever tried, I could not explain why. Please forgive me, but at the age of 7 and 8, I rather insufferably regarded myself as the measure of all things. *I felt that the world somehow needed me around to care!* Was it anxiety? Misbegotten vanity? An infantile tropism for order? Some kind of messianism? Whenever I heard the song "Moonlight in Vermont" — memory evokes a television image of perky Miss Rosemary Clooney in a big puffy chiffon dress giving her version of the hit — I was troubled by the enigmatic line, "icy finger waves." May one ask, first of all, is it a phrase or a sentence? Is the word "waves" a verb? A noun? Does it mean that waving is difficult for fingers nipped by cold? Surely it is not an allusion to some sort of icy gel for a lady's hair permanent. Nor could it possibly refer to the gesture of a breaking ocean wave -- certainly not in rural Vermont. Whatever the answer, it is a most unfortunate lyric, completely inápropos. (Why is "finger" singular?) It was all a muddle. I also believed that the line in the same song, "Falling leaves, a sycamore" — you cannot hear the comma — was an actual sentence, queerly, one that I came to understand! You know, taking the word "falling" as a gerund, whereby the act of falling (out of it) leaves the sycamore above you. Or, alternately, as in leaves the sycamore behind as in the distance. SeewhatI'msayin'? Oh, never mind.

Was I wicked mental (to use a Boston-ism)? I also used to think that Katharine Lee Bates in her famous lyric, "America the Beautiful" was using the word *majesties* as a *verb* when she wrote, "For purple mountain majesties above the fruited plain" — in this sense, that Mt. Washington majesties the landscape of New Hampshire. Frankly, an argument could be made for that belief; consider the grammar:

> O beautiful for spacious skies,
> For amber waves of grain,
> For purple mountain majesties
> Above the fruited plain!

The country is beautiful for the skies, grain fields, and for the purple mountain that "majesty" above the fruited plains, in other words. Was I any more out to lunch than the French poet Paul Verlaine who admitted in his *Confessions* (1895), in his early youth having come across Baudelaire's classic work — Verlaine was immediately thrilled to find words like "perversity" ("as they called it in seminaries for young ladies") and "nakedness" — "I was firmly convinced that the book was called *Les Fleurs de Mai*"?

Speaking of the unheard comma, I also entertained the belief that in the 1940s hit-song the refrain, "Bell bottom trousers, coat of navy blue" was an actual sentence, that the word "coat" was somehow a verb — you know, something like "covered with" or "sewn over by."

Elisions puzzled me, as well. "Missed the Saturday dance," the opening line of Duke Ellington's "Don't Get Around Much Anymore," I heard with a kind of dogged insistence as "Mr. Saturday Dance," probably because of similar songs around, like "Mr. Touchdown, U.S.A." and "Mr. Wonderful." In Lorrie Moore's novel *Who Will Run the Frog Hospital?* the narrator apparently shares my tin ear, for we read there:

> My brain worked stiffly, regrouped and improvised sounds. For a while I believed Sandra Dee was not only an actress but one of the French days of the week. I sang "Frere Jacques" with the bewildering line, "Sony, lay my Tina."

As I say, even as a kid I had the pedant's (and xenophiliac's!) compulsion to learn and understand the precise lyrics to various and exotic songs like "My Little Grass Shack in Kealakekua, Hawaii" (words and music by Bill Cogswell, Tommy Harrison, and Johnny Noble), especially any odd or evocative lines like "I can hear the Hawaiians saying *'Komoma1 no kaua ika hale welakakao'"* and "Where the *Humuhumu, Nukunuku a puaa* goes swimming by.'" I went to the trouble of buying the sheet music when I was in junior high school in order to check it out. I also had the equally peculiar compulsion, sometime later, to learn the correct spelling of the words in that popular 1940s *chanson de merde*, "Chickery Chick" (written by Sylvia Dee), the refrain to which, spelt as pronounced, goes:

> Chickery chick cha-la eha-la
> Check-a-la romey
> In a bananika, bollika wollika
> Chickery chick is me.

Even in my teenage years when in an unlucky moment I happened to hear that smarmy, operatic radio-pimp Paul Harvey — even his self-cherishing love of good diction made my skin crawl — conclude one of his bathetic broadcasts with, "And now you know The Rest of the Story," I knew as any discerning person should that the guy was a huckster and as salaciously oily and crudely over-familiar as he was ignorant. His signature codas were, in fact, not the "rest" of his loopy fables, but technically rather the *conclusions* to the stories, punch-lines, fabricated as finales, and "revelations" made to seem like the "rest" of something only by dint of this sad cheapjack's churlish over-dramatized pauses which, along with his penchant for reading commercials in his own voice without a break and so making ads seem part of the news, was integral to such shameless pitches.

Of course, I also used to believe, until I learned better, that H.G. Wells, Orson Welles, and George Orwell were all the same person, that the word Lourdes was an Old English spelling of the word Lord, and after my parents' gift to me of a copy of *Immortals in Music* that the word "Bayreuth" in the biography of Richard Wagner was a variant old-fashioned spelling of the capitol of Lebanon. Language meant a good deal more in broadcasting back then. For a broadcaster to misuse the word "hopefully" or scandalously to make grammatical mistakes of agreement ("Every*one* took *their* seats.") — this kind of sloppiness is standard fare on radio and television today — would generate piles of angry mail from listeners. Standards were higher back then. It was a different time. People would laugh watching the vapid *I Love Lucy* on television, and sympathize with the poor husband, whenever Ricky Ricardo with his comic Cuban accent would get befuddled over the confusing and contradictory pronunciation of words like *bough, rough, thorough, tough, cough,* and *dough*. It is probably one of their funniest episodes, if you found the show funny — I myself couldn't bear it. 1950s humor is to me, *mali principii, malus finuis*, the worst that ever was, all those pulled faces, clown shoes, spritzers-in-the-face, and people hitting each other with bladders. If you cannot connect with my complaint, look at a re-run of any *Red Skelton Show*.

It is ironic that I saw Ricky's grammatical dumb show on television, the "word-mangling medium that sucks in victims…perniciously," in the words of the theater critic John Simon, and which, in his opinion, along with the student rebellion of 1968, incompetent English teachers, and the utterly barbaric notion that "language must accommodate itself to the whims, idiosyncrasies, dialects, and sheer ignorance of underprivileged minorities," dealt one of the "four great body blows" to modern education.

Ricky Ricardo's private hobbles with words reflected a kind of cultural epistemology, for as W. H. Auden said, "The problem we have with our vocabulary reflects the problem we have with our lives," but it was more than anything a cognitive problem regarding accent. Accent, it should be noted, is only one feature of a dialect, which is only a variation in language that differs from other odd variations in its vocabulary, grammar, and pronunciation (phonology). Ricardo's phrase, "Lucy, you got some 'splainin' to do," (an overused part of our popular culture, Ricky never actually used this phrase,) may be called a sociolect or a kind of a regional topolect, but, technically, where a distinction can be made only in terms of pronunciation, the term "accent" is appropriate, not one of dialect. There are supposedly as many as 197 different — discrete — dialects spoken in the United States, including Spanglish, Cajun, Lumbee, Midwest, Chicano, Bostonian, Polish-American, African-American, etc.

To repeat, it was all somehow deeply important to me, all that music, all those lyrics, all those words. I will take a moment here to mention that the line from the ballad, "Danny Boy," although of course it is an Irishism — "It's I'll be here in sunshine and in shadow" — I'm still trying to figure out regarding the full heft of its grammar. That also goes for the bizarre line from "The Wabash Cannonball" — can anyone make sense of it'? — "From the great Atlantic ocean to the wide Pacific shore/ From the green New Hampshire mountains to the southland's Cajun lore." I have also heard "From the queen of flowing mountains to the south bells by the shore." I was also secretly bothered that in the sweet song, "There'll Never Be Another You," the Andrews Sisters sang the line, "There will be other lips that I may kiss," when it should more correctly be, "There may be other lips that I will kiss." Even at the verdescent age of eight or nine, while listening to the perennial "Home on the Range," I used to think — mistakenly, because I did not understand rhetoric — that the litotes, "And the skies are not cloudy all day," was fairly ridiculous. Speaking of "Home on the

Range," listening to *Gene Autry's Melody Ranch* on the radio on Saturday night CBS at 8 o'clock ("It's eeaaasy chewing makes those little jobs go a little easier. I like it!" drawled Gene of his sponsor, Wrigley's Doublemint chewing gum), I was constantly pondering the mystery, having been born and raised in Boston, Mass., of exactly where and what the West *was* when, say, the "King of the Cowboys" seemed to sing with equal passion and a kind of proprietary sectionalism about not only Texas ("Boots and Saddle," "Deep in the Heart of Texas," etc.) but also Kansas ("Sioux City Sue"), Mexico and California ("Mexicali Rose"), Kentucky ("Sleep, Kentucky Babe") — a particular song that Autry sang, by the way, with a (weak!) black dialect ("Silvery moon 'am shinin'/ in the heavens up above") giving the South plausibility — and about some other place in the mountains in "Silver-Haired Daddy of Mine" ("In a vine-covered shack in the mountains"), which I figured put him somewhere in either Colorado or Tennessee.

Were we supposed to know all of this?

Was some secret card with all the answers, all the solutions to all knowledge, been handed out at birth to people, but not to me?

What was I missing?

I for one was determined to know!

And I trust it will be patiently understood and forgiven that I was not anything close to being a racist as a boy but merely anxious when hearing these few lyrics to the old minstrel-song, "Bill Bailey Won't You Please Come Home,"

> 'Member dat rainy evenin'
> I drove you out
> wid nothin' but a fine-tooth comb

I questioned — forgive me — why woolly-headed black people would *need* a fine-tooth comb. I still do not know what a beguine[3] is, neither do you, nor do I have the foggiest idea what happens when one begins — or begins to begin. And of course the line from the 1950s hit "Golden Earrings": "And let this *pair* of golden earrings cast *their* spell tonight" [my italics], always bothered me for its grammatical disagreement. Although the lyrics to "What Are You Doing for the Rest of your Life" from the film *The Happy Ending* (words by Marilyn and Alan Bergman) has some splendid metaphors and images ("What are you doing for the rest of your life?/ North and south and east and west of your life?" "All the seasons and the times of your days/ All the nickel and the dimes of your

---

3    There was of course a pseudo-religious order called the Beguines ("stammerers") founded by Lambert Le Begue who died in 1177. The subject of Ellen Gilchrist's "1944," one of my favorite short stories, is this wonderful Cole Porter song and the magical epiphany of music.

days") I must say that I do have a bit of a problem with the line, "Oh, let me be the one to *hear* the *silent* wish you make." [My italics.] Growing up in the Midwest, the great singer Bobby Short has written of remembering local radio-announcers out there, stumped by the terminology or terrain of New York City, particularly Harlem's — and needless to say completely ignorant of the Eighth Avenue subway line that ran up to that well-known Negro section — who would introduce Duke Ellington's (and Billy Strayhorn's) great theme-song record as "Take Thee A Train"!

Speaking of the definite article, I found it quirky beyond words when in the seventh-grade we all sang in assembly from a Stephen Foster booklet "My Old Kentucky Home" — a lovely song, I felt, but inexplicably jammed with the definitive article, as many as seven of them in the first stanza alone where, notice, in the first line we sang in ensemble, "The Old Kentucky Home," stressing the generic everywhere, I gather, unlike the title which actually goes "My Old Kentucky Home:"

> *The* sun shines bright in *the* old Kentucky Home,
> 'Tis summer, *the* darkies are gay.
> *The* corntop's ripe and *the* meadows are in bloom,
> While *the* birds make music all *the* day.
> [My italics.]

On this same theme, why is it that in most radio commercials and TV advertising actors playing ordinary shills always, *always*, refer to the product they're selling or holding up by way of the unnecessary definite article? "I love *the* Ben-Gay." "*The* Clorox makes my floors shine." Are Madison Avenue men, *the* Madison Avenue men, convinced that this sounds somehow more homey, more real, stupid and so more authentic-sounding? Is this the locution for proletarian jerks like us? Isn't the dopiness of a person pointing at an object reinforced when he or she says *the*? "I looove *the* Bayer! It's a miiiiracle!"

As to the uncommon word "bromidic,"[4] as used — it pops up in the lyric always as something of a surprise in the Rodgers and Hammerstein song, "I'm In Love With A Wonderful Guy" from the hit musical *South Pacific*, "I'm bromidic and bright/ as a moon-happy night pourin' light on the dew," a line, let me add parenthetically, which exhibits a classic case of visual jabberwocky — *bromidic?* —

---

4        Last year, quite serendipitously, I came across Gelett Burgess' *The Bromide and Other Theories* (1933), a work in which can be found not only the definitive essay on that odd word, a Burgess coinage surely, but clearly Oscar Hammerstein's singular source for the lyrics sung by Nellie Forbush, a classic "bromide."

and with a particular word that I can assert that after a lifetime of reading, even with my own fascination with words, I have never once, *once* mind you, without a single exception, ever come across at any other time or in any other context, and that includes studying chemistry. I might also add that the word does not make an appearance in the classic *Webster's International Dictionary* (Second Edition), which is generally regarded as the most comprehensive dictionary in the world.

I was also convinced in my early listening youth that when Dean Martin sang "If our lips should meet, inamorata, kiss me, kiss me, sweet inamorata...," he was in love and having a blissful time in the little Italian town of Amorata, which, by the way, if there is no town there so named, there should be. I remember that I used to think, when I first began hearing the — at least to me — kinetic word Wyoming, it was what someone *did*, an action, out in the far West. Perhaps I never did get over my "hearing" problem for, jumping ahead to 1972, I believed for decades that the refrain of America's "Ventura Highway" — their run-on diction didn't help — was the encouraging exhortation, "Venture a highway in the sunshine/ where the days are longer/ the lights are stronger than moonshine," you know, go exploring a highway existentially — much more poetic, in my view. Checking again later in life my *Webster's Second International* also confirmed my nagging childhood suspicion that the word "slitch" in the line, "The kitchen took a slitch" from "The Munchkin Land Songs" (a.k.a. "Ding Dong The Witch is Dead") in the MGM film, *The Wizard of Oz*

> The house began to pitch, the kitchen took a slitch
> It landed on the wicked witch in the middle of a ditch
> Which was not a healthy situation for the wicked witch!

was not a real word but merely a sloppy rhyming-slug thrown into the lyric probably at the last minute — a further disappointment. Perhaps the lyricist was of the same mind-set of the mystic Bob Dylan who in 1967 nuttily told the director of *Don't Look Back*, D.A. Pennebaker, "All words that rhyme mean the same thing."

I love the subject of misheard lyrics, incidentally. We all remember that famous Christian hymn, "Gladly, the Cross-Eyed Bear," right? Most listeners point to the classic modern example in Jimi Hendrix's "Purple Haze"— when he sings, "'Scuse me while I kiss the sky," many people hear "'Scuse me while I kiss this guy" — and an entire website can be located that catalogs the funniest of them,[5] among which can be found The Cars' "Shake It Up," where you hear

---

5       http://www.kissthisguy.com

"Don't let nobody pick your bum" instead of "Don't let nobody pick your fun" and "She's got a chicken to fry" in the Beatles' "Ticket to Ride" and "There's a bathroom on the right" from Creedence Clearwater Revival's "Bad Moon Rising" instead of "There's a bad moon on the rise." It is technically known as a "mondegreen," a word that goes back to the poem "The Bonny Earl O'Moray" from Percy's *Reliques* (1765)

> Ye Highlands and ye Lowlands,
> Oh, where hae ye been?
> They hae slain the Earl O' Moray,
> And laid him on the green.

where for centuries people have misheard the last line of that opening stanza as "And Lady Mondegreen." — a verbal, and needless to say, comical confusion that has a person, for example, hear in the Twenty Third Psalm, instead of "goodness and mercy," "Surely good Mrs. Murphy shall follow me all the days of my life."

When I first heard "The Pennsylvania Polka," that old 1942 staple composed by Lester Lee and Zeke Manners, I was bedeviled by the opening exhortations, "Strike up the music, the band has begun." Was that not redundant? (I once apprised my mother that her saying "a pair of binoculars" was redundant, for if "binoculars" was plural, why say a "pair"?) With all of those phrasal verbs so popular in American speech, "stalled out," "sleep in," "lie down" "fry up," "write up," "drop out," "calm down," "stressed out," "separate out," there is an annoying aspect to that kind of usage, a kind of dopey, country-cuteness in the redundancy of the phrases. Southerners love such phrases, waitresses, ranch hands, those of the barnyard mentality. "Eat up them vittles, Bubba!" "You closin' up, hoss?" "What you up to, son?" "Where you at?" "I mone fry me up some taters!" I have always assumed that, at least to the normal individual, the phrasal verb — that verb in which a particle (usually a preposition) alters and narrows its meaning — was understood as crude. Worse than being bafflingly indirect, they tend to be informal, even slang. (It calls to mind phrases like "pre-recorded:" isn't everything recorded, *pre*-recorded?) "He put me down." "Are you having me on?" "Add up." "Back down." "Rip off." "Wear out." "Turn around." "Throw away." "Look forward." "Figure out." "Draw up." "Nod off." "Slip up." "Stand in." "Burn down." "Work out." The language is already precarious. Scruple rarely matters to people today. Listen to talk radio. Sports talk-shows are the worst offenders. I remember one caller in Boston on WEEI, using a snarky phrase, asked "How's that working out for him?" Within a week, everyone had adopted that pat phrase, callers, hosts, each and every parrot. In the same sentence sportscasters refer to the "Tour de France," which they pronounce Fra*wn*ce, as a sport taking place in France, which in the latter case they pronounce — why? — to rhyme with pants. The Prevent Defense, an alignment an American football that utilizes as many as seven or more defensive backs, all sports analysts on national television pronounce *pree-vent*, but in every other use of the word they will say *prevént*. American guys almost never say football — they prefer "*foop*ball." People constantly say "preventative" for preventive, "eriudition" for erudition, "sherbert" for sherbet, almost never use the phrase *per se* correctly — it means *by itself* — and do not know a number from a numeral. Almost everywhere foliage is mispronounced as "folage," women too often say "mens*tra*tion" for menstruation, and of course ill-informed goofballs still insist on saying "Eye-talian" for Italian and "Eye-ran" for Iran and "Eye-raq" for Iraq — always an indication to me that the person speaking is a perfect snool and a simpleton. How provincial is it in the year 2012 to be mispronouncing, and with no shame, the name of a country? The power of bad example set by public speakers cannot be stressed enough. The late ABC sportscaster/ buffoon Howard Cosell, ubiquitous on 1970s-1980s television in his canary-colored ABC blazer, earphones on his big ears that gave him the look of an insect, and a toupee that looked like the ruined pelt of a Tasmanian devil, by repeatedly — and incorrectly — pronouncing the word "defense" on the first syllable for entire decades succeeded by the virus of his verbal stupidity in ensuring that the word is now almost universally pronounced no other way by millions of sports boobs. His ungrammatical catchphrase, "I'm just telling it like it is," is another asinine Cosellism.

Good God, a clusterfuck of the 1970s, disco, and jug-eared Howard Cosell, all at once? I can't take it. I cannot take it. Have moithy!

Language has become debased. Clichés, threadbare phrases, inane word usage, trite expressions, verbal tics, stock terms, cheap slang, and grammatical errors that even third-graders would not make are indications of national brainlessness. Nowadays, Americans begin their response to every question with the word "Well." "Well, Tom, I guess…" "Well, the truth is…" When did this queer bit of bullshit begin, with Will Rogers? It had its rough equivalent in the 1930s, when almost everyone began virtually every sentence with "say." It persisted into the Fifties. Remember Buffalo Bob always opened *The Howdy Doody Show* with, "Say kids — what time is it?" People say irregardless, which is not even a word. "That's a whole nother argument!" everyone says. A whole *nother*! That isn't perfectly nuts? In general discourse nowadays, "absolutely" stands for "yes," "no problem" has replaced "you're welcome," and the slang expression "hanging

stands for everything from going on a date to socializing with your friends  
 having a "night over" with the girls to sitting around in a diner or driving  
around the back streets of Peoria in order to bash mailboxes with bats. "At the  
end of the day" is a phrase that virtually everybody now turns, like an hourly  
crank. Rank stupidity spreads on an epidemic scale. Intending (I gather) to say  
"hilarious," people say "hysterical." Is there anyone left in the world who still  
knows the difference between "lack of interest" and the word "disinterested"? A  
soul left alive who understands the distinction between "anxious" and "eager"?  
I cringe when I hear or read that a group of people may be "impacted" by a  
hurricane, a law, a recession. (The problem comes from people's confusion  
between the words "affected" and "effected" and the laziness of human beings  
to learn the difference.) Wisdom teeth may be impacted, but people are affected.  
Slovens, which now sadly includes most public broadcasters, are allowed to use  
that word instead of "affected" by even the *Chicago Manual of Style*, but in all  
formal writing — guides, journals, newspapers, white papers, certainly academic  
writing — its use is nothing less than abhorrent. The word *hopefully* is almost  
always used incorrectly: "Hopefully, it won't rain tomorrow." Hopefully means  
"with hope" and describes a subject who feels hopeful; it does not mean and  
never has and never will "it is hoped that." "Good to go," "I'm just sayin'" "I  
hope they find closure," and "go figure," are, among other phrases, echoed all  
day, everywhere, with box-ticking idiocy, and employed with insane abandon.  
(Closure is the practice of closing debate in a parliamentary body by putting the  
matter to a vote originated in 1882 in the British House of Commons. People  
nowadays like the word "closure," which is invariably misused, because it has a  
Gallic approximation and gives its addlepated users a sense of being highbrow —  
or of speaking French, but then how many parvenus who misuse and/or overuse  
the word realize that the French word for closure is *clôture*?) Why does no one say  
"resounds," a good Anglo-Saxon word? It is obvious that the Latinate "resonates,"  
a word that is used nowadays with mad abandon, sounds more full-throated and  
makes the ordinary Joe seem syllabically more muscular. There is also something  
kitschily pathetic in the rampant preference nowadays – as much a parvenu's as  
a sweaty, hustling real-estate agent's-- for the word "home" over "house." Finally,  
on the subject of wretched excesses, is every single dickwit of caller to a foolish  
talk-shows in the United States *required by fiat*, to say — parrotlike — "Thanks for  
taking my call"?

Then how woefully grotesque is it in this dubious. self-conscious world of  
ours that a politician is required to say, "I approve this message," in the very same  
commercial that he or she is *delivering*?

Cable pundits — and I hear broadcasters saying "pun*dints*" all the time — are addicted to words like "amazing" and "fantastic." One hears brain-dead variations of "X is the new Y" and "What happens in Z stays in Z." The slang word that is currently used for such conned, or canned, received phrases — rather like coins, flattened to the touch, that have been too long in circulation — is "*snowclones.*" Pop phrases everywhere proliferate: two easy payments, sum total, free gift, full quart, nice and hot, baby bump. Nothing is a "problem" anymore, it is nowadays a "challenge." The ridiculous word *parenting* is now, repugnantly, a verb. Then what the hell does "pro-active" mean — exactly what was wrong with the word *active*? The word *like* is now used as punctuation, an intensifier standing in for all the adjectives, verbs, and adverbs of which young folks are, like, you know, totally ignorant. At least half of the time when people use the word "literally" they mean "figuratively." ("We literally froze our asses off up at Moosehead Lake.") Does anybody on earth know how (and why) the word "parameter" should be properly used? Martha Stewart, American business magnate, author, publisher, and television personality, during a recent taste-test described something — and, what is worse, in that "coached" voice of hers, with *hauteur* — as "very excellent." This is pure ignorance. Then how about "By the way, I admire your pictures very much," as lawyer Tom Hagen, played by Robert Duvall unctuously tells the uncouth movie producer, Jack Woltz, in *The Godfather*. Although he is attempting to sound cool and articulate, especially after having just been insulted, Hagen's over-pastried compliment comes across as the opposite, pig-ignorant. "I admire your pictures" would have been quite enough, no? How anemic is it that all of the cooks on TV's *America's Test Kitchen* feebly resort to repeating the same insipid word "nice," over and over again, as the go-to word of praise throughout the show to describe everything, smells, taste, colors, tools — no verbal class — paradoxically employing the blandest, most vapid of words to characterize what are supposed to be the unique recipes they claim to perfect? "This thaw, took a while to thaw, it's going to take a while to unthaw," pronounced the addled President George W. Bush, speaking of liquidity in the markets in Alexandria, Louisiana on October 20, 2008. *Meet the Press'* David Gregory on the *Today* Show on March 20, 2012, truly embarrassing himself, mispronounced the word asterisk as "asterick." After a crucial loss, the Dallas Cowboys football-team owner Jerry Jones was asked by a local reporter on January 1, 2012 if the team would be rebuilding, and his answer was "Unequivocably." What about the Queen of Oprah's Book Club who cannot even spell? With her OWN network failing, Oprah Winfrey, who for years from a self-appointed position of literacy and intellectual discernment to puff her favorite books, took to Twitter on February 12, 2012 desperately to beg all

Nielsen watchers (ratings tabulators) to turn in to watch her TV special opposite the Grammys — a major violation in the broadcast world, by the way, not to speak of matters of taste — twitting, "Every 1 who can please turn to OWN especially if u have a Neilsen [sic] box." One does not have to reach far for grammatical horrors — notice that most of these are recent examples! On station WOMR in Provincetown on her Saturday morning show on May 26, 2012 disc jockey Tina Lynde, haltingly reading an obituary notice for Robin Gibb of the Bee Gees, solemnly referred to his "tackturn" manner, not — as it was written on her sheet — his "taciturn manner." Radio personality Lou Merloni on a WEEI sports show who in conversation has been repeating "like I say" virtually every minute for more than a year seriously declared on June 8, 2012 after several updates, "That's two breaking newses today." On the ESPN network Earvin "Magic" Johnson on the evening of June 3, 2012 brightly announced, "I'm feeling more better about the Boston Celtics than I am about the Miami Heat." (This same man is now in charge of a multi-billion dollar franchise, the new Los Angeles Dodgers ownership group!) Karl Ravech, a *Baseball Tonight* host, in an interview on July 13, 2012, responded to a question saying, "I don't know where those stories originate from." On June 29, 2012 MSNBC's jug-headed Joe Scarborough loudly and confidently declared that so and so "commentated on" such and such a thing. Critic Hilton Als in a small piece, "Have a Ball," in *The New Yorker* (July 2, 2012) — the snobbish magazine that for many decades has loftily mocked other peoples' gaffes — refers to the extravagant drag balls in Harlem where, he writes, "everyone dressed according to their fantasies — or talked about them." The egotistical, pushy, tendentious, and intellectually insecure Fox News pundit Bill O'Reilly, a self-stroking egotist whom Keith Olbermann calls "the Sisyphus of Morons," wrote in a column on January 30, 2012 that he "was slayed," instead of the correct "was slain." (His asinine book, *Killing Lincoln*, is so fraught with factual errors, incorrect dates, and grammatical gaffes — he makes reference, for example, to the Oval office at the Lincoln White House, a room that did not come into existence until 1909 — that the museum at Ford's Theater refused to sell it.) Running against then Senator Barack Obama in 2008 Hillary Clinton confidently stated, "But the differences between Barack and I pale in comparison to the differences that we have with Republicans." "The last time I checked, the Constitution said 'of the people, by the people, and for the people.' That's what the Declaration of Independence said," declared President Bill Clinton in 1996, in spite of the fact that the phrase comes from the Gettysburg Address. The obese radio talk-show capon Rush Limbaugh for the phrase "vice-versa" consistently — dementedly — says "vice-a versa." When the inarticulate and obnoxious grouchball, pea-headed Al Sharpton with his rude, confrontational snarl covered the Wisconsin recall-election, fueled by a struggle between Gov. Scott Walker and the state's labor unions, what was meant to be his rousing battle cry came out something like, "But resist we much... we must... and we will much... about... that... be committed!" After President Obama's stem-winding speech at the Democratic National Convention in Charlotte, N.C. on September 7, 2012, Sharpton on MSNBC gravely declared, "He was substanative [sic]." On January 3, 2012 after a spate of attack ads during the days of the Iowa Caucus when the tanking, angry Newt Gingrich publicly sneered at fellow candidate Mitt Romney and called him a liar, the weirdly inauthentic and animatronic Romney, shrugged and condescendingly replied of Gingrich, "I understand. He's a good guy. I like he and Calista [his wife]." "I'm very familiar with foreign affairs and topics of that like," said Donald Trump during the 2011 political campaign, boldly clarifying for citizens across the nation exactly how cultured, articulate and profound he is, a man perfect for the high prestige of the presidency. A formal White House press release outlining Joe Biden's travel plans to the New England area for the last week of February 2012 stated, in print, that the Vice-President would be traveling, on Thursday, for a campaign event to — wait for it —"Providence, Road Island." Talk about poor Froth in *Measure for Measure* having an empty head — try these!

We live in Cloud Cuckoo Land!

There was a time when a speaker would have been truly mortified to look like Mickey the Dunce. *But in public?* Being literate in a gathering was praiseworthy even *two thousand years* ago. "When you come together, everyone has a hymn, or a word of instruction, a revelation, a tongue, or an interpretation," St. Paul told the Corinthians (1 Corinthians 14: 26), encouraging the zeal he had already found in them.

I recall being bewildered when in that popular '50s hit-song, "Mona Lisa," Nat "King" Cole, apostrophizing the lady in the famous Da Vinci portrait, sings "You're so *like* the lady with the mystic smile" [my italics] when it is in point of fact *the* very lady with the mystic smile whom he is addressing! Was I — am I — being picayune? To me it was basically a cognition problem. In the same song, we also come up against the peculiar line — and image — "Many dreams have been brought to your *doorstep*." Given the painting, is it not utterly and gratuitously inexact? I mean, why not Mona Lisa's window? Or warm lap? Or front door? Or *chambre á coucher*? Most of the time, as I listened to music, I seemed to be hearing lines that I wrote myself. I thought for the longest time, for example, that Nat "King" Cole in the Victor Young song, "Love Letters Straight from the Heart."

was actually singing "Love led us straight from the heart" or "Love letters strayed from your heart." In the Four Aces' bouncy "Garden in the Rain," I was startled as a kid to learn after singing it my way — a way I preferred, I must confess — that the line, "But then the sun came out again/ And Santa's happily on our way" was in actuality, "And sent us happily on our way."

Inconsistency in lyrics has always bothered me. Is it not a bit of *Alice in Wonderland*-like unreason for Bill Haley and His Comets to sing, "We're going to rock *around the clock tonight?*" I can also say that for half a century I never knew what the last word was in the children's song, "This Old Man," so garbled it always seemed when sung,

> This old man, he played seven,
> He played knick-knack on my [*what?*]

— "oven"? "eleven"? — until I checked and found that, not surprisingly, odd variants still exist!

And what about that strange, unexplained, and befogging contradiction regarding the St. Louis Woman who, despite "all her diamond rings/ Pulls that man around by her apron strings." Tell me, exactly who with a bunch of diamond rings wears an apron like a waitress — Mae West? Jean Harlow? Marilyn Monroe? I rather tend to rather doubt it. I worried for ages as to which lyric, of the two aural alternatives allowed us, in the song "When I Fall in Love" is preferable, the phrase "to many" or "too many:"

> too many [to many?] moonlight kisses
> seem to melt in the warmth of the sun

In the opening lines of the song "When You Wish Upon A Star" from Walt Disney's *Pinocchio*, "When you wish upon a star/ makes no difference who you are," because the subject (it) is only implied, we are assured that no matter *whenever* you make your wish — whatever year, month, day, or hour — it will be fulfilled. On the other hand, adding a subject crucially changes the meaning of the line to the much more thematically egalitarian (socialistic?) idea, doubtless the song-writers' initial intention, that anyone (doctor, lawyer, Indian chief, or, for that matter, wooden puppet) has the democratic right to make a wish. Totally different meanings ride on it. I still tend to cringe whenever I hear the ungrammatical song title, "Who Should I Turn To," when "Whom Should I Turn To" would have just as properly fit the lyric.

Populism in the United States, however, often dictates what the common people prefer over what they choose to neglect. It is a class thing. When many Southerners, for example, would rather say, "I wadn't" for "I wasn't" and "I cain't" for "I can't" and "I'm feelin' hongry" for "I'm feeling hungry," plain, undisguised, open-faced ignorance is clearly preferred to the far more malignant charge of snobbery or pretension, an accusation that them there good folks feel would be leveled at them for using proper diction. An actual pride is taken in their misfit status. They do not want to seem citified. (One admonition I've heard down there is, "Now don't go gittin' above your raisin'.") Warm ol' phrases like "This is gooder'n grits" and "Have a cup of coffee, stranger, it's already been saucered and blowed" or "Butter my butt and call me a biscuit" and "I near liked to pee my pants when Jigger there come by" are some examples that come to mind. In the South, "y'all" is singular, while "all y'all" is plural. Every true Southerner knows, even by intuition, that "fixin" can be used as a noun, a verb, or an adverb. George Orwell in his long essay "The English People" addressed a number of problems in the usage of English and once declared, "The language of the BBC is barely intelligible to the masses." He noted significantly that the "English working people…think it effeminate even to pronounce a foreign word correctly." We are in familiar territory there.

Poor grammar may seem endearing in the right context, but to most of us it publishes stupidity. I remember back in 1974, for example, watching *Alice Doesn't Live Here Anymore*, director Martin Scorsese's fourth film, when in one scene Ellen Burstyn playing the would-be singer Alice Hyatt, a loving but earnest mother who desperately wants the best for her talkative precocious 11-year-old son, Tommy, says, "They called my brother and I...[etc.]" I forget how she finished the sentence, but I couldn't enjoy her character anymore. Fault me if you will, but her (inadvertent!) poor grammar — especially when all through the movie she yearns to improve her son — completely put me off.

Growing up, I managed to confuse the South with the West — was it because both were sun-drenched and so far away from New England? I dreamt about cowboys, and one book I particularly loved was *The Book of Cowboys* by H.C. Holling — a virtual encyclopedia of western lore — which taught me why horses buck, what a kayak was, how to make a bough bed, and how to tie a horse to bare ground without a stick, a stake, or stone. (Dig an arm-length hole, knot the long picket rope, ram it down, pack the hole with earth), along with lots of terms like "bit hole," "hackamore," "chaparajos," "quirt," "tapadero," and "snubbing post." I can still see the colored illustrations in my mind's eye to this day.

Logic matters to youngsters. I was astonished when teaching at Phillips Academy in Andover for a few years in the late '70s how earnest and rectitudinous young people can be (never lie to a teen-ager) and when, for example, coming across inconsistencies in a novel or a poem — or even in an unsatisfactory explanation coming from the teacher — how oddly surprisingly and uncompromisingly unforgiving they were. I gather a truism would be that you can get away with almost anything if you set it to music. In "South of the Border" from one of my favorite movies, *Down Mexico Way* (1941) starring Gene Autry and Smiley Burnette, there is a lyrical line that has always stood out for me — "Then for a tender while/ I kissed the smile upon her face." I have to repeat, I have always loved Gene Autry, "King of the Cowboys," and that rich melodious voice of his and so felt I could forgive him anything, including kissing a girl in the movies, even falling passionately in love with women, something I found out fifty years later, scandalizing me, that he did quite frequently and with an unconscionable indifference, but I must add, having the high-seriousness of the prepubescent, I strenuously objected to the inexactitude here. Has anybody ever tried, in fact, to kiss a smile?

A *smile?*

Doubtful.

I must admit there *is* that scene in Canto V of Dante's *Inferno* which treats of Paolo and his sister-in-law, Francesca, being condemned to be swept along together eternally through dark winds for their illicit but irresistible love. The lovers had been reading together of how Lancelot in a moment of passion and mastered by love kissed Guinevere, and Paolo, carried away in passion, then followed suit. When Francesca speaks to Dante as Virgil listens and Paolo weeps there is *perhaps* a smile that is kissed:

> *Quando leggemmo il disiato riso*
> *Esser baciato do cotanto amante*
> *Questi, che mai da me non fia diviso,*
> *La bocca mi baciò tutto tremante.*

> When we had read there how the longed-for smile
> Was kissed by such a lover, this one then,
> Who parts not from me this eternal while,
> Kissed me upon my mouth all tremblingly.

[Translated by J.B. Fletcher]

An equally irritating inaccuracy can be found in Paul Anka's song "Put Your Head On My Shoulder," in the line, "Put your lips next to mine, dear/ Kiss me." Exactly what happens when lips are put *next to each other*? Is it some kind of Martian ritual? The act of visiting futuroidals from Uranus? The bathos of this terrible song-writer! Paul Anchor; or the Art of Sinking! There are very few lyricists who can match him for the guaranteed, disjointed, fully hackneyed phrase. His "All Of A Sudden My Heart Sings" — listen to this poor thing sometime — shamelessly crams in just about every cliché in pop music. I would have slotted all his records for the lunar rotation (disc jockey slang for an infrequently played disc) from "Diana" right on down to "My Way," the favorite lobby song at the splashy Luxor in Las Vegas among the fake trees and faux sphinxes (and sphincters) where women look like poultry and the men are jiggling chips at the tables hoping to buy them feed.

It is remarkable what we hear if we listen closely. It has always been a source of dismay to me, as well, early and late, a twist of the knife of irony, that the lyrics to the bonny song, "You Are My Sunshine," are addressed by some poor herbert to a woman who has deserted him! (Could that have been the reason that once at a party in Hollywood, or so Marilyn Monroe told the writer Truman Capote, that the rogue actor, Errol Flynn, once blasphemously played the song on the piano with — as she put it — his "schlong"?) Or do I find myself alone in being wistfully surprised that the sad, epiphanic line following the apparently hopeful, "When the Moon Comes Over the Mountain," is "I'll be alone with my dreams"? (I am reminded here of Burt Lancaster and Deborah Kerr's hot passion for each other on the beach in *From Here to Eternity*, but let that scene play out, and you come to see them at each other's throats.) I wonder about the baneful effects of lyrics on adolescents. The song "Isle of Capri," words by Jimmy Kennedy, music by Will Grosz, beginning, "'Twas on the Isle of Capri that I found her," reveals the same letdown at the end ("She wore a plain golden ring on her finger/ 'Twas goodbye on the isle of Capri"). My hoodlum friends back in Medford, Mass. on any occasion of being dumped, would bitch, "She pulled an Isle of Capri!"

"I think love lyrics have contributed to the general aura of bad mental health in America," the lyrical outlaw Frank Zappa once explained in a long interview in *The Portable Curmudgeon Redux*. He continued to say,

> Love lyrics create expectations which can never be met in real life, and so the kid who hears these tunes doesn't realize that that kind of love doesn't exist. If he goes out looking for it, he's going to be a kind of love loser all his life. Where do you get your instructions about love? Your mother and father don't say, 'Now, son, now, daughter, here's how love works.' They don't know, so how can they tell their kids? So, all your love data comes

to you through the lyrics on Top Forty radio, or, in some instances, in movies or novels. The singer-songwriters who write these lyrics earn their living by pretending to reveal their innermost personal turmoil over the way love has hurt them, which creates a false standard that people use as a guideline on how to behave in interpersonal relationships.

When I was growing up, it always seemed to me that Southern or Western accents, especially in the faraway world of country singers, were actually speech-defects, seriously, flaws or pitiful imperfections of pronunciation that made the speakers wearing cowboy hats or singers with fringed or tasseled shirts seem a bit luckless or benighted or in need of remedial help. Many of their first names alone seemed to me in some horribly invented way — another doomed sample of what Karl Marx in another context called the "idiocy of rural life" — to be almost intentional caricatures of peculiarity and goofballdom. Merle. Porter. Del. Ferlin. Hylo. Webb. Cody. Lum. Foy. Narvel. Conway. Hargus. Slim. Krenn. Cooter. Billy Joe. Clyde. Trace. Finis. Wynonna. Penrod. Vestal. Ottie Lee. Cleavon. Delmont. Goodloe. Pervis. Bodean. Jim Bob. Fess. Obed. Hillous. *Hillous*??? I have also heard the names Elrod, Roscoe, and Saggory. But, I mean, even Hank and Slim and Dwayne seem totally cuckoo. How about Reba? Reba McEntire has a brother named Pake and a cousin or something named Belt Love! *Belt*! Were these creatures from other comets or constellations? Fess! Bewley! I always thought of Confederate soldiers whenever I heard such names mentioned, slack-jawed, shag-bearded anti-Lincolnesque semi-cretins who chewed tobacco and long-boned baleful farmers of the Nathan Bedford Forrest ilk who had bad attitudes and snarled in a feral way and in menacing grey uniforms were on the wrong side at the Battle of Gettysburg. Against them? No wonder we had to fight a Civil War. They were prone to teeth-whistle when they talked and hee-hawed and told "yarns" and wore over-hauls and duckbill feed hats and snapped their suspenders and would always lean on a word the wrong way when they said words like *ín*-surance or *cí*-garette or *úm*-brella, which they all clearly mispronounced, dopily putting the stress on the first syllable.

What ever happened to great, resplendent names like Cristobal Balenciaga, Walter von der Vogelweide, Christina Georgina Rossetti, Manfred von Richtofen? I am certain that anyone who was introduced as Mr. Fitzwilliam Darcy of Pemberley could not have failed, even if eventually, to win the hand of Elizabeth Bennett.

It all serves to prove the truism correct: "If God wanted Texans to ski, He would have made bullshit snow." It was so hokey the way country singers tried to seem so ass-kickin' tough, surly, and macho, monosyllabic and deep, meaningful and no-nonsensical when any fool could tell it was all show-business. Grizzled old Waylon Jennings once invidiously remarked that if David Allen Coe ever got in trouble with the cops it was because he had double-parked. (And if Waylon Arnold Jennings was an "outlaw," I am Pee Wee Herman.) But was jut-jawed Johnny Cash any tougher? Forget Folsom Prison. He spent a single night in jail once for drunkenness, and that scar on his chin was the result of nothing more than having had a *cyst* removed. All that wild rebellion and vaunted outlawry of his — followed by decades of a crazed and craven evangelism — were commercial masks adopted to sell records, and anybody with a half a brain could see through them. Look at this abortion recorded by Tom T. Hall, a fat Kentuckian clearly without a sign of a scruple:

> I love little baby ducks,
> old pick-up trucks,
> slow movin' trains, and rain.
> I love little country streams,
> sleep without dreams,
> Sunday school in May, and hay.
> And I love you too.
> I love leaves in the wind,
> pictures of my friends,
> birds of the world, and squirrels.
> I love coffee in a cup,
> little fuzzy pups,
> bourbon in a glass, and grass.
> And I love you too.
> I love honest open smiles,
> kisses from a child,
> tomatoes on a vine, and onions.
> I love winners when they cry,
> losers when they try,
> music when it's good, and life.
> And I love you too.

*Sunday school in May!?*

"Sentimentality is the emotional promiscuity of those who have no sentiment," wrote Norman Mailer. Nor is sentimentality an indication of anything like a warm heart. Nothing weeps more copiously than a chunk of ice.

Country singers, hillbillies, whose rustic way of speaking can twist words like taffy, seem to love hyperfabrications of sound. It is a marvel to hear them refane language by pronunciation, add syllables to one-syllable words, yodel and howl, and chamfer the fuck out of even the most normal words and phrases, the tongue working in a way that always remind me of what air pilots term pitch, roll, and yaw. According to A.C. Gimson in his book *Introduction to the Pronunciation of English*, there are forty-four individual sounds in the English language. (12 vowels, 8 diphthongs, 24 consonants — some phoneticians who disagree put the number as high as 50). But it seems to me that country singers — are they trying to mimic banjoes, electric and acoustic guitars, fiddles, and harmonicas? — have managed to invent many more. It is an aspect of populism, needless to say, but mis- or oddly pronouncing words has long been an ingredient of speech in the South, a kind of verbal handshake, redneck-style — "I *thew* the ball," "He *wadn't* kiddin,' son," "You *cain't* get there no more," "Y'all gone set a spell?" "I toad you twice!" "We howdied but we ain't shook." "Don't go cuttin' up in church now — that ain't fittin.'" "I'll allow them coon dogs do look right smart." "Bless Patsy, I plum dissermembered!" "She's a pistol." "Nearbout as I can tell." "Be-ins yore goin' to the store, get me some collards." "Aggervatin'? Purt near." Yup. Nope. Maybe. In parts of Wyoming or Texas or even Maine, that is considered a fairly lengthy conversation — same words! Speaking with poor grammar down South is more common than biscuits with white gravy. The folksy appeal of speaking lamely, wherein the "average guy" implicitly accedes to the general will by way of rustic group-speak, I would explain as a way of belonging and falls under the rubric of what the late Harvard political scientist Barrington Moore, Jr. in his *Social Origins of Dictatorship and Democracy* referred to as "Catonism," a rhetoric of extolling the peasant as the backbone of society. Such talk is big among the racing, raising hell, and how-to-turn-around-in-the-middle-of-the-road-at-75-miles-an-hour crowd, of course, yet it works for middle-brows, but, as I say, it essentially deflects the intolerable-to-be-borne charge that one is a snob.

Watch out for the bob waaar on that fence, hoss. He's all swimmy-headed. Ah'm standin' in need of a cold beer. Pass the sawt 'n' pipper. Want a Coke or a Sebmup? You can set them groceries down ratcheer. I'm commencin' to look. You in a big heepa trouble, boy. That women's jess eat up with jealousy. I like to near passed out. That's right nice. I'm fixin' to go shopping, yawl wanna Dr. Pepper? Gob Less Uhmurka!

Not talking at all of course makes a person seem even more genuine. The American cowboy always seemed deepest when he said nothing. It is one of the biggest forged checks ever made. What was inside, I remain convinced, was

cindercrete. Marshall Will Kane in *High Noon* is as monosyllabic as his name, ι
is, when he speaks at all. (It is completely fitting that Gary Cooper in interviews
often repeated that he had never read a book.) I don't believe that the hero in
*Shane* says a single word at all unless he is answering a question. Remember the
rural custom of people lifting only one or two fingers from the steering-wheel as
they passed, even though they didn't even know you? Bucolic eloquence.

Goobers in cowboy hats riddled with paradox were always either fobbing off
stories of how great it was to be back in the saddle again or selling us tall tales
about life on *el rancho grande* and home on the range. It didn't matter what they
were reporting, they all talked like they were from the Tall Grasses. I always had
to laugh over the eulogistic anti-urban-and-crime topoi being sold in country
music and lame but ongoing lyrical boasts of all that western wonderfulness. I
was perplexed. Most western songs, for example are always crowing about the
glory of the prairies. Whoop-ee-tie-ay-O! Whoop-ee-tie-ay-A! There, and there
alone, is peace and tranquility. So what's the story with that dying cowboy in
the old country classic, "Bury Me Not on the Lone Prairie" who fears a lonely
grave? The irony is that as he sings he is pleading to be planted anywhere on
earth *but* the lone prairie "where the owl all night hoots mournfully," where "the
blizzard beats" and "the wind blows." Bugger the prairie! He hated the goddam
place! This is followed with a total disregard for logic, never mind the dramatic
unities, by the line, "When I die, you can bury me 'neath the western sky on the
long prairie." There is not the slightest indication that the singer has changed
his mind, it is merely that by the time he gets to the end of the song, he has
forgotten the opening statement. An even grimmer irony is that the very people
he apostrophizes, perversely taking no heed of his request, proceed to plant the
poor bastard in a narrow grave, six-foot-three, right there in the damn prairie for
the dogs to eat! You have to listen to certain songs closely.

"There are two silences," observed playwright Harold Pinter. "One when no
word is spoken. The other when perhaps a torrent of language is being employed.
This speech is speaking of a language locked beneath it. That is its continual
reference. The speech we hear is an indication of that which we don't hear." I try
to listen to both as best I can. It is a moral act. The counterfeit is always a forgery.
So look for me, whether with approval or not, over there at the far table — one
chair — scribbling with a pencil.

Country music which was called "hillbilly" music when I was a kid is now the
most popular American music, extending far beyond the rural Southern United
States — it has both a huge Canadian and Australian fan base — and while its
roots lie in Western cowboy and southeastern folk music it now describes many

s, ballads, dance tunes, rock, honky tonk, rockabilly, gospel,
cal-type hymns, camp songs, and still of course, generally, the
harmonies that go back to the 1920s accompanied by mostly
s. It is a phenomenon. There are almost 3000 country music
juntry, pushing this kind of music and no other. It is hard to
believe but the fact is Garth Brooks from Yukon, Oklahoma has sold more than
60 million records, making him second only to the Beatles in total U.S. sales.

I feel honor-bound to confess, before we leave off Southern provincialisms,
that we have urban rednecks up north, as well — and in abundance. Sports
talk-shows reveal a good many. On the Dennis and Callahan Show on WEEI
radio in Boston, most of the callers seem so dim they could throw themselves
on the ground and miss. I would guess the average listener ranges from 20 to
50 year olds whom I picture thriving on the rituals of all-American manhood
like watching NASCAR races, collecting guns, swilling beer, and dyspeptically
fressing on heaped plates of Buffalo wings in front of the TV every night, clowns
and sycophantic dead-enders leading vicarious lives that seem to depend on daily
score totals and yards gained. The hosts are also low functioning dolts. John Dennis
is fatuously overspoken, while his partner is a perfect imbecile, a total fucking
numpty. "Who you rootin' for, caller? The Pats? You think them bums are playin'
good?" asks Gerry Callahan, "Mr. Thlipsis," a mean-spirited, anti-intellectual,
right-wing boanthrop who, filled with Irish anger, not only has a belittling voice
that is always on the edge of sarcasm which he conveys – vocal quotation marks
-- with a heated corona of breathy irony but also knows about forty-two words
and can barely finish a sputtering sentence. Can you fathom full-grown men,
guys in their 60s, seriously talking about *rooting* for a team — I mean, even using
the *word?* "You kiddin' me, right? Gedadaheah! The Pats shoulda punted an'
coulda done so without givin' up chunks a yahds! Run it? Nothun doin'. Let
them ketch it, *thennnn* nail 'em. Whattaya thinkin'? Now you gonna tell me, what,
they shoulda called a timeout? Huh? Whatizzthis? Woon't you expeck the friggin'
Giants are just as smaht and know what *you* wanna do? You carry a pockabook?
Like I say, you must be smokin' somethin', pal. You tellin' me they done the same
thing las' yeah, but oh, no, they dih-int! Lookit, in foopball, mosta them guys are
wicked dumb for stahtahs, OK? You go for it on fourth, I'd liketa see that. Wanna
know somethin'? The New York Giants suck! You learnin' anathin' about the
officiatin' meantime?" The level of conversation is beneath belief. They sound
in their banter like city workers with picks and shovels, standing in a mud-hole.

Incidentally, Callahan, also a late middle-age keypounder, actually writes a
sports column for the *Boston Herald*, a tabloidesque newspaper derisively known

among Boston wits as the "Wrestling News." To hear the hosts of sports talk-shows with IQs lower than a pro-golf score stepping on a soapbox to begin piously moralizing about athletes' bad behavior is painful enough — and stupid, ill-informed, unimportant people trying to look important will say anything — but to have to hear perfect dunces commenting on *world politics*, suddenly to be listening to Epsilon-minus semi-morons discussing international matters like the moral case for drones or North Korean nuclear ambitions or the danger of Basque ETA terrorists, is more than a body can bear. One fat little sports-porker with a triple-chin and an unfounded air of superiority named Dale Arnold – a true weasel -- passes judgment on everybody every chance he gets as if he were The Grand Inquisitor. But gossip is precisely what sports talk-shows are about, and all those meretricious and parasitical hirelings who batten onto the lives of athletes — private and otherwise— remind me of oxpeckers that hunt, peck, and nibble all of the filthy insects, larvae, botflies, and tics infesting the hides of rhinoceroses, feeding even on their earwax and dandruff. While the oxpecker gets free food, the rhino gets rid of all of his parasites. The horrible and unavoidable truth is, however, oxpeckers not only open new wounds but enhance existing ones in rhinos in order to drink the blood of their perches, just as the reputations of athletes are sullied by these dumbbells who, "clubby, stupid, and mean," resemble for me the "hard little men in hard little offices talking hard little words that don't mean a goddam thing," in the words of Raymond Chandler's in *The Long Goodbye*.

It is cliché city. *How's that workin' out for ya? You throwin' him under the bus? They gotta step up. He took it to another level.* Conversation is limited to "No way, José" "*Fannn*-tastic!" "*Unnn*-believable!" You hear athlete pronounced "ath-e-lete" and drowned garbled as "drownd-ed. It is a complete idiocracy. Everybody — *anybody* — with an opinion can be correct in sports. It is the toy department. I swear, sports have to require the least qualifications for a job across the entire spectrum of broadcasting. Sports talk-shows therefore empower the dumbest of callers who shout and rarely listen and have names like Jim Dandy, the Wrestling Goon, Mikie Nutzo, Charlie "Cha Cha" Ciarcia," Stevo "Reverso" Devlin, Big Neil ("Double Meal") Currant, Gerry "Nose Buds" Burke, Andrew Sufferfag, William "The Hack" O'Rourke, Petey "Fat Boy" Gailers, T.J. "Cheapo" Belk, and Frank "Dumbo" Drybell. At the outset of every morning, the WEEI hosts ask each other what each had watched on television the previous night. Reading T.B. Macauley's *History of England* or swotting up some amazing stuff in Palaeolithic studies or listening to Richard Wagner's "Parsifal" or reconciling gravity with quantum physics by way of string theory are not likely to be replies here, OK? "You watch that Celtics third quarter, Gerry?" "No, watched *American Idol*. You watchin' any of that?" asks Dino. "Nah, hey, what you watchin' tonight?" Watchin. Rootin. Living in the sports world is reduced to a Big Joe bean-bag chair, a jumbo bowl of corn curls, and the simple solicitation the next morning of "Wha joo watch?" *Watch?* Is that what manhood has come to, watching? To me there is nothing that can quite match for stupidity the activity of staring open-mouthed into a flickering TV box all night and mindlessly munching handfuls of orange fingerfoods. Willie Loman in *Death of a Salesman* felt reduced as a man growing vegetables at night in his back garden. How low have we fallen? Is this the act to which the New Frontier has been reduced, sitting home in your underwear on a couch watching other men play games? Is not *watching* strictly for simpletons and spazzes? Watching as an activity is almost by definition a goddam embarrassment, is it not? A feckless pastime and a time-suck? Apes watch. Proboscis monkeys watch. Fucking lemurs in the moonlight watch from trees. Ogle! I believe there is a gay subtext to sports shows, anyway, all those short, fat, little counterdimensionals, half of them with lisps and eyestrain and low sperm motility, spending hour after hour enthusiastically talking about tall, rugged athletes, admiring them, envying them, commenting on their lifestyles, discussing their salaries, analyzing their talents, speculating about their lives. What a eunuchoid activity — except that it is an utter *non*-activity. This is definitely a subject that warrants a social study. Do you not agree? On the morning of May 30, 2012, "D and C," these same WEEI hosts, spent almost an hour devotedly discussing the various hairstyles of handsome New England Patriots quarterback Tom Brady, asking him over a telephone call, clearly to his embarrassment, how and why he coiffed it in the several ways he has done so, which, I'm sorry, I find — in the words of *Village Voice* columnist Michael Musto, the "Hunter S. Thompson of snark" — "gayer than a home furnishings store on Super Bowl Sunday."

As I say, I love Gene Autry. I delighted in his odd pronunciations ("thar" for there, "I-o-way" for Iowa, etc.) and was always struck by the fact that his records all seemed to come, pointlessly, to an abrupt end — as if he had fallen off a cliff. Listen, for example to "Rudolph the Red-Nosed Reindeer." I loved his six-guns and smooth voice and fell for all those great words like "cayuse," "pommel," "hoosegow," "skedaddle," "goner," "bone orchard," "saddlery," "chow," and "chuckwagon." A metallic note was struck for me, nevertheless, whenever going into his loping theme-song, "Back in the Saddle Again," he sang about a peaceful land "where a friend is a friend" and "where you sleep out every night and the only law is right," as I detected something of a nutty paradox in that paradise, for, "ridin' the range once more," as he sings, he tells us he was "totin' my old .44" — the very size piece that "Dirty" Harry Callahan menacingly wagged at crooks in those violent films of his, blowing people away in California. I mean, was it peaceful out west there or not? Was it Eden or downtown Detroit? Was it all about the splendors of Melody Ranch or was it bumpkinville? As to jimson weed in that same Autry song ("where the longhorn cattle feed/ on the lowly jimson weed"), the whole plant *(datura stramonium)* is poisonous, of the nightshade family. What were they, devil cows? It was originally *Jamestown* weed, taking its name from the old town of Jamestown, Virginia, where British soldiers were drugged with it while attempting to suppress Bacon's Rebellion and spent weeks frothing at the mouth generally appearing to have gone insane.

Don't get me wrong. There is a West I love. I love the sacred Indian lore, the buffalo, the wind caves in the Black Hills, the eerie interminable coal trains with a hundred or more cars threading down from the Powder River in Wyoming through the sand hills of Nebraska to points east, the smoky cabins, the mysterious ghost towns, the tumbleweed dreamscape, endless rolling vistas of meadows, prairies, buttes, and hills evoked by those poignant melodies I have been hearing all my life like "The Call of the Faraway Hills" and "Jubilee" by George Whitefield Talbot and the theme from the movie, *Red River*, "Settle Down," and "Shenandoah," and the exquisite "Song of the Painted Hills" from the movie *Shane*, all of those deep, earth-evoking, wistfully-lovely, enchanting songs with something of a western ilk like the heartbreakingly pretty "The Last Roṡe of Summer" and "Return to Kinsole," mystic, evocative melodies of so lilting, so lambent a sweetness that they send a note of perfection to my yearning heart. I was simply put off by any preposterous and unlettered country hoopoe who with his antics made a mockery of such grace.

To me, Pat Buttram, Gene Autry's radio and film sidekick, was a perfect fool by dint of his accent, not merely for his clowning around. ("That-a-way, Mis-ter Orterrry? He's headed out to the arroyo!") Hank Williams, Ernest Tubb, Roy Acuff, Bob Wills, Little Jimmy Dickens, etc., though wonderful singers, seemed outlandish and goofy, hailing from dispirited outbacks where I imagined they never bothered to study diction or take out library cards or learn correct pronunciation or quote Shakespeare when necessary, definitely not citizens from the Greater Boston area. What was all that business of "Your *haar* is red, your eyes are blue, I'd swap my horse and dog for you"? (Throughout his entire life, into his late years Autry pronounced the word hair *haar*.) I considered that someone like George "Gabby" Hayes, although funny, was somewhat retarded, with his snuffy phrases like "consarn it," "yer durn tootin'," "dadgumit," "durn persnickety females," "Yessirree, Bob," and "you young whippersnapper." (It turns out that Hayes who was from the East was born, the third of seven children, in Wellsville, New York, did not come from a cowboy background — in fact, he never knew how to ride a horse until he was in his 40s — and was, in private life, a well-groomed, articulate man who was something of expert on wine!) Believe it or not, fairly toothless and gumming ol' Gabby actually sings — a duet with Roy Rogers, "We're Not Coming Out Tonight" — in the 1939 movie, *In Old Caliente.* I gotta tell you, I have heard worse, much worse.

Oh, I kept score in a hundred ways. I felt a secret scorn for the way Wyatt Earp, as portrayed on television by gnathic Hugh O'Brian, was glorified as "brave, courageous, and bold." He was valiant, intrepid, and plucky, no doubt, but that redundant wordiness nettled my priggish nature to no end. I think it was in *The Count of Monte Cristo* that Robert Donat's final line, spoken directly to the camera, was something about how the enemies of Monte Cristo had been brought down by those two fatal flaws in their characters — dramatic pause — "Avarice...and Greed!"

Touching on the Old West, as a kid I always found it curious that *loping* music always came up right away in cowboy movies, as background, to sort of nudge us into the mood of Westernism. It was kitschy seduction and irked me. Couldn't we feel moods rather than be *told* them? For fog music we were usually treated to snatches of Debussy. Tornado music in *The Wizard of Oz* — "*da dah da dah da dah (three times) DAAH!*" — was, what? Urgent Harold Arlen cueing trumpets. Composer and eccentric Oscar Levant once pointed out that the music of Frederick Delius was dished up not only for walks in the garden but for all bicycle rides in the country, as well. All train music, Levant said, seemed to come from Honegger's *Pacific 231.* The orchestral pattern of all carousels, he complained, was derived from Stravinsky's *Petrouchka.* Carefreeness, I've noticed, is often accompanied in film by the playing of David Rose's *Holiday for Strings,* the musicological equivalent of diarrhea. I would rather spend a week in the Mario Lanza Museum than listen to it once.

There is, of course, such a thing as poetic license. No, it shouldn't be "Love Me Tenderly" or "All Shaken Up." The song "Is You Is or Is You Ain't My Baby?" is exactly as it should be. *Vox populi.* Billy Paul sang "Me and Mrs. Jones?" Would "Mrs. Jones and I" have detracted from the back-street sordidness of the affair? Of course. Same with Wilbert Harrison's "I'm gonna be stand on the corner/ Twelfth Street and Vine" as heard in "Kansas City" and Sam the Sham's oxymoronic "I don't think little big girls should/ Go walkin' in these spooky old woods alone" in "Little Red Riding Hood." How can anyone not love it when Chuck Berry in "Promised Land" sings "working on a T-bone steak á la *cartey*/ flying over to the golden state"? The kind of hip jargon and flip soulfulness that as part of the cool aesthetic allows for Wilson Pickett to say "Yes, I Is" and Little Richard to sing "I Ain't Never" and Debbie Harry to state, "She moves like she don't care/ You gotta see her/ She's like a millionaire," language that grows from inner cultivation, hippitude, funky popular life, is a far different thing from the kind of artless boobery and almost malicious stupidity in a pop lyric that actually robs it of style — flat and unedited pretensions that provoke laughter rather than create mood. It is the organic make-up of the presentation that allows for it, one might even say requires it. And there remains one of the major distinctions in rock lyrics. Can the same be said, however, of Paul McCartney who in his song "Live and Let Die" possibly gave us one of the looniest one-line tautologies of Twentieth Century print: "...*in* this ever-changing world *in* which we live *in*"? A trifecta — all within ten words of each other. It doesn't get more artless than that. It recalls for me the line, "If I could take you *up* in paradise *up above*" [my italics] from the Chords' pop-hit from 1954, "Sh-Boom," a song recorded by both the Crew Cuts and the G-Clefs. Both gaffes find a match in the redundant line from "Small Town" where John Mellencamp from Bloomington, Indiana sings, "No, I cannot forget from where it is that I come from." As a youngster in my truth-mode I was sufficiently scholarly of course to be annoyingly confounded by Australia being referred to as the "The Land Down Under" — for isn't down *already* under?

How about two of my all-time favorites — Neil Sedaka's extra-helpful pleonasm, "I'm living right next door to an angel,/ and she only lives a house away." And Tommy James & the Shondells' clarifying, "I think we're alone now/ there doesn't seem to be anyone around"? There never seems to be a dearth of this comic blunder. A softball announcer during the Olympic Games in London in summer 2012 said, "If history repeats itself, I should think we can expect the same thing again." Paul Hamm, a gymnast, said, "I owe a lot to my parents, especially my mother and father."

Redundancy in popular music, which should not be confused with repetition, is not only one of its most glaring faults but to my mind is almost always less a problem of haste than haplessness. It is invariably the result of some poor dweeb sitting down and trying to "fill" a line for rhythm the way old linotypists used slugs of lead, and often with much the same result, such as in Dylan's "I'm ready for to fade/ into my own parade" or Paul Anka in "Diana" singing, "I don't care just what they say" or Junior Walker's "What does it take to win your love for me?" or the Beach Boys with that line in "Surfer Girl" that goes, "And so I say from me to you," that evokes something out of *Alice in Wonderland*! When the Rolling Stones sing the line, "It is the evening of the day" in their 1965 hit, "As Tears Go By," was it to distinguish it from the evening of the *month*? In the Everly Brothers hit, "Bye Bye Love," one hears the line, "Goodbye from romance/ that might have been," not only an intolerable clinker of redundant and ungrammatical usage ("goodbye from?") but a double pleonasm, for if nothing was ("that might have been") no goodbye — never mind from — is necessary or, needless to say, normal or rational! And when the Everlys in "When Will I Be Loved" sing the line,

> When I meet a new girl
> that I want for mine...

it is ungrammatical, redundant, and stupid all at the same time.

It can happen in the best of songs — and does. Take Eric Maschwitz and Manning Sherwin's "A Nightingale Sang in Berkeley Square." Just the opening line, for example, with its use of artless filler words: "That *certain* night/ The night we met/ There was magic *abroad* in the air." [My italics.] Certain. Abroad. The words do not belong and are quite clumsily haled in to carry the line, hobblingly so, as if on two crutches. No one in the late 1940s could avoid hearing the played and replayed popular song, "I've Got A Lovely Bunch of Coconuts" — it was written by Fred Heatherton — the refrain of which goes, "Every ball you throw will make me rich/ There stands me wife, the idol of me life, / Singing roll or bowl a ball, a penny a pitch,/ Singing roll or bowl a ball, a penny a pitch./ Roll or bowl a ball, Roll or bowl a ball,/ Singing roll or bowl a ball, a penny a pitch." My question: Roll *or bowl* a ball? May I presume to ask the distinction between the two? And in the cowboy classic, "Tumbling Tumbleweeds," sung by most western stars over the years, we hear,

> Cares of the past are behind
> Nowhere to go but I'll find
> Just where the trail will wind,
> Drifting along with the
> Tumbling tumbleweeds

I used to struggle with the ontological question: if cares *of the past* are not *behind*, my humble inquiry was, exactly where else would they be?

As to redundancy, what about the line, "the oldest established permanent floating crap game in New York" from *Guys and Dolls*? It is a gem of a song and a brilliant title. Abe Burrows came up with the phrase, and Frank Loesser pounced on it for what is formally the song, "Fugue for Tin Horns," that is sung by the three small-time gamblers, Nicely-Nicely Johnson, Benny Southstreet, and Rusty Charlie, but can't one make a case that *established* and *permanent* are near synonyms? I have the same problem in the same musical with the lovely song, "My Time of

Day," a true Manhattan lyric, a spot-on insight into Albion, but surely there is something wrong in the lines,

> My time of day,
> And you're the only doll I've ever wanted
> To share it with me.

Why the "with me" other than for rhythm?

I feel that Loesser makes the same mistake in the equally brilliant, "I Don't Want to Walk Without You" — of this song Irving Berlin actually told Loesser that it was the best song he ever heard — when, however, he clumsily writes,

> Oh, Baby, please come back
> Or you'll break my heart *for me*,
> 'Cause I don't want to walk without you, nosiree.
> [My italics.]   ·

Hearing those neo-tautological bunny-hops gives me much the same relatively queasy feeling I always had, watching *Mr. Rogers' Neighborhood* on PBS — it was both a soporific and an anodyne for me back in the terror-fraught late-1960s — when, singing "It's Such a Good Feeling" at the end of every show, Fred said,

> It's such a good feeling to know you're alive.
> It's such a happy feeling: You're growing inside.

But you're also growing outside, right? Or was Fred making a much deeper point touching on spirituality? Doesn't it perfectly bookend his other daily redundancy where after fastidiously unzipping and hanging up his sweater, plucking off his blue sneakers to swap them for shoes, then donning his jacket, he signs out with the goony remark, "I'll be back next time" [my italics] — thus endowing generations of kids with a tautological valediction? (I have always also been leery about the redundant name of the cinematic company Universal International Pictures, by the way, if you want full disclosure.) A dear heart, Mr. Rogers surely was — a logician he was apparently not. His "There's only one person in the whole world like you. And people can like you exactly as you are" is a head-cracking non-sequitur, first off; what people can do or may do are different things, but does he not undercut the very point that he is trying to make about a person's uniqueness? When he sings "There's only one person in the whole world like you," he is reductively stating, by the misuse of a deductive argument that the dear man never intended, that "Someone else is out there like you!" It's a beautiful day in the Dunderheadhood!

In the Mills Brothers' "Up a Lazy River," how about that reference to a "kind old tree"? *Kind*? Then there is the line that they sing in "Cab Driver": "There's a little place we used to eat," where they presume, I gather, we are supposed to supply the word *where* before the word *we* — or should we be taking the lyric literally and assume that is why, devouring entire restaurants, all four members of that mellifluous but almost paranormally tubby Fifties quartet, Calorico, Diabeto, Musso, and Elephantico, were so appallingly fat? ("Close?" went one of Joan Rivers's jokes. "We were closer than the Mills Brothers' thighs!") What about the gibberishesque opening line, "Since she put me down, I been out doin' in my pid," from the Beach Boys' "Help Me, Rhonda"? Or am I mistaken and does it go, "I've been out doin' in my head," that is, "doing in" — as in killing — my head? How is one supposed to know? I have often thought that the title "The Sound of Music" is redundant — I mean, exactly what does music do, at least regarding its elemental properties, *but* sound? Then there is the inane tautology, "You are the one love that I'll adore" in Kathy Young's old clutcher-and-hugger, "A Thousand Stars"? In Mel Tormé's "The Christmas Song," wonderfully evocative as it is, the odd line, "And every mother's child is gonna spy" manages to be, in one unforgettable but remarkably confounding image, sexist, redundant, and a ridiculous generalization all at the same time. And yet the song is warm, and it works. For me the surprisingly slothful lyric in Irving Berlin's classic "White Christmas":

> ...and children listen
> to hear sleigh bells in the snow

seemed redundant, even when I was a kid. It is as if, ontologically, the act of listening *causes* the children to hear. Can one listen *not* to hear? If Wittgenstein is not wrong when he wrote, "The meaning of a proposition is the method by which it is verified," are we not inevitably correct in finding that, if sleigh bells indeed are ringing outside in the snow and if children are listening, they will, more than likely, *hear* something?

In George Thorogood and the Destroyers' memorable song "I Drink Alone," we encounter some impeccable logic:

> With nobody else I drink alone
> Yeah, with nobody else

You know when I drink alone,
I prefer to be by myself.

(Am I the first to point out, by the way, how silly, how lame-brained in far too many cases, rock and roll lyrics look in cold print?)

There is surely no doubt that one of the classic redundancies of all time can be found in the song "I Gotta Be Me," in which we find the deeply metaphysical line, "What else can I be but what I am?" — a candidate, I've always felt, for the Lewis Carroll Award. The same goes for the fatuous line "...if I should tell you farewell and goodbye" in the hallowed 1952 hit "Lullaby of Birdland," music by George Shearing and lyrics by George David Weiss. And I still shake my head over the line in "A Cockeyed Optimist," again from *South Pacific*, "I could say life is just a bowl of Jell-O/ And appear more *intelligent and smart*." Come again? "Dear mother is waiting in heaven," sings Gene Autry in the song "Silver-Haired Daddy of Mine," "Just to *comfort and solace* me there."

What ever happened to our love?
It used to be so nice.
It used to be so good.

sings the group ABBA in the song "S.O.S." For me, it is the verbal equivalent of the ludicrously ostentatious (and wholly superadded) compulsion among peasant Catholics, especially in Mexico, South America, and Italy, to kiss their thumb — a peculiar populism, with not so much as a jot of theology behind it — after making the Sign of the Cross, what we in my family, when growing up, used to call "blessing ourselves." Creative tautology! The swirl on the cupcake! That extra little addition that means exactly nothing, the way, for example, all first basemen in the Major Leagues, after fielding a third out at first, almost superstitiously take an inspectorial glance at the baseball before they throw it to the umpire and head toward the dugout. Why? WHY? What is it with contemporary America with its need for panache to keep coming up with particularly annoying metallic phrases, such as "I'm going to sleep *in*" and "She's all stressed *out*" and "Fry it *up*" and "Dial it *up*?" Do you remember in that jingoistic song, "The House I Live In" how Sinatra sings about "the right to speak my mind *out?*"

There is a something disturbing about this sort of thing.

Way back in the '50s there was a song, "White Silver Sands," in which we hear the line, "We watched the sunset in the evening in a *far and distant* land." Remember the Rays' hit "Silhouettes"? "All the shades were pulled and *drawn/*

way *down* tight." [My italics.] Drooly time! The just plain dumbness of the poor cuckolded singer in the lyrical complaint of the song can be directly measured by the hardly surprising but surely compounded idiocies of his not only looking through the wrong window and the wrong building, but it turns out that the guy is also on the wrong block! I mean, such dimwittedness takes genius! No wonder that faithless girlfriend of his, revealingly silhouetted on the shade and cheating with someone else, was driven to find another lover. I am often reminded when I hear that idiotic tautology in "Silhouettes" of the laughably inane line delivered by swaggering John Wayne playing tough Tom Dunson in *Red River* (1948), "I don't like quitters, especially when they don't finish what they start" — quitters, you see, who *do* finish what they start are all right with the Big Guy! A remarkable note here is that the revengeful Dunson who sets out to kill young Matt (played by Montgomery Clift) does not only *not* finish what he starts — fulfilling his threat to hunt down and kill the upstart Matt — but ends up virtually cuddling with his rival after a preliminary fist-fight and — hold onto your hats — is *told by a woman* not to finish what he started! You can't make up stuff like this. (I could never stand leathery John Wayne, much as I love the movie, *Red River*. Was it because I liked Monty Clift so much more, in the same way women approve fat women celebrities: no threat?) What about the redundancy in "Up on the Roof" when the Drifters sing, "When I come home feeling *tired and beat*"? Or Clyde McPhatter in "A Lover's Question" pondering the profundities of love when he woefully asks of the sudden emotion that grips his heart, "How am I to know it's really real?" Well, um, because it's actually actual? Then there is the redundant howler, "And then we can cuddle up near" in Al Hibbler's "After the Lights Go Down Low." Cuddle up near and buss and kiss *in the dark with the lights out*!

One somehow can always count on the unendingly erratic Paul Anka for a great contribution in the matter of redundancy, when he writes in his garish "You Are My Destiny": "You are what you are to me." Yuh. How about the line in James Taylor's "Novelty Ride" the memorable exhortation, "Try not to try too hard"?

It goes on and on. Sorry: It goes on. Chuck Berry in "You Can't Catch Me" sings of "drizzling showers." "But in Camelot/ Those are the legal laws," we are assured by Alan Lerner in the musical, *Camelot*, reminding me of that idiotic line in "By the Time I Get to Phoenix," "For time and time I've tried to tell her so/ I would really go." "Make someone happy/ Make just one someone happy," sings Perry Como in the song, "Make Someone Happy." In their song, "Losing My Religion," R.E.M. superfluously sings, "I think I thought I saw you cry." Or try. Or lie. Whatever. I am reminded of the pharmaceutical company Pfizer's inane motto: "Life is our life's work." I call it the "Vim and Vigor Problem." I once looked up the word "vim." It means vigor! In the '50s song "Ready Teddy," the phrase "sock hop ball" ("All the flat-top cats and the dungaree dolls are headed for the gym to the sock-hop ball") is obviously redundant. And I am still not sure how I feel about the Beatles' line, "The kiss my lover brings, she brings to me." Doesn't she as his lover necessarily bring the only kind of kiss she *can* bring? If she is his lover, why is her bringing her kiss to him a matter of note, since her bringing it to him is the major premise of the song in the first place? Same with Elvis Presley's "Are You Lonesome Tonight," where he farcically asks, "Do the chairs in your parlor seem *empty and bare*?" Never mind the redundancy, what about the crazy word *seem*? Are we in the world of Looneyville? In Shep and the Limelites' classic "Daddy's Home" can be heard the comforting assurance, "Daddy's home to stay," with that laughable litotes added by the singer at the last moment as an inspired coda, just in case we are not certain, "I'm not a thousand miles away." James Taylor in "Shower the People You Love with Love," directs his song to those of us who during sad moments feel very much alone with the wonderfully memorable phrase, "when you're all *by yourself alone*." And did not James Brown, the "Hardest Working Man in Show Business," tell us in his song "It's A Man's World" that although it is a man's world — ready for it? — "it wouldn't mean nothin' *without a woman or a girl*."

"Sometimes we quarrel/ and maybe we'll fight," sings Jill Corey in "I Love My Baby." When Rosemary Clooney sings the lyrics, "Your arms open wide/ enclose me inside" in "Tenderly," I only wonder how arms can enfold anybody *except* inside. "I cried a tear," sings Anne Murray in her mooing hit, "You Needed Me," as opposed to what, Freon? Glycerin? Pine tar? "I held her hand/ She held mine," go the words in Guy Mitchell's "Sippin' Soda through a Straw." There's no end in pop-music of the "My heart's at your command, dear/ To keep love and to hold" — another pleonasm, this one from Johnny Ace's "Pledging My Love" — or the kind that we hear in Kitty Kallen's hit "Little Things Mean A Lot," in which I could never quite decide whether in the refrain that phrase was redundant ("And always and ever/ now and forever") or merely just plain ungrammatical ("And *always* endeavor/ now and *forever*"). One can hear amazing infelicities even in old chestnuts like Hoagy Carmichael's haunting "Stardust." We hear the redundant "And now the purple dusk of twilight" — as opposed to, what, the purple dusk of a spring morning or a winter afternoon?

In the song "Midnight Sun," we hear, "Your lips were like a red and ruby chalice." Red and ruby? I hate sloppy redundancy of the "And-suddenly-you're-sighing-sighs"-variety as in "The Tender Trap", which includes, I have to say, that clunker-dumb line in Frank Sinatra's "They Gotta Lotta Coffee in Brazil:"

"Why, they put coffee in the coffee in Brazil." Let's face it, the line is not very funny, neither is it visual, nor witty, nor inventive, and not even intelligible. In the pop-song "Mack the Knife," the line "Scarlet billows start to spread," always gave me pause — I mean, what else can billows do but spread? The Bee Gees in their song, "How Can You Mend a Broken Heart," sing, "I remember younger days when living for my life." But "living for my life" is pure jabber. On the other hand, I still consider "I Started a Joke" a brilliant song — and Robin Gibb's voice as good as Liam Clancy's. (Don't blame me, I also love Frank Ifield's "I Remember You," Slim Whitman's "Indian Love Call," and "One Christmas Catalogue" by Captain Sensible.) Another bust that amazes me is the line in The Hilltoppers' "P.S. I Love You," in which they sing,

> Write to the Browns
> just as soon as you're able;
> they came around to call

Hey, coming around *is* calling.

I was going to begin to write, optimistically, that way back in another time written songs were better, not like ABBA, say, who in their driving song, "Chiquitita," with its now encouraging, now despairing, often tautological lines ("Chiquitita, you and I know/ How the heartaches come and they go and the scars they're leaving/ You'll be dancing once again and the pain will end/ You will have no time for grieving/ Chiquitita, you and I cry," etc.), but from just about any angle I can see that would be wrong, to quote the late, lamented, honorable, plain-dealing President Richard Milhous Nixon. The artlessness of bad lyrics goes way back, as a matter of fact, and so does redundancy along with it.

"You've lost that loving feeling," loudly moo the Righteous Brothers, and just to be sure that we are alert add, "And it's gone, gone, gone." Then in Buddy Holly's "That'll Be the Day," we hear the clarifying pleonasm — almost as if it is a joke — "And if we ever part/ then I'll leave you." Johnny Mathis in his hit "Chances Are" redundantly sings, "You're the one and only one for me." "If I should tell you farewell and goodbye" we hear in "Lullaby of Birdland," which commits the same foolish fault. Since it is a love song, what would have been wrong with, "If I should tell you good cheer and goodbye"? Same hideosity in the pretentious Simon and Garfunkel line from "Mrs. Robinson," in which we hear, "Joltin' Joe has *left and gone away*." I will add by way of footnote that no one I have ever met over the last thirty years has a clue what any line in that song means. In their song "Homeward Bound," is it not tautological to sing, "I'm sittin' in a railway station/ Got a ticket for my destination"? As opposed to a ticket, say, for the second feature at the Regent? And in the 1970 pop-hit "Kentucky Rain," Elvis Presley sings, "Seven lonely days ago...I reached out one night and you were gone." Well, not one night. Precisely *seven* nights before his lament, no?

Hey, but don't blame Elvis. Put that one on composers Eddie Rabbitt and Dick Heard. Elvis actually never wrote a song. Close friends like Sonny West say that he was too impatient to do so, could not concentrate, and so forth. Why did Elvis never write a song? He owned over a hundred guitars (and 62 cars) and could noodle at the piano. (There is a DVD of his last public performance floating around in cyberspace that shows him playing a solo version of the Righteous Brothers song "Unchained Melody.") I simply do not believe that was his talent. Strangely enough, his close friend and long-time bodyguard, Robert "Red" West, a so-called redneck who was supposedly around strictly for his brawn, *did* write several songs — and good ones, as well — such as the hits "If Every Day Was Like Christmas" and "Separate Ways," a wistful song (about Elvis and Priscilla splitting) that in 1972 even reached the Top 40. Who knows, maybe Elvis did write an original song or two that got lost, like Shakespeare's original play that was called *All is True* — it was supposedly lost when a fire burned down the Globe Theatre in 1613, even while the piece was being performed. It is said that the Bard incorporated parts of it in his play, *Henry VIII.*

For lunacy, what about "...so I dropped my drink from my hand" in Jay & the Americans' song "Come A Little Bit Closer," which matches in brainlessness the equally hopeless thud in "The Trolley Song" from the classic 1943 musical *Meet Me In St. Louis*, written by no less a lyricist than Ralph Blane who actually wrote, "...as he started to leave/ I took hold of his sleeve/ with my hand..." As opposed to, what, taking hold with one's foot or ear or medulla oblongata? "And I could touch them with my hand," wrote Edna St. Vincent Millay in her poem, *Renascence,* who I suppose can be forgiven for her youth. The same cannot be said for the poet John Berryman who in "Snow Line" wrote, "I'd say my prayers out of my mouth as usual," reminding me of Nick's (Jason Calleia) snarling remark to William Bendix in the noir film *The Glass Key,* starring Alan Ladd, "You talk too much with your mouth." In "Mack the Knife" one can delight in one of popular music's great pleonasms, "When the shark bites/ With his teeth, dear." Or the Beach Boys in "Dance, Dance, Dance," where they sing, "I'm gonna dance/ right on the floor" — so much easier than doing so on the ceiling, don't you think? Paul McCartney in "Fool on The Hill" writes, "And the eyes in his head/ see the world spinning round." There seems to be no end of feed in this granary. One can explain it of course by the poetic impulse whereby a writer, highlighting concentration, as it were, can legitimately say, "I took her hand in mine" — for drama, for intensity. But too often, *most* often, we are looking at broadcloth that is shoddy. S-H-O-D-D-Y.

Is it the result of reinforcing an image? Underlining an action? Delivering what the lyricist hopes will be a twist of wit even? Who can say, except in most cases it is artless and even, sadly, comical. "I asked a pretty lady what time it was upon her watch," laughably sing The Spinners in "Does Anybody Know What Time It Is?" In the song, "Santa Claus is Coming to Town," what else could "The kids in girl and boyland" be as kids, one may ask, *but* girls or boys? And doesn't the mind boggle over the line in "Tonight" by New Kids on the Block: "Remember when we traveled round the world / We met a lot of people and girls"? And how could one forget "Only time will tell if we stand the test of time" in Van Halen's "Why Can't This Be Love"? Or that gem from "Gloria," by the Shadows of Night (their name arguably a pleonasm in itself, of course):

> She's five feet four
> From her head to the ground

As opposed to from her nose to her clavicle?

Flame imagery seems precarious in matters of redundancy. "You put the spark to the flame," sings Elton John and Kiki Dee in "Don't Go Breakin' My Heart." And Debbie Gibson is right behind with the line in "Red Hot": "I need your love like a flame needs a fire"? Isn't the title "Light My Fire," by the way, a tautology?

A line born of a very strange ontology is one sung by the O'Kaysions, almost classically moronic, in "I'm A Girl Watcher": "When I detect/ Girls of the other sex." What about the goofy tautological phrase "last sole survivor" in "Eye of the Tiger"? Or the line in "Smoke Gets In Your Eyes from *Roberta:* "So I chaffed them and I *gaily laughed.*" So much more convincing than *miserably* laughing, no? Or the line from America's "A Horse with No Name" that so poetically goes, "The heat was hot." But even in such well-established songs as "I've Got My Love to Keep Me Warm," we hear, "The snow is snowing/ The wind is blowing." Or in the perennial "Nice Work If You Can Get It," the ridiculous phrase, "sighing sigh after sigh." All wonderful tautologies — so easy to remember (as the song goes) and so hard to forget! In her ear-twisting "Big Girls Don't Cry," Fergie sings, "And I'm gonna miss you/ like a child misses *their* blanket/ But I've got to get a move on with my life." (That song also has the immortal line, "I need some shelter of my own protection, baby.") It is right up there with Katie Perry's "I Kissed a Girl" where we hear, "*us* girls we are so magical."

The "Clunker Department" in pop lyrics is well-fed and growing. The R'n'B trio, TLC, sang in "Chasing Waterfalls": "But all the praying just ain't helping/ At all 'cause he can't seem to keep/ His self out of trouble." Bryan Adams begins his song "Run to You" with "She says her love for me could never die/ But that'd change if she ever found out about you and I." Paradoxically, people who choose to say "between you and I" almost always quite earnestly imagine that they are speaking *elegantly*, falling into the trap of "hypercorrection," the name for a mistake made in the course of trying to *avoid* a blunder, of putting their fat foot in the middle of an ungrammatical mud pie. "Whom is fooling whom?" the actress Joan Crawford, unlettered but pretentious, supposedly once asked, trying just a bit too hard. (Whom-users are, more often than not, pretentious buffoons who rarely get it right. "Whom in Okinawa made you this steel?" asks the vicious O-Ren Ishii, leader of the Tokyo *yakuza* and a former member of Bill's Deadly Viper Assassination Squad in the movie, *Kill Bill, Volume 1*, attempting to speak eloquently — which gives us a good idea of writer/director Quentin "Every Scene is Too Long" Tarantino's literary IQ.) The group Savage Garden in "Affirmation" sing, "I believe the grass is no more greener on the other side," a song in which the group seeks to offer an abundance of philosophical tidbits but leave nothing but a gallimaufry of pure jibber-jabber. Paula Cole in "I Don't Want to Wait" pleads, "So open up your morning light/ And say a little prayer for I/ You know that if we are to stay alive/ And see the peace in every eye." In "Touch Me" Jim Morrison of the Doors — he claimed to be a serious poet — sings, "I'm gonna love you / 'Til the stars fall from the sky/ For you and I." (And what about "Try now we can only lose" in "Light My Fire"? Is that what Morrison meant when he speaks of "secret alphabets" in his song "Soul Kitchen"?) Wilson Phillips sing in "You're in Love,"

> And now I see that you're so happy
> And ooh, it just sets me free
> And I'd like to see
> *Us as good of friends*
> As we used to be
> [My italics.]

Then we have the Animals who in "The House of the Rising Sun" sing "The only thing a gambler needs/ Is a suitcase and a trunk." Trunk's not desperately there for rhyme? A gambler — of all people — needs *both*? One of the classic examples of repetition in pop music can be heard in the Drifters' "There Goes My Baby":

> I love her and I need her
> besides [sic] my side
> to be my guide

Not "side by each," as they say in Canada, notice. Not even "beside my side." But — *bleecch* — "besides my side." I wanna tell ya.

Illogical lunacies proliferate. Meaningless paradox. Nonsense. Illiteracy. In "America Is My Home," James Brown, who co- wrote the song, sings "The sun don't come out in rainy weather/ But when you boil it down they're still together." Consider then the lyric sloppiness of "Danke Schön," in which a line unbelievably goes, "Thank you for the waltz [sic] down lover's lane." Then there is the group Oasis with its truly psychotic line, "Take that look from off your face" ("Don't Look Back in Anger"). Mike Oldfield in his 1983 hit, "Moonlight Shadow," sings

> Four a.m. in the morning
> Carried away by a moonlight shadow
> I watched your vision forming
> Carried away by a moonlight shadow

We really do need that strong reassuring clarification of "four a.m. *in the morning*." Thanks a house! Burt Bacharach with his sideburns, robin's-egg blue tuxes, and cheesy E-Z listening style blithely proceeds to assure us in his hit "What the World Needs Now" that we need only love — and as opposed to? Why, "mountains, oceans, and hillsides," of course! You wondered? How perceptive! In "Alfie," one of Burt's many "loungapalooza" hits from the '60s — the kind of song that the critic Francis Davis says gives off the scent of Cashmere Bouquet — was it plain Jewish agnosticism or just plain nonsense in the lines:

> As sure as I believe there's a heaven
> above, Alfie,
> I know there's something
> much more,
> Something even non-believers
> can believe in...

that made me ask: much *more* than *heaven*? Is this not an example of hyperbole gone mad? In the standard "Just in Time," exactly what does the line, "When it comes/ My time is runnin' low" mean? *Low*? Time can be running down and, I suppose, even slow(ly), but use of the word "low" in the lyric is surely inexact and incorrect.

The main fault of the Bacharach/David songwriting team was not only the banality of their songs but also the unapologetic and incorrigible run-to-his-arms-the-moment-he-gets-home-to-you chauvinism reflected in them. Woman as delineated in their songs are fashioned for obedience, as Dr. Johnson (mistakenly) said they were for John Milton. In these mechanical songs, where women cannot cope when left alone and crumple when unloved, the imperious and frankly prehistoric message is to venerate men, to wipe their feet with your hair. A loveless woman — their female point-of-view always borders on desperate — is lost without a man. In "One Less Bell to Answer," the woman laments, "Though I try to forget it it just can't be done/ Each time the doorbell rings I still run/ I don't know how in the world to stop thinking of him." In "Who Gets the Guy," the frantic woman begs, "Woah, can't you see just how much I need you?/ It just has to be me./ Please tell me that the ending is a happy ending." Male adoration was lyricist Hal David's main subject. "Anyone Who Had a Heart" has a woman literally begging to be loved. In this absurd world, a woman must be dominated, must wish to serve the master.. Wishing, hoping, thinking, praying, planning, dreaming won't get you into his arms, no you must throw your whole self at him, hold him, kiss him, literally become a *slave* to him. Let one chorus of "Wives and Lovers" speak for itself:

> Hey little girl,
> Comb your hair, fix your make-up
> Soon he will open the door.
> Don't think because
> There's a ring on your finger
> You needn't try anymore.

Regarding the "three little words," some sort of drama always seems to appertain to them. When Olivia Newton-John sings in "I Honestly Love You" (written by Peter Woolnough Allen and Jeff Barry, 1974), "But this feeling doesn't come along everyday/ And you shouldn't blow the chance/ When you've got the chance to say/ I love you/ I honestly love you," shouldn't someone inquire what sort of cynical world we live in that the adverb is necessary to add to the powerhouse three? The line has the same nutty resonance that Troy Donahue's has in the movie *Rome Adventure* (1962), when at the end, smoldering — and, I might add carrying a candelabra and roses — he gushingly delivers to Susan Pleshette the deathless words, "I just wanted to tell you I love you *beyond belief.*" [My italics.]

In the opening lyrics of Sigmund Romberg's "When I Grow Too Old to Dream" — "When I grow too old to dream, I'll have you to remember" — was the lyricist, in this case the renowned Oscar Hammerstein II, trying to say that when the dreamer is too old and dotty to have dreams, he will — still? — be able to remember his (or her) past lover? It is sheer nonsense, except that, if it makes sense, it can only come across as an *anti*-romantic ballad, simply because it means the singer, with no alternative, is stuck with some kind of drab, undreamy, sad alternative. Oscar, get back to me on this!

The daring realism of the lyrics in Sam Cooke's "A Change is Gonna Come," the single from 1964 that came richly to embody the Civil Rights movement, is unapologetic and so politically-incorrect as is evidenced by the lines,

> Then I go to my brother
> And I say brother help me please
> But he winds up knocking me
> Back down on my knees
>
> Ohhhhhhhhh.....
>
> There been times that I thought I couldn't last for long
> But now I think I'm able to carry on
> It's been a long, a long time coming
> But I know a change gonna come, oh yes it will

The story goes that upon hearing various of Bob Dylan's socially committed songs, especially "Blowin' in the Wind," a poignantly relevant song about racism in America written by someone not black, Cooke went into his touring bus after speaking with a dedicated group of sit-in demonstrators in Durham, North Carolina following one of his concerts in May 1963 and wrote the first draft of what would become "A Change Is Gonna Come," a song that in its high seriousness was very much a departure for Cooke. The uncompromising lyrics in their frankness also reflect no doubt much of Cooke's own personal anguish and inner turmoil, addressing, as he supposedly was, two crucial incidents that were understandably badly effecting him at the time: first, the accidental drowning of his 18-month-old son, Vincent, in June of that year, and, second, the pain of a controversial incident that had taken place on October 8, 1963, after Cooke and his band had tried in vain to register at a "whites only" motel in Shreveport, Louisiana and were summarily arrested for disturbing the peace. Both incidents seem represented in the wistful tone and lyrics of the song, especially the final verse: "There have been times that I thought I couldn't last for long/ but now I think I'm able to carry on/ It's been a long time coming, but I know a change is gonna come." More well-known for his polished image and such light-hearted songs such as "You Send Me," "Bring It on Home to Me," and "Everybody Loves to Cha-Cha-Cha," Cooke strongly felt the need to address the violent conditions of racism, bigotry, and ignorance then prevailing throughout the States, especially in the scary, benighted region of the Deep South. Maintaining his pop image along with the fear of losing his largely white fan base had previously prevented him from settling any resolve that he might have had along those lines, but with this masterpiece of a song — its passion and beauty, the splendid far-seeing lyrics, the teasing of the sweet violin, the matching dramatic orchestration by the masterful arranger, polymath guitarist René Hall, with a symphonic overture for strings, kettledrum, and French horn, so mournful, so right, along with separate movements for each of the first three verses, the combination of those lambent strings and forceful drums for the bridge, and a concluding crescendo; and then that soaring vocalization by Sam Cooke himself at the peak of his genius, putting notes through the paces of a hundred splendid morphs ("It's been a loo-oong, a looong time comin,'/ But I know o-oh-o, a cha-a-ange is gone come") is just about nearly perfect. It has — literally — all of the resonances of Martin Luther King's incandescent "I Have Dream Speech" in its passionate pleas. It seems that for some generations the reputation of Sam Cooke has been carried, as T.S. Eliot has observed of Ben Jonson, rather as a liability than as an asset in the balance sheet of music. It is a pity. A black friend of mine one summer day in Charlottesville, Virginia assured me, "Ain't nobody gonna match that voice, and I'm talkin' nobody, jack."

A change *had* to come. Sam Cooke, like most anybody else who had taken a look around at social America in 1964, had found the growth slow and any real progress lagging. In the original Broadway performance of *Showboat* in 1927, with its themes of racial prejudice and tragic, enduring love, the chorus for the hit "Ol' Man River" began, "Niggers all work on de Mississippi/ Niggers all work while de white folks play." By 1936, in the film of that same musical, starring Irene Dunne, it was "Darkies all work on the Mississippi," etc. When a revival of *Showboat* was made in 1946, the lyric was nervously changed to, "Colored folks work on the Mississippi," etc. Finally, when full-blown MGM production was filmed in Technicolor in 1951, it went, "Here we all work on the Mississippi," etc.

Still, it is an uphill battle. Dizzy Gillespie once told jazz critic Gary Giddins that he felt there is a level beyond which no black man can rise in the United States — President Obama, given no Republican support for four years, is proof for not against this fact — and illustrated the idea by describing the apprehensive look he gets whenever he walks into a hotel lobby, which often changes into a withering suspicion reserved for blacks, that is, until he is recognized, a sudden transformation that is unappreciated as it is an acknowledgement given to his celebrity and not his race or his manhood or his worth.

I have strong memories of those Civil Rights days back in the '60s. We *believed* in progress. A classmate of ours at the University of Virginia — we had nicknames for everybody and used to call this guy "The Psychodynamist" — had been a volunteer helping blacks to register and vote in Danville, Va. a couple of summers earlier, where he encountered a vast amount of local white hostility. It was his belief that, as a result, Danville suffered that summer one of its worst heat waves in its history, an event in his unalterable view that it was generated in all likelihood by all the negative thoughts and emotions of the bigoted Danvillians. To him it was an established scientific fact that negative emotions like racism and prejudice caused natural disasters like earthquakes, hurricanes, and tornadoes, and in that he was not two jumps from Sam Cooke's conviction that a change was gonna come.

Ralph Ellison always claimed that large parts of American culture are built on black folklore. Sam Cooke, like others, embodied both the challenge and the change of it. He knew prejudice well. We looked to him for the voice, the style, the attitude, the vernacular of that "folklore." That black inflection has been the inspiration for America, musical and otherwise. As Berndt Ostendorf in his insightful essay, "Minstrelsy & Early Jazz," points out, "This is the deep irony of American popular culture: by confining the black man in a cultural stereotype primitivism and hedonism, the white man inadvertently permitted the black man to salvage large parts of a pre-industrial, anti-Victorian and anti-puritan working class culture which went into the making of 20th century American popular culture." In a way, Sam answered the questions that we were too afraid to ask, while we were happy to accept the answers he found that all along we were unaware we needed to know.

"The song lyricist's task is to provide excuses for onstage demonstrations of energy and also, at the top of his craft, to provide new phrasings for the ineffable and virtually trite," noted John Updike in his "Foreword" to *The Complete Lyrics of Cole Porter*, edited by Robert Campbell. "How many times can the discovery and proclamation that one ersatz creature is in love with another be endured? Infinitely many, as long as real men and women continue to mate: popular composers from generation to generation, if they do not teach us how to love, do lend our romances a certain accent and give our courting rites their milieux — proms, bars, automobiles and their dashboard moons — a tribal background, a background choir of communal experience." It was the task of the lyricist to speak for us, and eloquently, to stand in for us, so to speak, in the way that the golden-tongued Cyrano de Bergerac did for the handsome but thumb-tongued cadet Christian de Neuvillette in Rostand's play.

Updike waxes eloquent on how during Cole Porter's day songsmithing was a playground for great verbal ingenuity. He observes,

> This lighthearted era was a heyday for light verse: there were book reviews in verse, and sport stories; there were droll ballades and rondeaux and triolets. The plenitudinous newspapers and magazines published Don Marquis, F.P.A., Louis Untermeyer, Arthur Guiterman, Christopher Morley, Dorothy Parker, Ogden Nash, E.B. White, Morris Bishop, and Phyllis McGinley, not to mention such clever curiosities as Newman Levy's rhyming versions of opera plots and David McCord's typographically antic 'Sonnets to Baedeker.' Song lyricists were of this ingenious company: William Harmon's *Oxford Book of Light American Verse* includes, with poems by all the above-mentioned, lyrics by Porter, Lorenz Hart, Ira Gershwin, Oscar Hammerstein II, and Johnny Mercer.

It is a serious job, writing lyrics, and seriously, even if playfully, a job it was taken for decade upon decade by professionals and passionate amateurs who considered it as much a mission as a trade to write a song well. Jerome Kern called himself a "musical clothier — nothing more or less," and said, "I write music to both the situations and the lyrics in plays." His approach was to adapt his music to plots. According to Saul Bornstein, Irving Berlin's publishing company manager, "It was a ritual for Berlin to write a complete song, words and music, every day." Berlin has said that he "does not believe in inspiration," and feels that although he may be gifted in certain areas, his most successful compositions were the "result of work." In an interview in 1916, when he was 28, he said:

> I do most of my work under pressure. When I have a song to write I go home at night, and after dinner about 8 I begin to work. Sometimes I keep at it till 4 or 5 in the morning. I do most of my writing at night, and although I have lived in the same apartment for years there has never been a complaint from any of my neighbors.... Each day I would attend rehearsals and at night write another song and bring it down the next day.

According to the music historian Alec Wilder, it was generally well known that Berlin, who could not read music, ironically enough, and was unable to write down his own notes, always paid a professional musician to harmonize and actually to do the composition, but apparently it was a job that was always done under Berlin's close supervision. He notes that "though Berlin may seldom have played acceptable harmony, he nevertheless, by some mastery of his inner ear, senses it, in fact writes many of his melodies with this natural, intuitive harmonic sense at work in his head, but not in his hands."

I have always wondered if mobility encouraged ease in writing songs when I read that Frank Loesser often composed songs — actually worked best that way — while driving around in a car. So did Johnny Mercer. At what time does Elihu say that God gives songs? In the night — Job 35:10 — is the Scriptural answer, but I am beginning to think it may be while driving around in your Merry Oldsmobile! Bobby Troup composed much of his rhythm and blues hit, a mini-travelogue, "Get Your Kicks On (Route 66)," in his car, after almost writing about Route 40. Troup conceived the idea for the song while driving west from Pennsylvania to Los Angeles, California, and the lyrics, which include references to the U.S. highway of the title and many of the cities through which it passes, celebrate the romance and freedom of automobile travel. In an interview, Troup once said the tune for the song, as well as the lyric "Get your kicks on Route 66," came to him easily but that the remainder of the lyrics eluded him. More in frustration than anything else, he simply filled up the song with the names of towns and cities on the highway. The lyrics which include various major stops that Troup passed through, a virtual taxonomy of towns going west — St. Louis, Missouri; Joplin, Missouri; Oklahoma City, Oklahoma; Amarillo, Texas; Gallup, New Mexico; Flagstaff, Arizona; Winona, Arizona; Kingman, Arizona; Barstow, California; and San Bernardino, California. It turns out that Winona is actually the only town out of sequence; it was a very small town east of Flagstaff and might probably have been forgotten if not for Troup's bopping lyric, "Don't forget Winona/ Kingman, Barstow, San Bernandino." It was in 1950 that Harold Arlen, while driving around with Johnny Mercer, came up with the pop hit, "Ac-Cent-Tchu-Ate the Positive." It is part of popular legend of course that Arlen stopped in front of Schwab's Drugstore, after motoring down Sunset Boulevard in Hollywood, sat there for a while making a few inspired notations, and then created one of his greatest songs, "Over the Rainbow." I suspect that the great Hank Williams, always on the road, wrote many a song in transit. We know that he died in a car, a sleek baby-blue rag-top Cadillac, to be specific. At around midnight on January 1, 1953, when he left the Andrew

Johnson Hotel in Knoxville, Tennessee with his driver, Charles Carr, a 17-year-old college freshman on Christmas break from Auburn, porters had to carry Williams to the car, as he was coughing. A young man himself, only 29 years old, he was wearing white cowboy boots, a stylish blue overcoat, and a white fedora and sat in the back seat. The two who were on their way to a concert in Canton, Ohio crossed the Tennessee state line in an ice-storm and motored into the cold mountains of Bristol, Virginia where Carr stopped at a small all-night restaurant and asked Williams if he wanted to eat. Williams said, "No, I just want to get some sleep," and those are believed to be his last words. Carr drove on until he stopped for fuel at a gas station in Oak Hill, West Virginia, when and where he realized that Williams was dead. The filling station's owner called the chief of the local police. In Williams' car the police found some empty beer cans and the unfinished hand- written lyrics to an unfinished song.

It is reported that Mercer penned "One for My Baby (and One More for the Road)" — one of the great torch laments of all time — on a napkin while sitting at the bar at P. J. Clarke's when Tommy Joyce was the bartender. (The next day Mercer called Joyce to apologize for the line, "So, set 'em up, Joe," explaining rather self-consciously, "I couldn't get your name to rhyme.") Most of Cole Porter's songs with their glossy opulence and suave, matchless urbanity were written far from the environs of Broadway. His score for *Anything Goes,* which included "I Get a Kick Out of You," "You're the Top," "All Through the Night," and of course the title song, was composed while he was cruising down the Rhine. He wrote all the songs for *Jubilee* ("Begin the Beguine," "Just One of Those Things," and "Why Shouldn't I?" among others) during a round-the-world cruise with the show's librettist, Moss Hart. Porter was no mere dilettante composer. His mother, Kate, started his musical training at an early age. He learned the violin at age six, the piano at eight, and wrote his first operetta (with his mother's help) at age 10. She even falsified his recorded birth year, changing it from 1891 to 1893 to make him appear more precocious. He was keen to practice the piano, unlike the young Victoria who supposedly was not. Reprimanded by her music teacher — "There is no royal road to music, dear Princess. You must practice like everybody else" — the princess supposedly slammed her piano shut. "There! You see, there is no *must* about it!" Porter entertained lavishly. J.X. Bell notes he maintained a luxury apartment in Paris where he gave extravagant and scandalous parties with "much gay and bisexual activity, Italian nobility, cross-dressing, international musicians, and a large surplus of recreational drugs." But not even his busy social rounds interfered with his creativity. He did not have a hit show on Broadway until 1928, with the musical *Paris* — featuring such tunes as "Let's Do It" and "The Heaven Hop" — when he was 37 years old. Like all geniuses, he was always working, however, and he had the further ability, in the words of the critic John Lahr, "to turn discipline into a playroom." "I've done lots of work at dinner, sitting between two bores," Porter once said. "I can feign listening beautifully. I can work anywhere."

This was old 1930s Broadway, the days of Tin Pan Alley, of 55-cent theater tickets, the Old Algiers restaurant, Schrafft's, Gray's Drugstore in Times Square, of the Brill Building on 49ᵗʰ St., back in the time when sheet music sales were where the music industry made money and recordings were still a novelty. Customers walked into the music section of a department store and asked the song-plugger or piano-demonstrator — at one time it might have been a young Irving Berlin or Jerome Kern — to play you the latest song by Eddie Cantor or Al Jolson, Gene Austin or Bing Crosby. Record booths in shops lasted into the 1950s. Do you recall the scene in Miller's Music Store in *Strangers on a Train* (1950) when Guy Haines (Farley Granger) stops in to see his vulgar, unfaithful wife, Miriam (Laura Elliott) working there, when they remove to a private listening booth to talk?

I cannot say with any authority when lyrics began to take a turn toward the wrong direction and go south, when jejune composers found, you might say, a way of signaling profundity without having to demonstrate it. Slippage may have been constant. The '30s could be obvious and tinny, the '40s had a real loony gene, the '50s manufactured schmaltz, the '60s dumped a cargo of earnestness, the '70s were grim across the board — think disco! — and was there anything like music after that? I honestly cannot take modernity too seriously. I gave up going to movies around the time jugheads like David Schwimmer and Seth Rogen and Tom Hanks began to be considered movie stars, roughly when teenage boys started wearing — talk about a refrigerant —their droopy pants below their underwear.

Billy Joel who wrote both the lyric and the music for "Just the Way You Are" apostrophizes his lover with "I don't want clever conversation/ I never want to work that hard," but then says "I just want someone that I can talk to/ I want you just the way you are." Something's got to be wrong here. The Beatles, brilliant and fecund though they were, with their typical feel-good anthem, "All You Need Is Love," make the oversimplification of the song-title seem positively profound when compared to the laughably obvious lines that follow, each one so manifestly redundant — no wonder the refrain-line goes, "It's easy" — that it actually sounds like satire or a parody of one of those cretinous new-age blitherers like Norman Vincent Peale or Edgar Guest or Deepak Chopra:

There's nothing you can do that can't be done,
Nothing you can't sing that can't be sung...
There's nothing you can make that can't be made
No one you can't save that can't be saved...
There's nothing you can know that can't be known,
Nothing you can see that can't be shown.

Lennon and McCartney's logic, that if you can sing something, it can be sung, is as obvious as the fact of water being wet or fire being hot — the philosophical equivalent of someone hanging out a sign reading, "Tattoos while you wait"! Tell me, isn't the number 2 not so much an answer to but only another way of stating what the sum of 1 and 1 is? But the scandalously ridiculous line in the same song, "Nowhere you can be that isn't meant to be," legitimately puts Anne Frank in the Nazi camps of Bergen-Belsen or Treblinka.

King Illogic reigned supreme after Lennon met Yoko Ono. I love some of the later songs they did together, but my reminiscing smile dissolves when I recollect some of the insane songs she recorded like the "Kite Song,"

I frew a kite, I hewd on tight wis stling
Each time I go an-where, I hewd on tie
In za midduw ob da nait, I wake up in fwwwwite
Thinkin maybe in my dleam I let go mai kite
When I wa in restrau, talking to my flend
Watching zere mouse moo fast and faster
I sough of za kite that wa frying iza sky
And ma sure za my han was hording za stling.

"Death of Samantha," "What a Mess," or, say, "Namyohorengegyo." ("Her voice sounded like an eagle being goosed," wrote Ralph Novak, the luthier.) But all of that's another story. By the way, Yoko, dressed all in black and wearing a funereal hat, actually did once perform a solo of a screaming song, "Voice Piece for Soprano and Wish Tree" — literally howling and yipping — at a MoMA art show in summer 2010. Museum visitors were invited to take a microphone in the museum's atrium and according to a wall poster follow Ono's instructions: "Scream. 1. against the wind; 2. against the wall; 3. against the sky." The resulting screams, amplified throughout the echoing galleries, apparently invited some scornful responses. The lilting *lollapalooza* was one word used during World War II by American soldiers trying to catch out Japanese spies who might be posing as

Filipinos or indeed as Americans. Its *l* sounds were very difficult even for Japanese who were confident in English.

Words are weapons, indeed. I will leave it for you to deduce how well Yoko Ono would have done in Manila, ca. 1945.

Regarding Yoko Ono's screeching unpronounceable alphanumeric characters to the echoing galleries — I would have been tempted to call OSHA to ask about my rights — I am reminded of Old Solomon Gills, the ships'-instrument maker and owner of the "Wooden Midshipman," and the sad story he tells in Dickens's *Dombey and Son* recounting the tragedy of the "Charming Sally being wrecked in the Baltic with the crew, as the ship went down, singing "Rule Britannia" and "ending with an awful scream in chorus." Here's to you, Edvard Munch, and your crazy *Skrik* painted on cardboard!

I certainly do not mean that the Beatles were not innovators. "Day Tripper" with its opening roils is surely heavy metal. They did all sorts of musicological tricks and made no end of innovations: backward tape loops, as in "Rain"; subliminal mutters, as in "Strawberry Fields"; a wonderland of magical, upside-down lyrics filled with puns and prankishness. John Lennon cryptically says "I bury Paul" at the end of this song, although he later claimed (falsely) he was saying, "cranberry sauce." "Baby, You're a Rich Man" featured an unusual oboe-like sound which was created with a "clavioline" — an early forerunner of the synthesizer — and a *spin-echo* (feedback delay) effect which was used to fill from the end of one line of the verse to the start of the next. Experimentation they loved. They were even cheeky enough to write a song not only about a living man, "Dr. Roberts," but about a corrupt New York City physician who gave the Fab Four drugs. This beastly song was released on the *Revolver* album in the U.K. and on *Yesterday and Today* in the U.S. Lennon always claimed that Dr. Robert was in fact himself. "I was the one who carried all the pills on tour...in the early days," he claimed. The flat fact of the matter is the subject of that song was a real person, Doctor Robert Freymann, a "speed doctor" in New York who supplied drugs to many celebrities, including the Beatles. The lax Dr. Freymann died in 1987.

Beatle-worship aside, it must be admitted that there was a lot of bogosity and the nonsensical about the Beatles. "Revolution 9" is not really a "song" but more like a random group simply chanting "revolution 9" for eight minutes. "Being For the Benefit of Mr. Kite!" was a lyric literally stolen from a poster that Lennon saw, word for word. The words to the song "Michelle" mean little or nothing and lead nowhere. (Also the "steam organ" in that song was all George Martin — he took old tapes of Victorian steam organs and re-recorded them.) Then there was all that codswallop about the mystery of Beatle Paul McCartney being dead, all that empty, fruitless, psychoanalysis about "A Day in the Life" along with a minute examination, looking for symbols, of the album cover of *Sgt. Pepper's Lonely Hearts Club Band,* a fascination that began in the late 1960s and I believe is still going on. *The Magical Mystery Tour* album cover was also examined over and over again — black symbols. Ooo-wee-ooo! But for a person who grew up with Roy Brown, Arthur "Big Boy" Crudup, The Coasters, Big Joe Turner, Carl Perkins, Fats Domino, Bo-Diddley, Little Richard, Jerry Lee Lewis — turn up very loud "Whole Lotta Shakin' Goin' On" on a 45 r.p.m. record (always "cut hotter" than LPs) to experience the very definition of R 'n' R — Ray Sharpe, Roy Orbison, Gene Vincent, and early Elvis, I can say that the Fab Four were not quite in the mainstream of rock 'n' roll, either.

Stephen King in an oversimplified way felt the same. He wrote, "Lennon and McCartney co-wrote one joyous and overwhelming rock song, 'She Loves You." Lennon was responsible for another, 'Revolution.' McCartney was responsible for a third, 'Oh, Darling.' The great rave-up tunes of the Beatles' early days are all covers. The great Lennon-McCartney tunes of their middle and later periods are ballads, music-hall spoofs, or jumped-up skiffle tunes. Furthermore, although they looked pretty good in the rooftop sequence in *Let It Be,* they were by all accounts a mediocre live band coupled with many other British and American bands of 1963-70, most notably the Rolling Stones." I contest this and would quite happily put the boys' "Love Me Do," "Back in the USSR," "A Hard Day's Night," "All My Loving," "Bad to Me," "Tell Me Why," "Eight Days a Week," "I Saw Her Standing There," "I'll Cry Instead," "Please Please Me," and "Ticket to Ride," firmly in the rock 'n' roll empyrean.

It was through their lyrics, examining them, following their bliss, as much as through the joy of their music, that fans of the Beatles — them more than any singers I can name — sought the *darshan,* a word that is employed in India to describe the beneficial glow one feels from a glimpse of greatness. Reading *into* the lyrics of the Beatles was a 1960s pastime. *Sortes Beatleiana.* Many young people in what became a serious diversion, whether wearing bandanas and tie-dyed shirts or Pappagallo flats and madras dresses, would study the song lyrics of the Fab Four. It was a way of negotiating the turbulence of that agitated, rebellious age as much as ins and outs of one's own troubled youth, perhaps. But what about the soft-knowledge side of it, the pathetic passivity of pondering the impalpabilites in "Yellow Submarine," "Happiness is a Warm Gun," "Eleanor Rigby," "Being For the Benefit of Mr. Kite!" or, say, "The Continuing Story Of Bungalow Bill"? Was not that why the Jewish sociologist/ philosopher Theodore W. Adorno, who wrote about and initiated many discussions on the addictiveness of popular music in the 1940s and 1950s, saw the entire concept of pop music as a form of social control, a mindless diversion that killed any pursuit of real knowledge and turned "pseudo-individuals" into a nation of fatuous and self-indulgent bunny hunters? A "cross-eyed transfixion with amusement" was the result of what he saw had been made "consumable." Was it not true? Didn't it all lead to a reduction and misclassification of many values? Did not all of that navel-gazing validate Adorno's conviction that the culture industry, which produced and circulated stimuli-commodities through the mass media, manipulate a silly, vain, earnest, naïve dunderheaded population interested only in idle and conformist musical embellishments and expose them to little more than an unending series of mind-fucks? Vapid solutions? Easy pleasures?

A valid case could be made, on the other hand, that it was the young people alone, idealistic and indignant readers of lyrics and takers of them to heart, who brought an end to the insanity of the Vietnam War which the United States waged in vain, and lost, along with 60,000 American soldiers and 2 million Vietnamese. There was no direct threat against the United States. War against Vietnam was never declared by Congress. The goal of the war was unclear. There was never a clear indication that the United States of America would do whatever was necessary to win. There were no clear combat zones.; there was no front. In combat, there was no safety zone in the rear — there was no rear in Vietnam, only "R & R" in Thailand where you could get looped on drugs and alcohol and contract VD. The war was fought in a country whose history, culture, religions, and values were little known or understood by the general population of the United States. Territory was taken, lost, and taken repeatedly. Little emotional support was offered to soldiers returning home. As there was no formal conclusion to the war, soldiers did not return in any formal way but often came home alone and unheralded, many of them feeling sheepish. The Ambassador of Socialist Republic of Vietnam was given a standing ovation at the United Nations on September 20, 1977. It was a national abortion that lasted an entire decade.

Glenn Gould saw the Beatles as usurpers, to a degree, although it is no secret, least of all one that the "boys" sought to hide, that they "borrowed" much from Buddy Holly, Little Richard, and Chuck Berry. "Annexing such *vox populi* conventions of English folk harmony as the 'Greensleeves'-type nonchalance of old Vaughan Williams' lethargic parallel fifths," writes Gould, rather aggressively, "the new minstrels [the Fab Four, of course] turned this lovably bumbling plainspeech into a disparaging mimicry of upper-class inflection. They went about sabotaging the seats of tonal power and piety with the same opportunism that, in *Room at the Top*, motivated Laurence Harvey in his seduction of Sir Donald Wolfit's daughter." He goes on vociferously to complain,

Tonally, the Beatles have as little regard for the niceties of voice leading [sic] as Erik Satie for the anguished cross-relation of the German post-romantics. Theirs is a happy, cocky, belligerently resourceless brand of harmonic primitivism. Their career has been one long send-up of the equation: sophistication = chromatic extension. The willful, dominant prolongations and false tonic releases to which they subject us, "Michelle" notwithstanding, in the name of foreground elaboration, are merely symptomatic of a cavalier disinclination to observe the psychological properties of tonal background. In the Liverpudlian repertoire, the indulgent amateurishness of the musical material, though closely rivaled by the indifference of the performing style, is actually surpassed only by the ineptitude of the studio production method. ("Strawberry Fields" suggests a chance encounter at a mountain wedding between Claudio Monteverdi and a jug band.)

Maybe it is asking too much reasonably to expect one of the best-known and most celebrated classical pianists of the 20th century to forego maximum cogitation when sitting down to listen to the records of one of, if not the, most commercially successful and critically acclaimed acts in the history of all of popular music.

But when was cognition not part of listening to songs? When not fun savoring the lunacies encountered? What exactly is a "dukedom," as mentioned, for example, in Gene Chandler's "Duke of Earl"? A duke lives in a duchy. So does a duchess, for that matter. What about the line, "I could never stay away without you near" in Rosie and the Originals' hit, "Angel Baby"? Could the singer possibly stay away with her lover near? Away from what? Or does she mean that if the object was somehow near, the philosophical concept of staying away was by definition impossible? I wonder if that is what she had in mind, as, for example, staying in remote Alaska with her lover? But if her lover were near, where the deuce would she be staying away *from*? Don't you love the line in Nell Carter's "Hold Me, Kiss Me, Thrill Me," that goes, "Make me tell you I'm in love with you"? *Make me?* Now that's true passion, no? It is about as romantic as the ludicrous and farcically insulting lines in Jimmy Webb's "MacArthur Park" where in his shrill, high-pitched tension-wire of a voice actor Richard Harris screeches — category: dubious compliment — "And after all the loves of my life/ And after all the loves of my life/ I think of you." In the perennial song classic, "My Funny Valentine," what on earth do the lines "Is your mouth a little weak/ when you open it to speak" mean? Is not that lyric a moon-desperate attempt for a rhyme but in the end one fundamentally far removed from logic? At the beginning of

Neil Diamond's truly harrowing "Brother Love's Salvation Traveling Show," we hear, first, that there are "leaves hanging down" and then a few lines later we hear, "There ain't no trees." In his hit, "Please Love Me Forever." Bobby Vinton, the "Polish Perry Como," sings, "If I should die before I wake/ I'll come back to you, that's no mistake." What, come back as a ghoul or a duppy after he *dies*? Now, there's a treat. But I personally believe that Vinton quite legitimately redeems himself with his "Melody of Love," which with its Polish lyrics which he himself provided — literally, "I love you, my dear/ with every inch of my heart" — except that Vinton did adapt the song from a German not a Polish song, *"Herzen haben keine Fenster"* ("Hearts Have No Windows") that, composed by Henry Mayer, was a hit in Germany and Austria when performed by the Austrian singer, Elfi Graf. A version with newly written English lyrics was released in 1974 as a single called "Don't Stay Away Too Long" by the British duo Peters and Lee, but their version of the song failed to chart in the US, so Bobby Vintula (his real name) jumped on it, writing his own lyric

> I'm lookin' for a place to go so I can be all alone
> From thoughts and memories
> So that when the music plays I don't go back to the days
> When love was you and me
>
> Chorus:
> *Oh, oh moja droga, ja cię kocham*
> Means that I love you so
> *Moja droga, ja cię kocham*
> More than you'll ever know
> *Kocham ciebie calym sercem*
> Love you with all my heart
> Return to me and always be
> My melody of love
>
> Wish I had a place to hide all my sorrow, all my pride
> I just can't get along
> 'cause the love once so fine keeps on hurtin' all the time
> where did I go wrong?
>
> (Chorus)
> Oh, oh, ("la - las" for the first line of chorus)

My melody of love
("la - las" for the first line of chorus)
My melody of love
("la - las" for the first line of chorus)

(Fade)
My melody of love

I mention "MacArthur Park," one of the least bearable recordings ever made. It is not really a song but a kitschy drama, vocally acted out, explored like the five stages of grief. It is actually an insane dithyramb. You keep thinking *quit the bullshit* as you listen to Harris sing, especially as your eyes keep looking back, unwillingly, to the album cover where the "artist" appears unprepossessingly to be sporting a walrus mustache and wearing a headband very like Geronimo's! Throughout the interminably painful seven-and-a-half minute piece, a song written by Jimmy Webb and recorded with loud, heavily mawkish orchestration, the singularly untrained voice of the vain, thin-voiced, caterwauling Irish actor in his hippie period goes from dubious tenor to mooing baritone to just plain speech and then to a flatulently trepid, desperate *estinto* that rises to a screeching falsetto that sounds exactly like the ultrasound drill of a dentist. One of the lines in the song describes how lovers enjoy a "dance/ between the parted pages, and were pressed in love's hot fevered iron/ Like a stripéd [sic] pair of pants." No, I'm not making that up — the guy sings stripéd! All throughout the song, by the way, Harris repeatedly, moronically refers to the locale as "Mac*Arthur's*" Park. Sadly, because the LP sold half a million copies and the single 850,000 which gives you a melancholy idea of what the taste of people was back there in 1968, the actor, immune to irony and appearing on talk shows in his eye-killing floral shirts, seriously considered the recording of his song a watershed in music, a masterpiece, and placed himself somewhere up there in the league of Dietrich Fischer-Dieskau singing Arnold in Rossini's *William Tell* or Jussi Börling singing Don Ottavio in Mozart's *Don Giovanni* or Enrico Caruso singing Rodolfo in Giacomo Puccini's *La Bohème*. No shit.

Taste can be a funny thing. Albert Einstein supposedly liked country music. I have mentioned Theodor Adorno, the German sociologist. He traveled to the United States to sit out World War II and comfortably set up shop in the Pacific Palisades just in time to condemn the "culture industry" here and sourly express a priggish and vociferous disgust for jazz, swing music, and rock 'n' roll. Logician, philosopher, and mathematician Kurt Gödel cared little for classical music, according to his biographer John W. Dawson, Jr., and, wondering why good music had to be "tragic," he even claimed that Bach and Wagner made him "nervous," but the author of *The Consistency of the Axioms of Choice and of the Generalized Continuum Hypothesis with the Axions of Set Theory* loved "O Mein Papa," "Harbor Lights," "Wheel of Fortune," and many other pop songs from the '50s. Who would have believed that the brilliant Canadian classical pianist, Glenn Gould, renowned interpreter of the keyboard music of Johann Sebastian Bach, could be found disquisiting, and quite proudly, on the music of pop singer *Petula Clark*? Not Percy Sledge, not Barrett Strong, not Bo Diddley, not Wilson Pickett — but Petula Clark! He went so far as to write, "The Search for Petula Clark," a fulsome essay in which, "detailing an adjacent plateau of experience," he assesses four of her biggest hits, "My Love," "Who Am I?" "Sign of the Times," and "Downtown," songs which he sees are all of an integrated piece, a sort of small Bunyanesque pilgrimage through adolescence, denominating Clark "pop music's most persuasive embodiments of the Gidget syndrome." Get the picture. Here we have the most proficient performer of the majestic *Goldberg Variations*, as well as the complete *The Well-Tempered Clavier*, Partitas, French Suites, English Suites, and keyboard concertos, one of the greatest pianists of the 20th-century quite soberly, *musicologically*, assuming the role of, say, disc-jockey Alan Freed and proclaiming, "'Downtown' is the most affirmatively diatonic exhortation in the key of E major since the unlikely team of Felix Mendelssohn and Harriet Beecher Stowe pooled [their] talents for

> Still, still, with Thee, when purple morning breaketh
> When the bird waketh and the shadows flee…

A fellow who disliked and avoided playing the music of Liszt, Schumann, Chopin, and even Mozart — arguing (was he joking?) that Mozart "died too late rather than too early" — including the Beatles (for "bad voice leading"), Gould declared of Clark's voice, without irony, that it is "fiercely loyal to its one great octave, indulging none but the most circumspect slides and filigree, vibrato so tight and fast as to be nonexistent — none of that 'here comes the fermata, so hold on' tremolando with which her nibs Georgia Gibbs grated like squeaky chalk upon the exposed nerves of my generation." (Just for the record, John Lennon declared that she was also his favorite singer.) Gould praises Clark personally, who at 34 had two kids, for in his considered opinion "a well-ordered career in pop music should be conceived like the dramatic personae of soap opera." Gould takes her work very seriously. "'My Love' remains firmly persuaded of its nonmodulating course." "'Who Am I?'"... catalogues those symptoms of disenchantment and ennui which inevitably scuttle a trajectory of emotional escalation." "Motivically [sic], 'Who Am I?' plays a similar game of reverse 'Downtown'-ism," he observes. "The principle motivic cell unit of that ebullient *lied* consisted of the internal of a minor third plus a major second, alternately, upon occasion, with a major third followed by a minor second." And then "'Sign of the Times' ("I'll never understand the way your treated me,/ But when I hold your hand, I know you couldn't be the way you used to be"), reflecting "reconciliary concession," just like the others "emphasizes some aspect of that discrepancy between an adolescent's short-term need to rebel and a long-range readiness to conform." Gould approves Clark at all points. "The harmonic attitude is, at all times, hymnal, upright, and relentlessly diatonic."

Warning his reader that "such Schoenbergian jargon must be charily applied to the carefree creations of the pop scene," Gould was nevertheless brilliant and thought on his own two feet. A Presbyterian, he came to develop a singular aversion to what he called a "hedonistic" approach to the piano repertoire, concert performances, and music in general. Hedonism for him denoted a superficial theatricality, the cult of showmanship, gratuitous virtuosity. He was chaste in his way and wanted to ban applause itself, coming up with a doctrine of GPAADAK which stood for "The Gould Plan for the Abolition of Applause and Demonstrations of All Kinds." Live musical performances, especially classical or art concerts, he found were often delayed, ruined, and spoiled by audience members who coughed, hissed, wheezed, and even yelled during events. Over time he held the concert-going public in rather low esteem, finding them non-empathetic and hypercritical and, almost with a kind of social "dishing," all too ready to pit one musician against another in an inane and pointless competition

Stupidity in music — or anywhere — is a fascinating subject. Groucho Marx on *The Dick Cavett Show* while singing Gilbert and Sullivan's "Tit Willow" — he was a passionate Gilbert and Sullivan fan — suddenly stopped in mid-lyric to confront the audience with, "What does the word 'obdurate' mean?" An embarrassing, uneasy pause followed. The comedian badgered them. Still, not a single hand was raised. "What the hell am I singing this song for, if you don't know what the hell I'm singing?" asked the exasperated comedian. So he abruptly left off singing the song, walked over to Cavett, and began to talk about something else. It is truly a sign of the times that an old bald comedian from a past era in which that kind of ignorance was not only abhorrent but an actual source of embarrassment would be quizzing in vain a modern audience of lazy, poorly read, semi-anti-intellectual halfwits. "We need a leader, not a reader," the blustering presidential candidate,

Herman Cain, defensively snapped to an assembly of die-hard Republican wingnuts — and he was vigorously applauded — on the night of November 17, 2011 while campaigning in New Hampshire. When he was asked several questions about Libya, Cain, founder of Godfather's Pizza — I will leave it for someone older and wiser than I to explain exactly where the strict orthogonal lines meet for the ability to make a large anchovy-and-pepper pizza and to run for president of the United States — needed almost five full minutes merely to recognize even the *name* of that country. Convinced that the presidency of the United States was only the "fetus of monarchy," old John Randolph of Roanoke (1773-1833) in his day was greatly fearful that such power in the country should ever be invested in one man, and, looking at Cain, can anyone possibly wonder why? Cain is obviously a total ignoramus, but in these bleak days of political correctness even to say such a thing is surely to be accused of over-urgent exasperation and corrective contempt. Ignorance should be the cause of worry. I mention this here because I have always wondered, whenever the late Sammy Davis, Jr. was singing "Something's Gotta Give," whether that little guy actually knew what the word "implacable" actually meant. I offer this only because Davis, sad to relate, could barely write his own name. On a television quiz show I saw in the 1960s — the handwriting of a few celebrities was being analyzed — the hip singer, taking up and gripping the pen like a foreign object, could just about manage to write down a simple sentence that had been dictated to him, a very precarious TV moment, let me tell you, in that Davis who suddenly became tense, quite openly frustrated, very visibly angry — he begrudgingly held up a page of illegible scribble, just plain griffonage — and looked for a moment there that he might literally explode! I had to look away from the television set, it was that embarrassing for him.

"Oh, I never read," calmly replies Marguerite Gauthier (Greta Garbo) in the 1936 film version of *Camille,* when devoted Armand (Robert Taylor) offers her a copy of *Manon Lescaut.* One cannot help but find this courtesan, for all her beauty, a frivolous twerp with a mind as empty as her ready white smile. "I never read" has to be one of the most frightening admissions a human being can possibly make.

"I have given up flying with Great Literature.... I no longer take Great Literature on the road," wrote Dominique Browning in "Learning to Love Airport Lit" in the *New York Times* on February 21, 2012. "What I want on a plane trip is a loud, beefy — even vulgar — but scintillating companion. Someone like Scott Turow, who commands attention but is refined enough to respect my intelligence. This, not unlike any level of discrimination in matchmaking, narrows the field.... All I want now, from a good airplane book, is transport. A sense of propulsion. I want to feel the rush of plot against my cheek. I want to know where I am going, and why. I'm willing to trade transport for transportation." It is often noted that *moron*, as a scientific designation for a slow or feebleminded person, was the only word ever voted into the language, adopted in 1910, by the American Association for the Study of the Feeble Minded from the name of a foolish character in Molière's play, *La Princesse d'Élide*. This claim inadvertently overlooks another name: Dominique Browning.

What about the ludicrous line, never mind the logic — is it supposed to be a compliment? — when in his self-approving song, "After The Loving," Engelbert Humperdinck sings, "Thank you for giving me/ A one-way trip to the sun"? I mean was a songwriter with a pen in his hand, and sober, actually writing that with his brain screwed on tight? Is it not roughly the same kind of assbackwards compliment that we hear in John Denver's impossibly saccharine "Follow Me", which opens,

> It's by far the hardest thing I've ever done
> To be so in love with you so long.

A joke! Madness! Insane! Where — *how?* — did John Denver get his conception of flattery? Listen to his zany line in the song, "Shanghai Breezes." It goes, "I couldn't leave you even if I wanted to," an unintentionally mocking double-insult turgidly flung at his poor addled lover whom I see standing in a doorway scratching her head and asking like Jack Nicholson in *The Shining*, "Are you out of your fucking mind?"

Who can forget that Dan Fogelberg in "The Leader of the Band," I presume in all seriousness, leaves us the following memorable line,

> The leader of the band is dead
> and his eyes are growing old.

Isn't it only mad contradiction for the Elegants in "Little Star" to sing in one line, "You're the one I'm thinking of" and then a few lines later to say, "I need a love tonight"? Listen to the completely buggered-up imagery in Don Henley's hopelessly muddled song "End of the Innocence," when he confusingly writes, "Lay your head back on the ground and let your hair fall all around me" — what does his girlfriend have in that prone position, a form of *bilocation*? Hackery! Quackery! Flackery! In Tony Orlando and Dawn's "Knock Three Times," he sings, "Knock three times on the ceiling it you want me/ twice on the pipe if the answer is no," where -upon he proceeds to sing to this very same woman, "One floor below me/ You don't even know me/ I love you." Let me get this straight. If he doesn't know her, and so she him, presumably, how could she possibly know the secret code? Is it likely, furthermore, that his mad plea that he loves her, even falling on willing ears, would encourage her to *knock*? In the absurd song, "What a Difference a Day Makes," doesn't the line, "What a difference a day makes/ And that difference is you" constitute in fact a total contradiction? I mean, does the crucial difference that is made depend on her or on the day itself? If one is talking about one thing, why bring in the other? Or is she the day and that makes the difference, meaning that they are the same? I do not think I have to bring in Aristotle on the subject of modal logic to distinguish the lunacy here. It is the kind of daft reasonlessness that recalls for me an exchange that takes place in the Mickey Rooney film, *Andy Hardy Comes Home* (1958).

What about the following exchange:

> Aunt Millie: "Why don't we take a trip?"
> Ma Hardy: "Where?"
> Aunt Millie: "Let's go around the world."
> Ma Hardy: "No, let's go someplace else."

Then we come across the line, "Our share is always the biggest amount" — to share, as defined by Webster, means to divide and distribute in *equal proportions* — in the song, "The In-Crowd." Isn't that completely blinkered logic? Flatly moronic in their inaccuracy? Farcically facile? Almost comic? In the 1950s Jerry Vale's tawdry, tabloidal hit "Two Purple Shadows on the Snow" — the singer, being two-timed by the woman he loves and whom he sees kissing someone else behind a shade is bemoaning her perfidy — concludes his lament, "And as I ripped up two tickets for a show/ they turned to two purple shadows on the snow." It is all nicely symmetrical word-play and all, but frankly would not logic have it that if he ripped up two tickets there would be — at least! — *four* purple shadows on the snow? And, I mean, were the traduced singer in his heart-break truly furious in his crazy ripping-fit, might not one find more realistically *umpteen* little shadows on the snow? In Danny and the Junior's "At the Hop," we hear the line "When the record starts a-spinnin', you calypso when you chicken at the hop." Since both verbs stand for dances, might not one ask how anyone could possibly manage to do both at the same time?

I love Sam the Sham and the Pharaohs, but in the song "Woolly Bully" — words and music by Domingo Samudio (a.k.a. "Sam the Sham") — what is one to make of the puzzling and uncertain lines,

Hatty told Matty
Let's don't take no chance.
Let's not be L-seven.
Come and learn to dance!
Woolly bully — woolly bully,
Woolly bully — woolly bully

Exactly, what is an L-seven? Oh wait, I get it — if you draw an L and a 7 and put them together, they form — a square!

On the subject of enigma, has anyone ever asked who the speaker, Louie, is in the inscrutable 1957 hit, "Louie, Louie" (words and music by Richard Berry) and why he is even mentioned in a song which in no way depends on him? The famously cryptic song goes,

Three fine little girl is waitin' for me
Me catch a ship across the sea
Me sailed that ship, ah, all alone
Me never think how I'll make it home

Refrain:
Louie Louie, me gotta go
Louie Louie, me gotta go

Three nights and days I sailed the sea
Me think of girl oh constantly
Oh, on that ship I dream she there
I smell the rose ah in her hair.

(Refrain)

Me see Jamaica ah moon above
It won't be long me see me love
Me take her in me arms again
I tell her I'll never leave her here

Why is Louie's name used throughout the song and not the girls'? Is the time element of the song present or past? If the song is in the first person, how can he be using his own name? If he is or was alone, why the use of "we" in the song? Finally, if the singer is in love, how is it that as many as three girls are involved?

One of the stanzas in Paul McCartney's lovely "Mull of Kintyre" goes:

> Smile in the sunshine and tears in the rain
> Still take me back where my memories remain
> Flickering embers *grow higher and higher*
> As they carry me back to the Mull of Kintyre
> [My italics.]

I had always thought embers sank.

The mad contradictory images in Alan and Marilyn Bergman's abysmal "The Windmills of Your Mind," a meaningless mis-concatenation of snowballs, carnival clocks with spinning hands, a grotesque accumulation of muddled images of "apples whirling silently in space," all add up to — what? That the subject is deep? That human beings are confused? That modern man is thinking too fast? Too chaotically? Oddly? Pointlessly? It is an orgy of similes and mixed metaphors. And then we hear,

> When you knew that it was over
> you were suddenly aware
> that the autumn leaves were turning to the color of her hair.

Oak red? Hectic yellow?

Supposedly a love song, "If", as sung by David Gates, lead singer of the soft-rock group, Bread, writes,

> If a face could launch a thousand ships
> then where am I to go?
> There's no one home but you,
> you're all that's left me, too.

This is an exact quotation: I bothered to check the sheet-music. Is the first sentence a conditional juxtaposition that we are being asked to understand? First of all, is the singer a ship? Why would Helen of Troy, whose face is presumably matched by that of the singer's girlfriend, direct him to go anywhere at all? Then what exactly has war to do with this love affair, since that is what the Greek myth refers to? And if the girl is at home (cf. line 3), why in God's name should he be contemplating leaving to go anywhere? So, correct me. Is he not complaining that he is stuck with the girl he is miserably left with in contradistinction to the figure of beauty in the first line that seems to compel him to be going *somewhere*? And doesn't that reveal him in four short lines to be a person totally bugfuck?

In Kris Kristofferson's maudlin country-hit, "For The Good Times," a song that is an inexorable reminder to me of the '70s as clogs, yellow refrigerators, Maryland 100's (cigarettes), Jell-O cheesecake, dips, fondue sets, Mott's Snack Jars, the anti-static sock, Stridex Pads, Freakies cereal, pull-tabs, Van McCoy's "The Hustle," and the Dodge "Polara,"we have the pitifully inexact image of raindrops both blowing and whispering at the same time"

> Hear the whisper of the raindrops
> blowing soft against the window

Falling raindrops aren't poetic?

The '70s. The Disco sound. The Hues Corporation's "Rock the Boat," Biddu's "Kung Fu Fighting," the Bee Gees' "Stayin' Alive," KC and the Sunshine Band's "That's the Way (I Like It)," "(Shake, Shake, Shake) Shake Your Booty," Chic's "Le Freak," soaring, often reverberated vocals over a steady "four-on-the-floor" beat, a relentless eighth note (quaver) or 16th note (semi-quaver) hi-hat pattern with an open hi-hat on the off-beat, and a prominent, syncopated electric bass line sometimes consisting of octaves. Mullet music. David Cassidy. The Partridge Family and other phasianidae. This was the unmemorable decade where one never knew — and whether you cared or not was an open question — which was the song title and which was the group. Was it Toto that sang "Rosanna" or Rosanna that sang "Toto"? Mr. Mister that sang "Broken Wings" or Broken Wings that sang "Mr. Mister"? Styx that sang "Babe" or Babe that sang "Styx"? Then ponder the oxymoron "rock ballads"! That has got to be right up there with "paid volunteers," "exact estimate," and "act naturally." Thank the big hairs. It was an era where groups in satin floods with pastel colors loved to adopt questing names ("You guys are deep, maaan!") — like Survivor, Journey, Foreigner, Genesis, Supertramp, Rainbow, Nazareth, and other bands with one-word names that unimpressibly sound to the Midwestern wit James Lileks, like "Psoriasis, Seborreah, Pyorrhea, and Colitis." (At least a sense of group unity , a collective effort, adhered to Vito & Salutations, Barry & the Salutations, even Don & the Quixotes offered much more imagination.) Lileks in his highly entertaining book of essays, *Fresh Lies*, insightfully cites other wild group names that "frequently have umlauts over letters to indicate allegiance with Satan; thus, Higgly Piggly becomes the ominous Hïgglÿ Pïgglÿ," deathless rockers whose passionate fans, followers, and devotees can be frequently found in allegiance "raising their hands with the index and pinkie fingers extended, thinking it refers to the horns of the devil, when it is actually a sign expressing solidarity with the brother- hood of Careless Band-Saw Operators." (*Rrröööaaarr* is the second album by Canadian heavy metal band, Voivod, released in 1986 on Noise Records. The names of that band's members which are far more memorable than their music are Snake, Piggy, Blacky, and — wait for it — Away.) What a lot of polypharmalogical barking one heard back then, the dunderheaded lyrics in all of those "rock anthems" and "power ballads" — Boston's "More than a Feeling," Journey's "Open Arms," Air Supply's "The One that You Love" are several that come to mind — acataleptic love-howls that when crooned, at their very worst extreme, became, in the laughably oxymoronic parlance of the 1970s,"soft rock" or "lite rock," pretty much all like the lines of the following lax, slack, flaccid, and drooping offering from Yes' "Wonderous [sic] Stories" which would have been better sung by a flock of pipits:

> He spoke of lands not far
> nor lands they [sic] were in his mind
> of fusion captured high
> where reason captured his time
> in no time at all he took me to the gate
> in haste I quickly
> checked the time
> if I was late
> I had to leave, to hear your wonderous stories
> Had to hear your wonderous stories "la aha, la aha"

I still wake up in the middle of a sweaty *cauchemar* hearing the lyrics from "Eye of the Tiger," burned into me — *grooved* — like ugly, deep tribal cicatrices. I remember seeing the group Aerosmith in Boston back in the late '70s. "I shall only be glad to have seen it, for the reason...that it will be unnecessary for me ever to see it again," as Winston Churchill said of the city of Calcutta. The music of that decade sucked. It was false currency. What else can I add — that Meat Loaf had a good voice?

I like exactitude. Randy Newman in his plaintive song, "Louisiana," an account in song of a flood in Evangeline, identifies President Coolidge as a "little fat man with a notepad in his hand." Poor Calvin Coolidge, he of the wooden countenance, on his lumpiest day on earth in fact hadn't the avoirdupois of a bamboo splinter.

We're having a heat-wave,
A tropical heat-wave.
The temperature's rising.
It isn't surprising;
She certainly can,

goes the Irving Berlin song in the film, *There's No Business Like Show Business* (1954). Excuse me — she can do exactly *what?* And by the way who is *she?* Non-sequiturs abound. I can never watch this movie without being bothered by this pestilential song, even if it is performed by the beguiling Marilyn Monroe in one of her sweetest roles. (The rumor mill has it that Monroe who did not want to make this film was treated with disdain by her co-stars, and on the musical's LP she was, alone, not pictorially represented.) But what else can one expect in a crazy, hysterical cinematic mishmash — plot lines by Jackson Pollock — which, without blinking, cuts quickly from Donald O'Connor joining the U.S. Navy to Mitzi Gaynor butterfly-dancing to deaf Johnnie Ray being ordained a priest to Marilyn Monroe in a bare midriff sizzling with "Heat Wave" to Dan Dailey gulping whiskies in street-clothes to Ethel Merman in bon-bon pink after howling for the part ("But you can't cut that number, Lew — we need it!") reappearing in male drag as a fat sailor with even fatter sideburns belting out, "You Can't Be A Sailor Without A Tattooooooo"! It is one of the noisiest, most disjointed movies ever made, released the very same year that the first TV Dinner arrived on the scene, a turkey-and-dressing meal packaged in a segmented foil tray in a box printed up to look like a television screen. There is everything on the goddam menu of *There's No Business Like Show Business* but Judah Maccabeus of old being afflicted very sore by the enemies of Hebrewville! It was one of my earliest revelations that showbiz is all fake, as John Waters learned — happily in his case — when he discovered at an early age that as many as 10 Howdy Doody puppets existed, not one!

When Roberta Flack in "The First Time" sings, "The first time ever I kissed *your lips/* I felt the earth move *in my hands*," exactly what was she *doing?* In the dismal 1978 musical *Lost Horizon*, a total turkey, precisely what did Hal David and Burt Bacharach have in mind when writing the song, "Question Me an Answer," the ontological equivalent of "Problem Me A Solution," is it not? So many bits of obfuscation and inexactitude in popular music *irritate and annoy* me! When Hoagy Carmichael wrote of "love's refrain" in "Stardust," what on earth did he *mean?* In "Tumbling Tumbleweeds," how can the blowing weeds be understood as "pledging their love to the ground"? Oh, and don't you just love Ben E. King's lines in "Spanish Harlem,"

I'm going to pick that rose
And watch as she grows
in my garden.

No mean feat, right?

In "Cherish" by the Association, despite all the initial protests of unchanging love, the singer proceeds with a whine that he wants "to mold" his paramour into someone who would cherish him, turning a love-song into a charmless *jeu de chanson* of pure unadulterated vanity. Johnny Cash in "I Walk the Line" sings, "I keep the ends out for the ties that bind." Ends out of what? There is not a clue to the imagery in the song; if anything there is a mixed metaphor in the song title, which is total nonsense. *Orrrrrr* is he comparing himself to a woman's poke bonnet? "He uses all the great quotations," sings Jerry Butler in the song, "He Will Break Your Heart." Envying a more educated rival for his girl, isn't the singer actually trying to say, "He is well read" or "He can cite poetry"? What the fuck *are* all the great quotations? *Bartlett in toto?* Does his rival have an eidetic memory? I marvel at those approximation lines where someone subjectively intends what objectively no one else can understand, although I am convinced that I am the only person alive (and now you) to realize that Jewish Ted Geisel as Dr. Seuss, in having the Christmas choristers of Whoville sing, "*Da hoo doray, Do hoo ramus,*" was actually trying to effect the cartoon equivalent of Latin-chant — an area doubtless foreign to him — without in fact committing himself to anything spiritual or precisely Christian. In short, the approximation is an amateur's idea — or a Jew's — of Gregorian chant.

"I found her crying *needlessly,*" Bobby Goldsboro warbles in his hit song, "Honey," and then in the very next line she — *dies!* So much for her boyfriend's medical acumen. What are we to make of U2's logic (or a corpse's pride) in their lyric, "Early morning April 4th/ A shot rings out in the Memphis sky/ Free at last/ They took your life/ But they could not take your pride"? (Martin Luther King, incidentally, was murdered, not in the morning, but the early evening — and what good is his pride six feet under? "They" is also the wrong pronoun; he was shot by one man. Regarding the Vernon Duke song, "Autumn in New York," Gore Vidal shares my doubt about the phrase, "It spells the thrill of first-nighting" — surely not a reference to the Scottish New Year, "first-footing," but then to what? — when he writes in *Kalki,* "a mysterious phrase. Reference to the seduction of a virgin?" I suspect that Duke meant opening night at the theater. And is it overly fussy of me to point out that the hit from *My Fair Lady,* "The Rain in Spain," is a tango and that the tango came, not from Spain, but from Argentina? Frank

Sinatra's song, "That's Life," a defense of vitality, unadulterated excitement, and the sheer delight of living, ends not only on a distinctly morbid note but — right — with a threat of suicide. ("I thought of quittin' baby, but my heart won't buy it") One has to find that reference strange, since in this song from 1965 Sinatra really cranks it with a kind of tigerish all-out jive, chomping the words, growling out happy assertions of life, liberty, and living. In the Jive Five's rhythm-and-blues hit, "My True Story," the lovers' names are romantically chanted out with great verve by the Brooklyn group: "Her name it was Sue (yeah), his name it was Earl" in one stanza, and then in the very next stanza we are told — pointlessly — that those names in fact are aliases. Why? I also believe I hear the name "Lorraine" popping up. (The lyrics are remarkably muddy throughout most of the song.) In the end, strangely, *none* of the names ultimately seem to matter to the song.

In The Marvelettes' hit, "Please, Mr. Postman," a song whose theme is urgency ("Deliver the letter/ The sooner the better"), the refrain — inexplicably — goes, "Wait a minute, wait a minute!" "*Though* [my italics] a million miles away," sings Frankie Valli in "My Eyes Adored You," "you couldn't tell my eyes adored you." What? He is blaming her because she is not Wonder Woman? What about the calendrically-challenged Bobby Goldsboro who sings in "The Autumn of my Life:" — had he been drinking? — "And the years went by in the Spring of my life." Singing "Remember When We Made These Memories," Wayne Newton — his painful-to-hear speech-defect pronounces the last word "*memoriezzzjj*" — moronically sings, "Those two days in London town/ We yankee-doodled all around," when of course that old phrase "yankee doodle," British slang for the hated Colonials, evokes only the 18th-century enmity between the two countries! In their non-sequitur-filled song, "The Beat Goes On," the blessedly unaware — and I daresay undereducated — Sonny and Cher sing, "Bums still cries [sic], 'Buddy, have you got a dime?'" "Everyone is beautiful in their [sic] own way," sings Ray Stevens, allowing not only for the living legitimacy of bad grammarians, such as himself, but also people like Adolf Hitler, Vlad Dracula, and Pol Pot, as well. John Denver's "Leaving on a Jet Plane" is a love song, so why would either a husband or lover, passionately fixed to the woman he desperately hated to leave, sing,

> All my bags are packed, I'm ready to go,
> I'm standing outside your door to say goodbye...

"*Your door*"? The two did not stay together the night before he was to leave? Slept in different rooms? Or was it that he had to get up early, didn't want to bother

her, and so slept on a couch out somewhere in the living room? If so, does that mean that his sleep was more important than love and this is a *love* song, Mr. Deutschendorf?

Why would the Beach Boys in "Surfin' USA" sing the wacky line, "We're waxing down our surfboards/ We can't wait for June," when in California — their signature state, after all — it is warm virtually all year round. (Beyond that, ironically enough, the month of June in the city of San Diego is almost always the very *worst* month of the year: rainy, foggy, dull, horrible.) Dopey Steve Lawrence, whose lowing voice to me always suggests less of the crooner than an amorous cow, in his song "Portrait of My Love" manages with a kind of reverse genius to mispronounce as many as three words: it is "Mona Lisa," not "Moana Leeza," Michelangelo, not Mĭchael Angelo —,Ĭ not *eye* — and it should be "portrait" (as in "let") of my love, not portrait (as in "bait"). One would think that recording a song one would take enough care to do it right. But the Age of Shoddy is healthy and flourishing. What about that odd line Nancy Sinatra sings in her hit, "These Boots are Made for Walking" — "What you know you ain't had time to learn"? Come again? You can know something you have not been able to learn? Then exactly what was Bob Dylan's visual idea of a watchtower when he memorably wrote the song — and Jimi Hendrix sang — "All Along the Watchtower"? You cannot *walk* along a watchtower, dude — it is not a parapet or a castle wall or a road. It is a turret. Look it up. A simple dictionary — when used, of course — can be a songwriter's best friend.

In the thematically masochistic pop-song, "Angel of the Morning," the victim's national anthem, both Merrillee Rush and then Juice Newton — whose cover version taken by right of usufruct does not however exclude repeatedly confusing the same tenses — both proceed to sing with all seriousness the astonishingly buggered-up line, "It was what I wanted now" when the song's reflections are of and located (QED) in the past. P. F. Sloan, born Philip Gary Schlein in LA — whose ballads caused him to sometimes be referred to as "the poor man's Bob Dylan" — wrote in "The Eve of Destruction,"

> My blood's so mad, feels like coagulation
> I'm sitting here just contemplatin'

Look, forget the amateurish rhyme right there, which is bad enough, the unintentionally comic hyperbole of the song-title, consider merely the lack of inspiration of the song, the haste with which it was written, the bathos. The words must have been written in five minutes on the back of a matchcover with a crayon! What an insane and garbled image. Blood, personified — right there I have a headache — and so angry, so furibund, it doesn't want to flow which is what angry blood would do, it seems to me; meanwhile, the owner of the blood is simply just *sitting there*? Like a *fakir*? Just *contemplatin'*?

In Barry Manilow's headache-making "Ready to Take a Chance Again," he refers to the fact the he is "doing OK but not very well." Talk about cant. Try to picture Cole Porter or Ira Gershwin even *coming up* with such a lyric, never mind writing it down, and you will have some idea where taste, never mind literacy, is headed in pop music. Of every Manilow album, in which he artlessly eviscerates song after song with the gibbering mutterances of an auctioneer, it may be said, to plu-paraphrase the slick commercial slogan for the 1960s' John Schlesinger film, *Darling*, starring Dirk Bogarde and Julie Christie: "A little was too much. Too much was never enough" — to ridicule. Pure contrivance fails. What is not very often seen or understood is that composers like George Gershwin or Cole Porter were, more than anything else, boldly, sumptuously *un*systematic — you can feel it — and as they worked were disposed to serendipities and suggestions and ready for a move in any possible direction, but they never sacrificed quality in experiment or elegance in innovation.

Artifice, design, inventiveness for a great songwriter must all work together in harmony. Take Cole Porter's "Night and Day." The usual format for a pop song is thirty-two measures of music, broken up into eight measure phrases: AABA, or ABAB. So a tune starts with an eight-measure figure, repeats it, breaks in against it with a "release," and then returns to the original figure. For a new song written for specifically for Fred Astaire in *The Gay Divorcee* (1934) Porter made a new departure. Bill Adler in his splendid *Fred Astaire, A Wonderful Life*, explains it best: "The tune Porter had written for Fred followed the format, ABAB, for thirty-two measures. But Porter was only beginning After ABAB, he added C, a brand-new figure that played against the first two figures [ABAB], and then returned to B to wind up the song. ABABCB. It was a forty-eight measure song — unheard of! Plus which, the tune itself extended up and down an octave and a half — twelve full steps! — rather than the conventional maximum eight." Later, Porter claimed that the tune — strangely, for a song about sexual torment — was inspired by a Mohammedan call to worship that he had heard in Morocco. (He also said the same about "What Is This Thing Called Love?")

Although the song was tailored to Astaire (who in turn choreographed his dance steps to this haunting love song), the lyrics made Porter work. At a luncheon during a rainstorm at Mr. and Mrs. Astor's elegant mansion, according to an often repeated story, Porter supposedly had heard his hostess complaining about a broken eave on the house: "That drip, drip, drip is driving me mad.") In the film, as he courts Ginger in a smart hotel suite overlooking an English Channel beach on a moonlit night, even with a hint of his Omaha accent peeping through ("They're having a gāla night on the esplānade") Fred's voice is never richer, the couple never danced better, and the strange throbbing song soars:

> Night and day, under the hide of me
> There's an oh, such a hungry yearnin' burnin' inside of me
> And its torment won't be through
> Till you let me spend my life makin' love to you
> Day and night, night and day

A dog for exactitude, Ira Gershwin always fretted about lyrics and would work for days, weeks, on them. Words, their combinations, thrilled him. He often made wild bets on horse races based on fanciful word associations. Edward Jablonski in *Gershwin* gives Ira's very own account of working on "Fascinating Rhythm," putting words to his brother George's music, an intricate complexity in every way:

> I didn't think I had the brilliant title in Fascinating Rhythm, but A, it did sing smoothly, and B, I couldn't think of a better. The rhyme scheme was a, b, a, c-a, b, a, c. When I got to the 8th line I showed the lyric to George. His comment was that the 4th and 8th lines should have a double (or two-syllable) rhyme where I rhymed them with single syllables.

> I protested and, by singing, showed him that the last note in both lines had the same strength as the note preceding. To me the last two notes formed a spondee; the easiest way out was arbitrarily to put the accent on the last note. But this George couldn't see, and so, on and off, we argued for days. Finally, I had to capitulate and write the lines as they are today

> 4th line: I'm all a-*qui*ver
> 8th line: Just like a *fli*vver

> after George proved to me that I had better use the double rhyme, because whereas in singing, the notes might be considered even, in conducting the music the downbeat came on the penultimate note.

The strenuous give-and-take between the brothers, their dialogue of suggestion and counter- suggestion, was characteristic of their collaboration, an indication of their professionalism and how seriously dedicated and faithful both music-makers were to the task at hand, to the importance of truly creating something counter, original, spare, strange;

> Whatever is fickle, freckled (who knows how?)
> With swift, slow; sweet, sour; adazzle, dim;
> He fathers-forth whose beauty is past change:
> Praise him.

in the words of Gerard Manley Hopkins (an unsurpassingly brilliant lyricist himself), praising God in his poem, "Pied Beauty."

My own family, always studiously aloof — almost diabolically heedless and disobliging — has been nothing like the Gershwins in their cooperation, and in many if not most instances members have often not only never helped one another but knowingly stood in the way of assisting or even caring. I have always found myself more by strangers honored than by any true relations, to paraphrase Alexander Pope. A few years ago, one of my spiteful sisters in a fit of pique sold all of the books my brother Paul and I had inscribed and given to her and her family, a pathetic gesture calling attention to her own awfulness and in the process mocking only her own pusillanimity. Our private vulgarity is pragmatic and crude: ask no help, receive the same. No extra mile here. Cadets of Gascony we are not. I have always been moved that the magnanimous Theo Van Gogh could not live without his dear brother. After Theo died at age 33, a mere six months after Vincent, Johanna, Theo's wife of two years, realized only after reading their letters, that there was something so deep between her husband and Vincent that, in spite of her poverty and lack of options, his paintings must be saved. We owe the survival of Vincent Van Gogh's great paintings to Johanna Van Gogh, who ignored her parents' advice to throw them away, and just as much to the loving example of brotherhood her husband had. I mention all of this only because I believe that a working team such as the Gershwins, the Van Goghs is rare. Sibling rivalry. What is the surprise here? Jesus's very own brothers spitefully not only never supported his ministry — this is James and Joseph and Simon and Judas (not Iscariot), mentioned in Matthew 13:55 — but never even believed in him in the first place.

A noteworthy point is that, by simply taking an hour or two — or less — any songwriter worth his mettle can save a line or a lyric from a bad rhyme or a silly gaffe or an idiotic allusion. It would seem to be only a question of care and the requisite pride in doing something well. "I could never have done what I have done without the habits of punctuality, order, and diligence, without the determination to concentrate on one object at a time…which I then formed," the successful hero of *David Copperfield* explains, and surely his creator Dickens felt the same. Speed, however, seems to prevail in this age of shoddy. We live in an epoch of constant noise, blatant intrusion, infective fret, over-communication, incessant interruption, and availability — our world is the exact opposite of Henry David Thoreau's *Walden* — where even the smallest opportunities for thought, contemplation, meditation, never mind serious hard work, are now almost impossible to experience and where the fascination of young people is given over to what alone can capture their imagination technographically. Cell phones, email, computers, calculators, television, VCRs, DVD players, MP3s, video games, smart phones with e-lerts, GPS units, CDs, cassettes, mobile apps, iTunes, palm pilots, Facebook. It is a nothing less than a miracle that a human being living in the United States nowadays can entertain a single consecutive thought worth anything.

A most egregious example of filler can be found in the Beatles' "Strawberry Fields Forever," when out of its mixture of hippie argot, classical allusion, and baroque music comes this sequence of lines: "No one, I think, is in my tree; I mean it must be high or low; that is, you can't, you know, tune in, but it's all right, that is, I think it's not too bad." It almost reveals in the rabid agglutination of its madness not so much jabberwocky as a kind of polysynthesis! "I don't want to fake you out/ Take or shake or *forsake you out*/ I ain't lookin' for you to feel like me [my italics]," sings Bob Dylan in "Baby, Be Friends with You." Call them unlyrical road bumps. One of my favorite examples regarding filler can be heard in Dylan's "Mr. Tambourine Man" — "I'm ready for to fade/ into my own parade" — don't you love that *for*? It has its lyrical book-end in the group America's "A Horse with No Name," where we hear the dreadful lines, "In the desert, you can remember your name/ for there ain't no one for to give you no pain." The trick is, of course, scribble down the quickest word that comes to mind to fill out a line. It is the trick of the shortcut: true, not a felony, but still a fart. "You just sorta wasted my precious time," writes Dylan in "Don't Think Twice." David Gates with his "Baby, I'm-a want you, Baby, I'm-a need you/ You're the only one I care enough to hurt about/ Maybe I'm-a crazy," etc. proved himself just too lazy to write a lyric, in my opinion.

Another thudding instance can be heard (and heard and reheard) in the popular song, "Seventy-Six Trombones" from *The Music Man*, where Meredith Willson memorably writes, "…and they're marching *still right* today [my italics]."

As we have seen, even Alan Jay Lerner was not above shameless filler. In one of Eliza Doolittle's songs in *My Fair Lady*, "Just You Wait," the imaginary Dream King intones, "And whatever you *wish and want* [sic] I gladly will do." "Love walked *right* in," grudgingly wrote Ira Gershwin in "Love Walked In," notice, hating himself, as he later confessed — he was a lyricist far too expert for talentless padding — for having to use that filler-word "right." And surely it is for filler that Kenny Rogers, as if casually alluding to an old man or, say, a car that does not work, refers to Vietnam as "that ol' crazy Asian war." Stevie Wonder is wonderfully egregious in the forced-rhyme and filler department. In "Part-Time Lover" he sings,

> And if there's some emergency
> have a male friend to ask for me
> so then she won't be, for you,
> my part-time lover.

The last line is supposed to mean: "So that she [my wife] won't know you are my part-time lover." It makes no sense of course the way that Stevie Wonder has written it, and we have no idea to whom the singer he is speaking. Punctuation has not been more confusing since Evelyn Waugh parodied the postcards of English schoolgirls traveling on the continent. What ever happened to Strunk & White? And then to force a rhyme in the same song, Stevie Wonder ebonicizes "rang on the bell" for "called." Brrrr!

In Jimmie Rodgers's song, "Kisses Sweeter than Wine," does the line, "Our children, they numbered just *about* four," um, indicate that one of them was feeble? (This is a classic example of the need for a "filler" word, invariably the cause for ridiculous wordplay.) In "Make Someone Happy," we hear Perry Como sing, "Make someone happy,/ make *just* someone happy." Jackson Browne sings, "People go *just* where they will" in "Doctor My Eyes." Even the big dogs commit this sin. "We'll *just* glide/ starry eyed," writes Jimmy Van Heusen in "Come Fly With Me." "*Just* say the words, and we'll beat the birds/ down to Acapulco bay." The weak word *just* — a verbal factotum, bland as a parsnip — is a word in song lyrics that is virtually always used superfluously. A good example of that can be heard in the 1946 hit "Oh, What It Seemed to Be" written by George Weiss and collaborators, Bennie Benjamin and Frankie Carle and made popular by Frank Sinatra who sings, "And when I kissed you/ It was more than *just* a thrill to me." That *just* is not only unnecessary but actually screws up the very rhythm of the line. As I say, the word is laxity itself. For that, it is a — perhaps the — most highly popular filler-word of all for the hack lyricist. Hello again here to the lyrically-challenged Canadian box-head, Paul Anka, who in his '50s hit, "Diana," sings,

> I don't care *just* what they say
> You and I will be as free
> As the birds up in the tree.
> [My italics.]

In his song, "Honeycomb," Jimmie Rodgers gives us another great filler-word, "about," in the phrase "sounds *about* sweet like a turtle dove [my italics]." Irving Berlin himself, for rhythm commits the same kind of lyrical felony in "Have Yourself A Merry Little [!] Christmas," a ridiculous phrase — why *little*? — which reminds me of what the Beach Boys had to do to fill out a rhythm-pattern in their own Christmas song, "Little Saint Nick," where they are forced by lack of lyrical wit to repeat it over and over again as if on a drip-feed, "It's *the* little Saint Nick." Incidentally, in the song, "Have Yourself a Merry Little Christmas," we hear the line, "Have yourself a merry little Christmas *now*," a classic example of double-filler-nuttiness, for exactly when but on the feast of Christmas would one *be* having a merry little Christmas, right? The lame word "little," thrown in for rhythm, is for some reason constantly abused in the writing of lyrics. "And I wonder where she will stay/ My little runaway/ run-run-run-run-run-a-way" we hear in the 1961 hit, "Runaway" (words and music by Del Shannon and Max Crook). Why *little* runaway? Filler, plain and simple. In Chubby Checker's "The Twist" (words and music by Hank Ballard): "Take me by my *little* hand/ and go like this: *eeee ohhhh* twist, baby, twist," etc. *Little* hand? Chubby Checker has positively immense hands, each about the size of a pot roast of an Alaskan moose! Then in Frankie Avalon's "Venus" (words and music by Ed Marshall) we hear,

> Venus, if you will,
> Please send a *little* girl for me to thrill,
> a girl who wants my kisses and my arm...
> [My italics.]

Little? What, 10 years old?

In Elton John's maudlin song "I Guess That's Why They Call It the Blues," we hear him craw the magnificently bad line "...but more than else I simply love you." Surely he was supposed to be singing but more than *anything* else I simply love you, was he not? Who writes these lyrics, a Hottentot? Could it be Reginald

Dwight himself (Elton John's real name) or his collaborator and lyricist Bernie Taupin? I always experience a case of agita whenever I hear O.C. Smith sing the merciless "God Didn't Make Little Green Apples" and rhyme "little green apples" with "Minneapolis." The horrors of the 1970s — now there's a topic! It was all mainly Easy Listening, the "horse latitudes" of music. The great Irving Berlin, who was still alive at the time, confided to his biographer, Michael Freedland, that he would have written, "God didn't make little green apples" with "We don't pray in churches and chapels." But then of course Berlin prayed, if he prayed at all, in an entirely other building, did he not? For him, a Jew, how about "God didn't create for us many mystagogues/ to waste time chanting in synagogues"? But then as Gary Giddins points out in *Faces in the Crowd*, Berlin was once shockingly satisfied, not memorably, I daresay, to rhyme the words "queen" with "mandolin" and "beauty" with "suit me." Clunk! Clunk! Clunk! On the other hand, look at the smoothly brilliant way that man had with the lyrics and rhymes — parallelisms, chiasmus — in the splendidly melodious "Isn't This a Lovely Day (To Be Caught in the Rain)" which goes in part:

> Just as you were going, leaving me all at sea
> The clouds broke, they broke and oh!
> What a break for me
>
> I can see the sun up high
> Tho' we're caught in the storm
> I can see where you and I
> Could be cozy and warm
>
> Let the rain pitter patter
> But it really doesn't matter
> If the skies are gray
> Long as I can be with you it's a lovely day.

Nothing is smoother than that.

Then when sung by Fred Astaire, and danced by Fred and Ginger in *Top Hat* — perfection — smoothness never comes better. (It was Astaire who introduced more exceptional songs than any other performer, twenty-six by Irving Berlin alone.)

Mother Nature prefers *smoothness*. Look around. There just are not that many natural objects that have sharp points or jangling angles or bodkin-like spines, cusps, or claws. The glory of the universe can be found in its roundness. Cycles.

Orbits. Bubbles are round — spherical — because there is an attractive force called *surface tension* that pulls molecules of water into the tightest of possible groupings, and, as Robert L. Wolke points out in his *What Einstein Didn't Know,* "the tightest possible grouping that any collection of particles can achieve is to pack together into a sphere. Of all possible shapes — cubes, pyramids, irregular chunks — a sphere has the smallest amount of outside area." It is the distinct comfort of Muslims to know that a discarded Koran, while it can be piously burnt or buried — in a place that is never trod on — should best be placed in a flowing river.

How about the singer who adds words to ruin the rhythm? To seem hip, Lou Rawls always did it — badly. So did Sammy Davis, Jr. In Jerry Vale's fiendishly bad version of "Old Cape Cod" — the guy has no ear — he sings,

> If you're fond of *the* sand dunes
> And salty air…
> [My italics.]

immediately breaking the rhythm of the opening line, and then later in the song sings, ba-boomp, once again,

> …watching the moonlight
> on *the* old Cape Cod Bay.
> [My italics.]

when neither definite article was called for. It is truly painful to hear a singer, any singer, who has no rhythm, but you have to listen to this version which, compared to Patti Page's, is Coca- Cola detestably made with corn syrup (as it is now) whereas "The Singing Rage's" was the real thing, Coca Cola made with *cane* sugar. No, my *paisan*, Gennaro Luigi Vitaliano (Jerry's real name), for sheer rockiness is in a class all by himself when it comes to a tin ear. And that this was a seasoned singer all his life is hard to believe. You wanna cry. One maintained in vain the small hope that after multiple decades in the business Vale would have caught on and corrected himself after repeatedly hearing his arrhythmic gaffes on tapes and records. That it never happened makes me recall a remark the pragmatic Benito Mussolini made back in his day: "It is not impossible to govern Italians, merely useless."

Speaking of Elton John and Bernie Taupin, who in their songs so often prove to me the dark theory that William Burroughs advanced in *The Job* (1974) that the written word is actually a virus, they never fail again and again to come up with verbal bollocks. Take their flatulent 1972 pop offering, "Your Song," the singer's first hit, where the third stanza has the effect in a song's lyrics of an incorrect bite-alignment,

> If I was a sculptor,
> But then again, no —
> Or a man who makes potions
> in a traveling show.

Should we really be surprised to learn that Cole Porter himself once advised Jesse Stone, one of the guiding lights at Atlantic Records — and author of the Drifters' "Money Honey," Joe Turner's "Shake, Rattle, and Roll," and the Clovers' "Your Cash Ain't Nothin' But Trash" — to purchase a rhyming dictionary, helpfully noting, "If you're going to dig a ditch, you use a shovel, don't you?"

The deep lyric tradition in America has long since gone by, according to Gene Lees in his book, *Singers and the Song*. He believes it was destroyed by Elvis Presley as well as, even if less so, by the Beatles. No one in his balanced view can write lyrics without knowing and revering the language, the tonal possibilities of its croonable vowels, its aptitude for rhyme, its emotional vocabulary, the tint and variety of its accents. You may argue with him, but even if one thinks Lees is exaggerating, or is unfair, a good case could be made for the prosecution. Not only were lyrics once an integral part of music, and keenly listened to, they were in fact read. It must not be forgotten that the record industry initially began as a step-child of the sheet-music business. The popularity of tunes, prior to World War I, even into the '40s and '50s, was spread and appreciated primarily through that medium — through language and the quoted poetry that fueled romance. And yet it seems with a new sort of leveling we all have gotten further and further away from the notion of that literal integrity. The historicity of the full design seems no longer wanted.

It has gone the way of the Peak Frean.

I notice when checking out an item on *YouTube* that dates are rarely if ever supplied for songs of movies. Few seem to care much anymore for the complete story or permanence of a work, which seems to fit the "throwaway" aspect of living now in this world of planned obsolescence. Records, lyrics, *reinforce* permanence. Holden Caulfield felt that way when he bought that jazz record, "Little Shirley Beans," for his 10-year-old sister, Phoebe, which is why he was so crushed when he drops and breaks it. A broken record is "a common Salinger symbol of the irretrievability of the past," writes Kenneth Slawenski in his recent biography, *Salinger*. A record plays the same song always and never changes, in the very same way that Holden, even if irrationally, wants Phoebe not to change but forever stay a child. The broken record symbolizes a thwarting of that plan.

It might also be pointed out that music videos, in giving a new dimension to songs, have to some degree made lyrics even less significant, even though ideally videos should illustrate the lyrics. They almost never do. Michael Jackson was among the worst — his song "Smooth Criminal" has no consecutive three words that anybody can possibly understand. And how about the first line of "Bad" ("Your butt is mine...") to indicate the distance lyrics have come from quality, taste, or stylish invention. Pop music increasingly gets away with almost anything. Words *qua* words of course are not fully necessary to a song. "She's About a Mover" by the Sir Douglas Quintet is only one example of a song with a few couplets, but its relentless beat shows the true drive of rock-and-roll. What about rap music? One would expect inventive lyrics in any presentation which consists solely of words, no? I mean, since it is not singing? But rap is in the main just plain unadulterated blabberchatter coming down the chin. In Edwin Birdsong's "It Ain't No Fun Bein' a Welfare Recipient" (from the LP *What It Is*), he actually tries to rhyme the word "fun" with "recipient." "It ain't no funnn/ Bein a welfare recipiunn." That old country turkey, "I Can't Stop Loving You," I am reminded here, is another anti-paragon of muddled and incoherent "misery/ of the lonesome time."

Even the talented but neurotic gun-toting Phil Spector produced a Philles record for the Crystals called "He Hit Me and It Felt Like a Kiss," the lyrics of which, to say nothing of the sentiment, boggles the mind:

> He hit me and it felt like a kiss
> He hit me, but it didn't hurt me
> He couldn't stand to hear me say
> That I'd been with someone new
> And when I told him I'd been untrue
> He hit me and it felt like a kiss
> He hit me and I knew he loved me
> If he didn't care for me
> I could never have made him mad
> But he hit me, and I was glad.

This is an instance in song of what old fat cigar-chewing Hollywood moguls disdainfully used to call, regarding films, a "feathered fish" — a confusing story or plot with so many odd points and disparate parts that it neither flies nor swims. I suppose it is an example of musical *tremendismo*. Some people like it. The Spanish thinker, Salvador de Madariaga, convinced John Updike that Hamlet, uniquely, is the "callow, egocentric villain" of the play, so in his novel, *Gertrude and Claudius*, Updike oddly proceeds to see Hamlet's treatment of Ophelia as more shocking than Claudius's killing of his brother and the usurpation of his throne! What can I say? A sort of psychopathological bookend to that Crystals' song is Coffin and King's "Please Hurt Me," in which several of the charming lyrics go:

> If you got to hurt somebody, please hurt me
> And if you gotta break a heart, then
> Please break mine
> I won't cry if you deceive me
> I'll take it with a smile
> I know someday you will leave me
> But at least I'll have you for a while.

As one of the characters in Nöel Coward's *Private Lives* wittily observes, "Extraordinary how potent cheap music is."

Yet how it captures us — and reveals our proclivities.

I must say I feared for Phil Spector's sanity, long before reading about his manic gun-toting proclivities and the days of his virtually incarcerating pretty Veronica Bennett of the Ronettes, just from his trademark "Wall of Sound," that production technique that created a dense layered effect as background like overly feathered hair. I found those lavish, ginormous orchestrations of his — like the one he used on the Beatles' "The Long and Winding Road," which Paul McCartney hated, almost popping his cork when he first heard it — all had something fairly sinister, even imperial, to them, maybe even megalomaniacal. What happened to Spector? He is in jail, doing 19-to-life for murdering the actress Lana Clarkson. I myself would have been looking for him either there or, failing that, somewhere in the Erzgebirge forest where they make wooden nut-crackers and cuckoo clocks.

There is a list of howlers in popular music so long, clunkers of such scope and magnitude committed so often — but usually in songs of the Suzie-Is-The-Girl-For-Me school, a waste of shellac, invariably loping along after all those C, A minus, F, and G chords — that one has to wonder whether the composers were merely in a rush, being underpaid, simply had no talent, or were just plain stupid, for half the time it is as if when facing the problem to decide between rhyme and reason they in fact chose neither.

I am still trying to figure out the grammatical distinction in the old chestnut "Take Me Out To the Ball Game" between the two commonly rendered versions of one line (a) "I don't care if I never get back" and (b) "I don't care if I ever get back." Surely they do not mean the same thing or do they? Could it be that this is only another maddening version of flammable and inflammable? Neil Diamond, for example, one of the truly great fuglemen of vulgarity in pop music, may be famous for writing his own compositions, but I have been trying for years to figure out the language never mind the logic of virtually all of his songs. Take the lyric of his hit, "Sweet Caroline," that so unmemorably starts out, "When it begins, I can't begin to knowin." Is this pidgin? A translation of Gik-Gok? Urdu? Ptydepe? In an article regarding the singer in *The New Yorker* (January 16, 2006), Sasha Frere-Jones actually states that Diamond "grew up not speaking English." He was born in Brooklyn and is Jewish — did he grow up speaking Yiddish? When he sings in "Captain Sunshine," "Captain Sunshine, make me drink wine,/ Make me feel fine when I'm feelin' wrongly down," are we to understand such adverbial clusterfucks are from the Torah? "I got a song been on my mind," he sings. "Her words as such as the way they were sung it was the way they were sung," he sings. And when he sings, he *growlulates* — cuckoo emotional displays coming out in eructations, almost farting sounds, reminding me of what Nadezshda Mandelstam once said — surely not a compliment — of a Joseph Brodsky poetry reading, "This isn't a man, it's a wind orchestra."

Has Diamond's problem to do with his chinlessness? (He is as jawless as a lamprey.) Would a bronchial passage be somehow foreshortened by such an impediment? It did not seem to impact Queen Victoria, Percy Shelley, William Powell, Dorothy Kilgallen, Carole Lombard, Andy Gump, or Fred Rogers.

In his song, "I Am...I Said," one line goes, "And no one says a word, not even the chair." Let me ask, even charitably, can you honestly picture a person, pick anyone, seriously speaking that line, someone, that is, who has not stepped out of loony bin? That song is book-ended by Neil Diamond's similarly shlocky "And the Grass Won't Pay No Mind," which in exchange for his getting bumped by Elvis for a recording-session date at the American Sound Studio in Memphis in 1969 through a bit of hustling — a bit of log-rolling here — he actually got the King to record ("Your hair's softly falling/ on my face as in a dream/ and the time will be our time/ and the grass won't pay no mind/ saying nothing, lying where the sun is." The entire lyric is virtually soft-porn. Is it any news that Neil Diamond's distinctly psychoneurotic problems with personification surely warrant further study? I gotta say, I have always thought when it comes to lyrics that he has a head like a bowling bowl, a Brunswick Mineralite, probably the single most durable consumer good ever sold.

Diamond then describes a road in "Play Me" as being "thorned and narrow." A crazy image offered with a strained and nutty voice. Frere-Jones says that "he sings like a man who, though he experiences emotions intensely, must work too hard to express them; his words emerge with excessive force." He also insightfully observes that "there are very few settings on his voice machine: he can do less Neil or more Neil." My vote? How about (altogether) *less Neil!* The shamelessness of where musically or, better unmusically, he goes with his gimmicky lyrics and transparently unfelt growls — the vocal equivalent of his florid silk shirts — is painful. He is not only a chintz salesman but something of an affected and over-obliging varietist. I was once cajoled into watching him perform. At certain points he ludicrously wore capes, spangled flood pants, always the hideola of a bushy Jewfro. "Most of the songs that Diamond wrote back in the '80s and '90s," remarks Frere-Jones, "are mired in genteel strings and keyboards or, worse, harsh synthesizers, which made him sound louder but no hipper." Exactly how bad does it get with Neil Diamond? There was a time when the guy was on stage when he actually solicited people in his audiences to turn to their neighbors — no lie — and say, "I love you very much." *Very much!* Could it possibly get worse? To me, this focuses on the quintessential Neil Diamond vulgarity. Cosmeticist Estée Lauder cunningly claimed that when she first began hawking her lotions her very first principle for successful selling was, vilely — as if affecting something like concern, true matey-ness — to *touch* all of her prospective customers. Actually placing her hand on a stranger as a mercantile *ploy?* Employing frottage just to sell a *product?* This surely has to be tawdriness on the worst level, a meretricious display of bribery and deceit, the very definition of corruption and greed. (Who could possibly doubt that the same qualities that go into charming people also go into deceiving them?) It is also the needy, desperate habit of Craig Ferguson when giving his monologue on the *Late Late Show* on CBS to keep touching — virtually *groping* — the TV camera. Why so, to involve his listeners? It is a disgustingly skeevy maneuver. There is in its corrupt and hyperbaric neediness and special pleading the kind of narcissism that one weekly had to witness back in the 1970s watching the irrefragably stupid *The Carol Burnett Show* when all the actors with their trumpery, to sell their silliness — complete hypocrites — were always pretending to crack-up at what they were saying on the grounds that it was so hilarious the poor deludinoids watching should agree, a ploy so transparent and shot through with such cut-price brummagem I never believed it for a minute. That cheap, low-rent ploy of Lauder's, Ferguson's, and the Burnett boobs has its subfusc parallel in the Mattel company's Ruth Handler, she of Barbie

Doll fame, the woman who succeeded in taking that tarty little plastic figure with an adult body that she copied directly from the German Bild Lilli doll (which was not meant for children at all, rather a gag gift for adults) that she had bought in a Swiss shop, remanufactured, then sold directly to children by way of kiddie TV shows, cagily side-stepping the traditional role of the mother in choosing toys. (All four hustlers may be beat out by the Wrigley C ompany who in 1914, to promote its gum, mailed sticks of Doublemint gum to every single person that was listed in the U. S. phone book!) Diamond's greatest lyrical moment, all of his own devising, comes in that same song, "I Am...I Said," when he begins mooing with all the fake sincerity he can muster:

> Songs she sang to me
> Songs she brang to me,
> Words that rang in me,
> Rhyme that sprang in me
> Warmed the night...

lyrics which, I believe, had they occurred in a work of a Babu or been spoken by an Abo from the rim of the world would stand as a paradigm of comic English. Sprang? *Brang?* As Las Vegas hoodlum, Bugsy Siegel, in infuriated astonishment constantly used to remark, "You gotta be shitting me." I mean, this is Dickville Notch!

How did I like that Neil Diamond performance I attended?

I would rate it the way John Ruskin described *Die Meistersinger* in a letter to Georgina Burne-Jones in 1882: "Of all the bête, clumsy, blundering, boggling, baboon-blooded stuff I ever saw on a human stage... and of all the affected, sapless, soulless, beginningless, endless, topless, bottomless, topsiturviest, tongs and boniest doggerel of sounds I ever endured the deadliness of, that eternity of nothing was the deadliest, so far as the sound went. I never was so relieved, so far as I can remember in my life, by the stopping of any sound — not excepting railway whistles — as I was by the cessation of the cobbler's bellowing."

What Neil Diamond apparently never learned — forget the idea that he ever knew — was what Mel Tormé always understood. "The lyric is 98% of what a song is about," he told Kristine McKenna in an interview in *Book of Changes,* explaining,

> The melody is incidental, and if it happens to be attractive that's frosting on the cake, but the lyric is what's important. I choose songs that lend

themselves to being presented as little playlets because when I finish the song I want the audience to feel that it has been through some kind of an experience. And that can't be achieved with a lyric that's dumb and thoughtless — it has to start at "A" and end at "Z."

Little playlets? Hell, Neil Diamond's singing sounds like farm-animal imitations. A lathe shop! His live shows are all about stylelessly growling words and strutting about wearing capes like some kind of Transylvanian cryptid and constantly going up to the apron-lip of the stage trying to electrify any old lady groupies in savage pants-suits and faux-ginger hair who have remained in the auditorium fully convinced that talent is on display. He is the objective correlative in the full flush of her definition of Patti Smith's remark, "I don't listen to music by people I don't wanna fuck!"

Diamond, who often sings by dubbing his own voice in multi-tracks, begins to sound in a great cacophonous gabble like a Chinese nightclub singer under water, vulgarly howling five variables of music — melody, harmony, counterpoint, rhythm, and instrumentation — and with almost perverse anti-genius ruining them all at once, disproving even radical John Cage's questionable-in-the-first-place assumption that even noise is music if a person knows how to listen. I have to confess, applying it to music, it was the experience of my having inadvertently heard Neil Diamond sing that convinced me beyond all argument that Kenneth Anger may have been right when he declared that it was actually the *collapse* of censorship that has been bad for the movies. The horror! The horror!

What about his dim-witted "Cracklin' Rosie," where we hear, "You're a store-bought woman/ But you make me sing like a guitar hummin'"? Are not singing and humming two distinctly different things? Thematically, as to Rosie, it also may be asked why would a paid-for date *not* inspire? Finally, what about the lame rhyme-scheme? Someone once told me, I believe seriously, that this song of his was actually a loving paean to tobacco. (Leave it to Neil Diamond to serenade a cigarette.) No writer's lyrics are worse than N.D's. But why be surprised? Did not Norman Mailer explain to us in his novel, *Barbary Shore*, that if greatness is thrust upon certain men, thought is extracted from others?

Such shoddiness — shamelessness, really — did not always fly. Take Nat "King" Cole, for example, a real artist. In the original recording of his classic version of "The Christmas Song," he originally sang the last line of the bridges "To see if reindeers really know/ How to fly." After the first pressings were released and the song became a hit, Mel Tormé, who co-wrote the song, tactfully pointed out to Cole his grammatical error. Cole, a perfectionist, immediately returned to the studio and re-recorded the song, properly singing "reindeer" in the remake, the correct plural. The second version is virtually identical to the first, but those early flawed first-pressings have since become collector's items. By the way, just to show that such quality is not universal, the Melodeers, who made a 1960 doo-wop version of the Johnny Marks classic, "Rudolph the Red-Nosed Reindeer," throughout the song eight or nine times repeat the word "reindeers." Ouch.

On the other hand, in Nat "King" Cole's version of "Sunny Side of the Street ," he dimly sings (twice), "If I never had a cent/I'd be rich as Rockyfellow" and in his initial version of "Lush Life," he muffed the lyrics, ignorantly singing instead of "your siren song" the moronic "your siren of song," thinking of sirens, yes, as *signals* — a mistake only a hapless non-reader could make. (For a serious artist to re-record a song in order to correct a flaw is not a given, incidentally. Why, for instance, did Dinah Washington not correct her version of "Manhattan" when she heard herself on replay bluntly sing, "We'll turn Manhattan into a [sic] isle of joy?" Listen to it sometime. (The jarring effects regarding blunders like that, of indifferent or uneducated artists on the low quality of their work, from movie mogul Harry Cohn who never went to school to comedian Jerry Lewis who quit school in the 6th grade to the NBC Tonight talk-show host Jack Paar who had virtually no schooling — he contracted tuberculosis when he was 14 and dropped out — would be a good dissertation for some graduate student.) In the complicated song, "Lush Life" Billy Strayhorn's sophisticated and truly memorable lyrical masterpiece, there are as many verbal turns and phrasal challenges as there is a vast range of emotions. It is a song difficult to sing and in my opinion one just as difficult to understand, at least fully, being as sinuous as it is sensuous. Its strange and unusual structure gave even Sinatra a thorny time when he set out to record it back in 1958. But it frustrated him, and he gave up on it, laughing that he would "put it aside for about a year." He never did return to it. "Not everybody could sing it," says Andy Bey, the celebrated jazz singer and pianist with a strong personal connection to a song he has returned to repeatedly throughout a 55-year career. "A lot of songs had verses and refrains, you know, but it's like a mind-boggling thing. It's not about 'ring-a-ding ding' when you do 'Lush Life.'" It was in this song that Nat "King" Cole mistakenly, haplessly, also sang "strifling" for "stifling," as well as singing "those who lives are lonely, too," a real Ebonics gaffe forty years before that "slanguage" emerged in the semi-literate side of the black community.

A quick aside? If I were ever asked to give a sermon for young people and needed to find the right text (you know, in my John Bunyan mode) to inveigh against the subtlety of corruption, bad choices, the dangers of lapsing judgment

— an "occasion of sin," as we Catholics call it — I would point to jazz, citing its down-at-the-heel brokenness, the attention it gives to boozy despair, to lassitude, the blandishments of sex, drinking, smoking, as among its undermining elements. The word *jazz* has tawdry origins, being the Negro word for copulation, both as a noun and a verb. Only in a secondary sense did it mean vigor, cool energy, excitement. (We all know, furthermore, that the term "rock and roll" was also a black euphemism — one of the many — for sexual intercourse. One cannot fail to mention the classic Howlin' Wolf number, "Wang-dang-doodle," with its haunting refrain, "We're gonna pitch wang-dang-doodle all night long.") Jazz began as reechy music, indeed, and took root in the steamy atmosphere of the brothels of New Orleans where dancing, at least in the beginning, was little more than a species of African fuck bump. (That was nevertheless a good example of what James Brown meant when a half century later he earnestly declared, "The one thing that can solve most of our problems is dancing.") So my point is? In this context, I would notably cite the song "Lush Life" as quite specifically and significantly the kind of song/ music/ lyric that cajoles young people to visit the low life and to sink to the depth. It has all the earmarks of seduction, of soft allurement, of easy enticement, of irretrievable disappointment and depression, if not downright moral turpitude regarding temptation, let's face it. Straddling that soft line where the light meets the shadows, it calls to the mineral soul. It is dark and has a dissonance that more than hints at a loss of the spirit, of joy, of hope. There is a worldliness to it.

> I used to visit all the very gay places
> Those come-what-may places
> Where one relaxes on the axis of the wheel of life
> To get the feel of life from jazz and cocktails
> The girls I knew had sad and sullen gray faces
> With distingué traces that used to be there
> You could see where they'd been washed away
> By too many through the day,
> Twelve o'clock cocktails

The speaker is then tempted to "madness" with the siren song of a lover who comes into his life, briefly stays, then deserts him (or her), making his world dark and "awful again" and bringing on a case of such loneliness that he concludes, since "romance is much," he will waste away in some small dive" — doubtless the kind of place in which he sits — and "rot with the rest of those/ whose lives are lonely too."

In its relative sordidness, the setting of the song reminds one of that scene in the highly vulgar movie *Watermelon Man* (1970) directed by Melvin Van Peebles (who also wrote all the music) where in one scene idle and aimless Godfrey Cambridge is pointlessly sitting in a dark bar, smoking and drinking, while a slightly overweight half-naked stripper undulates, waggling her tassels, to the tune of the sleazy blues song, "Soul'd on You" [sic]." "Lush Life" makes such a distinct appeal to descend — for a young mind, any soft mind, especially — that one can find traces here even of the Original Fall. I slot it in the "Glad to Be Unhappy" mode, as sung by Sinatra in "In the Wee Small Hours" 45 r.p.m. LP. Do you recall the lyrical lines of "Music Makes Me" sung by Ginger Rogers (danced by Fred Astaire) from *Flying Down to Rio* (1933)? Indeed. I am talking about the caveat implicit in the confessional rhyme:

> I like music old and new
> but music makes me do the things
> I should never do.

So many race songs were heavily laden with drug references, like "Winnie the Wailer," "Mistah Paganini," "Reefer Man," and, among others, "Minnie the Moocher," that jazz classic first recorded in 1931 by Cab Calloway and His Orchestra. ("She loved him though he was cokey," "He showed her how to kick that gong around [smoke opium]," to which partying whites at nightspots like the Cotton Club would be singing along often totally clueless as to the subtext of the lyrics. Intemperate drinking and loose companions and crazy drugs and giving in to seedy indifference are major elements in the near-downfall of the characters in Lynd Ward's novels-in-woodcuts, *God's Man* and *Mad Man's Drum*, masterpieces from the 1920s. No, "Lush Life" is diseased romanticism, the sweet words — the honeyed enticements — of Sportin' Life in *Porgy and Bess*. The title of the sermon I propose would be, "It Ain't Necessarily So."

But now when I take off my moralizing Presbyterian hat, employ the "line item veto" to cancel out my spotty quibbles and complaints here and there — by the way, that is a Congressional tautology since each item is *on* a line — I find the song splendidly atmospheric, a perfect evocation of a certain mood, a "drama of literary anguish" in the way of T.S. Eliot's "The Love Song of J. Alfred Prufrock." As I say, it is a thorny song to sing, extremely convoluted as an arrangement, but it is a gem of a composition.

Folksinger Bob Dylan, troubadour of the '60s and general nonconformist ("Everybody must get stoned") surely did not deserve, or at least fully deserve, the contemptuous — and vicious, if you will — dismissal offered by Truman Capote who wrote, "I never liked Bob Dylan. I also thought he was a fraud. He's certainly not this simple-minded little boy with these simple little lyrics. He is an opportunist with a sharp, career-minded, knowing-where-he's-going. He is also insincere." I have to say here that Dylan's seemingly interminate mishmash of a novel, *Tarantula*, is without doubt one of the dullest novels ever published. He had the ability to write a truly beautiful lyric, I believe, and songs such as "Tangled Up In Blue," "Blowin' in the Wind," "Hurricane," "Rainy Day Woman," "Masters of War," "Don't Think Twice," "Man of Constant Sorrow," "Gates of Eden," "Lily of the West," are, among others, superb. But as a song-writer he was of the Natural Poet or "spontaneous" school of poetry and tended to rush writing his songs in the belief that, spontaneity being a natural gift, any undue deliberation would sully his craft and sullen art. (Novelist Stephen King, a subscriber to this same quantity-over-quality theory, once ludicrously proclaimed that any writer — has the guy never heard of James Joyce or Leo Tolstoy or Thomas Pynchon? — who does not write a book a year is basically a loafer.) Bob Dylan clearly had genius but disrespected the creative process and out of vanity badly needed to show himself to be a quick study, an easy as well as a prolific composer. Forget that his "Lay, Lady, Lay/ Lay across my big brass bed" has for almost half a century encouraged millions of muddleheaded young people to misuse the verb, "to lie." Or was he addressing a hen? But I was particularly thinking of — unfairly singling out, I admit — such Dylan lyrics as,

> If you're looking to get silly,
> You'd better go back to from where you came

a line that, at least to me, becomes the lyrical equivalent in music of having webbed feet, and lines like those in "Positively Fourth Street,"

> I wish that for just one time
> you could stand inside my shoes

Stand inside them? Are his shoes that big? He intended to say, of course, "I wish that for just one time you could stand *in* my shoes," not climb *into* one of them as if they were big as Mother Hubbard's! As I say, however, he was rushing. And how about the lines like that in his "Mr. Tambourine Man," "And but for the sky there are no fences facin'" — where the sky, for ages poetically the very definition of freedom, is the ultimate hobble? — or that in "It's All Over Now, Baby Blue," where we hear

> The empty-handed painter from your streets
> is drawing crazy patterns on your sheets

prompting one to ask, exactly how does an "empty-handed painter" paint? I take my hat off to the dynamic troubadour who, although poet Philip Larkin dissed him for having what he called "a cawing, derisive voice," did crash through the boredom of the Fifties. (Let me mention here in passing that the highly eccentric Larkin, at least according to his close friend and Marvell Press publisher, Jean Hartley, paradoxically considered Dylan's "Mr. Tambourine Man" — I am not making this up — "the best song ever written.") Still, what can you expect of someone — the too often hasty, psychobabbling, and occasionally over-facile Dylan — who once in all seriousness, indeed, temerity, pontificated that "All the great books have been written"?

To my mind that sentiment underscores the truth of the theory advanced in Fyodor Tyutchev's most famous poem, "Silentium," stating that a person should hide one's thoughts in silence since verbalization cheapens or simplifies them.

Must a person bothered by such lame writing, such unlyrical wanking, be sourly denominated a maniacal prescriptivist? Should we take the alternative tack and become instead like H.G. Wells' timid, quiet, and directionless Mr. Polly? ("He was uncertain about the spelling and pronunciation of most of the words in our beautiful and abundant and perplexing tongue...") Or emulate Shakespeare's fingerling Peter Quince who mangles the prologue to the play he is performing, causing Theseus to observe, "This fellow doth not stand upon points"? Or act like Bottom who uses words incorrectly? Should we follow the real-life eccentric, Lord Timothy Dexter, who at the age of 50 wrote a crack-pated book about himself, *A Pickle for the Knowing Ones or Plain Truth in a Homespun Dress*, a unique complaining about politicians, the clergy, and his wife, and which contained 8,847 words and 33,864 letters, but with no written punctuation and capital letters sprinkled seemingly at random? (At first he handed his book out for free, but it became popular and was re-printed in eight editions. In the second edition Dexter added an extra page which consisted of 13 lines of punctuation marks. Dexter instructed readers to "peper and solt it as they plese.")

I promise, the alternative is not to become a Punctuation Vigilante, some mad fanatical, punctilious, linguisticator of a bitter Javert with a spyglass and spite dogging the many peccadilloes of every illiterate fool. It is but to think of rules as protection against an infectious and slovenly lack of scruple modernity loves.

Awfulness in music — listen to Israeli disco, for example, (Israeli rock is not only bad, it is usually boomist twaddle about the virtues of the country itself:

nationalistic rock!) or French rock 'n' roll which all sounds like someone's chasing Edith Piaf around in circles with a pair of electric hedge-clippers — is often exacerbated not only by the way a song is sung but the voice singing it. And so does Sonny Bono. Why has Cyndi Lauper, who actually squeaks rather than sings, adopted the infantilized singing persona, as in her song, "True Colors," of a 7-year-old child? Somebody once apparently told the oleaginous singer Jerry Vale a long time ago that if on every other word he dramatically cracked his voice — an archaic use of the glottis used to accent fervor which in Caruso's day was known as the "Rubini sob" — it would somehow sound passionate and authentically Italian. But shouldn't someone tell him it only sounds like duckshit? And grizzled Willie Nelson with those nasal peckerwoodlike snorts when he sings sounds as if he has wandered in from a Goose Fair, his voice like those old horn-bulbs on a touring car which emitted bugling shelduckian sounds!

Nasal need not always be all bad. Vaughn Monroe, sometimes called "the Baritone with Muscles," who in the 1950s made popular such classics as "There I've Said It Again," "Ballerina," "Riders in the Sky," "Someday (You'll Want Me to Want You)" could sound extremely nasal, but it gave a bit of masculine force to his voice. Linda Ronstadt used to say that she was nasal and could never listen to her own recordings. To me she had perfect pitch. Other nasalites? Randy Travis. Carly Simon. Charlie Sheen, a fine actor who sounds, however, as if he has a perpetual allergy. (If the separation of the oral from the nasal cavity is incomplete, air escapes — leaks — through the nose, causing speech to be perceived as nasal; a paralysis of the soft palate makes all tones nasal.) Larry Fine of the Three Stooges. (You can hear all three sing — in rhymed couplets — in *Woman Haters* [1934].) Curly had his own "music" with his "nyuk, nyuk, nyuk!" — first heard in *Men In Black* — along with his famous "*Hhhmm*," his avian "*Woob! Woob! Woob*," the snarling "*Rrrrrufff*," and, invariably used when the Boys were being chased by a monster, "*Nyagghhh!*" Listen to Barbra Streisand sing the truly lugubrious "What Are You Doing for the Rest of Your Life?" — and we are talking about a real shnozz there — and you can learn what nasal really is. What is ironic in the nose department is that in singing Sondheim's "I'm Still Here," Streisand sings,

> But I'm here!
> Now I've kept my clothes and kept me space
> *I've kept my nose to spite my face*
> Still once you say you won't
> Keep your place loud and clear.
> [My italics.]

Barry Manilow, who was also not only notably nasal but who has not even the rudimentary trace of a good voice, never mind talent, literally shouts — in the deathless song "Daybreak" he actually *talks* off-key — trying to make up in volume what he lacks in finesse. Listen to his semi-psychotic para-version of "Memory" from the Broadway show, *Cats*, if you doubt that a song can be beaten up, mugged, virtually flayed, almost as if singing a song itself were a parody. His is a trudge, all uphill.

> Dayliiiiiight
> I must wait for the suuuuuunrise
> I must think of a neweeew life
> And I musn't give in…

It is nothing less than a fucking massacre. The thing is whenever Manilow turns up the volume, abandoning himself to, outstretching himself for, notes he cannot possibly reach in what I would call barely discernible fits of Long Island Dionysianism, he becomes even more painful to listen to. Scarifying. Wire-tight. Overheated. Not man-heat, needless to say. Nothing of that roiling, bold, incandescent sort, but the infantile screeching of a boy with an echoing nose. It reminds me of an arch question Noël Coward disdainfully asks in the movie, *Around The World In Eighty Days*: "How does one take the temperature of toast?"

As I say virtually every song Barry Manilow tries to sing he makes worse, and by that I mean *bad*, disconsolately unendurable — his neck-vein-straining talent-in-reverse, almost inspiredly anti-numinous, blindingly insufficient actually constitutes something like an ugly black halo over his head. The only sound you can make when your mouth is shaped that way is weird. His album, *Duets*, is truly too painful to listen to twice, pure twatwaffling, but, I assure you, his disconsolate rendition of "Memory" from *Cats* and his "Ready To Take A Chance Again" and "I Write the Songs,"

> I write the songs that make the whole world sing
> I write the songs of love and special things

are truly death-on-a-bun! I say the same thing goes with Neil Diamond. His gnawing "Turn On Your Hot Lights!" has not the musicality of a toothless busker on Bum-biter Street playing tissue-paper over a comb! His bad vocal scarifications remind me of Maurice Maeterlinck's description of the sting of a bee in his *The Life of the Bee* as "a kind of destroying dryness, a flame of the desert rushing over the wounded limb."

Which of us does not desperately rue the day when, at the age of 7, little Barry Alan Pincus (Manilow came later) was given an accordion as a gift by his mother or his grandmother? He daily practiced "Tico-Tico" and "Lady of Spain" and then when he grew up proudly graduated to writing ads and commercials for radio and television. His compositions covered all sorts of products ranging from acne-fighting face-wipes to sugary soft drinks to toilet-bowl cleaners to KFC ("Get a bucket of chicken…Have a barrel of fun!"), and, if that was not vulgar enough, he then had the cheek double-dippingly to work all of them into a medley of one interminable commercial jingle to perform in public performances, all, you know, with a wink, like "Ain't it vulgar? — but it really ain't me." "It's a craft writing a jingle," he explained, defending himself, "because you have twenty-two seconds to get the message across, and that's a whole lot different from writing pop songs."

So fancy the opportunistic and rapacious money-grubbing hog who does both and then, just to turn a penny, tries to combine them *as art*! It is no different than boorish loudmouth Rush Limbaugh who on the EIB Network is not satisfied with the multi-millions he earns from doing his show. No, El Corpulento insists on vulgarly, repulsively, consistently reading out his own commercials for cash and like a $3.00-an-hour carnival-shill hawking everything from mattresses to hair oil, carpets to vitamins, suppositories to (yes!) weight-loss programs. And this sackbut, this fat hustling man-balloon, unkind, bigoted, cruel, tendentious — "a man carved out of a turnip, looking out of astonished eyes," as a retaliating Yeats once described the critic George Moore — still yearns to be accepted in the nation as a serious political voice? As JFK once said about Richard Nixon, "He has no class." So big, so small.

Along with his braying, Manilow also has something of a speech-defect. Or is it simply his refaned and provincial Brooklyn accent? ("It's fa me, it's fa you, it's fa you, it's fa me, it's a world-wiide symphoneeee!") The subject of speech impediments regarding singers warrants further study. It is noteworthy how often in public broadcasting and on television and radio shows we get to see and hear so many examples of it. "We live out our grammars with our bodies," wrote the poet Charles Bernstein, and he is correct. It is an astonishing to find that so many national broadcasters and that interminable parade of endlessly chattering, nattering cable hucksters have speech impediments — glottal stops, lisps, slush-at-the-side-of-the-mouth, L/ R substitution, dysprosody, laryngeal gobbles, stuttering, cluttering, even denture-click. Sammy Davis, Jr., for one, had a constantly muddy *S*, an explosive meeting of tongue, lips, and teeth that ran into a highly audible glosso-labial lisp, a sort of weird cross between the annoying buzz of an insect and the hiss of a serpent, grimly coming out something like, "The folks*zzth* who live on the hill," "Try a little tendern*ess zzth*," "The candy man *szesszz*th," "That old black magic has me in its *sszzth*pell," etc. At times Sammy at his most extreme almost sounds like fat lisping Ed Wynn, that fumbling cross-eyed comic from the 1930s who wore tiny hats that, on his head, looked like a cup on a pumpkin and who as he went tromp-tromp-tromping into cardboard vaudeville forests always famously cried out, "Look — woodth!" "Be *wisszzth*! Be *sszz*mart! Obey your heart," intones Sammy D. in his popular hit, "Too Close for Comfort," and in the cretinistically pleonastic song, "I Gotta Be Me"[6] words and music by Walter Marks, (a song whose lyrics always frankly made wonder if the man was not certifiably loony) Sammy in full throttle madly bumble-bee-buzzes

> I wanna live, not merely *szthurvive*...
> That faraway *priszzth*,
> A world of *szthucceszzzth*...

with a frenetic cluster of S-and-Zs, culminating in the explosive word "success" — *szthucceszzzth* — giving us in its abrasiveness the effect of chainsavian insanity!

It is bad enough to hear Davis straining to negotiate words he can't quite handle, but what about hearing him sing in his late coked-up days? It doesn't get much more craptastic than hearing him sing *lyrics* to "Hawaii Five-O!" The words few have ever heard go on their raggedy way something like this:

> If you get in trou-bull
> Bring it home to me-ah
> Whether I am near yeeew-a
> Or across the sztheaaaaaa
> I will think of szthomethin' ta dooo-wa
> I'll be on the lookout for you
> And I will find yeeew-a
> You can count on me-ah

During this period, Davis performed other themes on his blessedly out-of-print album *Song and Dance Man* — a vinyl release from Germany in 1976 — the themes to *Mary Hartman, Chico and The Man, Kojak, Barretta's Theme*, and, a real gem, to *My Mother the Car*, one of the worst sitcoms in television history.

6        Regarding this song, one thinks inevitably of passionate Heathcliff's slightly schizo and creepazoidal remark in the film version of *Wuthering Heights* to Cathy, the woman he loves: "Not even you, Cathy, can come between us!"

Amazing to relate, actor Cary Grant who has always seemed to be the essence of perfection actually revealed a slushy S when he spoke, a speech-defect that for some reason seemed much worse in his earlier movies like *Holiday* (1938) and *I Was A Male War Bride* (1949) than in later films such as *Father Goose* (1964) and *To Catch A Thief* (1955) — but, I mean, in *Holiday* it becomes an actual distraction. Had Grant had some operation to correct the problem, do you think? Paid some physician to have a cheek-flap removed or a tonsil? Frank Sinatra unavoidably — was it an affectation or a speech defect? — gave the odd sound of a little J or CH before a D or a T: "The tender *ch*trap," "I concen*ch*trate on you," "You can't be *ch*true, dear." "I took a *ch*trip on a *ch*train, and I thought about you." "*Ch*try a little tenderness." Listen sometime to Ol' Blue Eyes singing the Merry Christmassy "Oh By Gosh, By Golly," when he jogs into the line, "Then comes that big wish/ Giving the *ch*tree the *ch*trim." *Ch*tree. *Ch*trim. "I love you for what you're *ch*ying [trying] to do," he tells Mibs (Jane Russell) in *Double Dynamite* (1951). The fact is that Sinatra could *not* pronounce the letter R correctly. In one of his early films, *Higher and Higher* (1943), his odd pronunciation of words like "marriage" and "stranger" and phrases like "on the run" come out sounding exactly like "mavvage" and "stainjer" and "on the vun." It's true! But the D problem he had was just as bad. Watch the movie, *It Happened in Brooklyn* (1947), and listen to find even the young Sinatra ask, "What are you driving at?" which comes out of course, "What are you jiving at?"

Curiously, ironically, if you insist, Sinatra who could be cruel and arbitrary if not downright vindictive once publicly disparaged — on stage in Atlantic City in between songs — the vulgarian interviewer Barbara Walters of ABC-TV. He described her as "Baba Wawa, a real bow-wow...a pain in the ass who has a lisp and should take diction lesson." He explained, "Baba Wawa doesn't need defense. She needs diction lessons. Did you ever listen to her? She says 'too-too twain' and 'I wuv a wabbit.' Diction lessons, not defense." I call Sinatra arbitrary because he never mocked Buddy Hackett's speech-defect but went so far as to ask the comic to be his opening act. Hackett sang, if you want to call it that — you haven't lived until you have heard him stumble through, "Itsy Bitsy Teeny Weeny, Yellow Polka Dot Bikini," this with his Brooklyn accent compounded with a voice that, mostly cheek, seemed to come out sideways through a mouthful of acorns — but he was best known for his humorless Chinese waiter routine, the epitome of racist vulgarity, in which he put a rubber band over his head and face so his eyes narrowed, whereupon he wrote down orders from a table, making L/R substitutions, and when it was time for dessert, he would crudely sing out in his Brooklyn-Chinese accent, "OK, who the wise-guy with the kumquat?" It is one of the saddest, stupidest acts in all of show business. In 1956 he also recorded s single on Coral, "Chinese Rock and Egg Roll," the flip side of which is "Ting Me a Tong" (Sing me a Song). It is the pits.

Oh, the 1950s was a real laff riot.

A serious PhD. dissertation could some day be written on the speech defects of popular singers. I am referring to the sort of things like Sinatra's buccal oddities as listed above, now, not the Rat Pack frankenslang that he and his gang dined out on — "clyde," "chicky baby," "bombsville," "the Big C," "gasser, "a Harvey," "cash out," "dig," "how's your bird?" "ring-a-ding-ding," "broads" (which included "mouse," "beetle, "twirl," "dame," "chick," "tomato," "barn burner") "fracture," "hey-hey," and "You're platinum, pussycat!" "The singer's voice was the voice of an angel, pure in diction. But the mouth was always Hoboken," wrote David Lehman in his wonderful essay, "Frankophilia" in *American Heritage* (Nov./ Dec. 2002) In the matter of speech defects,[7] it is endless.

Otherwise, God bless him, the man had perfect phrasing, always giving even seemingly unimportant consonants — who else would sing, "An*d* now the en*d* is near"? — their full due. What other singer took the time? The Chairman hits those two D's with the exactitude of a tapped Morse Code key. He literally bounces on "ring-a-ding-ding" and like a cool, stylish lightweight boxer punches out consonants, singing with classic pronunciation "Ju*sss*t in time." "And I suddenly turn and see/ your *fabbb*ulous face," he sings in "I Get a Kick Out of You." And notice kick-sung with quinch! He could deliver a word with the super-adrenalized whack of a Vod-Bomb (Red Bull and Vodka)! In "Once Upon a Time" we hear, "The world was sweeter than we k*nyew*." In his version of "Last Night When We Were Young" the *nnnnng* of "young" gets full attention. He stretches the word *"throuuuuugh"* in "Night and Day" — "and this torment won't be through / until you let me spend my life making love to you" — like a rich, tasty, salt-water taffy being puuuulled and streeetched. Listen also to that hoarse weariness that   Sinatra puts into his voice for a mere yoctosecond ("But I'll keep

---

7        Public broadcasting included. What about radio shockjock Howard Stern's shlightly shibilant S' like "falsch" (false), "horny shtrippers" (strippers), and "nysscch" (nice), etc.? It's grotesque, especially since, a major staple on his show is to mock the speech defects of other mentally-challenged unfortunates. "If shumone like you shlipped and fell on shum shtairs," declares Stern in a radio commercial for lawyers on Cape Cod's WPIXY, blah blab blah. NBA basketball's Bob Cousy ("He dwibbled and dwibbled," etc.); ABC-TV's Barbara Walters ("What a wocky woad to wun," etc.) — the letter R humbles many. Like Marlene Dietrich, actor Claude Rains also had trouble with Rs — two awkward thumb-tongued impresarios, dim ex-football broadcaster Frank Gifford ("Muhammed Ali, what a *thch*ampion," etc.) and talk-show host Phil Donahue with that tongue between his teeth ("Be *thch*eery, not sad!" "re*lidgt*heon," etc.); and, among other notably goofy examples, the alarming growing-more-numerous-by-the-day glottal-stop contingent: NBC's Tom Brokaw ("Uskama Bin Gladen of the Tglagliban"), science-reporter Robert Bazell ("Glady gluck, gluckily, was with him"). etc.

my head up high/ Although I'm kinda tired") in his blue masterpiece, "Cycles." It is the same with "It Was a Very Good Year" in which he gives the word *very* such power, gives the crisp T's in "twenty one" and "thirty-five" full value (rare for an American), and simply soars with "*caaaame* undone" and "*bluuuuue*-blooded girls." Sheer genius. There is real conviction there.

Who can knock Sinatra or any great singer who with extrapolating ingenuity had the brio, the joy, in "The Lady is a Tramp" to sing, "She loves the free fine wild cool knocked out groovy koo-koo wind in her hair" instead of the predictable and far tamer-as-written, "She loves the free, fresh wind in her hair"? It is called "kidding the lyrics," antically throwing in a bit of slang, bop, or simply repeating a word, kicking it, as he does, semi-sedately, in "A Foggy Day" when he repeats "the sun was shinin', shinin', shinin', shinin' everywhere." In "You Make Me Feel So Young," what better proves the persona of Sinatra's heel-clicking youth than his rich and self-delighting assertion — the man *felt* lyrics — "Wanna go and *bounce* the moon"? The critic Mark Steyn once noted, comparing the two vocal presentations, that in Ella Fitzgerald's particular version the verb simply passes unnoticed. Speaking of interpolations, N.Y. cabaret singer Michael Feinstein once told Mark Steyn that he personally always sang the line from "A Foggy Day," "I viewed the morning with alarm," the way George and Ira wrote it. With his own ear, however, Sinatra who found the rhythm flawed — with a monosyllable missing — always preferred to sing the line, "I viewed the morning with much alarm." According to Feinstein, however, Ira Gershwin hugely disliked Sinatra's addition. I agree with Steyn, who observed,

> The word 'with' is given far too much weight: it's accented, it's a minim, it's a preposition yet, as written, it lasts forever. Sinatra is too naturalistic a singer to be comfortable with that: his solution — the interpolated 'much' — seems perfectly acceptable. Singing, after all, is an interpreter's art.

At the same time, Sinatra tended at times to overvalue words. Some people may simply chalk it up to style. Panache. It was often, as well, the result of his high-spirits. Any real music fan or culture maven knows how Bing Crosby loved to sing, to croon, any words with the letter *B* in them. The more the merrier! He truly adored the letter, the bounce it gave, the lilting rosary of ba-ba-booms. He often even comically mocked or parodied himself in doing so. "When the blue of the night..." "Moonlight becomes you..." "Lock, stock, and barrel..." "Where children listen to hear sleigh-bells in the snow..." It animated the whole of his hit, "Swingin' on A Star" along with many others. It was a literal tic, let's face it. Many singers have them. Johnny Mathis loved to crack his voice, to split-level words. ("O-O-on my o-own, as I wander through this wo-o-o-nderland al-lo-ne.") With Mathis it can actually sound like an actual crack in a vinyl record. He was as shot through with crannies as a Thomas' English muffin. (A nook is a corner, a cranny is a crack.) t always reminds me of the macabre opening of *Journey Into Fear* (1943), the film based on the Eric Ambler novel, where in a seedy dark Istanbul hotel room the obese assassin, Banat, is combing his hair while the phonograph record skips. As part of his act, the American actor, comedian, and impressionist John Byner used to do a devastatingly funny parody of Mathis singing with that voice-rack, split-word technique. I don't know, an entire epistemology might be connected to breaking, cracking, and splitting — a way of seeing the world. In her novel, *The Waves* Virginia Woolf wrote, "Beauty must be broken daily to remain beautiful" — it is the very theme of that book, I suggest — and maybe that is the very point of waves themselves, no? As I have said, Jerry Vale not only fake-sobbed notes, but he also double-billed his words, just as Johnny Mathis did, riding them as much for extra value as for extra syllables. It leaves a gummy, slightly mucilaginous effect on songs, I have to say. Dinah Washington often sang by chat-talk. Bing Crosby who narrated (and played all the vocal parts in) the classic Disney animation, *The Adventures of Ichabod and Mr. Toad* (1949) opens that film — arbitrarily — with a drawn-out burble of onomatopoeic *B*'s, singing them with his typical casual style.

But nobody was better at back-phrasing than Sinatra, that stylistic technique where the singer is either ahead or behind the beat. Jazz singers typically use this technique, Ella Fitzgerald and Sassy Sarah Vaughan and Peggy Lee, to name but three, as do some pop singers. He almost seemed to *dare* musicians to follow him. No singer quite understood cadence, felt the rhythms *in* cadence, the cradle of tonality, better than Sinatra or for its patterns and progressions could orchestrate lip, jaw, throat, tongue, even ribs, to their best advantage in pitching the right overtones in a chosen song. He was vocally knowledgeable, could flex his vocal cords, and, expertly finding shadows in words and phrases, was able to whisper, coax, glide, explode forth, shout, cuddle a note, moan, hum, and generally take his voice through caverns of chest and head brought refinement to reverberation. As to pitch and phrasing, breaths and "stops" and in-between notes, the way he moved from note to note, that vocal slide he casually employed between two pitches Italians call *portamento della voce* — it is a passage, a glissando, involving anticipation — the way he teased a song's rhythm, his understanding of musical turns, commas, semi-colons, or colons, he was the master. Whenever he sang a song, it was not mailed-in but made a picture which he presented with a complex topology and registering something fine with almost photographic value of depth and detail.

Sinatra's vocal edge was to "declaim conversationally," as John Rockwell points out in *Sinatra: An American Classic*, one of the best books on The Voice, the Sultan of Swoon, Shoulders, the Bony Baritone, the Croon Prince of Swing, the Lean Lark, Bones, and of course Frankie. What informed the focused sharpness of attack that defined every note for him was his sense of clarity, enunciation, breathing. No explanation can surpass Rockwell's. "Unlike many singers, classical or pop, his voice rarely slips back in his throat, becoming more artificially rounded in tone — some opera singers, like Joan Sutherland, swallow everything into a mush of vowels — or more gravelly and vibrato-ridden. Sinatra hardly ever lapses into the frayed hoarseness of so many rock and rhythm & blues singers." It was also deeply about cognition. Sinatra heard lyrics, heeded them, devoured, apprehended them, acutely listened to what they meant. Not that he commanded the full field. "Sinatra's loud top notes were never secure in the operatic, proclamatory sense. Even late in his career, with audiences cheering coarsely at the climaxes, he holds something in reserve; he is almost always guardedly in control," notes Rockwell who is correct in pointing out that Sinatra was not a belter, never a belter. No one could interpret a song quite like Sinatra. If you doubt it, try to find his album, *This is Sinatra, Volume Two*, songs he recorded in the 1940s, ballads about dreams, mostly, like "You'll Always Be the One I Love," "Put Your Dreams Away," If You Are But a Dream," "Time After Time" — this is the voice Kitty Kelley described as "bedroom honey" — or listen again to him singing "All the Way," High Hopes," "You'll Never Know," "Fly Me to the Moon," "Young at Heart," "Nancy," "You'll Never Know," "I'll Never Smile Again," "The Brooklyn Bridge," "Cycles," "All or Nothing at All."

Style was his forte. His cuffs and cufflinks. That radioactive orange hanky, his favorite color. The affectation of the heavy pinky ring he wore all his life. I loved his jaw shift in between — and often pronouncing — certain words. His hands spoke. He often hung up one hand, dangled it, as he crooned. He would move rhythmically with an upbeat song, but when singing seriously, solemnly, somberly, he almost always kept his left hand, thumb to fingers, waist high, front. Panache. He presented himself, just as he sang, with lightness and grace, a style that had a softly elegant drape, like a Moss Bros. or Anderson & Sheppard suit, cut to show the natural look of the wearer's style rather than impose one on him. He had autobiographical gifts, could make a song authentic, deliver it from the heart. (Tony Bennett also had this gift. Admit it, didn't we all come to dislike the woman in his embittered torch song, "I Want To Be Around" who caused him to sing so vindictively, "And that's when I'll discover that revenge is sweet/ As I sit there applaudin' from a front-row seat/ When somebody breaks your heart/

Like you, like you broke mine"?) No other singer, by the way, went out of his way, more generously, to acknowledge for an audience the name of the composer of a song he sung than Sinatra. In a formal mode, when he introduced any guest or spoke in some official way, he always kept his right arm — right angle — clapped to his left. The rituals had serious rubrics. He had all sorts of repetitive locomotor movements, simple and complex, manual, and phonic.

The tic. Few ever talk about them. The sudden, repetitive, not necessarily rhythmic motor movement or vocalizations involving discrete muscle groups. A singer's tic can be invisible to the observer, or just barely seen. Common motor and phonic tics are, respectively, eye blinking and throat clearing. There are verbal tics and physical tics. Buddy Holly repeated a cute hiccup. Little Richard had a head-shaking *wooooooo* which the Beatles later adopted. The Who stuttered. Rod Stewart is hoarse. Shirley Bassey with outstretched hands would windmill her arms. Edith Piaf, a frail little trout, compulsively twicked at her dress. Tom Jones affected both the shoulder and pelvic shrug. Judy Garland at dramatic points in her songs would actually snatch at her hair, while Julie Andrews while singing liked to put her hand on her head. (Garland offered up a complete pathography of tics. How about the cocked hip? The stage-mother reach toward the audience? The dramatic arch-backwards, staring ceilingward? That raised arm across her face with open hand? Preparing to go on stage, by the way, she compulsively stood — and always entered from — stage left.) Celine Dion beats her chest to stress high seriousness. Joe Cocker went through a ritual of hand and arm spasms, twiddling them about like an epileptic. Whitney Houston oddly chose to close her mouth between phrases and, often, words, (as did JFK). Bernadette Peters has an endearing lisp. Sinatra employed a jaw shift on certain held notes, giving a gnathic kick to certain sung words and phrases. Bing Crosby often hung his arms out like a scarecrow on an upbeat song. Young Elvis loved to flash along with those pelvic thrusts a spasmodic leg wag, eliciting yowls from the girls. Rings, scarves, and capes were sartorial tics. What else was that glorious, self-indulgent array of martial arts — having sweet fanny adams to do with music -- but tics? There were the karate chops, the rolling arm-swivel, usually boosting a song finale, the sudden, swift double head-shift — a maneuver he learned from the singer Tom Jones — all sorts of kenpo hand-motions and footwork, the rising, raised all-finger-pointing hand, the wide-legged, single knee wag, the rapid reverse arm exchange like chess-castling his arms, and, among others, the revolving roundhouse swivel-kick. A favorite of his was a long kata-type sequence at the end of "Suspicious Minds" done to the accompaniment of mad, thumping drums. When he performed Roy Orbison habitually — compulsively — wore sunglasses. A particular favorite of mine, a tic that I have never heard anyone ever comment on, was one that the Rev. Martin Luther King at times employed to reinforce the gravity of what he was saying. It was a stabilizing gesture that involved a serious, inclusive, staring "don't doubt me" look filled with gravitas. I would place it somewhere under the heading of the vestibula-ocular reflex where the head goes one way, the eyes look another. It can be seen at its illustrious best, on film, at the exact moment when King utters the words, "I may not get there with you," during his prophetic final public speech on April 3, 1968 which he delivered perspiring and purposeful in that small crowded church in Memphis, Tennessee just hours before he was shot and killed at the Lorraine Motel, as passionately he spoke to the sanitation workers of the city who were then on strike protesting low pay and poor working conditions. President Barack Obama reserves this very same head and facial gesture, head one way, eyes another, for his momentous remarks, and if you pay attention you cannot miss it.

Luciano Pavarotti always refused to wear tights, greatly feared (like many Italians) the number 17, avoided wearing purple when singing (the color is considered bad luck in Italian opera), and would of course always superstitiously grab his testicles to ward off bad luck or the "*malocchio*" whenever he was unduly congratulated — drawing attention to good fortune can be dangerous — or if ever the word "*Forza*" was mentioned, as the mere name of Verdi's greatest opera, *La Forza del Destino* is cursed. Another bad-luck opera is *La Juive* by Fromental Halévy, an opera not only associated with legendary stories of misfortune but for Luciano, portentously, "the role that killed Caruso." Pavarotti also always carried a bent nail in his pocket for good luck whenever he sang. I believe that the way conductor Arturo Toscanini held his baton was a tic. Toscanini eccentrically held it down at its base with all four fingers of his right hand in a straight line. Nothing dainty, no artistic lifting of the pinkie like a dowager sipping tea. It was a solid workingman's grip, like a carpenter judiciously moving to place a shim, a movement coming largely from his elbow and forearm. He did not beat time in accordance with the traditional skeletal configurations, and his motion was criticized as being too circular. Winthrop Sergeant in a profile on the Maestro for *Life* magazine in 1944 described it as a "paddling" movement. Some said he was a slave to the metronome, others that though his beat was inexorable, his rhythms were rigid, that he was an enemy of Italian song and a wrecker of the art of bel canto, that he held the tempo and rhythm of the music firmly to its course and that it had the mechanical exactitude of a robot.

According to Gary Giddins, Billie Holiday's most overworked tic was ending so many of her songs with the interval of a ninth or major second down to the tonic. Sinatra had several other tics, in fact. He was addicted to the butterfly-like cruising of the A and O vowels. "*Aaaaa*-aand if I can make it there..." *Shoooze.* He loved the word "shoes" and when crooning it always gave the word an extra kick. He never failed to keep a song alive and kicking, investing himself in words that made lonely songs blue and "I'm-in-love" songs upbeat. Nobody put a song across — nobody could — better than Francis Albert. But, as I say, the fellow had that amazing T/ CH problem. A singer of exquisite phrasing, the Chairman of the Board (check on it) always managed to pronounce words like "chair" and "choose" and "children" rather peculiarly. "You've got a *tzip* on your *tszoulder*," he tells the gorgeous but snobbish socialite Tracy Lord (Grace Kelly) in *High Society* — watch the scene, pay close attention, and you'll hear it. "*Tsair. Tzoose. Tzildren.* "I'm *achrac*ted to all her *tzsarm*s." "The lady is a *chtramp*." It is hardly a matter of moment and at worse only mildly distracting, but the fact of the matter is it is there. Passionate for her, what did Ol' Blue Eyes particularly like about the main squeeze in his life, the lovely Ava Gardner? Why, that sexy hole in her chin — her *tsin!* Her *tsinny, tsin, tsin*! Actor Charles Boyer had that same speech impediment, trouble with his Rs, like many another Frenchman speaking English. "How stange," you can hear him say in *The Constant Nymph.* "Tuthfully, no," he says, instead of "Truthfully, no."

I cannot help but hear Sinatra sing "Stangers [sic] in the Night" whenever the song comes on the radio, a song, by the way, that he came to dislike for some reason. He refused to sing the song in concert. Was it for the pastiche-like coda, "Dooby-dooby-doo," which others compulsively parodied? Or was it the slightly louche gay subtext to Bert Kaempfert's dubious lyrics with their shady and disreputable subterranean flavor — "Strangers in the night exchanging glances/ Wond'ring in the night what were the chances/ We'd be sharing love before the night was through" — that made him uneasy?

As I say, Sinatra also had what I call a "DR/J" problem. "Want a *jink?*" he asks the Laurence Harvey character in *The Manchurian Candidate.* Want a drink? "You *jive* me crazy." You drive me crazy. "Cut the *jamatics!*" Cut the dramatics. "Your ass must be *jagging.*" Your ass must be dragging. What a strange if subtle speech-defect. The Voice, by the way, for all his style could never quite manage to sing scat. Did you know that? My friend, the late Peggy Lee over the telephone once hilariously imitated him — they were buddies — trying to sing scat, which, by the way, she herself could do to near perfection. Sinatra tried doing scat, but it went nowhere, nothing close to, say, Ella Fitzgerald's gift for it or Sarah Vaughan's — Sassy's soaring, incomparable "I Can't Give You Anything but Love" is a real trip to the land of Glossophilia. No, he could not sing scat in spite of all that famously loose, insouciant shoulder-rolling hippitude of his and all that ease with Rat Pack slang — "How's your Clyde?" "Hey, pallie!" "That's a gasser!" "Ain't that a kick in the head?" "He's got the Big Casino," "How's your bird?" and of course the inimitable "Ring-a-ding-ding," a universal phrase that he supposedly nicked from his comedian buddy, Fat Jack Leonard, and which incidentally is also the title phrase of the first LP (1961) he cut on his own label. "On his 1949 recording of 'It All Depends on You,'" observes Shawn Levy in *Rat Pack Confidential*, "his vocalese passages sounded like nothing so much as a kid blowing bubbles in milk with a straw."

I have always felt, regarding the astonishingly immature and at best farcical grammar-school hijinks of Rat Pack behavior both on stage and off, that it was the inane *schwarmerei* of a group of not only immature but egregiously uneducated guys — a group without a college degree among them. We're talking no schooling, none whatsoever. Dean. Joey. Frank. Sammy. Sammy Davis could barely write a sentence. Peter Lawford knew nothing. Books? *Books?* You mean those square things with pages in them and print? Surely that is one major reason why humor to them consisted of little but goosing "broads," inventing childish shtick, repeating silly phrases, throwing cherry bombs at each other, overusing stupid phrases (which all of them thought were ingenious), breaking up over insipid jokes, and not only getting sloppily drunk just about every night but to all the watching world insistently making the very *fact* of infantile boozing iconic. Did that not fly in the face of Isaiah, or am I being puritanical? The Apostles sang after the Last Supper before they went out to the Mount of Olives (Matthew 14:26). James indeed said that one should sing when anyone was merry (James 5:13). But Isaiah declared there should be *no* singing in the vineyard (Isaiah 16:10). But their fruit was the grape. Frank, who was cool, had a slight intellectual streak. He had a library and read widely, I have heard, later in life quite a bit. He certainly had a pronounced musical education. Was he ashamed a bit to have knowledge when, in the world of show business, ignorance to a large degree is a commonplace? I believe so. "He wants to be so many people that he doesn't know who he is," declared Judith Campbell Exner of Sinatra.

I think maybe the closest Sinatra ever came to rolling scat, if it was not the "dooby-dooby-doo" of "Strangers in the Night" — and it wasn't really close — was, oddly enough, his hip, unpredictable, loosey-goosey, finger-poppin' swinging version of the old chestnut "Ol' MacDonald" to which as a big superadded treat for his listeners he employed a lot of those extra-special Chairman-of-the-Board lyrics to transubstantiate the "chick" of the childhood version of the song we know into what in the lingo of the Rat Pack was dismissively called a "broad." And that is not saying much, believe me.

With his vocally inexplicable echo/ growl, pop singer Gene Pitney long seems to have had a seriously advanced D-T substitution problem, singing for example — growling, in fact, acrimoniously pushing hard on the beat — in his song, "A Town Without Pity," "When those *liddle* minds *dearr* you in *doo*." Did he suffer from borborygmia, the gassy noise in the bowels? He bizarrely pronounces his song-title as "The Man Who Shot *Liberdy* Valance." In another one of the several Burt Bacharach's songs that Pitney recorded — Bacharach commonly depended in his variety, like a peddler in the rag trade, on "volume" — "Twenty Four Hours From Tulsa," Pitney plaintively tells us in his thumb-tongued way how in being "*twendy*-four hours from *Dulsa*" he is looking for some*ding* to eat," when "all of a sudden," he cries — keens — "I lost *condrol* as I held her town" or "as I held the town" or "as I held a clown" or whatever word he is trying to sing at that juncture which, I must confess, no amount of listening over the years, even in a blind crouch, has ever made clear to me.

Good diction in singing, when called for it — clear pronunciation — seems to me to be a lost art. I would insist *long* lost. Gone with the buggy and the chimney sweep, the automat and the human pin-setter. Take the late Robert Goulet whose singing resembled talk, a kind of holding forth that one might mistake for good diction but was in fact "clipped speech like ice-cubes popping out of a rubber tray," as Frank Loesser once rudely said of the actor, Henry Stephenson, in the 1934 stage-play, "Sweet Aloes." With that chesty, blustering, rumbling, faux he-man cartoon voice of his, Goulet tried to sing with élan the holiday song, "The Christmas Waltz." ("Frosted window panes/ candles gleaming inside," etc.) Ya gotta hear this! He sounds as if he came from rural Arkansas — he was in fact born in Lawrence, Mass. — argue-singing like an Arkansas redneck with all sorts of wretched stresses and lazy elisions and poor grammar and, at times, deplorable diction, "It's that time *a* [of] year" and "and this song *a* [of] mine in three-quarter time wishes yooooou" and "every song *ya* [you] hear/ seems *ta* [to] say 'Merry Christmas" and "Santa's filled his sleigh with things *fa* [for] you and *fa* [for] me." [My italics.] It is a fucking nightmare, a textbook case for "Diction 101." Goulet struggled with language, wrapped it in hovering and irresolute self-interruptions. Every song he sang was a tractor-pull. In a way, he delivered a song the way John Wayne spoke, like a boar pisses — in jerks. ("We start tomorrow," growls Wayne in the role of Tom Dunson in the powerful movie *Red River* (1948). "We're going to Missouri with ten...thousand head...Most of you...came back from...the war and found...your land stolen by...carpetbaggers...there's no money and no work...in the South...because there's no...market for beef...So we're going to... Missouri.") It seems to be, but isn't, a variation of the so-called "Shatner comma"

— "You know, exactly, what, I mean" — the condition named after *Star Trek* actor who parses words out flit-like. No, Wayne, no genius, had probably learned his lines like that and doubtless never committed them to memory very well. It certainly fits in with my conception of Wayne. Who is surprised to find at the end of the movie *Stage Coach* (1939), when playing the Ringo Kid he sees the troubled, weeping Dallas (Claire Trevor) outside a brothel — she is a "fallen lady" whose sexual exploits have so unnerved the local women that they have banded together to oust her from their scandal-mongering society — that he clearly doesn't know what she is or where she lives? She tries to say her last goodbyes, but Ringo says, "We ain't never gonna say goodbye." (Speaking in that halting way of his, Wayne hazarded what is known as the "Donner Party" comma, you know, the crucial one that differentiates between "Let's eat, Grandma" and "Let's eat Grandma.") For another, sad, woolly-headed, predictably glaring example in the "failed diction" department, another Christmas bomb, by the way — and surely one of the prime nominees for the Annual Thumb-Tongue Award — listen to Madonna's cover of Eartha Kitt's 1954 hit, "Santa Baby," sadly a *de*-make and not a re-make, in which, unlike the sexy feline Kitt from North, South Carolina (that is correct), who loved to enunciate every word with almost cut-glass precision and whose diction was as crisp and even as the snow that lay round about when Good King Wenceslas looked out on the Feast of Stephen, the Material Girl not only crassly sings, á la *The Sopranos'* inarticulate Big Paulie, "wit' some decorations bought at Tiffany's (sic)" but does so through the song with a kind of mis-hitting genius, singing every single note off-key. Flat as flounders. It has to be one of the biggest mailed-in recordings in the history of pop music.

There are tiny voices with the stridulations of a katydid, like an insect singing in a single frequency at night — and who would deny that even that is not beautiful in its own miraculous way? — as well as large voices. When in perfect form all can serve the many rare and profligate definitions of beauty. Rita Streich, the splendid coloratura soprano with the crystal clear diction, had a small voice. So did Fred Astaire, Rudy Vallee, and Gene Austin, the Texas tenor, one of my favorite singers. "Many composers today don't know what the human throat is," the great soprano Elizabeth Schwarzkopf complained in a *Newsweek* interview on October 15, 1990. "At Bloomington, Indiana, I was invited to listen to music written in quarter tones for four harps and voices. I had to go out to be sick." Crooners, when they first came on the scene, were thought by many to be lacking in manly strength, and they do tend to have smaller voices than other singers. It was originally an ironic term, "crooners," and came in with radio broadcasting and electrical recording. Before their appearance, tenors held sway, like the full-throated world famous Irish tenor, John McCormack. Although McCormack made hundreds of recordings — the first on a phonograph cylinder in 1904 — you can actually see him in a Hollywood movie, the sentimental *Wings of the Morning* (1937) where as he sings several songs, notably "Believe Me, If All Those Endearing Young Charms," where as he performs he pathetically has to read the lyrics from prompting notes he is holding! (I have never seen that before or since. What explains that? He died from emphysema, not Alzheimer's.) Sophie Tucker and Ethel Merman with their leather lungs were true ox-killers, no felt slippers there, for sure. Dame Joan Sutherland, dubbed "La Stupenda" — Luciano Pavarotti said that she had the "Voice of the Century" — was noted for her contribution to the sudden renaissance of the bel canto repertoire from the late 1950s through the 1980s and had not only an enormous voice but in her prime a highly accurate intonation, supremely pinpoint staccatos, and a tremendous upper register. Then of course Birgit Nilsson had a voice so powerful with her clear ringing high notes, almost like metal, that, as they say, she could effortlessly drown out a large orchestra and fill gigantic auditoriums with her full extravagant sound. As the leading Wagnerian soprano of her time, Nilsson, notably as Brünnhilde — but in any of her other classic soprano roles, Leonore, Aida, Turandot, Tosca, Elektra, or Salome — clearly had to have impregnable pipes, force, and stamina. A light voice may be well suited for Rossini, not for Massenet, for Bellini, not for Wagner.

To hear songs sung as they should be, with correct emphasis, pitch, voices powered and enhanced by good diction, listen to young Ethel Waters and Julie London, Ella Fitzgerald and Karen Akers, Kay Starr and Mildred Bailey. (Did you know that the three singers, Bailey, Starr — born Katharine La Verne Starks in Oklahoma in 1922 — and the great Lee Wiley, were all Native Americans? Starr had both a full blooded Iroquois father as well as a Cherokee mother. Listen to Edith Piaf sing "Milord." Listen to Deanna Durbin sing "The Last Rose of Summer" — a Victorian standard but she is angelic and inimitable — or Wanda Jackson sing "Fujiyama Mama" and "Funnel of Love" or Karen Akers sing "Haunted Heart" or Adele [Adkins] sing "Hometown Glory," "Someone Like You," "Chasing Pavements," or "Rolling in the Deep" or Maria Callas sing "*O patria mia*," the big soprano aria from the third act of *Aida* or Annie Lennox sing "Why" or Sinéad O'Connor sing "Nothing Compares 2 U" or Aretha Franklin sing "Respect," "Chain of Fools," and "Natural Woman."

A singer obsessed with proper diction and every possibility of inflection was Dinah Washington who, incidentally, at least according to her biographer James Haskins in *Queen of the Blues*, loved — revealingly — *loved* all Bette Davis movies.

"Her [Washington's] articulation, the luxuriant correctness of her vowels, the *parlando* with which she emphasizes meaning, are among the fundamental joys of her art," declares Gary Giddins in *Faces in the Crowd*, in which he points out her vocal trick this way:

> It was a unique appoggiatura, an effect seemingly as natural to her as her stinging timbre — an upward glide pinned to or squeezed out of a note, usually at the end of a phrase.

Washington's voice, "a gritty, salty, high-pitched voice, marked by absolute clarity of diction and clipped, bluesy phrasing," in the words of Richard S. Ginell, had a distinct style that could incorporate all kinds of music, whether jazz, R&B, blues, or middle-of-the-road pop. It had the kick of a trumpet, that sort of popped or clipped technique of hers — "The leaves of brown/ came tumbling down/ remember/ that September/ in the rain" — "a brief gliss," Giddins again, "pressed with an extra dollop of vibrato...an echo of the pitched note that sometimes states and sometimes merely suggests an overture of a fifth or an octave."

I personally love the correctness of diction one hears in the music of Miss Vera Lynn, that pre-eminent World War II British favorite who had such a warm and beautiful voice. Too old-fashioned, you complain? There is astonishing timbre there. She had depth of delivery, sang with passion, and, enunciating clearly without a trace of pomposity, always gave each word she sang, each vowel, every consonant, its full and proper value: "Ju*st* keep on wish*ing and* care will go," "And Jimmy will go to s*l*ee*p* in his own l*ittle* room a*gain*," "Please give me someth*ing* to remem*ber* you by," "B*ut* I know we'll m*eet* a*gain* some sunny day," and so forth. Clear and clean and cool as cut-crystal.

Vera Lynn's singing — her speech — is non-rhotic, rather the way the English speak, clear of the kind of warbles, quavers, uvular trills, and alveolar or retroflex approximants that one often hears, for example, in Norwegian, Italian, Spanish, and Russian. One rarely finds in American singers her kind of precision or clarity. ("All my dreams/ pass before my eyes with curio*sidy*," grimly sings the group Kansas in "Dust in the Wind.") When Lynn sang the line "And Jimmy will go to sleep/ in his own little room again" in "The White Cliffs of Dover" — I have been assured many times that during World War II British listeners would burst into tears at the line every time — notice that she never milks the line or over-dramatizes it. That is *sprezzatura*. From a phonetic standpoint, little friction can be heard when Vera Lynn sings. While English as spoken in Great Britain is the arterial tongue, it is nevertheless a mistake to believe that the American accent is nothing but a coarse, second-hand imitation of the mother tongue, despite the conviction held by many abroad that this is probably the case. "An Englishman is always inclined to resent the unfamiliar when it is found under conditions for which he thinks he has some responsibility," Lord Tweedsmuir (John Buchan) wrote in his 1940 autobiography, *Pilgrim's Way*, pointing out that what might have been pardonable, even commendable in a foreigner, is blameworthy in a cousin. "There is no such thing as the Queen's English. The property has gone into the hands of a joint stock company and we own the bulk of the shares," wittily wrote Mark Twain in *Pudd'nhead Wilson*. It is the old "The British Grenadiers" versus "Free America" idea. So pipe it your way. What may sound like a curious or dubious fact is that before the American Revolution the two dialects were far more similar than what we hear today. Paradoxically, the American accent has changed only slightly since those days four hundred years ago, whereas, strangely enough, it is actually the British accent that has dramatically evolved. The British accent, which is known by linguists as non-rhotic speech, took hold as it is among the upper classes of England during the Industrial Revolution and slowly held sway just about everywhere. It is said that there are as many as thirty or forty major dialects and linguistic varieties in the UK which greatly differ from each other in pronunciation, vocabulary and grammar.

As to splendid voices, why not go all the way back to the days of Mlles. Galli Curci, Emmy Destinn, Hulda Lashanska, and Emma Calvé, the French operatic soprano, whose elegant voice was *sfogato* of 2½ octaves from G to C, always perfectly even throughout, with a contralto-like low register? The inimitable Ellen Beach Yaw, the American coloratura soprano known as "Lark Ellen" or the "California Nightingale," had a phenomenal vocal range that could encompass four octaves — a range that went from G to E1111 — and allow her to sing and sustain the D above high D. (Yaw was reportedly the only known soprano of her era to be able to do so. She was also able to trill in major thirds or fifths, trills which usually involved rapidly alternating notes over an interval of a minor or major second. Believe it or not, archival recordings of all of these singers are still available and can be heard.)

I should not fail to mention in this context Josef "Yossele" Rosenblatt, the Ukrainian-born *chazzan* (cantor) and a man whose fame in his day extended far beyond the Jewish world, earning him not only large concert fees — and in 1927 even a singing role in the *The Jazz Singer* — but also the sobriquet "The Jewish Caruso," the fabled opera singer whom at one time he eventually began to rival in Red Seal record sales. It was Enrico Caruso himself who came to acknowledge the cantor with praise as having a voice more like his own than any others. Rosenblatt's technique in cantillation was unique, the notes he hit being remarkably accurate at high speed and his *appoggiaturas*, similarly, struck near perfectly, both rhythmically and on pitch. He commanded four registers with a sweet timbre that went all the way from deep baritone through the tenor range and up to a controlled falsetto that, in the words of the critic Marvin Gelfand in *American Heritage*, "made the silver ornaments on the Torah scrolls jingle and dance." The cantor's accomplishments were so rare that Arturo Toscanini appealed to him to sing the leading role in Fromental Halévy's *La Juive*, but Rosenblatt quickly demurred, replying that he chose to use his vocal gift solely for the glory of God and in the service of his religion. Significantly, he turned down a "Golden Hello" from the Chicago opera house because he said that it violated his religious principles. It is said that upon hearing Rosenblatt sing "Elli Elli" Enrico Caruso was so moved that he ascended the stage and kissed him.

Speaking of the crisply pronounced final T, who can forget twitchy Bette Davis at her most arch in the film, *The Private Lives of Elizabeth and Essex* (1939) where in one particularly memorable scene, where the imperious balding Virgin Queen is addressing Robert, Earl of Essex, we hear Davis' odd, clucking New England aunty pronunciation with never a swallowed consonant at the end of a word: "Rab*art*, let's be kin*dt* for a mome*nht*!" And of course in her film, *The Letter* (1940) in which Davis plays the desperate Mrs. Leslie Crosby we hear in the usual clipped tones, "You've been — what? Trying to record my thoughts" and "Oh, I couldn't believe it, I wouldn't believe it. The last I saw her, I saw her walking in the village with those hideous bangles, that chalky painted face, those eyes like a cobra's eyes. But I couldn't give him up. I sent for him. You read the letter… so I seized the revolver and fired," and of course that mad, head-shaking, passionately succinct, crisply pronounced, "With all my hear*t*, I still love the man I kill*ed*." The late *Today* Show host and composer Steve Allen referred to the phenomenon as the "Bette Davis T." "It is a truism, I suppose, that Davis still holds the American T-pronouncing championship, and long may she wave," remarked Allen. "Her famous line, 'What a dump!' would not have seemed nearly as arresting had its first word been slackly pronounced. No, Bette Davis did not merely speak a word — she *e-nun-ci-at-ed it.*

Wayne Newton had fairly good diction, but to me his voice always seemed marred by a kind of gong-like quality, resonating like a computer, seeming at times inhumanly synthesizeresque with a pitch resembling Auto-Tune distortion. It was not rough or abrasive like Rod Stewart's, Bruce Springsteen's, Steven Tyler's, or even the later Bob Dylan's but rather a semi-futuroidal sound. Johnnie Ray had such a voice, almost a duck-quack. So did Al Jolson, Sophie Tucker, and

Ethel Merman (who often loudly gong-hit the same note twice!) and other song-belters whose larynxes did not oscillate in the normal way and who, narrowing of the aryepiglottic sphincter (the "twanger"), could very easily have got work announcing the arrival of ocean liners coming into New York harbor!

Are you aware we now have singing computers? A team of scientists in Japan have worked out various artificial algorithms in programs that now endow machines to have a more human-like sound, at least according to Chris Gayomali in *Time* (May 9, 2011), who explains that the notes from such machines are "built from a single type of frequency curve, meaning there's little variation when you go from note to note." Gayomali points out that what the researchers from the Graduate School of Engineering at the University of Tokyo have done, by innovatively programming "a new type of frequency wave that has a lot of the same tics as human singing," is to find a way to make the inflections sound more human, recreating the nuances that lend our voices their character. (Un?) fortunately, however, we are the *opposite* of computers. The human singing voice, never one thing certainly, can soar, descend, stress one note here, hold one there, extend a passage, rev up, become a marvelous basso profundo, soften to a throaty murmur at a low idle but then when fully activated rise with more torque than a Duesenberg into window-shattering thunder, becoming almost ultrasonic (tenor Stefan Zucker during a performance in Carnegie Hall in 1972 held a sustained A in alt-altissimo for as long as 3.8 seconds) — in short, a voice *stylizes* a song. Can you imagine any machine bringing even the highest of its sapience and swarm intelligence to the likes of George "Ol' Possum" Jones with his East Texan twangs and heart-stopping glissandi and melismata and trying even remotely to duplicate by cognitive simulation or nano-programming a codeform of him singing songs like "She Thinks I Still Care," "We're Going to Hold On," "The Grand Tour," or "My Favorite Lies" and expecting to get them right?

The human voice is so multifarious that of a piece it beggars description. How about trying to copy the sound patterns or odd chopfalls of John F. Kennedy, the guttural snarls of Hitler, the patrician vowels of FDR, the bulldog grunts of Churchill, the smart-alecky chirp of Harry S. Truman, just to take five? I wonder, were the particulars of this seemingly unlasso-able variable covered in Ray Kurzweil's popular book, *The Age of Spiritual Machines* (1999) in which he blithely predicted, not without hubris, "the emergence in the early twenty-first century of a new form of intelligence on Earth that can compete with, and ultimately significantly exceed, human intelligence"?

No, it was not. A further irony is that the kind of precise robotic "diction" from anything mechanized has always seemed, when heard beeping intervallically from a metal box or nerd-like bot, to be exactly what we *hated* in Computer Speak, that choppy, programmed, overly precise, non-emotional techno-speech that goes back to the days of Buck Rogers, the kind that is constantly parodied by humorless nerds and idiots at parties trying to imitate Devo, even if later smoothed out like Hal's from *2001: A Space Odyssey*. Joshua, the computer in the movie, *War Games*, sounds like the Mayor of Munchkin City. Aren't we talking Kraftwerk? Styx's "Mr. Roboto"? Input fed through band-pass filters? Tonal vocoders? Demo voices? "Hello. I am Mr. Skullball. I'm a brand new voice. Can I serve you?"

With the use of digital tools, let me add, even handwriting — writing itself — may one day become a lost art. A 2010 survey showed that 85% of college students, avoiding the negotiations of cursive, it would seem, are now printing when they write. Paper contact is decreasing! And language. One language dies every 14 days. A recent *National Geographic* (July 2012) estimate suggests that "by the next century nearly half of the roughly, 7,000 languages spoken on Earth will likely disappear, as communities abandon native tongues in favor of English, Mandarin, and Spanish.

Let me ask in all seriousness what actress had better diction than pretty little Patty McCormack in *The Bad Seed* (1956) playing the cute, pig-tailed killer, Rhoda Penmark? The articulation! "Could I have a peanut butter sandwich?" "Everyone knew I wrote the best hand!" "I just don't see how Claude Daigle got that medal." "Give me those shoes *back*!" "I love you, mother." "Good morning, Miss Fern!" Notice how in several places when pronouncing the single word "wrong," she gives full value to the *ng*" — an astonishing feat of perfect diction. It is matchless for brightness, directness, definition, precision, balance, and style, and wonderfully adds to the icy character of Rhoda.

I admire clarity of diction. Audrey Hepburn. Clifton Webb with his saucy disdain. Mohandas Gandhi. Robert Vaughn. Eve Arden. Laurence Olivier. James Mason. Almost all good British actors have good diction. Richard Burton, even when in his cups, had a voice as crisp as the docent voices on the audio guide-phones at the Frick Museum. Mickey Rooney enunciated every word perfectly. I would also point to Lena Horne, Dakota Staton, Brooke Benton, Mavis Rivers, and the husky-voiced Betty Carter. Although she had good diction, Katharine Hepburn tended to bray, even quack and, according to Liberace, everyday "sounds more and more like Donald Duck." Bea Lillie offered us almost a parody of good diction, as you can hear, in her witty song, "There Are Fairies at the Bottom of Our Garden," which another crisp enunciator, Noël Coward, said that he feared performing lest he mistakenly sing instead, "There Are Fairies in the Garden of My Bottom." What about CBS broadcasters Edward R. Murrow and

Richard C. Hottelet? Precise diction. (Compare their phrasing, their elocution, to the crass rubber-lipped excuses for broadcasters bringing you the news on cable television. today.) I would have to give credit to Pat Boone in this department, as well, both in his singing and in his films. That haughty clucking academy-taught rote-snap of Bette Davis or Katharine Hepburn is remarkable but still has a touch of the training-teacher about it, more than a hint of diction class.

Greta Garbo showed an extremely proficient *taught* diction, and, being Swedish born, she did not inherit many of the slovenly pronunciational faults many Americans have. Her shear-shaped, sharply distinct Swedish-American vocalizations in that low, husky voice were strange — she oddly pronounced the word happy as "hab-py" and "want" as "vahnt" — and she even sang her words to a degree. I love the way she said, "Rrrrussia." (Like all Swedes, she pronounced even her name differently: "Grraaaayta Garrboo.") "At vhat eenterval dos he vheeeestle?" "I have beeen memoriizing dees rroooom. In the futurrre, in my memorry, I shall liiive a great deeeaaal in dees rroooom." "I rrememberr. One sweems in a myshterious plue haaze, like the meest on a mountain in Sveeetzerland." She was very chatty, I've read — though she never called anyone buy his or her first name — and it would have been wonderful to be seated next to her as a dinner guest, a *mondaine* person with the patina of the world like Dr. Samuel Johnson and John Aubrey, T. B. Macauley and Oscar Wilde, James Joyce and Winston Churchill, Noël Coward and Cole Porter. In all of his speeches, the Rev. Martin Luther King almost always spoke with good diction. Who but King, it may be asked, to take the time — even bothered — to give full tri-syllabic plenitude to the word, "Catholic" — *Ca-th-o-lic*[8] — as so dramatically he did in his famous "I Have a Dream" speech at the Lincoln Memorial on August 28, 1963? (He always pronounced the word "movement" as though it had three syllables, as well.). Prejudiced though it may appear to sound of me, many celebrities of color like Vernon Jordan, the late Rep. Barbara Jordan (D. Texas), actor James Earl Jones, Eleanor Holmes Norton, Maya Angelou, Sammy Davis, Jr., despite his lisping buzz, and singer Della Reese — but *not* President Barack Obama — all seem to feel the need to *announce* their good diction by overenunciating, overstressing words. Sammy Davis, Jr. as Max Rudin points out in his essay, "Fly Me to the Moon," desperately tried to turn "every number that he sang into a drama of aspiration, to win over the audience, to have it accept him."

Pronunciation in a way has no rules. In *This Gun for Hire* (1942) two actors within a mere several minutes — Robert Preston playing Michael Crane and

---

8    Proper pronunciation is a subject for a full study. In *Casablanca*, for example, when Humphrey Bogart correctly pronounces the word "bourbon" as "borebun" — and not the conventionally heard "burrbun" — he gives us a true lesson in elocution and in elegance.

Olin Howell as Blair Fletcher — pronounce the name of Los Angeles differently, one with a hard G, the other a soft one. I believe it is a "generation thing." Sam Yorty, mayor of Los Angeles from 1961 to 1973, pronounced it with the hard G ("Loss *angle*-ese"). But he was born in 1909 and, as I say, grew up with that pronunciation.

Poetaster Maya Angelou has an almost hectoring and absurd over-pronunciation, as many class-conscious and comically pretentious types do. Angelou on the basis of nothing more than having been given an honorary degree or two always insists that she be introduced in public as "*Dr.* Angelou," in spite of the fact that she was born plain Marguerite Johnson in St. Louis, Missouri, on April 4, 1928. One senses as she speaks, that she is putting on the dog as a sign to the average uncritical dipshit, although it seems hard to believe, that she has wisdom, taste, and discernment, in spite of the fact that she was not only once a calypso singer with an ethnic headwrap but in the hardscrabble Depression-era South worked in a brothel as a pimp, prostitute, and later a low-brow supper-club "chanteuse." It is revealing, after reading Angelou's preposterous, self-inflating memoir, *I Know Why the Caged Bird Sings*, which is full of faux "elevated" and "arch" show-business mumbo jumbo about struggle and selling herself, to find black critic Paul Beatty, author of *Hokum: An Anthology of African-American Humor*, writing, "It would be 10 years before I would touch another book written by an African-American. As my wiser sister Anna says, 'Never trust folks like Maya Angelou and James Earl Jones who grew up in Walla Walla, Mississippi and Boogaloo, Arkansas and speak with British accents.'"

Comically, I have always secretly harbored the sneaking belief whenever I hear the Winchester, Virginia songbird, Patsy Cline sing "Walkin' After Midnight" — which she pronounces as "*minnight*" at every mention — that the departed lover she is looking for in vain probably left the poor thing because of her *bad diction*!

As I say, the late Sammy Davis, Jr. who, although he did learn from Sinatra to pronounce sung words after some study, still rather defectively buzzed all Ss with his tongue. But there were others. Old rock 'n' roller Jerry Lee Lewis could never repress that peculiar wet slur of his that, along with his mumbling Ferriday, Louisiana accent, often turns music lyrics into unreconstructed, indecipherable fugues and wails and trills. The perdurable Tony Bennett, still singing at the age of 86, has always had a relatively poor pronunciation problem, full degrees worse by far than any other of the slurring but hearty nightclub crooners like Tony Martin and Johnny Rosselli, Don Cornell (born Luigi Varlaro in the Bronx) and Russ Colombo, Dick Haymes and Jack Jones. From the very beginning Bennett was frequently off-key when he sang, a matter from what I have seen that is obviously not only linked to a singer not having the capacity to hear acutely or even correctly — hazarding in consequence the chance to fumble the values of both notes *and* words — but also in vocalizing which is, after all, only singing speech. It may sound faintly absurd, but Bennett even at his best has a problem with vowels, finds it difficult to comprehend or negotiate what vowels actually do or are supposed to do or, I don't know, should represent in any given word. He also has trouble with consonants. For example, notice how when singing, "If I Ruled The World" or "I Wanna Be Around," he rarely pronounces final Ds or Ts or Gs — a thlipsis problem that I would argue detracts from his style. He also has particular trouble with his Ch's and Sh's. "Darn that one chack" — one track — "mind of mine," he sings in "Darn that Dream." "You'll see the sun come *s-ining* through," he sings. Or "I know I'll go from rags to ri*tzes*." Or "But now I know your heart is *s-ackled* to a memory." Listen closely the next time you hear him belt out, "The Best is Yet to Come," when, singing to his lover, he refers to her "tsarms" — charms — and assures her, "We're going to drain the cup jjiiyy [dry!]." It is depressingly irremediable. The morning *faaarg* — fog — "may *tzill* the air," we hear Bennett sing in his signature song, "I Left My Heart in San Francisco," where in any public venue he stands forth belting out with a spread-armed, gusto-powerful conclusion *alla cantante Napolitano*, "The golden sun will *tssiiiiine* for me." Trust me, it is there. Listen to the man sing. Depressing as it may be to point out, had Tony Benedetto (Italian for "well spoken"!) been one of the Ephraimites (cf. Judges 12: 5 & 6) — suffering from the same vocal problem, they could not pronounce the SH in the Hebrew word *shibboleth* (they said, "sibboleth") — he would have been summarily slain.

"*See* gets too hungry for dinner at eight," we hear him sing even when at the advanced age of 85 he recorded his duet of "The Lady is a Tramp" at the Avatar Studios on West 53rd Street with the splendiferous 28-year-old Lady Gaga — brilliant voice — and "*See* likes the green grass under her *soos*/ what can I lose?" Hey, ya gotta love it. Tony can still handle the high notes, you have to admit. Writer Gay Talese in the *New Yorker* retails a story that Bennett once told him. "I remember Sinatra once asked Pavarotti, 'How do you sing a soft high note?' and Pavarotti replied, 'You keep-a your mouth closed.'"

Johnny Mathis, like Jerry Vale, sounds as if he has a palpable speech-defect by twi-noting words in a feeble attempt to give virtually every word a trill for "double-value." It is something of an Italian thing, a variation of the so-called "Rubini sob" — and it makes almost every song he recorded sound like a cracked record. Did he learn this vocal maneuver from Nat "King" Cole who also employed it quite often? (Mathis does it all the time, but infinitely more successfully.) Listen to the early records of young Nat "King" Cole: it could be Johnny Mathis himself, their voices were so very much alike. An interesting topic suggests itself here. Voice doubles. The Parallel Palate. Ever stop to think about it? George Bush, Sr. sounds exactly like the late actor Will Geer. LBJ with his raspy, ache-drawling voice sounded exactly like the old cowboy, Hopalong Cassidy. Then throw in moods! When LBJ was in high dudgeon he sounded like the orotund actor Eugene Pallette — see *My Man Godfrey* — with a deep, sonorous, rasping, fat angrification. Cowboy star Gene Autry's flattish, twangy, western Tioga, Texas/ Oklahoma voice was almost the literal duplicate of Harry Truman's, the man from Independence, Mo. Clark Gable and Dwight D. Eisenhower could be twins as far as their voices went. FDR when speaking sounded like hearty, jut-jawed actor Eddie Mayehoff of *That's My Boy* (1951) fame, the film-comedy in which that splendid character actor winningly played the overbearing, hyperathletic, domineering ex-football-star father of nattering nerd, Jerry Lewis. Gene Kelly sounded almost to a T like the late actor John Garfield. The late Andy Rooney of CBS sounded *quam proxime* like the bumbling character actor Henry Travers who played Clarence the Angel in Frank Capra's *It's a Wonderful Life*. Suave Kent Smith who starred in the 1942 film, *Cat People* sounds just like George Sanders. Governor Mitt Romney (R-Mass.) sounds like — and to a degree even resembles — the actors John Gavin and Tyrone Power, all handsome, resplendently wooden, inelastic. It is amazing how much Herbert Marshall sounded like Ronald Coleman. Actor Pierce Brosnan sounds like James Mason. Steve McQueen often sounded like Robert Mitchum. And Tommy Tune, Texas born, has the same voice as that on the MTA cars in New York City: "Stand clear of the closing *doorrrs*, please!"

There are of course many men whose voices are arguably unique, one-of-a-kind. The book of Acts in the New Testament reflects that it was written by a physician, probably Luke, simply from his vocabulary. Notice how much St. Paul comments in his short letters about work. (Converts were to earn their living quietly.) Paul's repeated use of the word "joy" in the book of Philippians characterizes him. (The book also contains no Old Testament quotations, since few Jews lived in that city.) What we discern of delivery, emphasis, vocabulary, tone, and topical circumstance is telling. There is a distinct literary style of Hebrew in the book of Ruth. It is curious, indeed paradoxical, that one of the most Jewish letters in the New Testament, the book of James, should have been written by an author apparently so much at home in the Greek language. Some unduplicable contemporary voices that come to mind are actors Strother Martin, Andy Devine, Arnold Stang, Eric ("We are Bates, sir") Blore, Al Jolson, Edward Everett Horton, Peter Lorre, Lee Marvin, Judy Holiday with her complaints-department voice ,Orson Welles, Don Knotts, Fanny Brice, Lionel Stander, Franklin Pangborn, W.C. Fields, Jimmy Durante — it sounded as if a potato were stuck in his windpipe — Frank Morgan, George Zucco, Lionel Atwill, Gertrude Lawrence, Cary Grant, ol' Casey Stengel, Winston Churchill, Jackie Kennedy, George Jones, comic Jackie Mason, Scarlett Johanssen, Carol Channing whose voice may be described as something like a cross between a Smurf and Chihuahua-like yelps, and although actor Ronald Colman had a voice as smooth as butter it seems unduplicable. There was Andy Warhol with that weird, flat, uncaring, robotic voice of his. One can understand why Buster Keaton, one of the two or three greatest stars of the silent picture era, never did well in talkies — he had a dull, leaden, bronchial voice, no matter what he said, one replete with an artless and unmagical honk. Was that why he was fired from MGM in 1933, only to be rehired sixteen years later for *In the Good Old Summertime* (1949), playing a negligible character? Drew Barrymore's voice ("Haow did ya-ou become a wedding thin*ger*?") is sheer Valspeak, replete with all of the characteristics of that sociolect, like "totally," "like," "whatever," "as if," her sentences spoken as if questions using a high rising terminal. Gwyneth Paltrow's nasal, queen bee voice is the very definition of vacuity, but when she puts on that smug, overweening, and airy English accent — she is a great hand for lording it over everybody ("I had my first bowl of gazpacho when I was fifteen in Spain, and the impression it made was a lasting one," she writes in her cookbook) — she comes cross as nothing less than detestable. How about the very peculiar voices of people in film like Jimmy Stewart, W. C. Fields, Joe E. Brown, Percy Helton, James Cagney, Elisha Cook, Jr. — Jack Nicholson not only sounds like the eccentric loner and Hollywood film fall-guy, Cook, but looks almost exactly like him — Ethel Merman, and neck-veined mesomorph (and, to me, vastly overrated) Kirk Douglas, with that weird throttling throat creak of his? I loved the hoarse voice of Claudia Cardinale, the Italian Tunisian actress and iconic sex symbol of the 1960s. And who else on earth ever sounded like Neil Young, whose voice with its twang resembles the harmonica he often plays, full of quivering movements like a Canadian aspen? There is something in it like cherry and chocolate making a Black Forest cake.

Certain voices are darker, more morbid than rainclouds. British actor Henry Daniell, with his haughty demeanor, dry, sardonic delivery, and near-Satanic, pulled facial features — the perfect screen "gentleman villain" — had a cold, pitiless voice in which diction *itself* seemed to pose a terrifying threat, the iron pronunciation of the scold. Rev. Al Sharpton with that muddy, thuggish delivery of his makes his every utterance sound like a crude threat, clouded, cryptic, and dark. When the bloviating Jesse Jackson, Sr. speaks, which for me is far too often, it is always an explosive malaphonia — a doggy uglification of unidentifiable grunts — which sounds as if he is not so much talking as actually chewing a rag. John Malkovich, the bald, cross-eyed actor, critic Rex Reed said, had a voice like an unbroken dial-tone. Would you call Gabby Hayes's voice breadcrumby or gummy or snuffy? There was that crazy carping bark of Northern Ireland's Rev. Ian Paisley in the heat of one of his disagreeably flaming rants. I had the dubious honor of seeing that man up close and personal in the summer of 1965 looking crazy as a shithouse rat while tooting his Orange flute on the City Hall steps in Belfast, Ireland: "Five tarms fufty yars of fulthy phusercal abuse fer our Prutersternt fa-erth" and "The Cartholicks? Have ye nart hard abite ert? Thare's no debeart thut thy're tryun' to run us dine in the vurry straits of Lundundarra! Way well knoo what thy're like, doon't way? Malarkey from the joomp, thuh-day, thuh-night, thu-morrah! What's the craic here? Duh all o them uglah, bog-trotting Carthelick hallions thunk I came up the Lagan in a bubble? Ut ain't Christuan — *und ut ain't notral!*"? No, but Paisley's honks were perfectly natural, right? It has to be incontestably the ugliest accent on the face of this planet. I have to say no human being has a more disagreeable speech pattern than the odd Golf Channel broadcaster David Feherty, a shirty little Ulsterman, born in Bangor, up in the Six Counties, whose every spoken sentence — always roosterishly delivered like a rising trademark that characterizes the voice of everybody from his region — ends as a loony question and always on the same note in mid-air. I hate to sound catty, but as John Adams said, "Facts are stubborn things."

I do not believe anyone could ever find actual voice-matches for, say, such oddly or uniquely spoken people as actor Trevor Howard, Liberace, boxer Mike Tyson, Wallace Beery, Rep. Barney Frank, Henry Travers, William Demarest, Vincent Gardenia, Alfred Hitchcock, Slim Pickens, Lee Marvin, Mr. T, Wallace Shawn, PBS's Garrison Keillor with his insinuating down-comforter voice, proffering (in the words of Prof. Stuart Hyde) "an intimacy that makes you accept gossip," Marjorie Main, Boris Karloff, Helen Kane ("Betty Boop"), the growly actress June Allyson, Marlon Brando, Chill Wills, Richard Simmons, Bette Davis, Louis Armstrong — his voice actually matched his trumpet, listen to both in his cool version of "Stardust" — Gloria Grahame, curmudgeonly Paul Lynde, Eartha Kitt, or even Gatling-gun-talking-people like film director Martin Scorsese, the Rosalind Russell of *His Girl Friday*, or the FBI's J. Edgar Hoover whose staccato speech back in the day was so machine-gun fast that he was the despair of all of his stenographers. (An early stutterer, he maniacally learned to overcompensate.)

Jane Russell had an odd speech anomaly. It was not a lisp but something like a dento-labial buzz. In the dreadful *The Outlaw* (1943), in which she appears as the vixen Rio McDonald, booby-front in her suspension-bridge bra and accompanying her every smoky appearance the irritating strings of the first-movement of Tchaikovsky's "Symphony No. 6 in B Minor, Opus 74, 'Pathétique'" as a moody backdrop. Throughout the film, the 19-year-old sexpot monotonously utters lines like "But you've been so fsick" and "You're not fsatisfied?" and "He difsappeared in the mountainfs." Her conspicuous jaw seemed to accommodate — indeed may have been the occasion of — her way of speech. To duplicate her scumbled Ss, try pronouncing the words "breasts" with your underlip ending in front of your top front teeth. Russell was big in her day. In 1950, she made a single for Columbia, "Kisses and Tears," with Frank Sinatra and the Modernaires. *Gentlemen Prefer Blondes* (1955) was her big smash, but later she also did a solo nightclub act and recorded torch ballads, Gospel, even spoken-word performances. ("These days I am a teetotal, mean-spirited, right-wing, narrow-minded, conservative Christian bigot, but not a racist," she frankly declared in 2003.)

Actress Kay Francis had a speech impediment. It was closer to a lisp than anything although she was known around the backlots of Hollywood á la Baba Wawa as "the Wavishing Kay Fwancis." Rumor has it that dialogue was carefully tailored to conceal this small defect, but the imperious director Ernst Lubitsch flatly refused to rewrite any of the key scenes in *Trouble In Paradise*, not only one of the best films of 1932 but "as close to perfection as anything I have ever seen," according to critic Dwight MacDonald, and if you listen closely you can hear traces of Francis's lisp. She sings with Harry Green, "I'm Isidore the Toreador" in a comic sketch in *Showgirls on Parade* (1930), by the way. Nor should one forget the lovely Marlene Dietrich who, with something of an Elmer Fudd problem, always pronounced — almost fetchingly —Ws for Rs. You can hear it in *Destry Rides Again* (1939) in which she introduced the song, "The Boys in the Backroom," singing,

> And when I die, don't pay the pweacher
> For speaking of my glowy and my fame
> Just see what the boys in the backroom will have,
> And tell them I sighed,
> And tell them I cried,
> And tell them I died of the same."

but it is effective, and she was a true star. As she once declaimed, "Gwamour" — glamour, not grammar — "is what I sell, it's my stock in trade."

For odd, endearing voices, the British are a treasure. Who could ever forget banjo-boy George Formby with his cricket voice? Or George Robey, the tubby music-hall star with his dark eyebrows and heavy emphatic voice? Or Ernest Thesiger with his spinster's voice? (Somerset Maugham once responded to Thesiger's inquiry about why he wrote no parts for him with the quip "But I am always writing parts for you, Ernest. The trouble is that somebody called Gladys Cooper will insist on playing them.") Or dapper cockney Stanley Holloway? Or Lonnie Donnegan and his skiffle-group snuffle?

Surely one of the weirdest voices ever heard — impossible to describe, except that it was a combination of goose honk, donkey bray, and the strained, incipient sounds of a case of strangulation — was the actress Jean Arthur's. There was more than just a husky pitch to the voice, for one could also detect a hint of a sexual catch at the back of the throat that suggested she was stifling or repressing something that couldn't come out. I suspect there was a mechanical box inserted in her larynx!

Eric Blore, Edward Everett Horton, Clifton Webb, Nathan Lane, Boy George, Elton John, Michael Stipe, and Robert Preston in the role of Carroll "Toddy" Todd in the movie, *Victor/ Victoria* (1982). What is with that gay sibilance? "Sometimes Jack would walk through a pack of gays, all sibilance and jingling and prancing, as if Santa's reindeer had been watered with champagne and gone off course," writes Edmund White in *Jack Holmes & His Friend*. One can assert that homosexuals try to sound like each other, simply choose to do so, with that stereotypical mix of sibilance and speed that makes so many of them sound like 13-year-old girls — the elevated phrasing, the variable pitch contours, the exaggerated breathiness, the mock shock — but what can possibly explain the sameness of that sibilant lisp in so many different places, how it has traveled all around the world as such an identifiably gay vocal signifier? Is there in fact a generic "gay voice"? Is it necessarily higher? Sweeter? More decorative and precious? Is a lisp always involved? There is often found in the speaker what has been called the "curse of the sibilant S" — a gay give-way, arguably. Paul Lynde, the brilliant character who not only gave us *Bewitched*'s wacky Uncle Arthur but also introduced the world to caftans and man-purses, is a good example of the gushing invert with all of that sardonic fluff of his and hilarious, nose-wrinkling fruitiness. Asked on TV's *Hollywood Squares*, "In *Alice in Wonderland*, who kept crying 'I'm late, I'm late?'" Paul Lynde with a limp wrist replied, "Alice, and her mother is sick about it!" Gay males do pronounce sibilants (*s, z, sh,* and the like) in a distinctive way by adding more sibilation, hissing, or stridency, a phenomenon phonologists call "assibilation." "I so badly want to de-ess myself," a gay friend of mine once saturninely remarked. "You know, the pitch trick — come in from the top?" The dangers of stereotyping should be avoided, of course. It is certainly not the case that one trait indicates a personality. "Gay men are not the only group whose members sometimes speak with assibilation. A habit of assibilating 'stops' like *t* and *d* is also a prominent feature of Quebecois French, for example, and the source of much derision from national French speakers," noted Joe Clark in *The Economist* in 1995. He goes on to observe,

> A word like *térébentine* ("turpentine") in certain Quebec French dialects is pronounced something like tsérébentsine. Many New Yorkers of all persuasions, and some American Jews, also assibilate in ways similar to Quebec French or stereotypical gay speech. Moreover, gay men who speak with what a North American newsreader would consider an "accent" — such as British, Australian, or even Texan gays — rarely assibilate at all. Nailing down just what makes a gay voice gay is as vague and slippery as human sexuality itself.

I would venture to guess that much of it is relatable to hormonal levels or chemical changes in similar ways between individuals (of either gender) being attracted to the same potential sex partner. This may have a deeper basis in the motivators driving observably favorable behavior toward potential mates being determined through natural selection throughout time. In other words, straight males may prefer higher pitched voices in their partners. It is instinctual for gay males, therefore, to have higher pitched voices more often than straight." Still, how strange the universality of a single such voice.

Many singers sound alike. Voices can bear an uncanny resemblance to each other, have you ever noticed? Is it the case that we too often look for the variation rather than the rule? Or is the pronouncement correct, as Ralph Waldo Emerson has it in his *Compensation,* that "Nature hates monopolies and exceptions"?

Frank Sinatra and Montgomery Clift, when speaking, sounded exactly the same. Ray Bolger and Buster Keaton — close your eyes and listen — could have shared the same vocal chords. Gene Kelly sounded like Fredric March. Martin Sheen sounds like the late actor and singer Gordon Macrae. Senator Hillary Clinton in her brassiness sounds like the older Ginger Rogers, both with a kind of sharp, snarping, midwestern, almost nagging wise-assery in their way of speaking. Wallace Beery toward the end of his life spoke almost exactly like the butt-plugged, bowl-shaped '30s actor Eugene Pallette who could anchor a scene just by walking downstairs and had the gravelly voice of a cement mixer, not unlike Louis — that is Lou*is* (he hated to be called "Louie") — Armstrong.

How is it that so many human voices in timber and tone seem also to *resemble* one another? Sportscaster Vin Scully who has a voice like a can-opener sounds like snipe-nosed Bud Abbott, the often angry, barking straightman-half of the comedy team, Abbott and Costello. Billionaire David Rockefeller sounds exactly like *The Simpsons'* wealthy skin-flint Montgomery Burns. Former Speaker of the House, Newt Gingrich, a man named for a lizard, sounds exactly like the late, double-chinned actor, Walter Slezak. Bette Davis, voice-wise, could of course have been Tallulah Bankhead. When he spoke, Norman Mailer sounded exactly like the late Trappist monk Thomas Merton, the celebrated poet and theologian who frankly sounded a lot like both Gene Hackman and the young Babe Ruth. NBC Reporter Mike Taibbi sounds exactly like former CBS anchorman Dan Rather — they could be clones. Actor Tom Cruise sounds like the late pop-singer Ricky Nelson. The great Boston Red Sox slugger Ted Williams sounded like a cross between actors Gregory Peck, Robert Ryan, and John Wayne, except that Williams was a true military hero, an intrepid fighter-pilot who defended his country in both the Second World War and the Korean conflict and was wounded, the exact opposite of the hypocritical, flag waving, starboard-leaning phony John Wayne who as a matter of fact spent not a single minute of his waking life in the United States Armed Forces during World War II with one exception, and that took place one afternoon greeting a handful of troops in 1943 in the safety of Guam into and out of which the reactionary actor was flown, under full cover of military protection, like a rich overindulged pasha.

The parallels can be uncanny. North Dakota Senator and 1972 presidential candidate George McGovern sounded exactly like the campy pianist, Liberace, both of whom in their speech had more than a touch of that of Dennis Weaver of TV's *Gunsmoke* fame. Liberace had not only had a wheedling effeminate voice but also a false, insinuating wink. His wink was almost as phony as Jimmy Stewart's in *It's a Wonderful Life*: his contrived winks — once at the black maid, Annie, while he's eating with his Pop, then at the end when he says, "That's right, that's right. Attaboy, Clarence!" Stewart's — and he was an *actor*? — are not so much winks as grotesque eye-yawns, artificial and completely manufactured.

There are also people, I swear, who look like they sound (Bob Seger = shaggy, Barbra Streisand = snouty, etc.), and even people of course who look like their *names* (Wilfred Brimley, Percy Kilbride, Babe Ruth, Primo Carnera) — in the field of psychology, it is known as "anchoring," and it can be applied in many different ways, such as associating someone's name with his or her physical appearance. Names, it has also been asserted, tend to be associated with certain facial features — Roys have rounder faces than Tims, I feel. Am I mistaken in also finding, by the way, that all Roys are fat? We would all agree, I'm sure, that such a thing as fat voices exist, people with that identifiably lardy "I've Just Eaten an Eclair" sound in the throat, very like that of that jelly-belly cartoon blimp Peter Griffin on *Family Guy* ("But where are those good old fashioned values/ on which we used to rely?") It is more than merely fruity and plump. There is a swollen, thick-set porcinity to it, a viscosity that suggests both stubbornness and a kind of unbudging stupidity. Burl Ives had one. So does that beachball-shaped, dugong-soft, right-wing broadcaster/ boob Rush Limbaugh on the EIB Network, his voice an over-resonant, filled-out, fish-oil-coated, swollen sound, at once fleshy and elephantine. (You do not have to listen closely either to notice that there is even a plodding corpulence to his theme song — I picture him slowly wobbling forward, shambling, to that effortful beat like a dumb, bewildered rhinoceros.) Fat-voiced speakers tend to have plap-plap lips like Charles Laughton and Edward G. Robinson and Orson Welles. Other fat voices: B.B. King, Dr. Hook, Wolfman Jack, Sydney Greenstreet, and Charles Coburn. I would also add Kate Smith, Mama Cass, Oprah Winfrey, and Queen Latifah. Do you happen to remember Tone Lōc singing "Funky Cold Medina"? That was another fat voice, at least to my mind, an obese, nasal, echoing, well, croak in his case, that I would put somewhere between Jack Benny's valet Rochester and a constipated bullfrog.

B-actors Whit Bissell and Hugh Marlowe not only sounded but even looked alike. What was my surprise, therefore, to find them both appearing together in the very same movie, *The Birdman of Alcatraz* (1962)! Why not throw into this particular mix those 1950s actors Richard Anderson and Richard Carlson, both of whom not only looked like but sounded like Hugh Marlowe and Whit Bissell — they always played dry, earnest, white, tweedy, buttoned-up, overly serious administrators and owlish cranks. As a matter of flat fact, both Bissell and Carlson appeared together in *Creature from the Black Lagoon* (1954)! Actor Donald Sutherland in every phase of every emotion — close your eyes — could be the actor Raymond Massey. Hopalong Cassidy's raspy voice had the same grating sound of the actor Victor Jory's. When he played a grumpy old bastard, as invariably he always did, in *The Fugitive Kind* (1939), Jory had the voice of an actual *grackle*. Didn't former *Tonight* Show host, bland Jack Paar and actor Bob Cummings sound alike with that same simpering smugness? Microsoft CEO Bill Gates sounds — and almost looks — exactly like that late goofy, bold-nosed, sandy-haired actor Sterling Holloway. Comedian Lou Costello, of Abbott and Costello fame, sounded sputteringly like the vaudeville comic, Rags Ragland. *Tonight* show-host Jay Leno sounds like ex-New York City Mayor Rudolph Guiliani, both of whom have the same lisp. With his braying and grig-like Leprecaunesque nasality, the thrusting Watergate felon and neo-fascist mediocrity and ex-talk show-host G. Gordon Liddy, sounds not only like a drunken version of the late actor Edward G. Robinson who sounded just like *The Simpsons'* cartoon police chief, Chief Wiggum, but with his inarticulate hemming, hawing and old geezerish dithering — er, er, um, ah! — almost a perfect verbal duplicate of the double-chinned actress from the 1950s, Marion Lorne, who seemed to be perpetually puzzled and perplexed!

The Three Stooges' Moe Howard sounded like James Cagney. Actors William Bendix and Jack Weston with their bunny lisps sounded as if they were twin brothers. Mickey Rourke sounded like tough Leo Gorcey, the Dead End Kid. Columnist Art Buchwald sounded like potato-faced comedian Buddy Hackett. British actors Michael York and James Mason shared the same sinusoidal voice and British diction. Singer Pat Boone sounded like '50s cowboy-actor Audie Murphy. William Demarest — close your eyes — could have literally been his contemporary actor James Gleason as far as similar voices go. Audible twins!

Eddie Bracken sounded like Jimmy Stewart. The poet James Dickey sounded like Orson Welles. Tony Randall sounded like Jack Paar. Both of them sounded like Ray Bolger. With his nasal New York accent, radio shock-jock Howard Stern sounds exactly like Alan Alda. The late motor-mouth radio gossip Walter Winchell sounded to a T like James Cagney. John Dean, President Nixon's lawyer and Watergate whistle-blower — he has the very same lisp and deep timber voice — sounds like Humphrey Bogart. Actor Noah Beery, one of the stars of the western, *Red River* (1948), sounded like Kirk Douglas. Quietly alias-dipping, many celebrities — actors, movie stars, television comedians — will often "try on," have often tried on, other voices, other sounds, other acts. "Sid Caesar was just an imitation of Danny Kaye as was comedian Dick Shawn," impressionist Will Jordan told the critic Gerald Nachman for his seminal book on 1950s comedians, *Seriously Funny.*

> Rickles is really Jack E. Leonard and Milton Berle. Bullwinkle was an actor imitating Red Skelton, just as Mel Blanc was imitating Art Carney as Barney Rubble, and as Alan Reed was imitating Jackie Gleason. Top Cat was Arnold Stang imitating Phil Silvers.

"I do Bob Hope all the time," says Woody Allen, who, when you think of it, is the constant coward Hope definitely was, scoring series of one-liners about his fears with the same old desperate metric quips from the side of the mouth, a stuttering rhetoric of nerd fear and comic self-deprecation that sounds less like the same voice than an actual dialect. Alec Guinness' walk was an exact duplication of Stan Laurel's dorky saunter. Jack Benny walked like Eve Arden. Robert Mitchum, in motion, had the same sort of crab-list that John Wayne had, a sort of odd, imbalanced, pre-encumbered slow slog trot. Regarding peculiar walks, both Charlton Heston and Dustin Hoffman — look some time — have weird legs of an almost wind-up character that never seem to allow either of them to move without jerking.

Are voices as fully variable as faces? Head shapes? Fingerprints? Or has there been an infinite variety of them down through the ages as unique to an individual as his or her DNA? It was often pointed out that when big, stocky, red-headed Mormon leader Brigham Young, successor to founder Joseph Smith, opened his mouth to speak, he was said to sound exactly — uncannily — like his charismatic predecessor. "Many in the crowd rushed the platform to see if their Mormon prophet had risen from the dead, only to be further mystified by the same 'supernatural radiance' that had enveloped Smith, now illuminating Young," notes Sally Denton in *American Massacre: The Tragedy at Mountain Meadows*.

Although the doomed flyer Amelia Earhart with her Atchison, Kansas twang sounded very much like the novelist Carson McCullers and Deborah Kerr like Anna Neagle and Miss Elizabeth Taylor with that insistent braying nasality of hers like the actress Carroll Baker, a case can be made, a sexist one if you insist, that women more or less tend to sound essentially the same. Betsy Drake sounded like June Allyson. And, well, Cindy Lauper does sound like the '30s actress, pert lemon-faced Una Merkel, OK? Both also sound very much like the late evangelist Tammy Faye Bakker. There are other exceptions. Television reporter Maria Shriver with that quavery, clipped, high-pitched, neurasthenic-sounding voice of hers channels the late actress Katharine Hepburn to a degree. I have often felt that actress Claire Trevor sounded like Tallulah Bankhead. The low-brow grating voice of Shirley Booth was Thelma Ritter's exactly. Lucille Ball sounded like Ginger Rogers. Mia Farrow sounds like Joan Fontaine — and also, listen closely, very like Deborah Kerr. Former CNN reporter Campbell Brown sounded like actress Jane Russell. Fat Rosie O'Donnell sounds of course exactly like the late Betty Hutton. Actress Lili Taylor sounds exactly like *Today* Show's Ann Curry. But surely no one could possibly duplicate the inscrutable voices of Jean Arthur, Marjorie Main, Jane Darwell, Jennifer Tilly, Fran Drescher, Julie Kavner, Gloria Grahame.

What about cross-sex voicings? I have mentioned that the Watergate burglar and sometime talk-show host, G. Gordon Liddy with his inarticulate, senile stammerings sounds like that chubby old ditsy actress from the old television show, Mr. Peepers, befuddled stuttering Marion Lorne. Didn't actress Bea Arthur sound like Lloyd Nolan and Steve McQueen who had a weird febrility touch to his voice sound like a woman? An eerie rain-in-the-voice sound connects Donald Rumsfeld to Glenn Ford. It is weird sound. Listen to Johnny Cash, Leo Gorcey, or Cliff Robertson. When they talk, you hear tears.

The novelist James M. Cain who happened to hate Joan Crawford's performance in the film-adaptation to his noir novel, *Mildred Pierce*, said that Pat Nixon, President Nixon's wife, who often, under stress, had a certain clipped and unhappy strain in her speech, would have been the ideal voice for his off-putting lean character. "Her voice is Mildred's," Cain once declared, who felt he had erroneously made his character Mildred "too smart," and as a result, he told David McCullough, "she struck people as being heroic. She was not heroic; she was just plain common." Then how about the pop-group, ABBA, with their Rote English? Those were voices that when speaking English were as odd as a rigid robot's! Was that why Greta Garbo, another Swede, after speaking for the first time on the silver screen in *Anna Christie*, supposedly burst into tears at the sound of her own voice?

A voice can be bad, but when it is conjoined, effortfully, to a song — look out. Needless to say, there are some truly hideous songs. Dastardly ones. But how about singers that as soon as they open their voices should be immediately consigned to the lower *bolgias* of dark Plutonian Hades? Did you ever hear *Star Trek*'s William Shatner sing "Lucy in the Sky With Diamonds"? Or Morris Albert sing "Feelings"? Or Paul McCartney sing "With A Little Help"? Or Willie Nelson sing "The Beer Barrel Polka"? Or Helen Reddy sing, "You and Me Against the World"? Or The Sex Pistols sing "God save the Queen"? Or Sid Vicious sing "My Way"? Or Barbra Streisand sing "Stoney End"? Or Cher sing "You Haven't Seen the Last of Me?" I would seriously rate the singers in the above group lower than the actor Peter Ustinov's intentionally parodic vocalization in the epic Biblical film, *Quo Vadis* (1951). Playing the part of the loony Emperor Nero, Ustinov musically apostrophizes the burning city of Rome as he plucks his lyre, singing — moaning — "O Lambent Flames, O Force Divine," a crazy megalomaniacal bit of high camp that surely has to be one of the great larks on celluloid. (He was nominated for an Oscar for his role in that movie.) In his very readable autobiography, *Dear Me*, Ustinov recounts how the runty director Mervyn LeRoy, by way of preparational direction for Ustinov's film-role, had the actor sent for singing lessons to the Rome Opera House where an overinvigorated Italian "professor" there dramatically (and madly) directed him to "breathe with the forehead," "think with the diaphragm," and "sing with the eye."

Erroll Flynn in *Montana* (1950) plays the guitar and sings, "Reckon I'm in Love" which turns into a duet with Alexis Smith, although frankly he more or less talks his lyrics rather than sings them. He also sings, "That's What You Jolly Well Get" from the 1943 star-studded film *Thank Your Lucky Stars*, and here he does a brilliant music hall turn, complete with derby and mustache and dance maneuvers.

Rosie O'Donnell got Hillary Clinton to sing "The Telephone Song" from the musical, *Bye Bye Birdie* — "Hi Nancy, Hi Ursula/ what's the story, morning glory/ what's the tale, nightingale," etc. — on the Rosie O'Donnell Show on February 3, 1997 just shortly after her husband's second inauguration that year. Wot larks! You can also hear Hillary Clinton massacre the words to the national anthem on *YouTube*, singing along to it as a candidate in Iowa back on April 12, 2008. What is notable is not so much that her singing voice sounds like dish-water gurgling through a sink but that her efforts are a political ploy. My only thought as to those performances are those of the quarry stone in Michelangelo's "The Sculpture of Night in the Medici Chapels:" "*Non veder, non sentir m'è gran ventura; Però non mi destar, deh!*" (It is my great fortune not to see nor hear. Please do not wake me up!)

But even Elvis Presley could kill you. Have you ever heard him sing "Glory, Glory, Hallelujah"? Hurting! I blame the media — they *make* you listen, they *make* you remember it all over again and again. Elvis Presley's songs from the movie *Frankie and Johnny* are intolerable (all but one): "Petunia, the Gardener's Daughter," "What Every Woman Lives For," and, "Chesay," especially, the latter memorably presented by The King wearing a Ruritanian costume to the accompaniment of Hungarian fiddles and tambourines. I would also randomly throw in, simply for the accelerating destruction of Elvis's oeuvre, a few others — "Ito Eats" (*Blue Hawaii*), "There's No Room To Rhumba in A Sports Car" and "Yoga Is As Yoga Does" (*Easy Come, Easy Go*), "A Dog's Life" (*Paradise, Hawaiian Style*) — he sings this song to four dirty slavering dogs, who end up barking — "Dirty, Dirty Feeling" (*Tickle Me*), "Harem Holiday" (*Harum Scarum*), "The Bullfighter was A Lady" (*Fun in Acapulco*), "Party" (*Loving You*), and, among others, the almost unbearably offensive "Old Macdonald" (*Double Trouble*) — remember that Vegasesque Sinatra version? — complete with animal noises and chickens clucking. Custom is a tyrant, as they say. It makes you want to cry. This from the man who gave us "That's Alright, Mama," "I Want You, I Need You, I Love You," "It Hurts Me," and even that brilliant diamond from the movies, the great exception, "If I Can Dream" from *Live A Little, Love A Little*, written by W. Earl Brown. Let us pause a minute, before moving on, to recall with contumely several of the musical grapeheads — pure hacks — who got rich writing most of Elvis's unfathomably bad movie numbers, Sid Tepper and Roy C. Bennett, for two, and Bill Giant and Bernie Baum, for two more — even Jerry Lieber and Mike Stoller provided a lot of rubbish — who with sheer hustle, an almost unhygienic greed, non-existent talent, and bad karma murdered both the man and the medium for unending decades. As the late Whitney Houston would snap, "Hell to the no!" — always her coldly emphatic if befogged way of expressing displeasure.

I would choose *It Happened at the World's Fair* (1963), directed by Norman Taurog, as the nadir of Elvis movies. The screenplay, written by TV sitcom hacks, Si Rove and Seaman Jacobs, is even for the early 1960s truly beyond brain-dead, stupid as mud, having the King, looking almost as ferret-faced as Journey's Steve Perry, zip about with stove-polish-black hair, canary-yellow make-up, and winkle-picker shoes while ogling the buttocks of every female in Seattle, exchanging inane quips with his buddy

> Danny Burke: "You didn't tell me she was put together like that!
> Mike Edwards: "Can't you tell a nice girl when you meet one?"
> Danny Burke: "Oh no! Now he's a cub scout. What happened, somebody steal your wolf whistle?"

and singing ten sapless, watery songs, among them, "Relax," "Cotton Candy Land," "Beyond the Bend," all headed for the RCA shitpile.

Americans dumbly lined up for all those bad Elvis movies all through the 1960s and 1970s, the kind of poor thick-headed deludinoids who in their Pollyanna-ish way think that Goldman Sachs is the Make-A-Wish Foundation.

A special award should be given to them. Let us call it the Norman Taurog Award. Taurog was the witless, avaricious hack who directed Elvis Presley in more of his Hollywood movies than any other director — nine, starting with *G.I. Blues* in 1960. One year after completing *Live a Little, Love a Little*, Taurog went blind — was that a cosmic punishment? Among some of Elvis's worst movie songs are "Do the Clam," "The Fort Lauderdale Chamber of Commerce," "Yoga is as Yoga Does," "He's Your Uncle Not Your Dad" from *Speedway* — a movie singularly cursed with some real clunkers — "Clambake," "[There's] No Room to Rhumba in a Sports Car," and "Who Needs Money." Will Friedwald singles out "All that I Am" from *Spinout* and "Almost in Love" from *Live a Little, Love a Little* as quality cuts and actually raves about "Everything but Love" from *Clambake*, stating — overstating, I feel — "It's worth at least half a dozen of the three-chord rock numbers he was cutting 10 years earlier." Six songs were recorded for the 1962 film, *Follow That Dream*, and Presley, upset, insisted that one of the most reprehensible duds, "Sound Advice," be omitted from release when it came time to assemble a soundtrack. As usual, Elvis was ignored. Either that or he acceded out of indifference. Both often happened. In any case, "Sound Advice" would be placed on the compilation *Elvis for Everyone* — or *Everyone Undiscerning*, if you will. It is truly the pits to have to see the King of Rock 'n' Roll capitulating to the bland insipidities of Hollywood in 1967, only a mere decade after he had recorded such great hits as "That's All

Right Mama," "Trying to Get To You," "Mystery Train," and "Blue Moon of Kentucky," climbing on a half-geodesic dome in a playground in *Clambake* and, while clapping his hands like a worried nun for a bunch of fourth grade brats who had been taunting one another, singing the song "Confidence"

> With a "C" and an "O" and a "N" and a "F"
> And an "I" and a "D" and an "ENCE"
> Put 'em all together and what have you got?
> Confidence

What is particularly skeeve-making is that all through the movie he is wearing black Beatle ankle-boots playing in thick Florida *sand*! For those songs he had to sing, I would have taken those Hollywood unmusical muttjacks named Sid Tepper, Roy C. Bennett, Randy Starr, along with dopey Ben Weisman and Sid Wayne — the two guys responsible for penning the deplorable "Dominick," a song Elvis literally had to sing to a bull — and banished them to the swampy area of salty lagoons in the Putrid Sea, a.k.a., the Sivash Sea, which lies ignominiously to the east of the Isthmus of Perekop between the Crimea and Ukraine! Composers? They were crapsters, non- musical drudges, talentless macflecknoes.

They got rich and fat, nevertheless. Mozart's final resting place was a pauper's grave. Beethoven was once arrested as a tramp, so shabby were his clothes. Giovanni Bononcini died in stark poverty. So did Antonio Vivaldi, in Vienna, without income, without friends, and without family and had a pauper's funeral in St. Stephen's Cathedral. The starving immortal Franz Schubert left an estate behind of less than ten measly dollars. But these spongeheads who sat around pools in Malibu and sold their souls for cash were raking it in by the armful and growing fatter than engorged ticks on oxen.

Free-wheeling young Elvis drew almost intuitively from the rich traditions of the Mississippi Delta, Nashville, and Tin Pan Alley. He creatively cherry-picked styles and sounds, reaching back to borrow bits from Big Mama Thornton and Wynonie Harris while also channeling Bing Crosby and Dean Martin. "Crosby directly anticipated Elvis's voice on his 1950 song 'Sunshine Cake.' On his 1956 'Memories are Made of This,' Dean Martin sounds exactly like Elvis, and when Elvis sings 'Angel' in his 1962 film, *Follow That Dream* he sounds exactly like Dino," notes Will Friedwald, who adds,

> It was only when RCA realized he was selling zillions of records to teenagers that a portion of his material was dumbed down to appeal to

adolescents and no one else. Such ephemera as 'Teddy Bear,' 'Good Luck Charm,' 'Wear My Ring Around Your Neck,' and many others represent most forgettable aspect of his legacy. In my head I can hear Louis Jordan or Ray Charles doing 'Blue Suede Shoes' but not 'His Latest Flame' or 'The Girl of My Best Friend.' These last titles are particularly puerile.

As early as 1961, Elvis had already been co-opted, even gelded, you might say. With his foolish, fussified pompadour — what happened to the *grease?* — on the 45 r.p.m. picture sleeve of *Blue Hawaii*, looking dumb, unhappy, and flatulent, the poor guy resembles a grumpy and recalcitrant soda jerk back in the 1950s who was asked to work late. In the movie, playing the role of Chadwick Gates, Presley has just gotten out of the Army and is happy to be back in Hawaii with his surfboard, his brainless beach buddies, and his girlfriend. Plot-wise, his mother (!) wants him to go to work at the Great Southern Hawaiian Fruit Company, but Chad who is reluctant to do so goes to work as a tour-guide at his girlfriend's agency. This was the rebel-rocker of 1956? The snarling hipster from Memphis who lit up rock 'n' roll? As Eric Hoffer wrote in *The True Believer*, "Every great cause begins as a movement, becomes a business, and eventually degenerates into a racket."

It went no better with the Beach Boys in late 1966. When the executives at Capitol heard Brian Wilson's new sound with their work-in-progress, *Smile*, an "impressionistic, vaguely psychedelic reflection on the American past," as described by Peter Ames Carlin in his essay "Brian Wilson's Wave," it was not only *different* — where were the waves, the surfboards, the groovy chicks? — but posed a threat. The teen narrative was a formula that worked and now they were forsaking it? Although chaos began to surround the group, drugs, in-fighting, illness, Wilson continued to write songs, "but now his songs played like miniature versions of what had come before," Carlin observes, "simply wrought tunes about going to the park, listening to the radio, or, as one 1968 track put it, being 'Busy Doin' Nothin'.'" They redeemed the time, to some degree, but it called for strenuous comebacks.

Certain pieces of music immediately make me have to run for a bottle of aspirin. Among them are the headache-making David Rose's "Holiday for Strings" — springy gabble for 1950s game shows — the "Green Acres" TV theme; the insufferable score to Steven Spielberg's *Raiders of the Lost Arc* by the shameless John Williams who although, he succeeded Arthur Fiedler as Principal Conductor of the Boston Pops Orchestra from 1980 to 1993, with a view to easy money had no qualms about double-dipping to be a composer in Tinsel Town. In 1984, a petulant Williams, being ridiculed, almost ended his tenure with the

Pops when some of the musicians in the orchestra actually hissed in a rehearsal while sight-reading only another one of Williams' ghastly new compositions. One would expect a yahoo like Barry Manilow, at best a commercial jingle writer, to shill for State Farm Insurance ("Like a good neighbor, State Farm is there..."), Band-Aid ("I am stuck on Band-Aid, 'cause Band-Aids stick on me!"), Kentucky Fried Chicken, Pepsi, Tab, Dr Pepper, and the McDonald's "You Deserve a Break Today" campaign, but for John Williams to be going commercial was truly beyond the pale. But what about classical composer Igor Stravinsky? In 1942, Stravinsky was approached by the Ringling Brothers Barnum & Bailey Circus to write ballet music for elephants. So what happened? Stravinsky adamantly refused, of course, correct? Wrong! The composer of *The Firebird* (1910), *Petrushka* (1911), and *The Rite of Spring* (1913) obliged — and sat down and pondering the big pay-off greedily wrote the "Circus Polka"!

The scabrousness of it all reminds me of the mercantile sticker message that Capitol Records added to a recording of Leo Delibes's opera, *Lakmé* in 1988 in a bid to boost sales among buyers not ordinarily interested in classical music? "Includes the Flower Duet from the British Airways TV Commercial."

For down and out abominable, have you ever heard Rod McKuen sing "Happy is a Boy Named Me"? Or Wayne Newton sing "Through the Eyes of Love"? Or Roger Miller sing "Italian X-rays"? Or Engelbert Humperdinck sing "Quando, Quando, Quando"? Or Lou Rawls sing "Three O'Clock in the Morning"? Or Gene Simmons sing "The Dodo"? Or Phil Collins sing "In The Air Tonight"? Or Neil Diamond sing "Song Sung Blue"? Or Cher sing "If I Could Turn Back Time"? Or The Osmonds sing "Where Does an Angel Go When She [sic] Cries"? (Theologically speaking, all angels are considered — by Canon Law — to be male.) Or Helen Reddy sing the teeth-aching, "You and Me Against the World"? ("I love you, Mawmy" "I love you too, Baby") How about Air Supply's gonadically challenged "All Out of Love"? Marty Balin's "Hearts"? Laura Branigan's "Gloria"? Mac Davis's "Baby Don't Get Hooked On Me"? Michael Jackson's "Ben"? The Righteous Brothers' "You've Lost That Loving Feeling"? Who would deny that Dave Loggins's "Please Come to Boston" is pure cretinous mewing? (Or his painful "This Is It"?) Who would not agree that Jeffrey Osbourne's "On the Wings of Love" is sheer dreck? Quarterflash's "Harden My Heart" nothing but heart-hardening horror? Pure Prairie League's "Falling In and Out of Love with You" a nightmare? I am also ethically bound to have to add here Three Dog Night's murderous "Joy to the World," with Messrs. Negron, Wells, and Hutton being the equivalent of a Waldorf salad: chopped apples, celery, and grapes (ugh). As black comedian D. Harvey says, "If yo' don't know how to commit murdah, then don'ts do it, OK? *Stay yo' ass at the house!"* Someday when you are really happy, too happy, content with the world, fully convinced of the real possibility, no matter how remote, of reason prevailing in the world, dare to listen to the country song, "Butterfly Kisses," by a singer named Bob Carlisle, OK? I nominate it for — ready? — THE WORST SONG EVER RECORDED! You will not believe bad can go as far as this. It is definitive pigtracks! Worse even than right-wing country peckerwood Toby Keith's unendurable, paradoxically *un-*American recording, "Courtesy of the Red, White, and Blue" which is delivered less as a song than the cocksure, red-faced, fist-pounding, dogmatic, fascistic pontifications of a barroom redneck, the kind of jackass who is a hero only to people who live in a places where the size of a truck is inversely proportional to the size of the head of the man driving it. I would rather hear a swill-bowl flushing. And why with his primal know-nothingism does Keith promise to a "put a boot in the ass" of all U.S.A. haters? His answer? "It is the American way!"

What a disrespectful dumbbell.

He and that bald cachinnating dwarf Lee Greenwood with their crude and pugnacious jingoism — have we not yet learned that these crazy, intemperate, embarrassing one-sided, boastful, bull-horn-blowing, eagle-waving extremes of nationalism start *wars?* — have made a career out of exploiting the flag. You heard the same kind of aggressive hydrofracking bullshit coming out of Nazi Germany in 1933.

No, to me certain songs are almost murderously bad. Things like O.C. Smith's "Little Green Apples" and Neil Diamond's hellacious "Turn on Your Hot Lights" and Marvin Gaye's "Sexual Healing" and Noel Harrison's "Windmills of Your Mind" and Chris DeBurgh's "Lady in Red" and Terry Jacks's "Seasons in the Sun" and Paul Anka's "Havin' My Baby" and Michael Martin Murphey's "Wildfire" and Yarbrough and People's "Don't Stop the Music." Then there is the apallingly bad "People," recorded by Barbra Streisand in 1964, lyrics by Bob Merrill — "the worst songwriter of all time," according to Mark Steyn (any relation to Jule Styne who wrote the music to "People"?!) — the guy who also gave us, among others, "How Much is that Doggie in the Window," "Mambo Italiano," and "If I Knew You Were Comin' I'd've Baked a Cake." Hardly the worst songwriter of all· time — his competition was in the thousands — he nevertheless went out to the driveway of his house on February 17, 1998, age 76, and shot himself. What about all those intolerable, unmanly, almost extravagantly bad, soft "Easy Eighties" songs — "power ballads," I believe they called them — all of them selling tubs of sincerity but each one thinner and more emotionally dishonest than the next, like Michael Bolton's "How Am I Supposed to Live Without You?," Paul Young's

"Every Time You Go Away," Jack Wagner's "All I Need," Chicago's "If You Leave Me Now," REO Speedwagon's "Can't Fight This Feeling" — a group named for a flatbed truck — John Cafferty and the Beaver Brown Band's "Hearts on Fire," Jefferson Starship's "Miracles," America's "Sister Golden Hair" — "Although the song is a message from a man to his lover, explaining that he still loves her despite being not ready for marriage," said the group's songwriter Gerry Beckley, as if speaking about manna from heaven, "the title was initially inspired by the mothers of all three members of the group, all of whom were blondes" — Seals and Croft's "Get Closer," Bread's "Hooked on You," the ungetoutofyourheadable "My Sharona," the debut single by The Knack, released in 1979. I am talking about the mediocre generic sound of England Dan and John Ford Coley's "I'd Really Love to See You Tonight," Phil Collins's "Sussudio," Rick Astley's "Never Gonna Give You Up," Color Me Bad's "I Wanna Sex You Up," Michael Bolton's "Can I Touch You," and things like Bette Midler's "Wind Beneath My Wings," a sort of turgid moose-calling display or so it always seemed to me. When she tried to put a song across, Midler always seemed to release a kind of toxic effusion like juglone, a compound that instantly wilts and kills tomato plants. I will also throw into this list for pure torture her adenoidal "The Rose," where we hear her clawing-after-the-lyrics chicken-diction trying to scare up passion:

> Just remem-be*rrrr* in the wint-e*rrrr*
> far beneeeeath the bitter snows
> lies the seeeeeeed
> that with the sun's luv
> in the spriiiiiiiiing
> becomes the roooooose.

She should have stuck to doing the voice of "Woody the Spoon" from the 1970s children's television show *Vegetable Soup*.

These are the songs that can get stuck in your head and really do serious damage to your mind, what critic and wit James Lileks in another context would call "interior desecration." No pleasure, merely pain, the insistent groove — grind, grind, grind — that scoring-wheels your poor brain with ever-deepening ruts. It is like the scary, to me neo-suicidal narrator ready to go off her dot in "The Man That Got Away" — you know, Judy Garland at high morbidity singing zombie-like, "The winds grow colder/ and suddenly you're older." That doesn't burn a hole in your sleep? I fear reprisals. Don't laugh! In a short story by Julio Cortázar, "Continuity of Parks," a man is killed by one of the characters in the novel he is reading! While we are on the subject of the Hall of Heaves, I would just for the record also immediately dump anything from radio stations that call themselves "Hot," "Alternative," "Cutting Edge" or that break in (over crash music) screaming, "We have the best mix!," "The Christian Rock Experience!," "Your Easy Listenin' Addiction!," "Play us in the office all day!," "Less static, more music, no n-o-i-s-e!," "Voice of the Prairie," "Sunshine Station in the Heart of the Nation," "The Gospel Messenger of the Air," "The Biggest Little Ten Watt Station in the World," "Only Bank Owned Station In Indiana."

Noise permeates our world. Maria Sharapova grunts at every tennis stroke. Glenn Gould hummed while he played the piano — his mother had taught him to sing everything he played, an unbreakable and notorious habit. There is a constant noise heard in New Mexico, the "Taos Hum." Where does it come from? Bat fish? Sonic hypnosis? Is it a government signal? An ELF frequency employed to communicate with submarines? I walk around half the time taking in otoacoustic emissions! The question is where *doesn't* noise come from? Take for example that saucy passage found in Vladimir Nabokov's novel *Bend Sinister*, regarding the housemaid Mariette; we read, "She sat with parted hips, slightly moving her tightly crossed thighs, producing a tiny sound, soft labiate with an alternate crepitation as if she were rubbing the palms of her hands which, however, lay idle." But what is not noise? Television is noise. Signs are noise. Yakking loudly on cellphones in public is noise. Traffic is noise. So are relentless telemarketers. Horse laughs are noise. Crowds repeatedly chanting "de-fense" at NBA games for an hour are noise. Birdbrains who scream "Get in the hole!" at golf tournaments are noise. The pathetic, self-admiring "Forewords" that Nabokov appends to his novels are noise. Politicians — "There are no great politicians in my book," said William S. Burroughs, "they are all liars" — are noise. I find that certain *names* can be noise, at least many of them, Newt Gingrich, Benjamin Netanyahu, Spiro Agnew, and, among others, Robert Abplanalp — President Nixon's rich crony. Noise is of course pollution. For sheer, unadulterated musical pollution, rating right up there with a cat in heat, someone twisting a piece of Styrofoam, or the truly unearthly rattling sound of a "*gragger*," the Jewish wooden musical instrument that is used at Purim (I was once invited to a celebratory meal in London) and other tactile aversions, I would specifically have to list: "A Perfect Day" by the Constellations — called "psychedelic soul-rock" — Beck's "Gamma Ray," The Violent Femmes' "Country Death Song," The Mighty Mighty Boss Tones' "Let's Face It" — a genre called "ska-punk." — "We're On the Road to Nowhere" by the Talking Heads, "Short Skirt Long Jacket" by Cake, Stevie Wonder's "Never Had a Dream Come True," Journey's "Separate Ways," Blue

Öyster Cult's "Burning for You," and, among others, Florence and the Machine's "You Got the Love." I would throw in the Beatles' "You Can't Do That." Are you scandalized to read that? Hey, as we hear in the song, "The More You Ruv [sic] Someone" from the musical, *Avenue Q*, "The more you love someone/ The more you want to kill them [sic]." Right? I recall a quip of Quentin Crisp's: "Being loved can never be a patch on being murdered. That's when someone really gives their all for you."

There are moist voices, voices that plead, obsequious voices, like the clunker "Dear Heart" as sung by Andy Williams who with that unbearable, almost *wet*, Bubba-the-Love-Sponge voice that in its desperate shlockiness seems proof of that Original Sin never seems to cease clammily laving at your neck. He candifies it, sugars every slow word, cow-moos it out like a smarmy cheapjack. It is so false, so miserably styleless, crude, insincere, artless. Williams's appalling rendition of the song "I'd Really Love to See You Tonight" (cf. above) in which you can hear the poor, lost, bewildered aging crooner wandering around inside the song as if trying to feel the walls of it, going up and down scales looking to resolve mis-hit notes — it sounds like he is dissecting it — added to his singing gaffes and ludicrous dead-ends. It is truly frightening. Please do not even mention his daft version of *West Side Story's* "Maria," a beautiful song, needless to say, but in his version an interminable, crucifyingly slow, grotesquely milked loop of fraudulent, missed, overvalued notes, sugary trills, and vocal glugs. Williams has some serious competition in this genre with songs like Conway Twitty's prurient "You've Never Been This Far Before," George Strait's "I Cross My Heart," Porter Wagoner's "I Thought I Heard You Calling My Name," Kenny Rogers's sappy "Lady," and Bill ("Whisperin' Bill") Anderson's "Still," a smitten spate of love-bug confession-talk ("I wancha to know/ I'm still here") the *sine qua non* of this grouping, just to name a few.

I have to say that having to hear Henry Mancini and Andy Williams at the same time truly approaches torture. Please God, spare me consciousness! Listen sometime to that last tasteless note that Andy Williams delivers — in an attempt at panache? — at the end of "The Days of Wine and Roses." Pure trumpery. Crassness. Vulgarity itself. Almost lewd in its over-suggestive pleading, like bad paperback art from the 1950s. I gather that all of that hammy emotion and soggy, smothered-in-molasses yearning is an Iowan's idea of sensuality. Bumpkin-chic. I mean, Andy Williams loved schmaltz more than a fat kid loves a lazy dog. There is a hunger to it, a shamelessless, almost prurience. With its desperate urgency, voracity has to be, more than anything else, easily one of the lowest, least attractive of all human impulses. I am reminded as I think of it of all of those interminably crude, exploitative talk-people you cannot avoid on radio or television, don't try to change the channel, it's useless, they're always in your shirt, like a fusillade, an interminable conga-line of pushy, wheedling, unappeasable, yammering, opinionated Jewish interviewers and shoved-down-your-throat manufactured-by-committee celebrities — where the fuck do they all come from? — with their needy, overly familiar, merchandizing voices ringing through the airwaves with crude and bottomless zeal like Larry King, Howard Stern, Roseanne Barr, Rikki Lake, Barbara Walters, Bill Maher, Jerry Springer, Wolf Blitzer, Sally Jesse Raphael, Maury Povich, Bill Mazur, Michael Savage, Jon Stewart, Gerry Nachman, Paula Zahn, Andy Cohen, Judge Judy Seidlin, Chris Wallace, Dr. Drew Pinsky, David Gregory, Andrea Mitchell, Gloria Allred, Marv Albert, Geraldo Rivera, Jerry Springer, William Kristol, Daniel Pipes, Kathie Lee Gifford, Charles Krauthammer, Joan Rivers, Frank Rich, Andrew Goldberg who goes under the alias A.J. Hammer, Mort Zuckerman, Ed Shultz, and the arch-vulgarian Chelsea Handler who are neither fascinating people nor talented reporters nor serious investigators but simply heartless and insensitive ghouls one can't avoid. There is a kind of pleading as invoking that does pass muster.

Pleading?

Slim Whitman is a good example.

A quick aside here. I positively love Slim Whitman's music and so, know this, please, I have absolutely nothing personal against the likes — even the excesses — of sartorial peacockery like Porter Wagoner's trademark rhinestone Nudie suits or even high-swept pompadours or rail-thin frames or spectacularly weathered faces in country singers. Slim was in that category and sported an outmoded 1930s mustache, to boot, nor had he qualms about trilling notes, using falsetto, or even yodeling — he was also a left-handed guitarist (he lost much of the second finger on his left hand in an accident) — but who else on earth could have sung "Indian Love Call" or "Rose Marie" or "Secret Love" as deftly as that man? The late Michael Jackson cited Whitman as one of his ten favorite vocalists.

There are so many bad songs. Gordon Lightfoot's "Beautiful," Helen Reddy's "You and Me against the World," Dan Hill's "Sometimes When We Touch," Dave Loggins's "Please Come To Boston," which is pure hell. Robotic. Merciless. As Jean Harlow tells Clark Gable in *Red Dust*, "Shake out of it, Fred!" Then there is Carly Simon's execrable version of "My Funny Valentine." Not a single note is hit right. She tends to talk-sing, the way that the terrible actors Nelson Eddy and Kevin Costner, to pick two egregious examples, deliver every wooden line as if they were sitting next to you, tired, in a train or bus station, just reporting bland facts like laundry lists. "If a horse could sing in a monotone," said the always charitable critic Robert Christgau, "the horse would sound like Carly Simon, only a horse wouldn't rhyme 'yacht,' 'apricot,' and 'gavotte.'" There are worse sins, of course, than being talky and off-key. How about the pseudophilopatristic cant of those aboriginal country songs, "I'm Proud to be an American" and "God Bless the USA," written and recorded by country singer Lee Greenwood, which, obviously written strictly for cash, actually exploit the country rather than ennoble it? I would much prefer to buy a Crudely Painted, Not So Funny, Plywood, Cut Out, Folk Art Garden Gnome from Al Harrington's Wacky Waving Inflatable Arm Flailing Tube Man Warehouse and Emporium as advertised in *Family Guy*! It is my belief that any pea-and-thimble-rigging cheap-jack who goes about making a commercial living out of draping himself in the American flag as a career move, the way that most used-car dealers famously do all the time, waving pennants and farting out slogans and hysterically honking about big door-buster deals, should be deported on the first leaking submarine. Significantly, Dr. Samuel Johnson in his dictionary defines the word patriotism as "The last refuge of a scoundrel."

As I have mentioned, a notable lulu was Richard Harris' voice-straining "MacArthur Park," a classic late 1960s song as posturing and pretentious as General Douglas MacArthur, for whom the park was named. When once asked what was going through his mind when he wrote the lyrics, Webb replied that the lyrics were meant to be symbolic and referred to the end of a love affair, but a song with more round-about, puzzle-headed delusions or buggered-up imagistic concoctions cannot be found. The single ran for a length of more than seven minutes, with a long, climactic orchestral break rising to a crescendo-like build-up that sounds like the Lone Ranger and Tonto might come riding by at any minute.

When disc-jockeys had to go to the toilet while on air, they often played "MacArthur Park," which is one reason, in my opinion, it became so popular. Some deejays hearing the call of nature went with the Sugar Hill Gang's 1979 "Rapper's Delight" ("I said a hip hop, the hippie, the hippie to the hip hip hop,") the original hip-hop record. Or Quicksilver Messenger Service's 1973 version of Bo Diddley's 1956 "Who Do You Love." Or Nigerian multi-instrumentalist Fela Kuti's "Beasts of No Nation," a full 28 minutes, 21 seconds of jazz-rock Afrobeat. Another popular toilet-track is Goldfrapp's "Ride a White Horse." I myself might have gone with Pink Floyd's mystical rant, "Echoes," a 23-minute-plus jaunt. Or the Rolling Stones' "Miss You," the 12-inch disco mix from 1978. Or The Doors' "LA Woman" (8 minutes). Or the long version from 1975 of Donna Summer's "Love to Love You Baby," which ran for 16 ½ minutes. (I also love her driving "I Feel Love," 15 minutes.) Or the Velvet Underground's rocking "Sister Ray" — the song they always closed with, live — over 17 minutes long. But why not go with Wagner's full Ring Cycle, 14 hours long, and take the day off?

"Wichita Lineman," another Jimmy Webb offering from 1958 — Dylan Jones has referred to it as "the first existential country song" — has to be one of the most lugubrious recordings ever made. It was recorded by Glen Campbell who sounds dead singing it. In 2004, *Rolling Stone* listed that morbid song as one of the "500 Greatest Songs of All Time," ranking it at #192. To show further proof of Original Sin, music journalist Stuart Maconie fecklessly called it "the greatest pop song ever composed." Prosiness came easily to Webb, not so much poetry. Shakespeare — why not pick the best — had the full arsenal of punches, jab, straight right/ left hand, hook and uppercut knew all the ins and outs of rhetoric. His *Julius Caesar* is mostly blank verse, with little prose, whereas *The Merry Wives of Windsor* is just the opposite. There are well over a hundred songs in Shakespeare's canon. His fancy for music was deep and comprehensive. The only Shakespearean play which does not contain at least one song is The Comedy of Errors, although the play has been adapted as a musical several times, first as The Boys from Syracuse with a score by Richard Rodgers and Lorenz Hart, then in 1976 in a version by Trevor Nunn, scored by Guy Woolfenden, for the Royal Shakespeare Company; and also in 1981 as Oh, Brother! with a score by Michael Valenti and Donald Driver. Lorenzo who elopes with Jessica unequivocally summarizes the importance of music and song in *The Merchant of Venice*:

> The man that hath no music in himself,
> Nor is not moved with concord of sweet sounds,
> Is fit for treasons, stratagems and spoils;
> The motions of his spirit are dull as night
> And his affections dark as Erebus:
> Let no such man be trusted. Mark the music." (V.1.91-7)

Even a master can write bad songs. How about the great Irving Berlin's "Fella with an Umbrella"? It is a song recycled in the movie *Easter Parade* and sung so weakly by Peter Lawford that one gets the sneaking impression that the actor just made it up as they were shooting. I cannot find a thing to recommend it. Its facile lyrics and mechanical, kitschy, and melody-less turn honestly makes me wonder whether its composer was actually sober when writing the thing. As to bad songs, what about Bread's "Baby I'm-A Want You," Orleans' brutal "Still the One," Lobo's "Me and You and A Dog Named Boo" — singer/songwriter Kent Lavoie supposedly chose the name Lobo ("Lone Wolf") for his billing so that if the record flopped he could start a career again without any baggage — Ray Price's drainingly maudlin "For The Good Times," The Ides of March's

"Vehicle," Bill Conti's "Gonna Fly Now," Barbra Streisand's "Stoney End," "Cradle Me," "Don't Rain On My Parade," anything she sings, Stevie Wonder's "Yester Me, Yester You," Paul McCartney's "Listen To What The Man Said," John Denver's "Shanghai Breezes," The Four Seasons' "My Eyes Adored You," Seals and Crofts' "I'll Play For You," or Christopher Cross's "Sailing"? *Arrest them all for noise pollution! For aural assault! For battery of the ears! Sentence them to beat hemp in dark dungeons! Slaughter them all! Be unsparing and make no pardons! Behead them in public squares and sell their heads to waiting customers like Baldwin apples!*

Many celebrities have tried their hands at singing — hard to believe in some cases, scarcely endurable to hear in most. Some notable examples? How about Mae West's "Twist and Shout"? Jack ("Dragnet") Webb's version of "When Sunny Gets Blue" or "Try A Little Tenderness"? Sebastian Cabot's "It Ain't Me Babe"? Everybody has tried singing songs and recording. Actors. Cowboys. TV stooges. Grade-D actresses. Eighth-rate celebrities. Bruce Willis. Leonard Nimoy. Anthony Perkins. Jack Palance. Fat, puffing, red-faced William Shatner. Jeff Bridges, Danny Bonaduce, Tony Danza, Kevin Costner, Clint Eastwood, Barbara Eden, Robert Downey, Jr., Russell Crowe, David Hasselhoff, Scarlett Johansson, Jennifer Love Hewitt — are you with me? I'm talking about *putting out record albums!* — Juliette Lewis, Christopher Lee, Alyssa Milano, Robert Mitchum, the Olsen Twins, Tony Perkins, Burt Reynolds, Esther Rolle, Steven Seagall, Frank Stallone, Mr. T, Jack Webb, and Tina Yothers. You have not lived until you have heard Cybill Shepherd sing "Let's Do It" or Jayne Mansfield croon "Little Things Mean a Lot" or the 1960s gossip-columnist Rona (née Burstein) Barrett limp in with "Lullabye of Broadway," all of whom remind me of one of my all-time favorite lines from the movies when Greta Garbo in *Romance* extravagantly states, "Ven I vas young, ve vere very poor. But ve has lots of friends — all of them mices."

That line is right up there with several other totally loopy film favorites of mine, like Van Heflin's in *Shane* (1953), "Don't you ask nothing but questions?" and Victor Mature's in *I Wake Up Screaming* (1942), "If I ever catch you around here again, they'll have to pick you up with a sieve"[!] and Richard Conte's minatory threat in *Thieves' Highway* (1949) "Touch my truck, and I'll climb into your hair."

I still insist that actors, always desperate for attention, are the neediest, most self-exalting assholes on the planet, never mind the most overpaid and grotesquely over-indulged, shallow, vainglorious hucksters who mime and lisp and dissemble before cameras strictly for money, their craft, as someone once described it, being "something between a black art and a form of manual labor." The movie *Fame* (1980), a pandering and sycophantic fable retailing a lot of fudge about the New York High School of Performing Arts, shows in a truly unintentionally disturbing group-portrait that documents some of the vainest, overindulged, beaver-chewed trivialists on earth just exactly how actors and performers are bred. They are almost to a one devoid of idealism, competitive, not collaborative, barking in hunger for attention, unconcerned for anyone else — forget those trendy photo-ops showing them in Africa or Haiti helping unfortunate children, it is always a career move — and poverty-stricken as to any ideas or thoughts. They crave winning plaques and awards of shiny metal, even in old age, desperate ascot-wearing applause-freaks and bounders who live only to see their faces in magazines. A mere fart or fanfaronade on a television show gets them an Emmy nomination. Everyone well remembers the song, "Hi-Diddle-Dee-Dee" from Walt Disney's *Pinocchio* (1940) sung by scheming con artists Honest John and Gideon,

> Hi diddle dee doo
> You sleep till after two
> You promenade a big cigar
> You tour the world in a private car
> You dine on chicken and caviar
> An actor's life for me!

Why do actors — sorry, *artistes* — always end up marrying other actors? Narcissists need mirrors. They are all rabid for compliments and hogs of vanity, meteorologists of their inner selves, except that their weather is always predictable because in an infantilized and desperately regressive way they desire basically only one thing, to be applauded. "Look, most people in entertainment are that way — they all act like children. Nobody I've known in the business — including myself — had an emotional age above fifteen. We are not normal people," declared the American television producer Don Ohlmeyer on the immaturities of Howard Cosell in Mark Ribowsky's biography of that mouthy old sports-broadcasting relic, a sad, self-regarding piece of human kohlrabi.

Incompetence in singing has a hundred or faces and voices. A film star could be screechy — Jane Powell singing "Open Your Eyes" in *Royal Wedding* — or plain flaccid — Red Skelton singing "Spring has Sprung" in *Excuse My Dust* — or truly manic — Betty Hutton in *Annie Get Your Gun* singing "Doin' What Comes Natur'lly." Did you know that comedian Redd Foxx — John Elroy Sanford — also began working in a musical group called the Bon Bons in 1939 which lasted only a few years? John Garfield sings, "My Momma Done Told Me," the line title for the song "Blues in the Night" in the movie, *Thank Your Lucky Stars* (1943), making every note sound flat as a baking sheet. I can report that the young Sean Connery had a splendid singing voice. He sings "My Pretty Irish Girl" in *Darby O'Gill and the Little People,* while working a scythe, and, although has since gone on record as saying that singing was one aspect of the role that he was not too fond of — he liked the song well enough to cut a 45 r.p.m. of it (a rarity, I'm told, among record collectors) we know it is his real voice and not a leprechaun's. (A leprechaun, according to legend, can never use his magic in the daytime.) He also sings in "Under the Mango Tree" — only a few bars — in the James Bond movie, *Dr. No.*

How about Sylvester Stallone's turgid "Too Close To Paradise"? Or Lorne Greene's maudlin version of "The Place Where I Worship"? There was his ponderous, mostly spoken pop-hit, "Ringo," a bout of faux-western twaddle that shameless Hollywood "composer" Henry Mancini once actually lauded for its "pure, naked virility." I once heard a record of Greene singing "As Time Goes By," which sounded like a rusty radiator fan in an old Chrysler Newport. Debonair Omar Sharif sang in movies, "You are Woman, I am Man," "Pink Velvet Jail," etc. He more or less talked the few songs he ever recorded, *recitativo*-wise — "Whaaad does a mun nid/ some shirts aand some neckdies...You're lawcked in a piinnk belbet jaaaaail" — in his case with major head-cavity resonation which always made him sound like he was sitting in a barrel. "I am proud to represent my country, Egypt," the "Egyptian Muslim" Sharif often declared, except that his real name was Michel Shalhoub, he was born to Lebanese-Syrian parents, was baptized a Catholic, attained stardom in the Arab world only by marrying Egypt's top actress, Faten Hamama, converted to the Islam religion, and then he came to Hollywood to enjoy fame by himself. The bane of Sharif's English was always elided words. He would say "ge-treel" for "get real" and "lee-pup" for "leap up." Speaking of "As Time Goes By," no one who has heard it can ever forget the fractured English of it as sung by tenor José Carreras, a version in which he croons in a kind of Euro-Babu, *"Dee woooorl weel ohlwez welcum loafers...."* I would contend that the late actor Robert Mitchum's take of the calypso song, "Mama Look a Boo Boo" — his LP *Calypso - Is Like So* came out in 1957 — is in the reedy owl-sounds of its strained presentation surely the nadir of "Jamaican" art, and in the cliché department — like Belafonte singing about banana boats or Louis Farrakhan (when he was a Calypso singer known as "The Charmer") singing "Ugly Woman" — not two jumps from a lady from Kingston, Jamaica asking, "You go back recent. If I go, me I doan tell nobody I come. Me cyan have no holiday there no mo'. Jamaica change. Ooo-wee. Them got no respeck for nuttin,' I tell you. I vexed!"

Do all movie stars yearn to sing? More to the point, do they all believe by some kind of show-business fiat that they all can? Dashing Robert Taylor who tried to sing a duet in *Broadway Melody of 1936* had a flat, cardboard-dry voice of an autosexual and from what I have read of him — his priggishness, his infamous appearance as a starboard-leaning witness in front of HUAC in 1947 to rat out people — it fit. Comedienne Lucille Ball's singing voice in *Too Many Girls*, the 1940 film version based on Rodgers and Hart stage-hit about college life, while being ogled by four guys, including a young Desi Arnaz who looks about 13 years old, sings "Nearer" with what I would judge are fairly good pipes if — note *if* — she is not being dubbed. I say that because it sounds a bit too smooth, too glossy, too professional. Almost all actresses seem to feel the need to give their voices an airing in movies, just in case they prove to be brilliant. Diane Keaton. Bette Davis. Arlene Dahl. Mamie Van Doren. Kim Basinger sings the standard "Let's Fall in Love" in *The Marrying Man* (1991) with a kind of exultant courage, but then is that her actual voice? As they are traveling by car Karen Black in *Five Easy Pieces* beautifully croons a Tammy Wynette song to Jack Nicholson — and it's a lovely voice. In 1959, memorably introduced by an enthusiastic Paul Lynde, Linda Evans with a big dimple and a weird, sort of glued-on, upswept, plastic, directionless hair-don't sings a song called "Love" in the movie *Beach Blanket Bingo* — which is high up on the list as the worst movie ever made — with the distinct aural menace of a completely weak voice, the kind one hears in all its threadiness, say, with the late Richard Harris with his wobbly, reedy, where-am-I-going-with-it, onion-skin voice in the film version of *Camelot*.

Forget Jimmy Stewart's brief sally into song in *It's A Wonderful Life* when with Donna Reed he seems to be imitating a dying coyote ("Aaaaaaaand... dance by the light of the moon") while singing "Buffalo Gals." In an earlier movie *Born to Dance* (1936) Stewart sings "Easy to Love," and truly butchers it — truly, no worse voice ever bollixed up a prettier song. In the perfectly rotten western, *Night Passage* (1957), Stewart, while playing an accordion yet, sings (twice!) a weak version of a weak song, "You Can't Get Far Without a Railroad." Grade: C- But in its leathery way, it is sort of home-spun and masculine. The same cannot be said of Burt Reynolds who in 1974 recorded an album, *Ask Me What I Am*, a collection of shlocky seduction-songs of the cheap valentine-candy variety, proving at best only a pitiful and unremitting lack of self-awareness. That was the year, along with chart-toppers like Paper Lace's "The Night Chicago Died," Terry Jacks' "Seasons in the Sun," and Paul Anka's predatory "You're Having My Baby," that the Ramones came out with their scintillating "I Don't Want to Walk Around with You," which goes in part:

I don't wanna walk around with you
I don't wanna walk around with you
I don't wanna walk around with you
So why you wanna walk around with me?

The thing is a song does not have to have anything like a spectacular lyric for it to succeed, no indeed. The lyrics to "Please Please Please" do not exactly rise to the standards of Cole Porter, but James Brown singing it puts it into orbit:

> Please, please, please, please me (You don't have to go)
> Baby please, baby please, please me (You don't have to go)
> Baby please, baby please don't go (You don't have to go)
> Don't go, I said baby, don't baby
> I love you so (You don't have to go)
> Baby, you know you broke my heart when you went away (You don't have to go)
>
> I said, I said, I said I'll see you some other day (You don't have to go)
>
> I said, baby, baby, please, don't go (You don't have to go)
> Don't go, no baby, no baby I love you so (You don't have to go)

It was to the Argentinian Latin-lover Fernando Lamas, born in Buenos Aires, that we owe one of the great shlock-seduction offerings of all time when he came out with the same kind of cheesy boudoiresque LP on the Roulette label as *Ask Me What I Am*. Lamas' album was called *With Love* — virtually a book-end to Reynolds' album — with the added romantic bonus, for all the women of the world, of Lamas' soulful, love-sponge of a face, shown life-size, gracing the album cover. He sings a bunch of old standards, not badly, with a sort of Julio Iglesias-like tremolo, such as "I Love Paris" ("*...in da sprintine, in da fall, in da winter, in da sommer, when eeeet seeessles*") and "Tenderly" ("*The ivninnnn briz carays da triz....your arms opin wide, enclos mee iii'side*"), but I have heard a lot worse. Lamas hits duds, of course, which is to be expected in amateur singers. Jimmy Durante's versions of "As Time Goes By" and "September Song" are clunker-full — I mean, he does not hit a single note bang on — but, hey, that effectively became his style.

Meryl Streep who droned "Amazing Grace" at the end of *Silkwood* (1983) — a tailing-off flattish version with gratuitous country yodels — sings (and dances) throughout *Mamma Mia!* (2008). She studied singing as a child, although she was supposedly assailed with a bad case of stage fright when asked to perform songs at the Hollywood Bowl while promoting 2006's *A Prairie Home Companion*, at least according to Christine Fenno on *Popwatch*, a blog of *Entertainment Weekly*. Actors in their narcissism insist they can do anything, and, of course, to be able to sing fills a huge vanity quotient. So Streep sang in *Ironweed* (1987), *Postcards from the Edge* (1990), *Death Becomes Her* (1992), and *Dancing at Lughnasa* (1998), and she would have sung in the musical *Evita*, after a year of preparing to front that cast, until she learned that Madonna had landed the lead role. According to a 1991 newspaper report, Streep said, "I could rip her throat out. I can sing better than she can, if that counts for anything." Reese Witherspoon and Joaquin Phoenix rose to the challenge, doing their own singing in the Johnny Cash biopic, *Walk the Line* (2005). One hunger for actors that beats-out singing is to imitate foreign and domestic accents. I think I can take Streep in any morph except that one — one that she exercises in just about every single movie that she makes — and would cross an ocean to avoid having to hear her pretentiously repeat, "I hod a fohm in Ofrica.'

Does it say anything about television, never mind the state of American taste, that the man who holds the Guinness World Record for the most time spent in front of a television camera, has not a trace of talent — dancing, singing, acting — in ANYTHING? Regis Philbin has, nevertheless, recorded at least four albums — *When You're Smiling, It's Time for Regis, Just You, Just Me* (with his second wife, Joy) and the inevitable *Christmas Album*. He has been the interlocutor of such indispensable programs as the *Joey Bishop Show, Live with Regis and Kelly, Who Wants to Be a Millionaire?, Million Dollar Password, America's Got Talent*, and appeared as a celebrity contestant on *Are You Smarter Than a 5th Grader?* He has hosted *The Neighbors*, took work as a "field reporter" for ABC's *Almost Anything Goes*, worked New Year's Eve programs in Times Square, popped up in sit-coms, judged Miss America Pageants, vocalized for animated series, sat as a guest on panel shows, went on talk shows, and has done everything but fart into a Dixie Cup and call it music. From what I have seen in the way of his TV commercials the guy is utterly shameless and willing to shill anything from pelvic belts to hemorrhoid creams to Velcro balls to goose-horn sirens!

How best describe Philbin's paranasal voice? His "voice" is actually part throat, part nose, but a swollen tongue is involved, as is — no lie — the jaw. One hears ululations, but are they blocked, dammed up, nasally occluded all at the same time? What we hear is a fat sound, a lumpfish gagging, something broken in the mandibles. Sinusoidal does not do justice to what seem to form a voice about to cack up gristle, or spit, while being strangled at the same time. An absence of diastemas between the teeth is suggested, causing tight teeth, a conjoining, it would appear, of the hyoid to the cartilage of the larynx, producing an echo vaulting into the snout. His is the voice of a butt trumpet. Speech for him seems to echo from — resonate in — the bone-box of his actual skull. But speech here is only a euphemism. The human head is made up of sinuses, maxillary, frontal, ethnoid, sphemoid, but in this guy's case they all seem empty for he appears to be talking out of humid turbinates, all blocked.

I cannot imagine anyone having a more pointedly nasal voice than that strange anchorman Shepard Smith of Fox News — he is the spitting image of short, red-nosed Charles VII, the French king who abandoned Joan of Arc in 1430, letting her be burnt at the stake a year later — whose brontosonic honk is unhappily aligned to his short size and what is also a horrid lack of formality, an awful chumminess, a familiarity that involves an overreaching absence of ceremony so vulgarizing in its casual chattiness it seems to assume that you are both having a chat standing at a urinal.

Were you even aware that the likes of Kevin Bacon, Corey Feldman, Jeff Bridges, and Don Johnson have also tried their hands at what, to be charitable, may be called "celebrity" musical recordings? In this great pantheon may also be numbered track star Carl Lewis, gigantic ex-Miami Heat basketball center, Shaquille O'Neal, and the big-titted, long-haired cheesecake buffoon, Fabio, to say nothing of Mae West whose 45 r.p.m. single of "Twist and Shout," recorded at the age of 75, is replete with orgasmic huffs and snorting sex sounds. In the category of celebrity singers, who can forget Art Linkletter's "We Love You, Call Collect?" a maudlin spoken-word recording that he addresses to his dead daughter, Diane, who committed suicide at UCLA by jumping out of a window but in which one can hear him subconsciously *scold* the poor lost girl, implying that the sin she committed in her despair let *him* down, thus unwittingly reflecting not only the pomposity of a cold, incompetent parent ("I've read there are/ Thousands just like you/ searching for something/ they failed to find at home... Why were we never able/ to unlock your frustration/ and talk it away...Where is this thing/ For which you search/ Is it found by rejecting your heritage?") but proving past all consideration that she could never have come to him, that she was one of the last people who could or would have helped her. I am well reminded here of the movie *The Little Foxes* in which someone despairingly asks, "What must God think when he sees us all?"

Not all movie stars are bad. Playing the composer Sigmund Romberg in the amazingly-bad-at-least-for-MGM musical, *Deep in My Heart* (1954) dramatic actor José Ferrer who, visibly brimming with confidence, proves to be not only a just decent enough dancer but manages to carry a note as well, as witness his doing a workman-like job on the peppy "Leg of Mutton Dance." He makes himself look quite attractive when, in real life, I am told, he was quite the opposite. Good looks guarantee nothing in the musical department, of course. On the other hand, it helps. While Lauren Bacall sings — well, sort of raddles off — the song, "How Little We Know" in *To Have and Have Not* (1944) with one of the weakest, most inexpert voices in film history, Jane Russell with near perfection ties up her solo of "Five Little Miles from San Berdoo" in *His Kind of Woman* (1951), singing with confidence in an intimate room with very few people in attendance. Robert Mitchum is there, ogling her with admiration — or is it lust? In *Macao* (1952), also starring Mitchum — the two perfect a film mood of indolent insolence — Russell wearing a golden dress and shiny earrings and rafts, *slews*, of jewelry sings "One for My Baby" with typical sass and a real sense of panache.

Robert Mitchum, whom I somewhat knocked before, did manifest some fairly good pipes, if of a limited range. Listen to him in *Night of the Hunter* sing, almost croon, that old evangelical hymn, "Leaning" — a haunting baritone — as well as "Bringing in the Sheaves," which he does superbly, scarily, with eerie conviction. His recording of "Thunder Road," sung in the movie of the same name, sold well. But it depends on which picture you see to evaluate his singing voice. A rough-edged Mitchum sings "The Wild Colonial Boy" in a bar in the movie, *The Sundowners*, (1960), and more out of tune you cannot get. I gotta say, literally every note is sung off-key, and utterly leaden.

I had always thought that Gloria Grahame in *A Woman's Secret* (1941) sang quite credibly, indeed with sexy smoothness, first "You Take Me to Paradise" and then "Estralita" just as winsomely as she had sung "I Cain't Say No" in *Oklahoma!* (1955) until I found out that she could not only not a sing a note but that a botched surgery on her mouth had weirdly "frozen" the upper lip and left her with a very strange speech — never mind singing — pattern which caused her to be known as "The Girl with the Novocaine Lip." Sexy Ava Gardner actually had a lovely voice, but because back in the days when filming the musical, *Showboat*, every film department always arrogantly insisted on having its own way, and the dubbing people, to flex their technical muscle, I gather, insisted that Gardner not be allowed to sing "Can't Help Loving That Man of Mine." One of the very first thrills of my life came one summer night when my then young parents took their kids to see *Showboat* (1951) at the Meadow-Glen Drive-In in Medford, Massachusetts, and I recall standing up behind them in the backseat of our car in my blue pajamas, leaning forward with folded hands, being smitten with Ava singing that song, as well as Howard Keel and Kathryn Grayson — in high Technicolor — singing "Make

Believe" in that lovely duet. I could not quite believe the rich color and music and frankly thought that I had died and gone to heaven. On the movie album LP, however, Ava's actual voice was allowed to stand — and a beautiful voice it proved to be, almost as beautiful as her film replacement's. In her brassy role in the film, *Mogambo* (1953), incidentally, Ava in a sweet moment sings a few bars of the classic, "Coming through the Rye," and is nothing less than note-perfect. Janet Leigh gets to sing only a few lines of "Put on A Happy Face" in *Bye Bye Birdie* (1963), and the result is pure mud. She is Audrey-Meadows-waitress nasal, at best. Paul Lynde who in the same musical sings the witty and upbeat "What's the Matter with Kids Today?" is in fact only marginally better, barely holding the tune. I remember a particular *F Troop* TV episode in 1966, "The Singing Mountie," where with unapologetic fruitiness Lynde hilariously played a cop on the trail of an elusive criminal, the "Burglar of Banff," on the show repeatedly pronounced *Banff-ff-ff* of course by way of a labial spit-spray.

Actor George Sanders (*All About Eve, Rebecca,* etc.) had a rich, mellifluous baritone and from what I have read could have actually had a career in grand opera. In the 1950s he made a guest appearance on the Tallulah Bankhead Radio Show where he sang the aria, "*In lacerato spirito*" from Verdi's *Simon Boccanegra,* and so authentic was his performance that most people in attendance, and surely most listeners, believed him to be mouthing a recording. In 1958, he came out with an LP, *The George Sanders Touch,* singing, among other hits, "More Than You Know," "September Song," "As Time Goes By," including even one of his own musical compositions, "Such Is My Love."

Did you know that Telly Savalas, TV's lollipop-sucking detective *Kojak,* in a fit of rare optimism to say nothing of megalomania covered the Beatles' "Something" in 1974, his version a fat-witted melodyless jaunt into the realms of cacophony that sounds as if the actor had a severe eating disorder? Or that Leonard Nimoy, *Star Trek*'s Mr. Spock, has recorded about a dozen albums? (The character that he played had pointed elfin ears and, I believe, convinced him that he himself had acute — and sensitive — hearing.) Or that chic diabolist and cultist Anton LaVey went so far as to make records, notably in 1995 the hokey LP, *Satan Takes a Holiday*? Or that boxer Jake LaMotta recorded a grim *a capella* version of "My Way" in 2002? Or that heavy- weight champ Muhammad Ali in 1976 actually recorded *The Adventures of Ali vs. Mr. Tooth Decay,* which also starred as indiscriminate co-contributors — talk about a mixed bag — both Frank Sinatra and Howard Cosell? That the hustler Uri Geller, that preposterous Israeli nutball from the 1970s who became famous for supposedly bending spoons and forks with his mind, recorded an album of his own atrocious songs?

There is no accounting for the acute and ongoing shamelessness of people in the world of show business. They get up and sing, blow up balloons, start tap-dancing, or do a spate of animal imitations at the drop of a hat. Van Johnson in *The Romance of Rosy Ridge* (1947) with an accompanying banjo sings, *brays* — harshly, gravelly, unbearably — "When You Are Far From Your Darling" to the winsome and clearly over-obliging Janet Leigh. Gary Cooper unselfconsciously sings "Marry Me, Marry Me" in *Friendly Persuasion* (1956), not quite his first and only recording. Gary Cooper is credited with performing the song "Here Comes Cookie" in *Bluebeard's Eighth Wife* (1938). He also sings a few lines of "Old Joe Clark" in *Along Came Jones* (1945). (Is that why his name is Melody Jones in the film?) Clint Eastwood sang "I Talk to the Trees" in the movie musical, *Paint Your Wagon*. Clunked notes. Almost as bad, the late Lord Laurence Olivier over the opening credits of *The Entertainer* (1960) sings — in a weak, wayward, wobbling voice — "Why Should I Bother to Care?" In his case, I daresay, it is a voice clearly arranged — programmed — to sound comically weary and decadently enervated. Mickey Rooney in *Words and Music* (1948) sings a duet with Judy Garland, "I Wish We Were in Love Again," and although he goes flat a lot he has pizzazz and a middlingly good voice. Singing under the pseudonym Ruth Haig, Betty Grable who starred in *The Dolly Sisters* (1945) made one record with husband, Harry James, quite credibly singing "I Can't Begin to Tell You." In the kitschy movie, *Valley of the Dolls* (1967), Susan Hayward actually sang, "I'll Plant My Own Tree," a song that had been written initially for Judy Garland in a projected movie that was to parallel Garland's own many tragic mésalliances and personal excesses. Angela Lansbury playing the lovely Sibyl Vane sang, "Goodbye, Little Yellow Bird" in *The Picture of Dorian Gray* (1945). Not bad, all things considered, but Lansbury has an airy voice, something like a cardboard-horn with a hole in it. Nevertheless, she did go on to star in the lead of the musical *Hello, Dolly!* And I have to say that the veteran Irene Dunne sings "Why Was I Born?" in a rather sweet way in the movie, *Sweet Adeline* (1935).

Playing the banjo and singing in *Cool Hand Luke*, the actor Paul Newman gives us several choruses of "Plastic Jesus" — a humorous folk song written by Ed Rush and George Cromarty in 1957 — but delivers it, sitting on his bunk, in a sad monotonous moo. It was Newman with a perfectly straight face and all of the gravitas of a funeral director who always seriously referred to his "instrument," by which he meant his voice, as if he himself — in the flesh — were a Guerneri violin. The poor fool didn't know that Leonardo Da Vinci once sent puffs of air through the larynx of a dead goose and produced a honk?

Which of us is not spooked when hearing the song "Where I Come From" that Jennifer Jones sings in *Portrait of Jennie* (1948), a monotonously creepazoidal and ghostly chant performed with a kind of mentally-ill child's delivery? She seems to have tried to get away with singing the entire song in the same long dull repeated note, but it goes badly awry. Maybe if she had been less traitorous to her despairing first husband, Robert Walker, throwing him over with her eye on the main chance in order to make a dirty financial alignment with the rich Hollywood mover and *macher,* David O. Selznick — the two were living together in concubinage that very year — goodness in the form of fate might have made her voice more mellifluous. "Everything he did was for Jennifer. His whole life centered upon her, to the detriment of his good judgment," said John Huston in *An Open Book.* "Selznick never did anything worth a damn after he married Jennifer." Their daughter, Mary Jennifer Selznick committed suicide at 22 by jumping from a 20th-floor window in Los Angeles on May 11, 1976.

Does that sound extravagant? You don't believe in karma? Lionel Barrymore ascribed the sad, alcoholic decline in the life of his brother, the actor John, to the fact that John once brazenly brought back a totem pole from an Alaskan holiday to be placed in his Hollywood garden. Up to that point, apparently, John could do no wrong. After that, however, his luck badly turned, and Lionel attributed this solely to the totem pole. John Barrymore had handled this object casually and thereby angered some Eskimo god.

I have alluded above to the song "I Talk to the Trees." We were taught dancing back in junior high school in an old closed gym at the Roberts Junior High School to that record ("Ladies choice!" "Men's choice!"), and I mention this only because records, old music, are portals to deep memories like nothing else, smells included. I can still recall the big old 78 r.p.m. Slim Whitman version of that song that our seventh-grade teacher played on a portable turntable. Those old shellacked records, table-thick and yet brittle as ribbon candy, cracked easily. Record collectors still look for odd variants in 45s, red vinyl, hologram records, and rare picture discs, the vinyl equivalent among bin-monkeys of book collecting and looking for, say, such rare Stephen King collectible hardcover editions as the asbestos-bound *Firestarter;* the Bible-paper, zipper-closed Scream Press edition of *Skeleton Crew*; or the rare original limited artist edition of 250 with a stainless steel and leather cover of *My Pretty Pony* with its fey digital clock inserted in the cover that sold for $2,200 back in 1989 and now a fortune. I know, I know, did the mercantile King know Colonel Tom Parker?

Pretty Miriam Hopkins sings in the film *24 Hours* (1931) as a glamorous and world-weary chanteuse. She demonstrates no voice but lots of gusto as she belts out, "I'm yours to the end/ That's what's makin' me rave/ Baby come and get me/ You're the one that I crave." (It was so strange how often young women used baby talk in early '30s movies, calling their men "papa" and themselves "girly," and always speaking in those squeaky tones. It was oddly fashionable — and they all did it.) Lovely Myrna Loy in *Love Me Tonight* (1932) sang a verse of "Mimi" wearing a negligee, but, according to Mick Lasalle in his book, *Complicated Woman* (2001), the bit was cut from all prints for its raciness. The urge to sing, to be recorded, is a common enough drive. Were you aware that the strange, apocalyptic David Koresh (born Vernon Howell), the innocent altruistic minister who while holed-up in his Waco retreat was harassed, brutalized, and then on April 10, 1993, along with his devoted religious followers, harmless men, women, and children, tragically incinerated by the insane attacks of ATF agents and U.S. government thugs — thanks, Janet Reno! — once played guitar with his messianic group for an album called — sadly, morbidly apt — *Voice of Fire*? Or that the late great Divine, the blimpish cross-dressing star of several John Waters' movies, in his *My First Album* (1982) left us such memorable tunes as the raw "Jungle Jezebel," "Native Love," and "Shoot Your Shot"? (You can hear the actual avoirdupois in his beach-ball-fat voice!) Or that Louis Farrakhan, for years known as "The Charmer," made dubious history with his calypso miss-hits all through the 1950s? Or that former PTL queen Tammy Faye Bakker, famous for her raccoon-eyed makeup, recorded an album for quick cash called *Building on the Rock* in 1975, several years before she and her troll-like husband Jim were dragged before the law for simony, theft, graft, corruption, and general fleecing of their gullible Christian flock of millions of dollars. Jake Austen in *Playboy* (March 2005) describes her album this way: "This is one of several albums on which Bakker plays Susie Moppet, a pig-tailed pig girl who explains in a high shrill falsetto how the act of smiling protects you from sin, which probably isn't true." As I say, the hugely talentless TV gadfly Regis Philbin put out a CD of songs in 2004 called *When You're Smiling* — an amazing dud that was sold with an "actual" photo of him ("Free!") along with a treasured "special appearance" by his wife, Joy — and there is literally not a word or phrase sung when the man does not sound like he has a blow-fish stuck directly in the center of his glottis. Blockheaded stand-up comedian and moronic Rat Pack anomaly, Joey Bishop's "Your Cheatin' Heart" with its ungroovy ad-libs fecklessly ends with the sage homiletic advice, saccharinely tucked in as a thoughtful coda, "Nobody likes a cheatin' chick." Were you aware that the late actor Walter Matthau sang? His mewling version of "Bring Her Back to Me," sounds like actual goshawk calls. Bette Davis actually cut a 45 r.p.m. record, singing "Life is a Lovely Thing." Bette Davis. Can you imagine? There is a CD covering a 1976 recording that she made for EMI Records in London with eleven tracks featuring the then 68-year-old legend performing her memorable songs from *Whatever Happened to Baby Jane; Now, Voyager;* and *Hush Hush, Sweet Charlotte* which includes — go figure — her famous car speech from *All About Eve*. Others tracks include "Until It's Time to Go," "Loneliness," "Mother of the Bride," and more. Digitally Remastered! Her "I've Written a Letter to Daddy" is a camp hoot, of course, and although her version of "They're Either Too Young or Too Old" sounds a bit floppy, flat, and talky, her voice is fibrous and reveals that old Davis clipped diction. Lucille Ball was a decent, if not quite stellar singer in real life. (This was a running gag on TV's *I Love Lucy*.) I once saw her in Boston breezing through the Ritz, an elegant hotel frequented by, among others, the late doomed Edie Sedgwick who frittering away her life in exhibitionistic ways characteristically to amuse her friends, notably the Andy Warhol crowd in New York City, once stood on top of a table and in her breathy voice sang Richard Rodgers's "Loads of Love:" "I never have been handed much, I never have demanded much, I just want money, a nice position, and loads of lovely love."

Certain actors play at being bad. This is the "Jack Benny Violin Persona" Syndrome. It is a well-known secret that in reality Benny was a very talented violinist and counted virtuoso Isaac Stern among one of his close friends. Barney Fife, for example, had a whole episode devoted to how bad of a singer he is on *The Andy Griffith Show*; he had sung awkwardly with Andy on earlier shows, but Don Knotts actually had a fine country tenor voice. Katey Sagal from TV's *Married...with Children* is an excellent singer — she actually got her career start as one of Bette Midler's Harlettes — although her character, Peg Bundy, is not. I have heard that the late Jean Stapleton, in spite of that "opening" to *All in the Family*, sang quite well in real life. When a character is supposed to be a bad singer, I have noticed, he or she will often use a transparently fake voice to simulate a supposedly "tone deaf" sound. Sliding the notes up and down randomly and screeching at the top of your lungs, often complemented by bad lyrics, helps and contributes to the popular portrayal of bad singing, even though it is blatantly fake to anyone who has ever heard the real thing.

Hollywood has always been Showoffville. Who in Tinseltown did not sing? Boris Karloff sang. So did Will Rogers. Peter Lorre, believe it or not, sang in the 1928 Brecht-Weill musical *Happy End*. Walter Brennan who in something of a unique pitch always tried to get listeners of his music to cry made a small career throughout the 1960s singing maudlin trash like "Old Rivers," "Mama Sang a Song." "Little Son," "Riders in the Sky," and "Cool Water." John Payne, a 1940s "heartthrob" from the From the Bob Eberle/ Tex Beneke era sings "Love is Where You Find It" in *The Garden of the Moon* and manages to hit not a single note right. Buster Keaton found the occasion to sing in movies. He had an untrained, metallic — almost twanging — singing voice, but his version of "In a Little Spanish Town," during which he accompanies himself on a ukulele, is a lovely turn. His bit in the movie *Doughboys* singing and playing the uke with Cliff ("Ukulele Ike") Edwards tapping the strings, for musicality, has to be pound for pound one of the great musical scenes in film history. Cliff Edwards was a nonpareil. "I Can't Give You Anything But Love." "I'll See You in My Dreams." "A Bundle of Old Love Letters." "Me and the Man in the Moon." "Dream Sweetheart." "Hard-Hearted Hannah," "Paddlin' Madelin Home." Cliff Edwards. You will not see his like again, trust me. *Dragnet*'s Jack Webb cut an LP called *You're My Girl* — he poses smiling on the jacket, wearing an open shirt, holding a cigarette — on which, "talking" the lyrics of the songs parlando-style over chessy easy-listening background music, he gives sexy, low-voiced renditions — it is strictly a pressured voice — of such classics as "Try a Little Tenderness," "But Beautiful, "I Thought about Marie," and "When Sunny Gets Blue."

On the *Golden Throats: Great Celebrity Sing-Off* series you can have the thrill of hearing such gems as Leonard Nimoy singing "Proud Mary," Mae West "Twist and Shout," Andy Griffith "The House of the Rising Sun," Eddie Albert "Blowin' in the Wind," Jack Palance "The Green, Green Grass Of Home," Telly Savalas "I Walk the Line," Sebastian Cabot "It Ain't Me, Babe." Slim Pickens "Desperados Waiting For a Train," Rod McKuen "Mule Train," William Shatner "Lucy in the Sky with Diamonds." Joe Pesci "Got To Get You in My Life," "Big Girls Don't Cry" by Edith Massey and the Eggs, "Michelle" by the sex-book author, Xaviera Hollander, and the inimitable Phyllis Diller singing "(I Can't Get No) Satisfaction." Be still, my heart! *The Rhino Brothers Present the World's Worst Records* is a compilation album, re-released in 1983, which features mostly novelty songs, parodies and cover versions of popular songs, performed very poorly (in some cases perhaps intentionally so). The rare original album included an airsickness bag and a warning that the album "may cause internal discomfort." Dr. Demento wrote the liner-notes for the album.

Rude, malapropistic tough guy Leo Gorcey actually sings in *Blues Busters*, a Bowery Boys cheapie from 1950. In the movie, "motorlips" Satch (the great Huntz Hall) develops an uncanny ability to sing after having his tonsils removed. The fact is, all of his songs were dubbed by John Lorenz. Huntz however did have the distinction of appearing (top row) on the cover of the Beatles' *Sgt. Pepper's Lonely Hearts Club Band* album. Then again, so did a Sony TV set, a Hindu doll, a garden gnome, and a tuba.

Why, even John Wayne sang! Early in his career, he appeared as "Singin'" Sandy Saunders in *Riders of Destiny* (1933) and seven more films for Monogram Pictures. Wayne's version of the singing cowboy was much darker than the later ones; his ten-gallon hat was black instead of white, and he would chant about "streets running with blood" and "you'll be drinking your drinks with the dead" as he strode purposefully down the street toward a showdown. I have already mentioned the Three Stooges in *The Women Haters*, their very first short, in which they sing — painfully, croakingly — "For You, My Love, My Life, My All." And of course their "Swinging the Alphabet" — to be seen in *Violent is the Word for Curly* (1938) — is an American classic. Andy Devine whose voice had a blasted, pitted hoarseness to it sings, "Jesus Loves Me" to an audience of children. Marjorie Main sings in *The Harvey Girls*, while Percy Kilbride gives it a go in *George Washington Slept Here*. Sex symbol Mamie Van Doren sings "Like a Rolling Stone" in *Untamed Youth* in 1957 — she was the first woman to sing rock-and-roll in a Hollywood musical — and it is just short of bearable. Gina Lollobrigida sings. You can hear Charlie Manson singing all over the Internet.

Charlie Chaplin sings in *Modern Times*, the first film where his voice is actually heard. He performs Léo Daniderff's comical song, "*Je cherche après Titine*" — a version that is also known as "The Nonsense Song." His character has to sing it in gibberish since, due to losing the shirt cuff on which the lyrics were written, he is making up the words on the spot The lyrics are ridiculous but actually appear to sound like words in French and Italian. Chaplin's dexterous use of half-intelligible wording for comic effect points the way towards Hynkel's idiotic speeches in *The Great Dictator*, to me one of the unfunniest movies ever made — second-grade humor — and, as far as I am concerned, a total failure. Sentimentality was his vice, a failing at its most extreme late Victorian kitsch as can be found in much of the music he composed such as "Smile," "Eternally," "Weeping Willows," "Without You," "Mandolin Serenade," etc. Katharine Hepburn had a terrible voice, hard, overfried, nagging. Have you seen film footage of her playing Coco? She wanders around the stage wearing a black hat in a black-waif ensemble looking like a thin, slightly berserk cat-o-nine-tails, and when she begins singing she sounds like Walter Brennan! "Get out your Tums, kids, because this one's gonna hurt," wrote the acerbic but witty Michael Musto. "You see, in 1969, screen legend Katharine Hepburn played designer Coco Chanel in the splashy Broadway musical *Coco*. I will always regret having missed that one, but with a truckload of thanks to the *YouTube* clip from that season's Tony Awards I need no longer lose sleep over the loss," Musto goes on to say,

The number has a mind-numbing array of svelte women (and one semi-chubette) parading around in red outfits to drearily over-arranged elevator music. Stick that out, though, because then comes the prize: La Hepburn croaking out a few show-stopping lyrics with a lack of musicality that makes Rex Harrison look like Caruso by comparison. No wonder the Tony voters decided that Lauren Bacall's slightly less atonal belch-singing in *Applause* was more palatable that year. They should have called this show *Loco*!

Hepburn lustily crow-caws,

> Who the devil ca-ahs,
> What a woman wa-ahs
> Is it werth a stitch
> Packing up a witch
> In a golden sh-ell?

Her singing, "I Can't Give You Anything But Love" in *Bringing Up Baby* apparently drove her co-star Cary Grant absolutely bonkers. She hits the word "love" so flatly that one may say in all charity that it may possibly be — literally may be — the very worst single note ever sounded by an upright human being. I would rather listen to Hepburn sing that, however, than have to watch her again in that stupid, gender-bending farce *Sylvia Scarlett* (1935). Of all the grating voices of Hollywood actresses, hers had to be among the worst, tremulous, harsh, loud, and faux-patrician all at once, although Jean Arthur's comes close, an almost indescribably snarping high-clipped snort from the nose, always off-key, that with a good deal of Munchkin in it always wavered unpredictably in a crazy frailty just right for screwball comedy. There was a constant *honk* in it. Arthur played and sang the lead in Leonard Bernstein's 1950 musical version of *Peter Pan*, which co-starred Boris Karloff as Captain Hook, but you have to hear her claw-singing her duet with the late humorist Fred Allen, "In My Merry Oldsmobile," to be legitimately brutalized, to feel you are in the midst of Canada geese.

I have mentioned Marjorie Main, the character actress known for the raw, domineering, salty roles she played at MGM. With her masculine manner and "sack-o'-taters" figure, she was fairly unprepossessing. Damon Runyon once remarked that she had a "voice like a file and a stride like a section boss." ("Between you and me and the world," she once said, "Ma Kettle was the real man in the family"), I would have to point to her cacophonous singing in the hectic song-and-dance number, "Swing Your Partner Round and Round" in *The Harvey Girls*, playing the tough old western stick "Sonora Cassidy," as the closest rival for sheer abrasiveness to Kate Hepburn's scrawking voice in *Coco*. Be prepared for it. It is a voice that lands like cold wet wash-flannels on your face. Work it, girlfriend!

Almost as bad were the musical crullers Red Buttons offered like the "Hi Ho Song" and "Strange Things Are Happening" which he recorded in the 1950s and continued to sing the rest of his life, as only the ambitious little Aaron Chwatt (his real name) could, every single chance he got — on stage, on television, in movies, live in Las Vegas, on the Borscht Belt, on street-corners, for Bar Mitzvah groups, you name it — always energetically bouncing up and down on one leg with one hand held behind an ear, giving us a good idea of how unfortunately corny the Eisenhower years had been. (Does it not signify in a rather large way that Ike's favorite dessert of all time was prune whip?) The talentless Buttons would be doing this bit 40 years later — strutting, cupping his ear — when the sad fact remained that a whole new generation had no a clue to who he was or what he was doing.

This is all hard to believe? Not in a country where folks are a few Bradys short of a bunch, where people line up three months ahead of time to watch a *Star Wars* movie, where year-in and year-out devoted TV listeners sent off letters to that great impresario Lawrence Welk — read his *This I Believe*, if you doubt me — with requests for him to play such songs as "White Clips of Dover," "Dunker Shane," "Aisle of Capri," "Tip Top Through the Tulips," "Sam Lewis Blues," and the romantically haunting "When You Walk Through A Store." God bless America! Surprised Spiro Agnew became one of its leaders?

But then of course these are all cartoons. Perhaps I should say most of them. Gregory Peck's surprising rendition of "I'm A Rambling Wreck from Georgia Tech" in *The Man in the Grey Flannel Suit* (1956), where he accompanies himself on a ukulele, is not bad. The man could carry a tune. I also think that Marlon Brando does a more than passable job singing "Luck, Be a Lady Tonight" and "Woman in Love" in the musical *Guys and Dolls*. Lee Marvin's growly version of "Wanderin' Star" in *Paint Your Wagon* is masterful, as well. Andy Griffith had a first-rate voice. Listen to his songs in *A Face in the Crowd*, notably "Free Man in the Morning" — brilliant. Were you aware that the late actress Joan Crawford also sang? Indeed she did. In the early MGM film *Mannequin* (1937) she croons,

> Always and always I'll go on
> adoring the glory and wonder of you;

> Always and always my love will go
> soaring to heaven far under the blue

Far *under* the blue! That's what she sang. Don't blame me. Music by Edward Ward. Lyric by Bob Wright and Chet Forrest. Right. Far under the blue. I have personally checked the sheet music ("You Can't Go Wrong With A Feist Song" is the boast on their logo, although in this case we may have found a major exception.)

Seth MacFarlane, the creator of the satirical television show *Family Guy* has recorded a solo album of American standards and, vocally relaxed, does a good job with "Two Sleepy People," "You're the Cream in My Coffee," even the schmaltzy "Something Good" from *The Sound of Music*

Does pop music *have* to be bad? The great bluesman Robert Johnson was a savvy pop musician, remember, interested in hits, not some way-out esoteric Delta folk or jazz rarity. Blues was a hot new style for him, contemporary, hip, coming down from the north from the likes of Bessie Smith, Ma Rainey, Lonnie Johnson, Leroy Carr! He had a feel for the times he lived in! Listen to "Come On In My Kitchen," "Terraplane Blues," or "Walking Blues." What happened to the *quality* of pop music?

Was it Noel Harrison who sing-sang "The Windmills of Your Mind" in *The Thomas Crown Affair*? I was truly convinced that nothing on the planet could possibly sound as bad as that, with the glaring exception perhaps of Petula Clark's almost incandescently dreadful version of "Old Devil Moon" or the almost stadium-filling stink of Eric Carmen's droning "All By Myself" or the uniquely monstrous Jerry Vale's coyote-howling version of "Be My Love" which with its incessant voice-lilts and tired, greasy twi-kicked note-squawks and primitive Sicilian yelps is almost comic in presentation, a neo-operatic farce carved out with what comes across as wavy undulating lines rippling oddly off each missed note like the rascela lines on an old woman's buttocks! No, I'm afraid that even in his best songs he was always leaking oil. You find you have the sudden urge to want to shout at the top of your voice, "*Piantala! Mi raccomondo!*" (Stop it! Please, I'm begging you*!)* With its pleading servility, it has a distinct aspect of obsequiousness about it, something along the lines of that absurd gurgling doofus, the late Paul Harvey (thank *him* for the stupid portmanteau word "guesstimate") and that pocket fascist radio-cretin/commentator, G. Gordon Liddy. On his phisopolemical talk show he would resort for actual entertainment — apparently nothing was ever planned for the daily program — to reading over the airwaves lame right-wing articles others had written, not even his own thoughts. His smarmily servile opening question to all the cretins and blockheads and Hitler Jugend and Bund Deutscher Mädchen and Hausfrauen who compulsively called him up to rant on Radio WXTK (Cape Cod) was always his unctuous greeting, "How may I serve you?" Aside from a dull program that had been averruncated of anything at all like common sense, crazy Liddy's raddled voice alone, a senescent one characterized by flustered and distracted pauses, halting phrases, and inattentive stammerings, sounded like that of a grunion. There was in those metallic, almost midget-sounding clucks of Liddy's not only a good deal of the Hollywood Munchkin, as well as a discernible strain of anger and self-disappointment, but also the constant attempt on his part to try to assume a British accent. He would say *been* (sounding like seen), *rawther* instead of rather, *a-gain* as rhyming with rain, etc. Unbalanced. Who was it that said, "Every Irishman wakes up every morning depressed to find he is not an Englishman"? Were you aware, by the way, that during the unjust, immoral American invasion of Iraq in April 11, 2003, Liddy, a flaming bigot, a token-Zionist who prejudicially inveighed against Arabs, a cultural divider, a paranoid, and a shirty little deludinoid who also believed that he could sing, repeatedly played over the airwaves his own zombiesque recording of "God Bless America"? But back to Jerry Vale — not the coolest cat who is what am — OK? He knows little or nothing of musical rhythm, which is bad enough, but, worse, he cannot and never could feel any given song's *values*. The fact is that Jerry Vale with a kind of rudimentary deafness did not *hear* his voice. "Old Cape Cod"? *Che macello!* He was desperately bad, imponderably untalented, almost matchless for unbearable. He who never goes away, I gotta be frank, embodies that venerable old Chinese vaudeville act, On Too Long. There is no question that he is solid proof of Dr. Linus Pauling's truism, "No vital forces, only chemical bonds, underlie life."

If you think Vale is bad, listen to Noel Paul Stookey's rebarbative lowing on that *come si chiama* called "Wedding Song." Oh please God, I think, stop singing, *stop singing*, STOP SINGING! How did that man ever *begin* singing and why? Was he once a wedding singer, someone that was actually paid for it? Why can't he find a right note? I mean, even a blind pig occasionally finds an acorn. Hey, Paul Stookey, stop singing! The telephone you don't hear is me not calling. Wasn't it the actor Charlie Sheen who once declared, "I don't pay hookers for coming over, I pay them so they will leave"? I have nearly driven my car off the road upon hearing the "Wedding Song" come on the radio. It is worse than a vocal somnifacient. It is artlessness itself instanced. I have grown dark and depressed and angry, bewilderedly trying to locate the lump of wrath and the precise reason for it that could elicit such elemental disgust, nausea, and unabated fury all at once. I swear to God, I want to strike out, throttle someone, bash my head on the car steering wheel not so much in the knowledge that this incalculably sterile song exists — he supposedly wrote it for his partner, Peter Yarrow — as that I can never quite reach the off-button on the car radio fast enough before hearing

> Where there's a something something
> there is looooove.
> Aw, there is *loooove.*

Aw? Aw? *Aw!!!!!!*

There are certain recorded songs, even worse than maddening instrumentals like David Rose's "Holiday for Strings" and "Elephant Walk" and "The Pink Panther Theme" and "Spanish Flea" and "Hawaiian War Chant" by Billy Vaughan, that are so elementally bad, a combination of a brutally bad singer coupled with cheesy or brainless arrangements, that every single copy of any of them should be found and burnt. All such bad songs seem to share spates of over-jovial sax-zaps or trumpet zings or violin-runs. (Tell the truth, don't you always find yourself, as I do, mentally throwing darts at a target during the brisk flourishes whenever you hear Beethoven's *Violin Concerto in D Major,* 1st movement, part three?) These songs stick in thrilling memory like those of the bloated and swag-bellied Imelda Marcos, Queen of the Philippines, sporting cherry-size drop-earrings of yellow pearls and concentrating her starry gaze on President LBJ in 1967, singing "Because of You" in Tagalog — or her mewling version of the incommunicably bad song, "Feelings," sung in a woefully out-of-tune voice to semi-comatose President Reagan and his wife Nancy. (Talk about the nadir of show business.) Of course I have never had the luck to hear, live, Calvin Coolidge squeak out "Love's Old Sweet Song" or catch the old Boston mayor, "Honey Fitz" Fitzgerald, wheeze "Sweet Adeline" — or descry the mating calls during love-spring, for that matter, of a parliament of capuchin monkeys in the branches of the high rain forests in desperately green Guatemala.

I am thinking here of such unmusical abortions as Barbra Streisand's "Don't Rain on My Parade," Gordon Lightfoot's "Softly" — a true nightmare — Captain and Tennille's "Muskrat Love," Wings' "Band on the Run," "On and On" by Stephen Bishop, Three Dog Night's "Jeremiah Was A Bullfrog," Lou Rawls's "Unforgettable," Bette Midler's "C.C. Rider," Paul McCartney's "Silly Love Songs" — a particular title that reminds me of what Courtney Love once told MTV's Kurt Loder, "I'm not psycho, but my lyrics are" — Kenny

Rogers's hoarse "She Believes In Me," America's "Believe In Me," Harry Belafonte's cancerously croaky "And I Love You So" — I always wondered if Belafonte's decade-long public commitment to Civil Rights was not done as an active penance to redeem the time for having spent just as many decades singing reductively brainless calypso and bongo songs — Helen Reddy's "You and Me Against the World" or her truly crackbrained version of "Look Down (That Lonesome Road)," Glen Campbell's cacophonic "Rhinestone Cowboy," the Clark Sisters' "I'll Get By," Toby Keith's fascistic "An American," and, as I say, things like Mr. Paul Stookey's indefensibly bad "The Wedding Song," such eerily jolt-headed, deathful examples of a musical breakdown in taste and quality that, taken altogether, sound in their unconscionable din like a crazy ill-conceived soundtrack from Hieronymus Bosch's cacofornopornological hell in his painting *The Garden of Earthly Delights.* Streisand's dubious version of "Speak Low" is a sort of begging screech, a preposterous serving of strained, unlistenable artifice like 'N Sync's "God Must Have Spent A Lot of Time on You," a tuneless, melodyless, featureless piece of scat and scatterchat with lyrics composed as if by a 6-year-old cretin. The nonpareil of shuddersome. Horrendous. Streisand's "Stoney End," finally, ending with those maniacal chicken-crows at the very top cockloft of her shrieking voice,

> Cradle me, mama, cradle me again
> (Cradle me, mama, cradle me again
> Maaaaaaaaaaaaaaaaaaaama, cradle meee agaaain…)

somehow can never quite quash the echo in my head, repeating over and over, of the name of the group, Screeching Weasel. "Many singers make my teeth ache from Rudy Vallee to Britney Spears, but none is taken so seriously as the incomparably ersatz Barbra Streisand," writes Gary Giddins in an article, "Most Overrated Singer" in *American Heritage* (May/June 2000). "Everything she sings is charged with self-loving vulgarity; worship me, she bellows, and forget the song," adding that her "primary technique consists of heavy breathing, which turns tenaciously aspirate on vowels or *h* words." Giddins admits that she has a "huge" voice but not only does she not know what to do with it but is always too egotistically intent on "stopping the show." "*Classical Barbra* exposed her hubris, yet her pop singing is every bit as garish." Citing her lack of "emotional generosity" — which is why, he says, she "has never joined the ranks of the great hearts-on-their-sleeves emoters, from Jolson to Garland" — Giddins compares and contrasts her with the "unparalleled versatility" of the *committed* and highly popular, indeed revered,

Bing Crosby who, with his perfect timing and articulation, "could be equally affecting in country, cowboy, Hawaiian, and standard songs."

I can forgive Jule Styne for the wretched "People" which of course was a Streisand hit back in 1963, the lyrics of which are insane, because he also gave us — as if crying out, "*Ralliez-vous à mon panache blanc!*" — such musical gems as "I Don't Want to Walk Without You," "Let Me Entertain You," "I'll Walk Alone," "Let It Snow! Let It Snow! Let It Snow!" "Just in Time," "I've Heard That Song Before," and, among many others, Miss Lorelei Lee's theme song (lyrics by Leo Robin):

> He's your guy
> When stocks are high.
> But beware when they start to descend.
> It's then that those louses
> Go back to their spouses.
> Diamonds are a girl's best friend.

Whenever I hear in "People," Merrill's cloying passage, "We're children needing other children/and yet letting our grown-up pride/hide all the need inside," I develop a serious toothache. I think of the scene in *The Simpsons Movie* (2007) when Marge sententiously says, "Sometimes you have to stand back to appreciate a work of art," a dubious if anti-intellectual Homer snickeringly replies, "Way back."

"I have put all my heart into this song ["Feelings"], my own personal creation," declared Morris Albert (born Mauricio Albert Kaisermann) in 1976. "It is what I think I will be most remembered for. I have even gotten fan letters from big stars like Diana Ross and Cary Grant." It is bad enough that the song is horrendously bad, nothing more than agglutinated repetitions of the same tired lyric, "Feelings/ Whoa, whoa. feelings/ Whoa, feelings," but it turns out that it had been plagiarized. Kaisermann was sued for copyright infringement. A Federal District Court in New York City ruled in 1988 that over 80% of "Feelings" had been stolen from "*Pour Toi*" ("For You"), a French song that had been written in 1956 by Loulou Gaste, the real composer who by a court-ruling received a $500,000 settlement from Kaisermann the Brazilian thief, as well as 78% of the royalties generated by the song. The amazing detail, at least to me, is that anyone would claim to have written what has to be, hands down, one of the worst pieces of rubbish in music history, a true party killer.

David Soul's "Don't Give Up On Us, Baby," Ambrosia's "The Biggest Part of Me" and "How Much I Feel," and "Diary" by Bread — the '70s were a cesspool of bad music — are impossibly bad. Do you realize how in a very real way these songs have intruded on your *life*? The list goes on. Def Leppard's "Pour Some Sugar On Me," Liza Minnelli's strangulated, hair-pulling, hysterical version of "New York, New York," Paul Anka's "Love Me Warm and Tender, Dear," Bobby Darin's "You're The Reason I'm Living," Michael Jackson's "Don't Stop Till You Get Enough," Earth Wind & Fire's "September," Paper Lace's "The Night Chicago Died," Mac Davis's "Baby Don't Get Hooked on Me" — all intolerable. "On The Wings of Love" composed by Peter Schless and Jeffrey Osborne is pure braying. Listening to Joni Mitchell sing "Big Yellow Taxi" is like hearing fingernails down a chalkboard. I cannot bear Ben E. King's "On the Street Where You Live," Marvin Gaye's "Sexual Healing," and Sergio Mendes's "The Look of Love." "Courtesy of the Red, White, and Blue" by Toby Keith is of course a category all of its own, "Musicological Jingoism," hype costumed as hope. Rubbish like that. The toilet bowl of popular music. Waving Old Glory for mercantile reasons.

> Now this nation that I love is fallin' under attack.
> A mighty sucker-punch came flying in from somewhere in the back.
> Soon as we could see clearly through our big black eye,
> Man, we lit up your world like the fourth of July...

By "lit up your world" Keith means the unconscionable shock and awe bombing on March 22, 2003 not only of Baghdad, but of Mosul, Iraq's second-largest city, and the southern city of Kirkuk as well where as many as over 100,000 innocent Iraqis were savagely incinerated, an even greater blasphemy when it became common knowledge almost immediately that the Iraqi government and the Iraqi people had nothing whatsoever to do with the attacks on the World Trade Center or the Pentagon on September 11, 2001. But all of that is show business of which Irving Berlin assures there is no business like, right? The rhyme-crippled, sub-poetic, truly repellent doggerel that Keith slaps onto his music — fourth-grade bad — are reason enough to take away his ASCAP license:

> Oh, justice will be served and the battle will rage:
> This big dog will fight when you rattle his cage.
> An' you'll be sorry that you messed with the U.S. of A.
> 'Cos we'll put a boot in your ass, it's the American way...

Do you happen to recall Roland Barthes' definition of *plastic*? "A disgraced material, lost between the effusiveness of rubber and the flat hardness of metal." That is exactly how I would describe Toby Keith.

What about the flip-side of Toby Keithism? His pandering jingoism would not have endeared him to Timothy McVeigh who was, by the way, a pop-music lover. McVeigh loved the song "Bad Company" by the band of the same name. The terrorist responsible for the April 19, 1995 bombing of the Alfred P. Murrah Federal Building in Oklahoma City, Oklahoma was later quoted as saying as he fled the site of the bombing that he thought of a specific "Bad Company" lyric, "...dirty for dirty," a phrase heard towards the end of the song. He bombed the building as a retaliative response to the federal government's pointless massacres at both Ruby Ridge (3 dead) and Waco (76 dead). He had painted "Bad Company" on the turret of his Bradley M3 Fighting Vehicle with the U.S. 1st Infantry Division in the First Gulf War — he was a top-scoring gunner on the 25mm cannon — and listened to the song frequently through his armored vehicle's stereo. Other favorite tunes of his during the Gulf War were the Jefferson Airplane's "White Rabbit" and songs by Queen.

There is literally no end to musical horrors. America's "Tin Man" ("Oz never did give nothin' to the Tin Man/ that he didn't, didn't already have") *Didn't, didn't!* The Bellamy Brothers' "Let Your Love Flow," Hall and Oates' "Rich Girl," Dave Loggins's "Please Come to Boston" — so incalculably bad a song, a singer, a lyric, an arrangement, and an *idea all at once,* that I am struck dumb in thought's astonishment — Orleans' "Dance With Me," Todd Rundgren's "Hello It's Me," Styx's "Come Sail Away," Randy Vanwarmer's "Just When I Needed You Most." It is a midden heap. Even the great Judy Garland singing "I Am Loved" is pure hideola, scarcely identifiable as a song sung by a *sane* person. Her young voice, so clean and strong with barely any grit, was an angel's voice. She cannot be blamed for the lyric, but it is a bad paper, turned in late, and I grade her an "Incomplete."

Magnets, according to *Magnetic Therapy* and other health tracts, are said to be efficacious as to curative powers in helping alleviate certain physical complaints such as toothache, stiffness of shoulders and other joints, pains and swellings, eczema, asthma, as well as chilblains, injuries, and wounds. *What about earache?*

I hear these bad singers and by way of simple juxtaposition ruefully ponder how so many beautiful songbirds are slaughtered in the millions around the world. Did you know that over 50 million songbirds are trapped, killed, and eaten every year in the Great Britain? The very same thing in Cyprus, where millions are annually captured by cruel glue-traps, sticks from which the birds, unable to free themselves, and then executed by a toothpick to the throat, to be pickled or boiled for Cypriots in a national delicacy called *ambelopoulia.* The Swedish physician Axel Munthe in his book of memoirs, *The Story of San Michele* (1929), describes how in Capri on the slopes of Monte Barbarossa, poachers commonly killed singing birds — thrushes, waders, stock pigeons, quails, wagtails, swallows, larks, and others — packed them and sent them off to France to be eaten by unethical and unprincipled gourmands.

I think Elvis Presley's "Daddy (Please Don't Cry)" added a new low to music. It is the B-side of "Rubberneckin'," from his movie *Change of Habit* (1969) in which Elvis, playing a doctor, at one point earnestly tells one of the three volunteers at his clinic in an urban ghetto that two of their predecessors had been raped, adding in all seriousness, "One even against her will." The pre-Army Elvis lost his freedom to the Hill and Range music publishing company founded in LA in 1945 by Austrian-born Julian Aberbach and his business partners, Milton Blink and Gerald King, along with their wily younger cousin, Freddy Bienstock, fast-shuffling Hollywood hustlers, sedulous promoters of their own interests and no one else's, who were responsible for much of the country music produced in the 1950s and 1960s. *They* had control over his material, *they* decided where he would head, *they* chose the frightful and undignified, atrocious and beggarly songs the poor gullible goober had to sing in all the 31 movies he made, setting up an unprecedented arrangement in which the publishing rights to every one of the songs that he recorded were split 50/50 between the Hill & Range Co., his management, and Tupelo Boy himself. Between all of them and Col. Tom Parker, Elvis hadn't a snowball's chance in hell. He just took the sheet music for all those movie songs and punched in. I must say that Elvis, for decades the highest earning dead celebrity, in his late maudlin morph had a terminal illness. The boy once had dreams. He loved black music. He loved ol' Wynonie Harris. He loved Southern Gospel of the Homer Rodeheaver/ E.O. Excell variety. He could never hear enough of the Blackwood Brothers, the Golden Gate Quartet, the Statesmen. Elvis once told Sonny West that when he first started out he wanted more than anything else to sing gospel and had even auditioned for a chance to be the lead singer with a local gospel group but was turned down. "I like to sing with the Methodys," FDR used to say of a Sunday, surrounded by G-men and the Secret Service heading for the Foundry Methodist Church on 16th Street in Washington, D.C. So did Elvis. He lived to sing rudimentary harmonies and do *a capella*, call and response, but sadly descended into all sorts of redneck mewing. God, at least musically, seems to have had a bad effect on Big E. Precious Lord, take my hand!

But it got even worse than that. Toward the end, after the *Physicians' Desk Reference* became Elvis's personal bible, when he began the long, dark descent to the lower reaches, taking "uppers" (Dexamyl, Escatrol, Desbutal) and "downers" (Valium, Percodan, Tuinal) in pitch-black bedrooms, sleeping all day in phantasmagoria, there was only a phantom shell of the King of Rock 'n' Roll.

Barbra Streisand's fault as a singer — hysterical, piercing, glassy — is that she turns every song into a piece of megahyaline architecture. She cannot leave a simple song alone but teases it, expands it, *worries* it. In the end, she leaves a song swollen with theatricality, a macroturbulence that is only exacerbated by plosives coming through a nose shaped like a piton hammer or a fawn-foot axe-handle, and it rarely gels with any true feeling. It is rug-chewing. Scenery hurling. She thrives on back-up choruses as hot antiphonal barrages. In contrast, listen, say, to Doris Day sing the Les Brown classic, "Sentimental Journey," a real voice-stretcher of a song with a demanding range, but Dodo with that voice of hers that was as fresh as a bandbox does it to perfection, no bansheeing, no extra advertising. Any singing voice can be as crazy and as imperfectly odd as a human face. Carly Simon with her voice often hit clunkers. I cannot think of a song more leaden, uninspired, out-of-key, or more unsurpassably bad than her version of the standard "When Your Lover Has Gone."

Streisand, Diamond, Jerry Vale. What they do is over-egg the pudding when they sing. They *pester* songs — in a very real sense made them unchaste. Neil Diamond is Velveeta by the pound and orange as a gumball. I mean what do you do with a guy who wears all black (at times a cape) and plays a black guitar while standing on a riser that is shaped like a pentagram with a band futzing behind him that is more of a small orchestra and then, while humping, singing "Holly Holy" and "Cherry Cherry" and nauseating polka-clap-alongs like "Forever in Blue Jeans." (Cue hysterical laughter.) This is not merely schmaltz but the essence of mawkishness. As Jean Giraudoux once said, "The secret of success is sincerity. Once you can fake that you've got it made." Beautiful noise, my ass.

Forgive what may seem overly unkind, petty, or in fact trivial. The British philosopher Alfred North Whitehead once declared that it requires a very unusual mind to undertake an analysis of the obvious; I suspect he said it because what is obvious may say a good deal about our culture, not only of rock, but of our country. We cannot live on the blind side of illusion or of absurdity. As Jimmy Durante says, exasperatedly flinging up his arms in the movie, *Music For Millions* (1944), "That's the conditions that prevail."

I mention Durante. "In discussing his many songs, the Schnozzola has confessed that he doesn't know exactly how to analyze them," wrote Gene Fowler in *Schnozzola*. In his own inimitable way, Durante explains,

> I think it's the drive that puts 'em over, and the no-rhyme, like sometimes when you're only talkin'. Anybody can tell which is my songs, like "I Was Walkin' Down Broadway the Other Day" or "I'm Home the Other Day and I'm Sleepin'." It's like, what do you call it? Narrationin' little stories.

I try to get a little story in each song….Some of the songs [that I sing] are very pretty and would be a big hit if anybody else sang 'em. But nobody else seems to sing them after I get through. It's the truth…. Now I think when I sing a song I roon it for anybody else. It's like the kiss of debt.

Almost every song that Dinah Shore sang — whole albums of songs — was sung off-key. If Dinah Shore was a legitimate singer, to borrow H.L. Mencken's quip about Dr. Johnson, then a cornet player or bagpiper is a musician. (Remember Noël Coward's quip, "A gentleman is someone who knows how to play the bagpipes but doesn't"?) Try to catch Dinah Shore's version of "Bye Bye Blues," for example — she ingeniously manages to hit not one note right. She had what is called "bad intonation." Rosemary Clooney came very close to the same thing far too often but had more style. There was an absence at the heart of Dinah Shore; to me, she was "a grin without a cat." Possibly her dresses were too tight when recording. Do you know the IRS' "Dinah Shore Ruling"? To wit: "*A dress can be deducted as a professional expense if it is too tight to sit down in. The ruling was issued after singer Shore deducted gowns worn in public appearances as business expenses and insisted, when challenged by the IRS, that they were only worn on stage while performing.*" My feeling is that Liza Minnelli is close to tone-deaf and sings virtually every song off-key — has a real pitch problem. I suggest she cannot hear herself well and tries to make up in volume what she lacks in finesse. Johnny Cash, who sang so often off-key, had a sort of dead-drop in virtually every song he sang, a swerve off melody into a rut rather like a sputtering auto taking an unfortunate mis-turn left or right into thick sand. There is a *dumbness* to it, forgive me. It is faintly disturbing in "I Walk the Line" to have to hear him hum several times just to stay on key. Cash seemed to have short breath, a gasping quality as he sang. I always felt, neurotically, that whenever watching him sing I had to sort of co-breathe with him, *help* him out bronchially, the way I also do, say, when watching what I can only call "gaspers," people like the eerie-looking, right-wing, dark-souled political pundit, Charles Krauthammer, that baleful, bow-tied figure who constantly appears on Fox News looking like a funeral director. When he makes his glowering political points, he has to draw heavy, laborious breaths after every five or six words or so, gasping like an aging musk-ox, very like the late chef Julia Child, the big tall wheezing television lady who, in demonstrations of walloping a dead fish or whipping up a syllabub or hacking up carrots, always seemed to convey a very serious oxygen deficiency. I have already made the point that, except for certain songs by Slim Whitman, Kitty Wells, Hank Snow, Hank Williams, Gene Autry, Bob Wills, and a few others, I have always considered the subjects of country music — and, forgive me, even the genre, at least a great deal of it — tired, trite, vapid, corny, hackneyed, insipid, and for the most part platitudinous. Who of us is surprised that Tim McGraw in "I Like It, I Love It," sings,

> Spent forty-eight dollars last night at the county fair
> *I throwed out my shoulder*
> But I won her that teddy bear
> She's got me sayin' sugar-pie, honey, darlin' and dear.
> [My italics.]

No, we're not talking intellectuals. Schooling is not even in the argument here. I gotta say, it does throw a little light on Johnny Cash getting Cs and Ds in school, right? Remember his single, "Straight As in Love"? he sings, "If they gave me a mark/ for learnin' in the dark/ I'd have straight As in love."

Kill me! A big grinnin' country dunce sporting bared arms and an oversized killer black Stetson with an outlandish 4 ¼" brim crunched up on the sides and pulled down in the back winning a teddy bear at a county fair *and actually singing about it?* I well recall in my early teens hearing Ernest V. Stoneman and the Stoneman family singing in their bird-bill voices over the radio, "The Sinking of the Titanic," with the — to me — dopey, because over-obvious, refrain, "It was sad when that great ship went down." Ya think? I recall they sang the truly memorable line, "They were going to build a ship that the water could not go through." Well, yuuuhhh, that sorta works in the navigation business. But that was by no means the worst of it. How about little ol' pea-picker Archie Campbell's recorded comic (!?) recitative of "The Three Little Pigs?" "*The Pee Little Thrigs*"? Hilarious, don't you think? Spoonerisms. This was perfect entertainment for teenagers who like fart jokes. "He huffed and he puffed and he hoed her blouse down"? Oh, I was a hard marker. I hated yodeling. I hated self-pity. I even hated the cornball "shave-and-a-haircut-two-bits" twanks at the end of the Flatt and Scruggs classic "Foggy Mountain Breakdown," which spoiled it for me. Cheesy. Then throw in Merle Haggard's "Mama Tried" or his "Okie from Muscogee," with its lowbrow philistinic passages:

> We don't smoke marijuana in Muskogee;
> We don't take our trips on LSD.
> We don't burn our draft cards down on Main Street;
> We like livin' right, and bein' free.

and you more or less dot the i.

To me, all country music can be summed up with lyrics like: "On the night I let down Momma and Daddy by drankin' and cheatin' on Linda Bee 'stead of truckin' hogs as I was supposed to find me doin' I found Jesus who give me to boot-scoot back into the US of A of her heart." or "It's OK you cheated on me with that skank down in the holler, 'cause, beggin' your redneck pardon, I since done hitched my trailer to the Lord back in Tennessee and am now bowlin' strikes with them Reparation Angels up abooove."

It is a country *topos* to portray most things urban, complex, scientific, academic, secular, European, northern, or poetic as either ridiculous or evil. On the unendurably insufferable television show *Hee Haw*, Roy Clark, wearing a frilly Elizabethan Age collar and playing the role of "Claude Strawberry, Poet of Cornfield County" — his face resembled a cab with the off-duty light on — used to read with a gay sibilance to mock poets, *poetry*, in fact — the way, I gather, a number of benighted folk up in the hills of Arkansas or Tennessee possibly actually do judge that genre of literature — a "furrin" language — as being conceived, written, and spoken, with a fey, lisping delivery and a limp wrist. I would certainly point to this 1970 show in empathetic support of the imaginative science-fiction writer Philip K. Dick's contentious judgement that "the world we actually have does not meet my standards." There has long been a vigorous, anti-intellectual sub-culture in many areas of America that thrive on the belief that most things outside one's community state and nation are inferior and threatening, from Joe ("Deer HUnting With Jesus") Bageant's "Guns are the warrior ideal" to *Family Guy*'s Peter Griffin's "Books are jerks." (I would add that the suave Humphrey Bogart in that one anti-intellectual scene in *The Big Sleep* also shocked me with his belittling caricature of a book-collector when, arranging his hat to look like a nerd and slipping on thick glasses, he walks into a bookshop to order a rare volume with the same gay prissiness, as if all readers of books were unmanly, weak, simpering, and foolish.)

Was it for such people that the instructions for a medical thermometer advise, "Do not use orally after using it rectally"? That the side of a Slush Puppy cup warns, "This ice may be cold"? That the box of a 500-piece puzzle reads, "Some assembly required"? That cans of Easy Cheese contain the instruction, "For best results, remove cap"? That a label on a nighttime sleep-aid reads, "Warning: may cause drowsiness"? That cans of self-defense pepper spray caution, "May irritate the eyes"?

One can occasionally hear in country music a unique turn-of-phrase, usually a regional or Southern peapickerism with, often, silly song titles to prove it, such as "Venom Wearin' Denim," "Elvira," "Dropkick Me, Jesus, Through the Goal Post of Life," "A Boy Named Sue," "Remember To Remind Me I'm Leavin'," "We

Never Killed Each Other (But Didn't We Try?)" "I'd Rather Be Picked Up Here Than Put Down at Home," "Is It Cold in Here, or Is It You?" But you rarely hear an original phrase in Gospel music. What rules there are pious clichés. Words are "received," taken from the Good Book, yes, but flattened to the ear from overuse and merciless repetition, sanctioned, as it were, by Baptist piety, the legacy of churchy minds. If you listen to some of the old Gospel standards, "The Eastern Gate," "Sheltered in the Arms of God," "I Bowed on My Knees and Cried Holy," "Farther Along," "When God's Chariot Comes," "Oh for a Thousand Tongues," "I'll Fly Away," "When We All Get Together," "It is Well With My Soul" — nary the habitus of a unique lyric, never an original line to savor can be heard. But why should that be? David's Psalms are positively filled with poetry. ("Over Edom will I cast my shoe; over Philistia I shout in triumph," "All your robes are fragrant with myrrh and aloes and cassia," "There on the poplars we hung our harps, for there our captors asked us for songs," etc.) Still ballyhooed are the Gaither and Homecoming Friends TV Gospel Shows, now sold as videos — much of it brilliant American music — a stage, rocking with godly zeal, filled with happy, unputdownable, energetic chubby people, oldsters wearing wigs, groups with string ties, singers propped up on canes, women wearing gingham brocaded dresses, old ladies sitting back in chairs clapping hands and shouting, rednecks wearing suspenders, all bellowing and praising God. You will never see these people eating lobster *carpaccio* at Le Bernardin or shopping on Seventh Avenue in New York City. At times, however, they can really rock, and that is an undeniable fact. Vocals with them come every which way — it is an otolaryngologist's banquet — whistle registers, falsetto registers, head voices, a sudden and occasional deep vocal fry that is sure to set everybody to stomping approval. It should also be said that a lot of these folk — "witnesses" — are also as faithful, as godly, as Trappist monks, even if they are a bit credulous and somewhat presumptuous. Doubtless, some are not. In his autobiography *It's More Than Music* — a book in which he intimates that the Holy Spirit, visiting the studio, virtually co-wrote the "devout" Gaither Vocal Band's 1991 album *Homecoming* — Bill Gaither, leader and director of the group and winner of as many as four Grammys, 20 Doves, and the first Gold Record ever awarded to an "inspirational" album, proudly mentions that its signature song of which this is the repeated chorus

> Let's just praise the Lord! Praise the Lord
> Let's just lift our hands to heaven, and praise the Lord!
> Let's just praise the Lord! Praise the Lord!
> Let's just lift our hands toward heaven and praise the Lord!

is used to close their concerts each evening and for its force has less to do with music than with proselytizing. There is in effect no lyric, by the way. It is a Chautauqua drone, the equivalent of Gospel fast-food. Preening, however, Gaither explains how aboard a bus all of his musicians got together and "with a yellow notepad" came up with this signature song, which "begged for audience participation." The same could be said for the zealous chant of the God-haunted and intransigent Carrie Nation who opposed alcohol in pre-Prohibition America — she was 6-feet tall and weighed 175 pounds and described herself as "a bulldog running along at the feet of Jesus, barking at what He doesn't like" — and whose hectoring keen, "Smash! Smash! For Jesus'ake, smash!" carried more masculine quinch than Gaither as she campaigned through the beery saloons of dry Kansas hatcheting open kegs of demon rum and destroying bars, a drama she would later re-enact for vaudeville audiences while also selling photographs of herself, collecting lecture fees, and marketing miniature souvenir hatchets. Show business and religious zeal have always happily conjoined in the United States. One thinks of the marriage of tiny General Tom Thumb (who stood only 25 inches tall and weighed 15 pounds) to just-as-small Mercy Lavinia Bump, also a dwarf — "The Loving Lilliputians" — that was arranged by showman and scam artist P.T. Barnum on February 10, 1863 at Grace Church, the elegant Episcopal cathedral at the corner of Broadway and 10th Street in New York City. It was a mercantile event sold to the public and, as Barnum well knew, it immediately became front-page news and drew immense crowds in the tens of thousands. The very nature of selling *anything* constitutes counterfeit piety.

Which is faith, what scam in Gospel groups? It is difficult to determine unless you choose to decide the differences physiologically by scanning the various faces on stage. Many of them seem sweet. Other faces appear too bright, slightly insane, sadly set in a certain way as if belonging to someone who never expected anything again, as James Purdy said of a character in his grim novel, *Narrow Rooms*, visages set in a certain way so that they resemble a door that has been nailed shut in a deserted house. Where some seem truly blissful, for others it often seems like the wrong kind of happiness.

Clothes figure widely in gospel, indicating almost as a giveaway that a rustic or sort of provincial unstylishness — string ties, wide 1940s skirts, gingham dresses, bows in the hair, etc. — is properly non-citified and innocent. It is precisely the *details* in dress that telegraph so much, no? We know right away that Robert Ryan in *Beware, My Lovely* (1952) is a dangerous schizophrenic by the clipped necktie he wears. We grasp immediately that Jack Palance in *Sudden Fear* (1952) is a loony killer — along with the fact when they meet that he tells Joan Crawford he is wearing his mother's wedding ring! — by that insane off-the-wall white ankle-length coat/bathrobe/jacket that he has chosen to wear when he sits by her bedside reading, pausing only to whisper (twice!), "*Are you asleep?*" I will match it for horror with Joan as the mad, shiny-faced, schizophrenic Louise Howell in *Possessed* (1947) with her dark drab dresses and slingback shoes, a movie in which her auditory lunacies like hearing chirping birds, clocks, raindrops, even her own blood pulsations constitute a grotesque music all its own. We are not surprised at anything that screwball Richard Widmark would do or the nature of his frail-to-say-the-least mental state in *Kiss of Death* (1947) after glimpsing him wearing that wide-brimmed Borsalino when he says, "For a nickel, I'd grab him. Stick both thumbs right in his eyes. Hang on 'til he drops dead."

Oh no, clothes quite aptly tell us what we see is what we get.

Gospel music from an older time had some passion. As time passed, however, the music became more devotional and less daring — I am talking now about the power of lyrics — and, while the faith may be present, we find neither the salt nor the savor. ("The best lack all conviction/ while the worst are full of passionate intensity," as W.B. Yeats wrote.) It reminds me of how, over time, Charles Schulz's *Peanuts* comic strip grew increasingly bland, too cozy, I suggest, too institutionalized, the way all tired acts end up, in Branson, Missouri or what Meredith Willson in *The Music Man* refers to as the "hailstone and sarsaparilla" belt. Gospel has become a kind of Bransonification of God. Discretion — in its core sense of separate, distinct — becomes invariably what it means in its more extended sense. I have always admired Thomas Jefferson for instituting the splendid Rotunda, the centerpiece of the University of Virginia, to serve as a library rather than a church, which was an innovation for an American college at the time. Jefferson's departure from the usual and accepted practice was both risky and audacious, but it presaged a new spirit in American life.

Southern and country gospel is a wide category, with duets and quartets from the Blackwood Brothers, the Dixie Four, and the Harmoneers to the Praise Brothers and Junior Hawkins & the Gospelaires to Fearless Fife Ministries to Randy Ward (Gospel on Wheels) to the Happy Goodman's to Clowns for Christ to Soul Purpose Gospel — and how about the uniquely named group called the Bo Conrad Spit Band? — so I cannot go on record as legitimately saying that *all* of the lyrics are hackneyed, banal, or commonplace, but most of what I have heard reinforces Mark Twain's remark, "I've never read an account of heaven that, should I go there, didn't make me want to turn right around and come right back."

I do not believe that cheesy Lou Rawls in whatever song he tried to sing could manage to hit any note straight on, and so, trying to be cool, he tried to compensate with on-the-spot-ad-libbing, not to try to jazz up classics, but rather weakly to circle notes he could never quite hit directly. It was a weak, desperate attempt, serendipitously, to try to nail the thing, which, as I say, he almost never did. He is not Brook Benton. Nor is he Billy Eckstine, not even close, no way, two black singers preceding him who in the music world are legends and whose service — as President George W. Bush the Texan said on May 25, 2004 of General Sanchez — has been "exemplerary." Rawls had a wackadoodle voice, to begin with. Zoo-esque! There is no question the man had "pipes," timber. His trouble was — with finger-snapping incompetence — always trying to improvise, which he did very poorly. I would always be thinking: *would it kill you to stop doing that?* His unfortunate versions of "All the Way" and "Let's Take It Nice and Easy" are just plain protrudingly goofy. But when the man offers up his crooning version of "Have Yourself A Merry Little Christmas" — flat notes, missed notes, whiskey-sour notes, notes he cannot reach, clunkers, melodyless flights that crash, laughable reaches for panache, pickle-sour offerings of words, fucked-up scat, attempts at style that go nowhere — it sounds like long drunken grunts coming from a shower stall!

Extreme attempts to stylize can appear phony. What else was Liberace trying to do with his ankle length chinchilla coat ("You paid for it," he always gushed to the audience) and all those candelabra and kitsch? Elton John for all that bygone harlequinade was only a buffoon, manifesting what the French call *voulu*, a word that denotes both too much effort and the vice of artificiality. Jerry Lewis, trying for effect, butchered his songs with the specious pummeling of a sinister clown, bullying laughs out of audiences not knowing they wanted to cry. ("The guinea's not bad, but what do I do about the monkey?" asked the always tactful MGM mogul Louis B. Merde — as they called Mayer — when he first saw Martin and Lewis perform.) One has one's own dreams, I understand, I do. I rowed the Rhine with Richard Wagner in the same way when, listening to the Moody Blues, I pictured in my imagination pterodactyls flying about over forests of wild, unfamiliar vegetation. But there is a custody of the self, a reining in at some point, that — truly to be cool — must be maintained.

I remain convinced that Willie Nelson virtually never recorded a song not wildly off-key. Listen sometime to his skin-crawling versions of "Moonlight Becomes You" or "The Very Thought of You." Tony Bennett, listen closely, is almost always just a smidgen off-key and always has been and at times can sound as bad as Hurricane Smith or Kenny Rogers or Michael Jackson or Richard Harris, losing himself in ear-thumping over-orchestrations to try to get drowned out creatively. If you doubt me, listen to his strident and unmusical recording of "I Can't Believe That You're in Love With Me" or his dissonant version of

"Indian Summer" — he misses almost every note in true amateur fashion — or his unbelievably obnoxious recording of the classic "As Time Goes By."

Bennett's wretched version is superceded in sheer atrociousness perhaps only by two others, Carly Simon's leaden-flat offering of the same song and tenor José Carreras' strangulated version, one that I have cited before, that sounds — "*the wooorl weel ohlwez welcomm loafers*" — as if he is in actual combat with the lyrics with which he is trying to seduce us. Octogenarian Tony Bennett in his duet with Celine Dion sings, "If I Ruled the World" with a croakiness, an almost grave-like grasping for air, that is painful to hear. Why at the age of 86, Bennett is still found attending Hollywood events like a foolish teenager, hobbling on stage at the paracme of his career, be-wigged and be-corseted, to pick up gimcrack awards and to be seen pathetically blowing kisses to his public is more than I can understand. Is it so hard to see that one's sell-by date has expired? Applause-freakism is truly a disease. That Dion badly overcrowds him with a voice that sounds like a screeching weasel in a foot-trap seems to be what he deserves. Why do certain entertainers not have the grace to stand aside, call it a day? Applause-freaks can never sit back and chill. No, they pull on wigs, strap on corsets, stick in shoe-lifts, paint their cheeks, scream for softer lighting, and just never fucking go away!

When I recently described to a friend of mine, playfully requesting him to guess my subject as I spoke of a slapdash assemblage of mismatched legs, bristly hair, beady eyes, an idiotic pendant dewlap, called a "bell" in the deer world, along with a fleshly flexible snout, my friend thought I was describing a *moose*, but I was in fact speaking of *Tony Bennett* — everything but palmate antlers! Bennett's unmemorable recording of "My Favorite Things" is, if anything, an undisciplined comic-operetta of missed notes and unhealthy failure, a wrong-headed attempt at trying to lay down a hip version of a classic which, ruining a good melody, he tries, by improvising, to rewrite/ update/ improve, like Lou Rawls's abominably nutcase version of "Silver Bells," a convoluted bit of flat, unmusical terrorism in which virtually not a note can be identified with the traditional melody.

Then there is Celine Dion, "Canada's revenge on America for decades of acid rain," according to critic Ed Brayton. Dion, who has been a celebrity guest on the *Oprah Winfrey Show* a record 27 times, more than any other celebrity — double self-promotion in the Mediocrity Sweepstakes — seems unappeasably insistent, with almost frightening drama, that every note she hits radiate light. (I would have thought that the lights would have gone *out*, due to the macro-psychokinetic phenomenon known as the "Pauli Effect," a term (coined using the name of the Austrian theoretical physicist Wolfgang Pauli) referring to the apparently mysterious "anecdotal" failure of technical equipment in the presence of certain — mediocre? cursed? overrated? — people.) Dion's singing reminds me of Thomas Kinkade's cloying paintings, glowing, over-saturated, commercialized, with every last window lit to lurid effect as if the interior of the structure might be on fire. At its worst it has something in it of the desperation of a person maniacally washing glass, swipe swipe, roundabout swipe, the kind of singing with its pastel-like qualities, its unrelenting poshlust, resonating perfectly with the kind of entertainment that goes down big in the ramparts of Las Vegas where it so happens the diva performs nightly as the *prima assoluta* soprano of a highly ornate five-star theatrical show at the Coliseum at Caesar's Palace. (She hugs people in the crowd.) The volume of her voice is thin, full of tricky melismas, with coloratura and multo lirico-spinto, and the kind of nasal backing that, when raised to the heights of witchy penetrating timbre she can reach, can make you have suddenly to pee. She seems not to have a head voice but rather uses a vibratoless falsetto which is disconnected to the normal voice-body. Lop off all but the first twenty or so seconds of her monster ballad "My Heart Will Go On," and it merits a slot on any legitimate list of howler-monkey music recorded in Coiba Island or the wilds of Guatemala. Throw in the unconscionable crime of adding pan-flute solos and lilting pastel-like Irish melodies to the heightening emotion she is selling, and it can quickly pass from rank sentimentality and pretentious bad taste to an intensity bordering on truly diseased neo-Wagnerian kitsch!

With a voice full of doily-esque quivers and trembles, all at once timid, sexual, and slightly crazy — "*Neeaaaah, faaaaaahh, whereeeeever you aaaaare*" — Dion has the firepower to drive the intensity of her phrasing, spooky schmaltz much of it, into an almost terrifyingly high register, first by cutting her syllables preciously short, then by drawing each one out like a shawlie keening. As to that signature song, never has the subject about devouring love sounded so threatening and yet so vulgar — it reminded me as it spread of invasive Japanese knotweed which is eating New England! — in spite of "powering the *Titanic* soundtrack to a year-topping 10 million copies sold," as one critic points out, "[and yet] made millions more pray that an iceberg would somehow hit Dion." It is a kind of song that in such a place as secular, glitzy, immoderate Las Vegas *would* constitute a hymn, a deity-less worship, actually, granting Dion something of spiritual status. She draws big crowds. But in the strictest sense, quality cannot be quantified, since if it could be perfectly translated into quantity there would be no basis for the distinction between the two in the first place.

One can only wonder how all of those fans and ultrafidians of Celine Dion or Barbra Streisand would respond hearing the indescribable magic of Renata Tebaldi, Elizabeth Schwarzkopf, Joan Sutherland, or Montserrat Caballé singing the great bel canto heroines like Bellini's Somnambula, Rossini's Semiramide, or Donizetti's Lucia di Lammermoor or had the experience just once of being in their electrifying presence or hearing their soaring notes and ascending scales, their clear, ringing, stunning high E-flats.

Are these the last ramparts of powerful music?

Not quite. Such power, rare, can be heard today. I was lucky enough this year to hear at the Met the extraordinary new work called *The Enchanted Island*, its splendid new libretto by Jeremy Sams, in which, uniquely, the lovers from Shakespeare's *A Midsummer Night's Dream* are shipwrecked on his other-worldly island of *The Tempest*. Inspired by the musical pastiches and masques of the 18th century, the work — in English — showcases arias and ensembles by Handel, Vivaldi, Rameau, André Campra, and others. Lovers of Baroque opera could hear the world's best singers, glorious music of the Baroque masters, and this masterful tale of the Bard's. The eminent conductor William Christie led an all-star cast with David Daniels (Prospero) and Joyce DiDonato (Sycorax) as the formidable foes, Plácido Domingo as Neptune, Danielle de Niese as Ariel, and Luca Pisaroni as Caliban. Lisette Oropesa and Anthony Roth Costanzo play Miranda and Ferdinand. The utterly inventive, dazzling, production was directed and designed by Phelim McDermott and Julian Crouch with choreography by Graciela Daniele. I only wish I could confront the squads of folk going out to see Streisand or Dion and make my case, asking with The Shangri-Las in "Leader of the Pack," "Do you get the picture?" only to have the group reply with what we hear on the record, "Yes, we see."

But what people fail to understand is that people who "pilgrimage" to Vegas are for the most part straight, conventional, unimaginative, family-oriented, highly conformist, easily pleased beangooses and casual and unexacting middle-brows, uncomplicated clucks out to feel a little daring and throw away some money. In their one-dimensional way they feel exactly as Barrett Strong did in his big hit, "Money": "What it don't get, I can't use." They may feel playfully sinful coming to Sin City from Lodgepole, Nebraska and Rice, Virginia; Norphlet, Arkansas and Bounceback, Montana; Burnt Corn, Alabama and Hawbottom, Maryland, but the truth is they are not at all decadent. Their values are square and for the most part unsubtle, and to real crudeness they much prefer schmaltz, imitation, maudlin sentimentality, and boat-sized deliveries of slush and hokey emotion.

I see them as simple, contented souls. They are not fashion plates, have no interest in the little *quelque choses d'autre*, and find no saving irony in anything like intellectual exchange. The men sport pinky rings, grew up driving leather-roofed

Gran Torinos, love the buffet at Circus Circus, and admire, even revere, the music of John Tesh and Kenny G. and Yanni and Zamfir, King of the Pan Flute. The ladies wear wigs and ground-grippers and lots of lavender perfume and scream when they laugh. Wrote the social snob Diana Vreeland in her autobiography *DV* — and she moved in distinctly different circles — "My favorite dinner parties are the English because they never laugh." She adds,

> I am so spellbound and overcome by the mood they create through their language. Their wit is what is so supreme. A funny person is funny for so long, but a wit can sit down and go on being spellbinding forever. One is not meant to laugh. One stays quiet and marvels. Spontaneously witty talk is without question the most fascinating entertainment there is.

So much for the effete elite.

Curiously enough, while not universally true, most people who go to Las Vegas prefer vulgarity *without* crassness. Be raucous, not crude. The middle-brow mind can be easily embarrassed. A bladder-wagging comedian may amuse them, buffoons running amok with seltzer bottles, but the city is also ground-zero for what the late Walter Winchell bitterly called "vomics," the filthiest comedians alive. No greater discrepancy exists between normal people and the show business scum who gather for so-called "celebrity roasts" so popular there, where actors in verbal *saloperie* mock each other with the vilest obscenities, and, although hurt by the wretched and embarrassing indignities, get caught up in the casual evil and have to pretend to love it by doubling over in spasms of fake laughter. I witnessed one on TV given for a pencil-necked geek named Bob Saget that would have offended barnyard animals.

The off-color is different. The prurient, the libidinous, the risqué, the coarse is what most visitors want. To me the ultimate Las Vegas movie is *The Silencers* (1966), starring Dean Martin who throughout wears ugly jackets with pastel turtleneck jerseys ("Sy Devore wardrobe!"), which can only be summed up as a vulgar, dated gallimaufry of clumsy strippers, fake fights, a brassy soundtrack with detestable songs, an inane plot with mercilessly stupid dialogue by Oscar Saul (words like "gasser" and "computer tape") and all of it filmed through yellow filters which makes it look like Columbia Pictures shot it through an aquarium glass filled with old fishwater. It is made for zooplankton to enjoy, just the dopiest stuff imaginable — fare for real gumballs.

Vulgarian Bette Midler, in any case, never really hit it big in Las Vegas, because she *was* too raunchy and low-brow. It was too sedate for her, for one thing, but the crowds were shocked by her brazenness. "I want sleaze, I want sequins" has always been a familiar Midler battle cry all through her career, big with the boys in Provincetown but not so in the purlieus of Lost Wages. A singer who started her career in 1970 singing at the Continental Baths in the basement of the Ansonia Hotel at Broadway and West 74<sup>th</sup> St., Midler could not help but accept early in life that she had a flat, leaden voice, and that as to looks she somewhat resembles an umbrella with a broken handle did not — does not — help very much, either. Judging depth of character by a person's looks or estimating the worth of an individual by the exigencies of his or her facial bad luck is not a particularly charitable thing to do, perfectly understood, but in the shallow world of show business it is a metoposcopical fact that explains a great deal in determining one's success (or lack of it), and, to be quite truthful, it is the main thing. Now throw in her size, her definitive genome, and we're talking a moose, what the Chinese rudely call a *you tong* ("pillar box") or *wan dun ju lun* ("ten-thousand-ton ocean-going ship"). She was fat, let's face it, a creature broad in the beam with walloping great cheeks, visible speedbag armfat, an owl-beak nose, and what I would call even a fat smile. In my opinion, like a good many rather desperate people in life she was plagued by kakorrhaphiophobia, a morbid fear of failure, and would have done virtually anything to become more than just a face in the crowd. Therefore, since music makes the space it takes place in, as William Gass has pointed out, when in a quick assessment Midler saw what she lacked[9] she decided to adopt that big loud fruity persona — a juggernaut of big ear-rings, gold lamé pedal pushers, and Spring-O-Later shoes — and chose to become the brazen, bawdy, and bodacious creature we know her by, a "broad" who transcending her homeliness and less than average voice worked up a show business "character." It matched her style of mockery and pastiche. No buffoonery was off the table for her. Anything for money. The name *midler* in German means cash, funds, money. "My name means the shape I am," said Humpty Dumpty in *Through the Looking Glass.*

There are worse things than being off-key, however, and that is to put oneself on display as a fundament of tacky noises, embarrassing excesses, and stupid jokes, "Did you hear that Dick Nixon bought a copy of *Deep Throat?*" crudely asked

---

9        Do not look for my approval here, although Midler herself, obviously immune to irony, in one of her stage shows once cattily declared of Britain's Princess Anne, "She loves nature in spite of what it did to her." Who would deny that physiognomists are for the most part generally prigs? Frankly, I have always found it nauseating in the film, *Sabrina* (1953) that we are asked to accept the depraved moral that a poor girl can not only be courted but can win the hand of one of her "betters" only if she is pretty. Her decency, intelligence, virtue, grace, and honesty do not signify, merely her beauty. I was going to say such was life back in the days of Kreml hair tonic and Lilac Vegetal after-shave, but then Erica Jong, a Jewish writer, declares in her 1973 novel, *Fear of Flying*, "All Arabs look like Nasser."

Midler of an audience at the Palace in 1973. "He's seen it ten or twelve times. He wants to get it down Pat." *A View from A Broad*, her crude memoir from 1980, features an array of grinning, wide-mouthed photos of her, all lipstick and big nose, dressed like a hot dog, hugging a kangaroo, and of course showing off her breasts, a gesture that over the years became for Midler her signature move — no singing, just out-flopping. At a New Year's Eve Show in LA in 1975/76 in the staid Dorothy Chandler Pavilion, sitting in the hand of a giant King Kong prop, she decided to bare all. "So at the stroke of midnight, I duh-ropped my dress and exposed myself to 3,600 people," Midler with typical modesty explained. "I don't think they even saw it, you know. It was just my little chest: nipples to the wind. When in doubt, go for the jugs!" This from a woman with the body consistency of a box jelly-fish. It never seemed to matter where she was performing. She bared her breast in September 1978 to a full audience at the Palladium in London. At the Academy Awards a few years, after losing to Sally Field, Midler stood up and said, "I bear no grudges…This is the Oscars. We have to be dignified, as dignified as humanely possible. That is why I have decided to rise to the occasion." Typically, she then put her hands under her breasts and pushed them up. Now that's class, don't you agree?

Why is one surprised at such popularity? The top-selling beer in the United States — Bud Light — is the shittiest. Wonder Bread, white, gummy, innutritious loaf-feel, leads all other brands in sales. Best-sellers in both fiction and non-fiction for decade after decade have been the trashiest of published books. Cars are now all shaped alike and invariably catlap gray, dung-brown, or off-white. Gravestones that were once elaborate and beautiful are now godless and utilitarian. There hasn't been a brilliant movie script out of Hollywood since *All About Eve* (1950). As the shallow and artificial editor of *Vogue*, the late Diana Vreeland always said, "Give them what they never knew they wanted."

Being off-key. It may be the bane of the discerning auditor with perfect pitch be he a composer or a carillon-tuner, to hear — agonizingly — when someone hits a clunker. Robert Schumann, an aesthete as well as a great composer who was for years subject to deep melancholies, suffered perpetually from imagining that he had the note "A" sounding in his ears and on February 27, 1854 attempted suicide by throwing himself from a bridge into the Rhine river where he was rescued by a boatman. He spent the following two years, his last, in a mental hospital. "A" or "La" is not only the sixth note of the *solfège* but is generally used as a standard for tuning. When the orchestra tunes, or so goes the formality, the oboe plays an "A" and the rest of the instruments tune to match that pitch. Every string instrument in the orchestra has an A string, from which each player can tune the rest of his instrument. "A" is also used in combination with a number (e.g., A-440) to label the pitch standard. The number designates the cycles per second of sound waves. A lower number equals a lower pitch. I tend to believe that poor Schumann went through a noisy, cacophonous world that never met his ideal "A."

Again, Tony Bennett's diction is legendarily piss-poor, in the song "As Time Goes By" actually slurred and slang-born and rude. I have an educated friend in New York City who particularly hates the rhetorical short-cut called thlipsis — runnin' for running — and has told me with utter sobriety that she would never date a man who slips up on this matter merely *once*. She finds it mortifying. I can see her point. It is a slothfulness that denies a kind of intelligence. I remember finding it hugely unattractive and apish when in the movie, *Living in a Big Way* (1947), a very young Gene Kelly, the romantic lead and would-be lover, seriously confesses to Marie McDonald at the movie's most significant — and passionate — moment, "It hadda be you."

To me, Tony Bennett almost always seems to try too hard to put a song across, *hard-selling* it, so to speak, in the sweaty urgent way that belies his age and makes him seem as if, no matter how many years he has been singing, he is still engaged in some sort of audition. No better example, to let the one stand for the many, can be found in his hopelessly murdered version of "Santa Claus Is Coming To Town," a song in which when referencing the toy-like "rootie-toot-toot" and "tummy-tum-tum," obviously embarrassed, he self-consciously *giggles*, throatily winking to us, as it were, sub-textually giving us the heads up, that *he knows* the lyrics are childish and that of course he is hip in spite of the immediate job at hand, so madly desperate is he to break through the wall of the song for this entirely vulgar acknowledgement. The man cannot take being infantilized, even for a nanosecond. The innocence is missing. Tony B. has no *sprezzatura* at all. Should we not make it a truism that no singer should ever, *ever*, be allowed to improvise a Christmas classic?

Needless to say, even at his extreme worst, Bennett is nothing close to as bad as Anne Murray or Florence Henderson or the truly preposterous Kathie Lee Gifford who in absolute terms has arguably the most inartistically baleful voice ever, *ever*, to get picked up by a standing microphone. It is partly the unbelievably pretentious gravitas with which the deluded Gifford *surveys* herself as she sings, almost always desperately trying to put across the worst songs, finding God in them, she suggests, by draping a kind of chintzy aura around each and every unrealized note she attempts. With all of that growling and gribbeling of hers? Puh-leeze! It was the same with Anne Murray with her housemaid sighs and Anita Bryant, the Nightingale of Barnesdale, Oklahoma, whose faux-fervor and sense of rhythm like a tuba burping on the first and second beat was seriously meant to mime celestial intoxication. Old wacko LPs of Bryant's like *Abiding Love* and *Mine Eyes Have Seen the Glory* — a photo on the back of the album shows her obsequiously kissing President Lyndon Johnson during the Vietnam War — are frightful. I remember one song of hers, "An Angel Cried," I can barely abide and compared to which, for its insincerity and backhanded and dissimulating false piety, I'd prefer to watch an impromptu display of fart lighting. Then there was Della Reese with her obnoxious over-phrasing, Joan Baez with her airy strains, singers like Cher or Madonna and her sleazy carnival act or Sheryl Crow with voices like trumpets growling rat-a-tat-tat and glissing over all creation. Auto-Tune was used to produce the prominent altered vocal effect on Cher's scrimp single, "Believe," giving a metallic patina to an already impaired voice, a palimpsest that is half echo, half howl. I have heard her sing at times when she seemed almost barking mad, a perfect cognate to all the kinky, kooky, kicky headgear and leopardskin pants and harlequin hairbows and freaky frockery that she affects, getting down with her bad self, as I imagine she thinks of it, but, sadly, making her more and more a figure of fun, always a sign of a career heading due south. Recorded in 1998, "Believe" was the first commercial recording to use the *software* for this purpose. Why do I always feel that when Cher sings any song she keeps hitting *the same note* over and over again?

More to the point, why am I listening?

*Quare id faciam, fortasse requiris?*

Miss Bowers in *Death on the Nile* comments, "It has been my experience that men are least attractive to women who treat them well." Madonna won all of her plaudits this way, in my humble opinion, and like Cher always offered a sort of overlording jungle-like importance to swarms of willing, desperate, obsequious men, rabid and masochistic fans who love to be dominated. Madge from Flint, Michigan with her array of sacred/profane corsets and crosses, rosaries and raunch — the dopey Lesbian social critic and mustachioed feminist Camille Paglia in 1990 worshipfully declared Madonna "the future of feminism" — has been presenting herself for decades as a variation of the mysterious, domineering white queen, a self-cherishing and narcissistic sextress, H. Rider Haggard's *She*, who is worshipped as *Hiya* or "she-who-must-be-obeyed," an emotional imperialist who in a diva-like way quite expected and frankly *exacted* cringing from all of her pursuivants, mostly teenage boys but also a large gay contingent, who, feverish and fetishistic alike, were all too willing to provide it. "Attention must be paid!" I have never felt for a single minute that La Ciccone was original or in any intrepid or constructive sense truly speaking her mind (a mind I never saw) or offering anything like strong opinions, the way ingenious persons do, but rather scolding fans, hectoring them, musically and otherwise, and always with that scornful and contemptuous disdain which craven types love. "Express Yourself." "Justify My Love." "This Used to Be My Playground." "Don't Tell Me." "Bad Girl." "Fighting Spirit." "Give It 2 Me." "Hey You." "I Deserve It." "Power of Goodbye." "You Must Love Me." "Nothing Fails."

Papa Don't Preach *this!*

Still, I promise you I like all sorts of singers, as disparate as Joni James, Aretha Franklin, Edith Piaf, Pearl Bailey, Joan Jett, Etta James, Alison Krauss, Annie Lennox, Debbie Harry, Lucinda Williams, even Little Peggy March. I am certainly not arguing, beyond that, that style need be perfect, textbook, academically symmetrical. Quite the opposite. In its uniqueness, true style will often daringly flirt with the odd, the eccentric, the canted, the original, the strange, the spare. Listen sometime to Billie Holiday sing "Solitaire," "God Bless the Child," "Am I Blue?" "I Cover The Waterfront," "Love Me Or Leave Me," and "Gloomy Sunday" or Odetta sing "Roberta, Let Your Hair Hang Low" and "Deep River" or Ella Fitzgerald sing "720 in the Books" and "What's Your Story, Morning Glory" — Ella had a blue voice, whereas Billie Holiday had a blues voice, which is a very different thing — or Caterina Valente sing "*Je n'avais pas compris*" or Sweet Emma Barrett sing "A Good Man is Hard to Find," "Bogalusa Strut," and "I Ain't Gonna Give Nobody None of My Jelly Roll" or the great Carmen MacRae sing "When You Get Around To Me" and "I'm Putting All My Eggs In One Basket" and "Baltimore Oriole" or Timi Yuro sing "Hurt" or Booker T. and the MGs play "Green Onions" and "Jelly Bread" and "Chinese Checkers" — John Lennon called that great Stax house-band, "Book a table and the Maitre D's" — or Irma Thomas sing "You Can Have My Husband But Don't Mess With My Man" or Johnny Preston sing "Cradle of Love" or The Joe Jeffrey Group sing "My Pledge of Love" or The Grass Roots sing "Temptation Eyes" or Freddie King sing "Pack It Up" or Aretha Franklin sing "Think" or Johnny Rivers sing "Baby, I Need Your Loving" or Peggy Lee sing "That's All There is" or Verdelle Smith sing "Tar and Cement" or Mabel Mercer sing "I Am Ashamed That Women Are So Simple," "Grow Tall My Son," and "Fifth of July," or Lenny Welch sing "Since I Fell for You" or Dion & the Belmont's sing "I Wonder Why" or Ricky Nelson sing "Poor Little Fool" or the Skyliners sing "Since I Don't Have You" or Thomas Wayne sing "Tragedy" — a song also brilliantly done by the Fleetwoods — or The Fleetwoods sing "Come Softly to Me" or Joni James sing "Have You Heard" or Bo Diddley's "Road Runner Man" (Beep Beep)" or The Sheepdogs sing "I Don't Know" or The Doors sing "People

Are Strange" or The Passions sing "Just to be With You" or "Terry Stafford sing "Suspicion" or Tina Turner sing "I'm Gonna Do All I Can" or Ray Charles sing the incomparable "Night Time is the Right Time," and you will see my point and come to understand the difference.

We are talkin' masterpieces here.

Have I mentioned James Booker, the black one-eyed gay Player Prince of New Orleans who made his recording debut in 1954 on the Imperial label with "Thinkin' 'Bout My Baby" and "Doin' the Hambone"? Then let me do, "*twicet,*" as he'd say. He was a session man for people like Fats Domino, Smiley Lewis, and Lloyd Price. In 1958, Arthur Rubinstein gave a concert in New Orleans, and afterwards, 18-year-old Booker was introduced to the pianist and played several tunes for him. Rubinstein was astonished, saying, "I could never play that... never at that tempo." James was also a heroin addict, a terrible alcoholic, and on November 8, 1983 he died of renal failure while seated in a wheelchair waiting to be seen at the emergency room at New Orleans Charity Hospital, but the cat knew every piano style on earth — jazz, stride, blues, gospel, and Latin — had a killer left hand, could piggyback Schubert onto a blues tune or launch classical rockets and in his lifetime cut only three albums, but — to quote the Beatles — he was the toppermost of the poppermost! "Walked with no one and talked with no one," he sang. "And I had nothing but shadows."

I have touched upon Tina Turner. The late Ike Turner always claimed to be her Svengali. "I always showed them what to do. I can go and record any girl you bring in here right now, and you would swear to God she's coppin' off Tina, because there *is* no Tina. You hear *me* through Tina. I do it all," he told Scott Raab in *Esquire*. "I do every bit of it. Every note that's played. When you saw Ike and Tina, every step came from me. All that shit came dead out of me." Arguably, Tina's implicit reply to this in songs like "All I Can Do is Cry," one of several of her efforts that reveals her at her rawest, her most outraged, her most angrily soulful — strictly cat-scratch-cawing blues that opens with a scream and is filled with bitter jealousy. It purports to be about losing her man but is mainly an attack on men in general. Her nose is wide open, she is storming, pissed off, offended, accusatory, and taking no prisoners. In his own right, Ike was embittered by the tendentious and one-sided movie, *What's Love Got To Do With It* (1985) in which he was one-dimensionally portrayed as an abusive thug, while his wife, Tina — Ike always claimed that the two of them had never married ("As God is my judge, of all my wives, Tina is the only one [of 13 wives] I was never legally married to") — is presented as an innocent victim who triumphantly breaks free of him. His name suddenly became a synonym for wifebeater, overshadowing any and all of his contributions to music. It all quite fit in with the way that he saw the world. "To me, the onliest two people that ever had freedom in America is a white man and a black woman," Ike would say later. "They can do what the shit they wanna do. A black woman in Mississippi could slap the shit out of a white man — there ain't nothin' gonna happen to her. Rosa Parks, if she hadda been a black dude that done that, they woulda hung him on the highest tree. I'm just bein' real about it."

Who can be surprised that Ike's final philosophical position came down to — "Everything is a hole." "When you're born, two holes — there's a hole at the head of your penis, and you come out of a hole. So you come out, and everything is about holes. When you eat? Hole. When you breathe, it's a hole. When you see, it's a hole. When you hear, it's a hole. And when you die, where are you goin'? Right back *in* the hole. If you get too much money, you gonna be in a hole. If you don't get enough, you're definitely gonna be in a hole. So to me, the best thing to do is stop tryin' to stay outta the hole. Get in the hole and find out what's happenin' with the hole and try to control the hole. And then you can have the whole, because you understand the hole."

Immanuel Kant could not have expressed it better.

The usually competent Jack Jones nevertheless made the cheesy "The Theme to *The Love Boat*" — to me, the curiously dreadful theme song of the 1970s — and sings his version of "Stranger in Paradise" like a jump-rope song, his truly ghastly interpretation of which goes flat and then lounge-lizardly without a trace in his version of the original melody. No mention of '70s music can omit the name of the melancholy gnome Paul Williams, who not only wrote "The Theme to *The Love Boat*," but other rainy songs — wistful to a one — like "You and Me Against the World," "Waking Up Alone," and "Rainy Days and Mondays." (One deep bow for "The Rainbow Connection," however.) Singers Dinah Washington, Blossom Dearie, even Joni James as she sang often went thumpingly flat. Actually, there are recordings where to be off perfect-pitch does not really matter all that much and in fact can even add a certain hip or jazzy *je ne sais quoi*. One thinks particularly of Fred Astaire here, whose flat notes often had a certain kind of dash, of élan. "Isn't this a lovely day it is/ to be caught in the rain," he sings, hitting the word *rain* flatter than a flounder, but it seems right. (I would miss a plane, any day or any week, just to sit and re-watch that refulgent scene on television.) The same can be said for his version of "Pick Yourself Up" from *Swing Time:* "Work like a soul inspired till the battle of the day is won/ You may be sick and tired, but you'll be a man, my son" — sung fairly flat and weak. You hear the same bittersweet flat notes in "A Fine Romance and "The Way You look Tonight," two songs, curiously, that have the same chord sequence. Mel Tormé who rarely delivered a song the same way twice cared such a great deal for vocal styling, looking for every chance to put a bit of a twist of French pastry to a lyric, that he always — even if at times over-lushly — delivered the goods. I have always admired the voice of rich tenor Allan Jones, father of American pop singer Jack Jones, who starred in many film musicals during the 1930s and 1940s – listen to him sing "Oh! Paradis" from Meyerbeer's *L'Africaine* to hear perfect power and intonation. What resonance! The timbre of his voice – his incredible *tuyauterie* – was fabulous. (Jealous Nelson Eddy, who considered him a potential threat, spitefully asked that most of Jones's footage in the film, *Rose Marie*, be cut, including his rendition of the great Puccini aria *"E lucevan le stele,"* and MGM acceded to Eddy's demand.) Bing Crosby had perfect pitch. So did Frank Sinatra and Nat "King" Cole. They could and often did dare to sing such sinuous, key-shifting, unimaginably difficult songs as "Puttin' on the Ritz," "I'll Never Smile Again," "Lush Life," "Isn't It A Lovely Day," "Indian Summer," and "China Gate" which an amateur singers should never attempt.. (I cannot say whether Jackie Evancho, the 12-year-old American child-prodigy who first appeared on *America's Got Talent* is still an amateur, but her sweet *a cappella* performance of Puccini's lovely *"O Mio Babbino Caro"* from the opera *Gianni Schicchi* is truly soulful.) It would be a task indeed to find a more difficult song to sing than "Love of My Life," but in the movie *Second Chorus* (1940) Fred Astaire sings it to Paulette Goddard with such flair and aplomb that you are transported. The lyric, with cool internal rhymes, is nicely balanced:

> Would you like to be the love of my life for always, and always watch over me?
> To square my blunders and share my dreams
> One day with caviar, next day a chocolate bar.
> Would you like to take the merry-go-round I'll lead you?
> I'll need you wait and you'll see.
> I hope in your horoscope there is room for a dope who adores you.
> That's what makes the only dream of my life come true.
> For the love of my life is you.

Johnny Mercer and Artie Shaw (who also handsomely co-stars in the movie) wrote this song one day over lunch at Mercer's house, and when the excited Shaw wanted to show it to the studio, Mercer persuaded him cagily to wait three weeks explaining, "If you tell them you just wrote it over lunch, they won't think it's any good." It managed to garner an Academy Award nomination in the Best Song category that year.

No, no one can speak of perfect pitch without mentioning the versatile Mel Tormé. He had the smoothest voice a man could have, and he combined it with a flawless sense of pitch. "As an improviser he shames all but two or three other scat singers and quite a few horn players as well," wrote Will Friedwald in *Jazz Singing*. He was short and fat with a face that, while amiable, looked like a blocked punt, his wide smile showing a pendulous lower lip that somehow seemed to indicate that the calls of the flesh had yet to be subdued. The talented Tormé wrote more than 250 songs, several of which became jazz standards, and also arranged many of the songs he sang. He often collaborated with composer Bob Wells, and of course the best known Tormé-Wells offering is "The Christmas Song," often referred to by its opening line "Chestnuts roasting on an open fire." The song was recorded first by Nat "King" Cole. Tormé said that he wrote the music to the song in only 40 minutes but also claimed that it was not one of his personal favorites. Tormé was a rare example of a singer who could not only deftly paraphrase the original melody of a song — it was his signature in a sense — but in his case seem to perfect it, adding "sauce" to it, always with taste and respect to the vision of the songwriter. Sinatra did it as well, but not with the deftness of Tormé or Ella Fitzgerald who could often cut loose during a swinging up-tempo number and "sing" several scat choruses by doing nothing but using their extraordinary voices — without words — to improvise a solo like a brass or reed instrument. He claimed to have hated his nickname "The Velvet Fog," but it suited his agile genius to an odd kind of perfection. His "gassy" 1962 song "Comin' Home, Baby," arranged by Claus Ogerman, led the jazz and gospel singer Ethel Waters to say that "Tormé is the only white man who sings with the soul of a black man." His fabulous album, *Songs of New York*, would be one of my ten choices to take to a desert island.

Years ago there was a wonderful magic place in popular music where style, meaning, and art all converged in a successful way but that seems nowadays to have completely disappeared. Songs are no longer even written the way once they were, with a kind of universal meaning to them. The same goes for the *art* of singing, I feel. I wonder how many female singers nowadays could manage the difficult "Early Autumn" the way Jo Stafford so beautifully sings it. (Henry Watson Fowler in his classic, *Modern English Usage*, states that the word *fall* is more vivid than *autumn*, surely one of lyricists' — and Americans' — favorite words.) Listen to Sinatra's "I Concentrate on You" and tell me anyone with a microphone in his or her hands these days could even manage to get it off the ground. Hear Sinatra sing "Violets for Your Furs" or "Your Beautiful Face" or "Lover Come Back to Me," his brilliant duet with Dorothy Kirsten — amazing. The Chairman of the Board who himself considered the song "My One and Only Love" one of the most difficult to sing — a song that many other singers have attempted and fudged (although Joni James happens to do a version that I love) — does a superlative job of it with Nelson Riddle. Also truly difficult was the great song "What Is This Thing Called Love," which Sinatra did *after twenty-one takes* with Nelson Riddle after Sinatra himself, experimenting for perfection, changed the tempo, rearranged the chart, and shortened the composition. Frank's version of "It's So Nice to Come Home To" with Billy May, a virtually impossible song to sing, is positively matchless, and when you listen to it notice how the man effortlessly *gliiides* like a true balladeer from one impossibly, delicately, shaded flat or sharp note to another, from one oblique note to another, never flinching, never self-consciously searching about for them with fake trills and phony sallies as so many vocal *bruggioli* do as if fumbling for a key at a door in the dark! It is astonishing how Sinatra goes from one rich cruising phrase to another without flaw. "September of My Years," really a terrible song — overwritten and silly — a very difficult song to sing, as well, Sinatra does flawlessly.

It is profitable to listen to the early, middle, and late '60s and to hear the changes in timbre and texture of Sinatra's flutelike, parachuting baritone, to catch the subtle nuances of his mature voice. Alex Ross in *The New Yorker* (May 25, 1998) accurately sees the essential paradox:

> The voice was veering in the opposite direction of the legend: Sinatra was a thin young man who grew wealthy and stout, but it's his younger voice that sounds plump and his older voice that sounds lean and hungry. He knew all along — or, at least, until his erratic years — that his voice was what counted in the end.

And, with exceptions, the diction.

How he felt those lyrics that he mesmerizingly sang, interpreting our own lives so well. Then there was also the way that Sinatra always ended a love song, softly, gently, easily. A creative delitescence was involved, flaperons down. It was a soft deceleration, imperceptible newtons mildly reversing, in much the same way that an expensive elevator, with a smoothing but inconspicuous buss, adds a final slow rise as it settles at the lip of your floor.

Paul Anka moos. Neil Sedaka shouts. Lesley Gore whines. Helen Reddy brays. Linda Ronstadt is nasal. Frankie Laine absolutely hooted. Olivia Newton-John's voice is 95% air. Britney Spears is adenoidal. Cher ululates. So does Buffy Sainte-Marie, Dolly ("It takes a lot of money to look this cheap") Parton, and lovely Yma

Sumac, the notable Peruvian soprano whose extraordinarily wide vocal range could reach notes of slightly over four octaves from $B_2$ to $C\#_7$ (approximately 123 to 2270 Hz) as well as descend to notes in the low baritone register as well. Does not the British pop-singer Sade also have a voice that zooms up and down with the speed of a hydrodynamic fish? Phoebe Snow vibrates. Dean Martin when he sang — for comparison listen to recordings of him talking — assumed a kind of lazy toy voice, a facetious persona, that seemed almost embarrassed, sort of spooked, to be actually singing for a living, and so he shruggingly circled words and phrases in any given lyric with a mirthful, sometimes faux-Italian, sometimes almost Negroesque, sometimes mock parodic — needling — treatment to a lyric. It rarely sounded sincere, but in the end that was of course part of the intended style, the essential Dino persona. Casual chic. No heavy lifting. Parody as style. How different from the earnest, almost credulous, tight vocal presentation, for example, of Roy Rogers whose voice, as James Horwitz points out in *They Went Thataway*, his book on old movie cowboys, "seemed to come from somewhere near the back of his head and out of his eyeballs." Della Reese barks. Pert Teresa Brewer used to squeak. Just as Steve Lawrence lows (as with a cow) and Eydie Gormé bellowed (as with a bull), the two merged, smatchet to smatchet. ("One face, one voice, one habit and two persons...An apple cleft in two is not more twin," as Shakespeare put it in *Twelfth Night*.) Connie Francis wailed. Al Martino always managed to give off an aura of cheap vino, cannoli, and Neapolitan cinema. (One of his earlier singles, the somewhat overly grand and rather stagy Italo-operatic *cantino romantico*, "Here in My Heart," a Bill Borrelli / Pat Gennaro/ Lou Levinson composition, I consider, at least in the pop music department, one of our true musical treasures.) Carmen McRae sang behind the beat, with irony. Tony Orlando with that more frenetic than energetic but fake bonhomie and frozen smile always reminded me in his overweening smarminess of all those pie-faced, completely insincere, cut-from-the-same cloth, TV game-show hosts who came frantically jogging out to the mike as the show began and whose faux joviality and desperate soullessness, instantly obvious, immediately annihilated any possible trust in them. When Rex Harrison sang/ talked in the musical *My Fair Lady* — it is called *"parlando,"* a style where the rhythm (and often the pitch) of the tune are usually observed, but the "singing" sounds more like the speaking voice and notes are often shortened with the ends of phrases often having a downward inflection, simulating natural English speech — one could discern something of a melody, except that in his case it was one querulous, slightly nettled melody. *Parlando*, of course, is precisely what was one of Jimmy Durante's techniques when he was trying to put a song across and exactly what he was referring to when he spoke of his own narrational method, saying, "I think it's the drive that puts 'em [my songs] over, and the no-rhyme, like sometimes when you're only talkin'."

Bob Dylan's "You Ain't Goin' Nowhere," an example of country rock that he wrote in 1967 and recorded with The Band (then known as The Hawks) in Woodstock, New York during the self-imposed exile from public appearances that followed his July 29, 1966 motorcycle accident — it was issued in 1975 on the album *The Basement Tapes* — is a brilliant embodiment of *parlando*, a masterpiece. His "Just Like A Woman" — subject: poor little rich girl, Edie Sedgwick — is basically spoken, no?

Walter Huston introduced "September Song" to the world in *Knickerbocker Holiday*, the 1938 version, but he did not sing it so much as speak it. Walter Brennan could not be called a singer by any stretch of the imagination, but there was a sad, rainy, wistful quality to that old, befrazzled, goldminer-like voice. James Cagney who walk-paraded instead of danced fluidly also relied heavily on the use of *parlando* in the memorable film, *Yankee Doodle Dandy*, when he sang "Mary," "You're a Grand Old Flag," and "Give My Regards to Broadway," but it is probably the case that no one ever did it better. Robert Preston used the same half-sung, half-spoken technique in *The Music Man* in songs like "(Ya Got) Trouble," "Marian the Librarian," and "The Sadder-But-Wiser Girl," with an emphasis on rhythm rather than melody. The dead-flat Robert Goulet merely talked when he sang; without even a trace of melisma, only declamation; he always delivered — vocalized — lyrics in a stubborn, bleak monotone and even in his attempts at being upbeat in a song came across as wet-weather gloom. I think he wanted to sound magisterially, magniloquently virile. The drone of a bagpipe — a bourdon — had more diversity. He always recalls for me Maurice Ravel's remark about his most famous composition, the tour de force "Bolero" — "It is my masterpiece. Unfortunately, it contains no music."

In Charles Boyer's album called *Where Does Love Go?* the French actor did not so much sing "All the Things You Are," "Once Upon a Time," "La Vie en Rose," "What Now My Love?" and "Softly as I Leave You" as recite them with heavy Gallic resonance — narrated, with big, lush orchestration. One would like to mock, but the album is actually quite impressive. It was the album, incidentally, that Elvis Presley himself loved and during *Clambake* (1967) handed out copies to the whole cast and crew.

Remember Rudy Vallee? He sounded with that extreme Down East nasality of his just like a nanny goat, some kind of quat that in dry season wandered down the rocks of some mountain off the coast of Bar Harbor, Maine! He was a great star back in his day, when crooning through a megaphone seemed to stimulate the girls. Comedian Jerry Lewis who in the late 1950s effortfully tried to peddle old Al Jolson chestnuts, songs accompanied by stabbing, brass-driven arrangements, often ended up in a puddle of maudlin and embarrassing farce. Lewis was under the false illusion that "belting" mattered — it was a 1950s thing, I think — pushing the natural chest register beyond its normal limits. Most "belters" can carry it fairly comfortably up to around B-flat in the middle of the staff, but Jerry Lewis always punked out before that. Elvis Costello who disconcertingly tends to yodel has a voice somewhat like one of those uneven terraced hillsides in rural Portugal, a decline jutting down to balance by abrupt, uneasy, non-discernible steps rather than by anything at all like a seamless flow. The late Anthony Newley with his hems and hoots and boggles had no vocal range at all but with a bronchial honk always seemed to be singing the same note, sounding to me like the Cowardly Lion ("If I-I-I were the kiiiing of the fo-or-orest") from MGM's *The Wizard of Oz*. I recall him singing the title song from *Sweet November* opposite hiccupping Sandy Dennis where he played a cloddish, maudlin lover with what Truman Capote would call a "case of the cutes." Rocker Rod Stewart — the man actually looks avian — sounds like a prehistoric Patagopteryx giving sudden hysterical birth in a sandpit, exasperated wings a flap, as it were, hauling out each weird, crackled note as if he were hatching a mottled egg! With Stewart still there is the remnant of a melodious voice beneath all that gravel. I think of Aerosmith's Steven Tyler as a synecdoche for all hair bands, mousy guys with tall coiffures — he has the further subtracting but still apposite feature of having a face like an upturned canoe along with the looks of guy that would knock up a girl in the back seat of a Camaro — and the name *Ruidoquedito*, meaning "little noise" in Spanish, comes to mind as a suitable tag. It is a variation of the name, *Rumpelstilzchen* which in German means, literally, "little rattle stilt". (A *stilt* is a post or pole which provides support for a structure.) A *rumpelstilt* or *rumpelstilz* was the name of a type of German goblin, also called a *pophart* or *poppart* that makes noises by rattling posts and rapping on planks. When Tyler, the "Demon of Screamin,'" in heavy make-up, wearing more scarves than Sarah Bernhardt, goes pipping about the stage, crepitating like a tiny firework, and howling from that monstrous letter-box of a mouth, "Walk theees waaaaay," who else in that grotesque, over-fussified, bisexual sub-world of tightpants-wearing looneytunes is a better rumpestilt?

Another belter was Frankie Laine. Full of face with a big sensual mouth, and wide shoulders, Francesco Paolo LoVecchio (his real name) put a lot of hoot and jive — he never needed a microphone — into big 1950s hits of his like "That's My Desire," "Jezebel," "Mule Train," and "The Cry of the Wild Goose," and he even sounded black. He was emotional, but then he was Sicilian, so what do you want from me? As jazz critic Richard Grudens wrote, "Frank's style was very innovative… He would bend notes and sing about the chordal context of a note rather than to sing the note directly, and he stressed each rhythmic downbeat, which was different from the smooth balladeer of his time." As he sang, he swerved and used to claw the air, *grab* it with both hands. Why not? They are tools of drama. D'Annunzio wrote an entire play for Eleanora Duse's beautiful, expressive, histrionic hands.

Speaking of hems and hoots, listen to Ben E. King's greaseball version of the old standard "Amor" with all of its revisionary — substitutionary! — grunts, growls, and groans in surely what is one of pop-music's most feeble and failed examples of hipster ad-libbing, a raw declamatory three-minute yowl scarcely identifiable as song but what I take to be the otherwise talented King's idea of cool scat, reminding me of ex-Red Sox manager Jimy [sic] Williams's enigmatic if not nonsensical remark, "Everything's as important as when it happens." In his attempt to simulate sex, King sounds like he is actually *eating* something, reminding me in its hideosity of the way in movies that the rather repulsive-looking comedian Woody Allen kisses a girl — he revoltingly *chews* them!

Do kissing patterns not reveal things? Fifties pop-singer Pat Boone could never conceal a kind of banal flatness when he sang and with no range gave a monotonous flatulence to every song he ever recorded. But I was going to say, you knew the guy was lame from the jump. Remember how in the movie, *April Love*, when gorgeous Shirley Jones hugs and kisses Boone in that stable scene, he merely stands there as useless as a box of rocks without so much as single physical movement. Grotesque!

With her oddly clipped and broken delivery, the irascible Dinah Washington, from all reports "a mean, tipsy, powerful rotten-egg lady," as Mercedes McCambridge once said of Joan Crawford, could not really hold a note — or perhaps merely out of patience refused to — as if doing so were too much work or cost too much effort, offering a style that gave a sound of scolding to her voice. (Whenever in a recording studio, as live bands waited for her, she would supposedly throw off her coat and bark, "All right, motherfuckers, one take!") Seals and Crofts sound like drunken grigs or munchkins weeing away in high report. The truly unbearable Kenny Rogers, the most hackneyed singer in the history of all country music, moves from the low register of growls to a high upper register of what I can only call Western Quacking — I mean, it sounds to me like an Alabama redneck practicing animal calls in an old backyard shed. As I say, Barbra Streisand, who at times literally screeches, has the sharp oxyphonic sound of a dentist's drill. Olivia Newton-John who has no strength in her voice alternately squeaks and thinairishly sounds with those faux-meadowlark trills as if she was high on valium, and she cannot hold a note for a hemidemisemiquaver. Frankie Avalon is nasal. (He recorded his first hit, "Dee Dee Dinah," literally holding his nose.) Cher's unbearably philistine vocal tremolos, sexless and unmagnetic and more than a bit simian, sound very much like that of old country singer A.P. Carter, husband of Sara, who all his life trembled with a mild palsy that informed his quavering voice. (The best word to describe the vocalizations of Cher — you hear it with Rhesus monkeys — is "ululation.") Nancy Sinatra is monotonic in the main but does seem to use it to her catatonic advantage in all those low-rent, atonal songs of seduction that she sang in the mid-'60s, a period that recalls for me The Walker Brothers' "The Sun Ain't Gonna Shine Anymore" and the Sir Douglas Quintet's "She's About A Mover" and the Fuzztones' "Oh Those Eyes" and the Hollies' "Bus Stop" and The Remains' "Diddy Wah Diddy" — a particular group I thought was fairly good. (Speaking of gaffes, in Nancy Sinatra's big hit "These Boots Were Made for Walking," should she perhaps have sung "What I know you haven't had time to learn" and *not*, as she mistakenly does, "What you know you haven't had time to learn"?) To me, Cher with her gross unmusicality is so bad in virtually everything she sings [sic] validates the assertion that Al-Qaeda leader, the fanatical Puritan Osama bin Laden, makes when he darkly stated that music being played in a house is "unethical." Cher always seemed to think that she needed more heft, more tuft, in her voice. How someone could sound like a decrepit old woman even at a fairly young age truly puzzles me — adenoids? echo chambers? double tracking? — but it is always there, that kakidrositic moaning, the sex-yodels of a crazed Arctic tern, and can be found in every single Cher record from the very beginning, all the cheesy mickeymousiana that once used to be heard, say, in the over-feverish orchestrations of the Blue Barron [Harry Friedman] Orchestra with the vulgar over-slurring, indefensible kitsch, and quavering horns. Neil Diamond, finally, mu-shu-porks all of his lyrics with greasy fattitude, in places throwing in growls he farcically thinks add male authenticity to his music. Now picture him on stage wearing a cape and looking like a nightmarish theropod, capable of flying! Total vulgarity. I would rather hear the Lawrence Welk Band play their favorite old standard, "Boo Hoo," even with that loopy bandleader gummy-grinning, winking, and waving that broom-long baton. At least what he wore wouldn't terrorize a heron.

With Diamond's unfetching growls, I am always reminded of the musical (mis?)attainments of Quilp, the malicious hunchback dwarf moneylender in Charles Dickens's *The Old Curiosity Shop*. Quilp who probably got his voice from eating hard eggs, shell and all, devouring gigantic prawns with the heads and tails on, and drinking boiling tea without blinking. As Dickens points out, Quilp

> …occasionally entertained himself with a melodious howl, intended for a song but bearing not the faintest resemblance to any scrap of any piece of music, vocal or instrumental, ever invented by man.

Dickens and song, now there's a subject. Mark Tapley would cheerily burst into sprightly vocalizations. For all his faults, Mr. Micawber could both sing and hum — he loved the song "Auld Lang Syne" — and his son, Wilkins, you will recall, loved nothing more than to break into "The Woodpecker Tapping," although he suffered regrettably from a "head voice." Mr. Bucket gained a wife with his vocal talent. Captain Cuttle sang naval ditties. Harold Skimpole himself, for all his mooching and misguided vanity, composed half an opera. No, in his novels Dickens offered us some unforgettable singers.

The unearthly sonic tremolos of folk-singer Buffy Sainte-Marie's voice — isn't it even more depressing to learn that they are natural sounds? — literally approximate the roars, crowings, girneys, and k-alarms of a desperate mandrill in heat. She reminds one with that raw, unsettling, whining vibrato of hers of the ghastly trumpets of Lawrence Welk which always went whinging along like the temperature graph of a pneumonia patient. Her tremulous voice always recalls for me old the joke:

> Patron: "Do you know 'The Road to Mandalay'?"
> Singer: "Yes. Would you like me to sing it?"
> Patron: "No, I would like you to take it."

Englebert Humperdinck, whose singing style gives one the impression that he has inhaled massive doses of sulphur dioxide, once made me destroy a radio. He often sang/ spoke between his teeth, like a dentiloquist. (And why anyone merely to break into the music business would adopt, to mock, the preposterous name of a 19th-century German composer alone makes that person certifiable.) Engelbert's unintentionally comic crooning — listen to the oil in "After the Loving" — becomes funny, and as Ella Fitzgerald insightfully sang in "You're Laughing at Me" — no small bit of wisdom — "Humor is death to romance."

Country singers like Merle Haggard and George Jones and Johnny Paycheck and Waylon Jennings and hearty Don Williams with his tugboat basso, while they are not bad, trying to sound virile and tough, often come across in a snuffy, snarling way only as angry, illiterate — almost IQ-less — simpletons. Willie Nelson most of the time sounds as if he has just wandered in from a Goose Fair. (His crack-pated version of "White Christmas" is a crime for which, were I on the jury, the punishment would be cutting off his pigtails. (He looks the kind of guy who used to be beaten up by guys like him! A quick but apposite aside here? On certain rare occasions, improvisation on a classic can be done brilliantly, as for example with the Drifters' brilliant version of "White Christmas," the Harmony Grits' "Santa Claus is Coming To Town" — compare this version to Tony Bennett's hopelessly sleazoid version or the Carpenters' cheesy exploration which is done as a *torch* song — or, say, the Orioles' cool "What Are You Doing New Year's Eve," but I have always had a real problem with singers who with vain but feeble attempts at creative noodling desperately try to improvise Christmas standards — one of the worst areas of horrendous singing — *rewriting* them, as it were, like Natalie Cole's "Sleigh Ride," Lou Rawls's "Silver Bells" (truly as bad as it gets), Robert Goulet's "There's No Place Like Home for the Holidays," Leon Redbone and Dr. John's costive "Frosty the Snowman," Barbra Streisand's neo-Christmassy "My Favorite Things" in which, yowling like a constipated crane, she painfully presumes to improvise on Rodgers and Hammerstein, and Paul McCartney's "A Wonderful Christmas Time," the entire song of which consists of the repetition of the line, "We're simply having a wonderful Christmas time," and so, as I say, in this particular department, believe me, I was going to state that Willie Nelson has to be Captain of Awful. But then that would leave out a few other major contenders like Neil Diamond who in attempting to sing "We Three Kings of Orient Are," I swear, virtually performs a partial-birth abortion on it. Listen sometime to Paul Anka's would-be bop loungelizardization ("Hey, come on it's lovely, yeeah, weather, oooh, for a...") of Leroy Anderson's "Sleigh Ride" — it is *crazily* bad. And what is the name of that black group — girls? guys? *oxen?* — that recorded the swinging version of "Rudolph the Red-Nosed Reindeer?" Too, too fearful words.

But did you ever stop to think regarding so *much* bad Christmas music that the worse it is the bigger our advantage in demanding that each singer's horrid album match or undercut the competing prices? A monopsony controls the total demand for a commodity. Thus a "monopsonist" can reverse the abuse and ingeniously dictate terms to its suppliers in the same way that a monopolist controls the market for its buyers, so that in the end we can shut them all down and never have to hear them again!

We all know "The Twelve Days of Christmas", the carol of English origin that enumerates a series of increasingly grand gifts to be given on each of the twelve sacred days of the holiday. It invites parody, of course. The Muppets did a version, with Miss Piggy adding her long drawn-out "Five golden rings." So did The Simpsons. Shrek, too. Alvin and the Chipmunks covered the song for their album *Christmas with the Chipmunks, Vol. 2* (1963) in which the furry little scamps grow tired in the middle and accidentally flub the lyric on the eleventh day. On one Christmas episode of *The Lucy Show*, Lucille Ball conducts a boys' choir who sing this song, and because the boys forget the words, Lucy acts out each part of the song which seems to get faster and faster as the song gets longer. (Gale Gordon, who played Mr. Mooney on the show, is also in the choir and finishes each round of the song with his bass version of "and a partridge in a pear tree.") One of the worst versions, if it is not short, dumpy Allan Sherman's intentionally mocking, anti-Christmas-holiday hatchet-job which he wrote and performed for a 1963 TV special and in which the listed gifts are tacky items, such as a cheap transistor radio (the punch-line being that on the twelfth day the butterball Sherman decides to exchange the eleven previous gifts for other items) is probably Da Kine Lyrics — Hawaiian-style — to "Numbah One Day of Christmas," as strange a version of this song as the eerie one that appears in Ellery Queen's novel, *The Finishing Stroke*, a brain-teasing tour de force in which the song actually figures in the plot.

> Numbah One day of Christmas, my tutu give to me one mynah bird in one papaya tree.
> Numbah Two day of Christmas, my tutu give to me two coconut, an' one mynah bird in one papaya tree.
> Numbah Tree day of Christmas, my tutu give to me tree dry squid, two coconut, an' one mynah bird in one papaya tree.
> Numbah Foah day of Christmas, my tutu give to me foah flowah lei, tree dry squid, two coconut, an' one mynah bird in one papaya tree.
> Numbah Five day of Christmas, my tutu give to me five beeg fat peeg... foah flowah lei, treedry squid, two coconut, an' one mynah bird in one papaya tree.
> Numbah Seex day of Christmas, my tutu give to me seex hula lesson, five beeg fat peeg... foah flowah lei, tree dry squid, two coconut, an' one mynah bird in one papaya tree...

Were you aware that catechists, earnest ones, if you will, actually assign spiritual interpretations to those enumerated gifts ("Four calling birds" for the Four Gospels, etc.), the partridge in a pear tree being the Baby Jesus?

Among some of the truly classic disastrous Christmas records are: Kay Brown's "Daddy, Is Santa Really Six Foot Four?", Alice Cooper's "Santa Claws is Coming to Town;" Frank Zappa's "Holiday in Berlin" — the entire song comprised one word: *booooh* — the Three Tenors' version of John Lennon's "Happy Christmas/ War Is Over", Twisted Sister's "O Come All Ye Faithful" — true unmusicological piggery — where a possum-snout-faced, cross-eyed, slavering person-thing of indeterminate sex named Dee Snider wearing misapplied lipstick and creepy make-up along with wild, garish, yellow medusa Klimt-like hair leads a group-sing in a dining room, literally howling out the lyrics. (Heavy Metal Christmas music need not be fully dismissed. "Run Rudolph Run," as sung by Motörhead's growly-voiced Lemmy Kilmister *et alii* [ZZ Top's Billy Gibbons and Foo Fighters' Dave Grohl] is a little gem.) The cool stylings of the upbeat "Merry Christmas Polka" by Sonny Cash (actually an Italian guy born in Canarsie) with all of its bells, whistles, piano, and farting farfisa accordion, is close to a potpourri of total insanity. Japan's Hikaru Utada offers a unique blend of Nippon/ American and dog-yipping sounds to her inexplicably named "Merry Christmas Mr. Lawrence FYI," which is a "crash blossom" of lunacy and which goes in part:

> NYC, NYC. Woah, woah
> Tokyo, Tokyo. Woah, woah
> Send it off from the streets to the highest
> To the highest high.

Among the list might be added the inspired and heartfelt lyrics of "Ghostface Christmas," sung by rapper Ghostface Killa (a.k.a. Dennis Coles who did time for attempted robbery in 1999), prominent member of the multifarious Wu-Tang Clan from Staten Island with its magical cryptic slang and non-sequiturs:

> It's the season for sharing, season for the gift
> Season of snow, it's December 25th,
> That time of the year, we dress like Saint Nick
> Stirring whipcream into that hot cup of Quick.

I have heard better stuff on African 45 LPs sung in Luo, Lingala, Efik, Kiswahili, and Kisii. Am I mistaken in thinking that rappers are all clones? They scandalously all get away with using the n-word, everyone from NWA to Jay-Z to Notorious B.I.G. to Ol' Dirty Bastard to black rapper Me'shell Ndegeocello whose "Dead Nigger Blvd. (Part 1)" — she suffers from photosensitive epilepsy and is susceptible to seizures induced by flash photography when she is performing live — is not the least of her problems. But what about the conformist dress code? Is it not possible that that every last ghetto fab and playah since the very first rants of DJ Kool Herc or Afrika Bambaataa, with their gold chains, bling pendants, big limousine sneakers, velour suits, prison shorts, Stunna shades, sideways hat all turned to 7 o'clock like Soulja Boy, bucket hats, hoodies, headwraps, name belts, and stylin' jabbing hand-gestures that I'm certain must carry something of import — all weird twisting finger gyrations and configurations — all came to us by way of the Bokanovsky Process of human cloning described in Aldous Huxley's novel *Brave New World*? If not, why do so many in the Hip Hop world all dress the same. like Snoop Dogg, Mix Master Mike, Chamillionaire, Li'l Scrappy, Tiga, X-Clan, Da Brat, Bubba Sparxx, Dead Prez, Floetry the Songstress, Roscoe P. Coldchain, Del Tha Funky Homosapien, Insane Clown Posse, E-40, Knocturnal, Silkk the Shocker, Jagged Edge, Waka Flocka Flame, or T-Nutty who explains the tribalism in "Flowmastermouth":

> And yes, I'm gonna confess
> Like the rest, of my people
> My niggaz, that be runnin niggaz over like a diesel
> Got everybody humpin', the same way the beat go
> Makin it a gangsta party
> Cause there's nobody wit us, but hoody rats and killa.

These are muzzle-loaded head-bangers, mouthy, boastful, yammering — revealing themselves in the flash-smoke like rank, inexpert amateurs and so open to return fire — not anything like authentic breech-loaded, maggot-nuking guns, full of solid shot and true aim and accurate fire-power, the true *boomsticks*.

I suppose one may insist that all of this has grown out of lyrics from long ago like Jerry Lee Lewis's "I wants to love you like a lover should" and Louis Jordan's "We chickens tryin' to sleep/ And you butt in/ And hobble, hobble hobble hobble" and Big Bill Broonzy's "She built up round, lay on the ground, she can look up as long as you can look down" (from "Trucking Little Woman" — rock 'n' roll in 1938!). Box it about as you will, I still see the barbarians at the gates. I am not alone in this, by any means. Please, I am not looking for Kate Smith, OK? We all flipped over Ernie K-Doe singing "axed" for the word *asked* in his big hits, "Mother-in-Law" and "Can't Tell You" — just as we disliked Billy Joel's pathetic attempt at trying to be cool in his 1980 hit, "Don't Ask Me Why," when in a feeble attempt at "wiggerism" and in a pitiful imitation of Ernie *et cie*, he sings

"Don't axe me why" — but Ernie was the real thing, "Mr. Naugahyde" from the Big Easy, "The Emperor of the Universe," etc., and when he died in 2001, after a traditional jazz funeral in New Orleans, was even interred in the 200-year-old Duval tomb in Saint Louis Cemetery. C'mon!

What bothers me in the crudities of Hip-Hip is what particularly nettled the English poet Philip Larkin about certain aspects of modern jazz with what he felt were its irresponsible innovations. "I dislike such things not because they are new," he wrote rather scoldingly in *All What Jazz* (1985), "but because they are irresponsible exploitations of technique in contradiction of modern life as we know it." He goes on to say,

> This is my essential criticism of modernism, whether perpetrated by [Charlie] Parker, [Ezra] Pound, or [Pablo] Picasso: it helps us neither to enjoy nor endure. It will divert us as long as we are prepared to be mystified or outraged, but maintains its hold only by being more mystifying and more outrageous: it has no lasting power.

A fondness for what we know is one thing, bringing about lamentations for the old, tried and true rock-and-roll, but one can find serious animadversions nowadays against the random, the unpolished and rough-cut, the unrefined in music, where amateur and unskilled hacks and hirelings are turning out bad product.

"Where's the Ray Charleses, the Sam Cookes, the Jackie Wilsons, the Louis Jordans?" complained Ike Turner several years ago. "Where? It's no more. Black radio died. Kids took to the street with rap and hip-hop. 'Shoot him. Kill him. The bitch this. The bitch that.' This is what they had to do to sell records. So they did it. But the rest of this life that I got in me, man, I'm gonna use it to get black music back on radio. Because there's very few of us left. Motown sold out — that's dead."

Chuck D of Public Enemy summarized the mentality of hip-hop fashion and some low-income youths as "Man, I work at McDonald's, but in order for me to feel good about myself I got to get a gold chain or I got to get a fly car in order to impress a sister or whatever." In his 1992 song "Us," Ice Cube rapped that "Us niggaz will always sing the blues/ 'cause all we care about is hairstyles and tennis shoes." While they tend to dress the same and to use the same finger motions to get the audiences or crowds real crunk — the "Mos Def Hand-Wave," the "Slim Shady Chop," the "Down Jab," the "Ninja Star," the "Tonedeff Fast-Finger Piano-Playah," and, among others, the "Poison Bullet," where the arm is bent at around a 90-degree angle out from the body and moves up and down as it is goes higher in the air (some of them might actually be gang signs like the "Compton Crip," the "Kitchen Crip," the "Underground Crip," the "Hoover Crip" and the "Mafia Crip") — what has made each gangsta *personally* more extreme or funkier, on the other hand, may be attributed to "antecedent denial," the fear, or taboo, of a guy copying his predecessor, and so each performer down the chain becomes freakier and freakier, cruder and cruder, dumber and dumber.

On February 24, 2012 long lines of "sneakerheads" queued up outside of stores overnight got their first crack Friday at a new space-themed Nike basketball sneaker, the $220 Foamposite Galaxy with glow-in-the-dark soles and a purple and pink galactic swirl pattern — only 1,200 pairs went on sale at a handful of stores across the U.S. to coincide with the start of the NBA All-Star Game weekend. An angry mob of blacks raged into the early morning after a Footlocker at the Florida Mall in Orlando cancelled the midnight, first-come first-serve release of 200 pairs of the shoe due to "safety concerns." Gathering crowds became so unruly in other major cities that deputies in riot gear were called in.

Just for sneakahs, duuuude! Know'm sayin'?

I daresay those Hip Hop names are no crazier than Black Metal names like Fleshcrawl, Cryptopsy, Abruptum, Krabathor, and Cradle of Filth which, in terms of dubious extremism, hearken back to the Vanilla Fudge, Strawberry Alarm Clock, etc. bizarrerie of the 1960s, but in any case all of them seem to convey in terms of slanting horror the same creepy relation to music as those "veganized food" monickers like Quorn, Gardein, and Soyloaf do to those extrusions of skinless, boneless, meatless faux-chicken that is made out of soy and pea protein, tofu, beans, carrot fiber, and mouthfeel. My question is what is behind the diabolical names they choose like Rotting Christ, Impaled Nazarene, God Dethroned, Christ Agony, Black Crucifixion, Judas Iskariot, Atheist, Sabbat, Lord Belial, and, among others, Pentagram — the need to frighten mommy and daddy?

I have a serious problem with some of the "radio journalists" on NPR, let me confess right off, so my specific complaint here touches deeper issues. But really, what about those fruity, self-cherishing voices of Robert Siegel, host of *All Things Considered*, and Scott Simon, of *Weekend Edition*? Their preciosity is truly unbearable, so affectedly mellow with yeasty timbre that their every word is not so much spoken as rather giggled and gurgled and so pleadingly saccharine and pleased with itself that the two of them sound like nothing more than human clafouti. Are they ballet dancers? Their voices are pie-soft, they speak to coddle what they never seem to say and fiddle with words that pause to value themselves, like girls waiting for a kiss. They bubble like waterfalls. It is not "Now for the news" with Siegel, but "Now for the noooge [news]," not "Trade Center" but "Trade Centirrr." "The vasht ashembly took up the entire shtreet." "Yes" comes out "Geshe." Simon's overly precious voice sounds frumpy and frumenty all at once. He has a tongue/uvula combination that I cannot stand. He gives one the, not distinct, but indistinct impression that rather than speaking a language he is browsing it like a wading moose for leaves and soft buds and lilies. Neither Siegel nor Simon can enunciate a clear or crisp S. The word "others" with Simon becomes "otheeriz." He says "analysheesh," not "analysis." But let me get to my point.

Each and every Christmas Scott Simon irreligiously reserves a segment on his NPR show *Weekend Edition*, with the conniving assistance of a dunce named Jim Nayder, host of Chicago WBEZ's *The Annoying Music Show*, to play a bunch of perfectly terrible songs to mock the holy day — or holiday, if you insist — of Christmas, in order to annoy and insult Christians and take the mickey out of them. Simon and Nayder are cute and cozy with each other — *mishpocheh*, I believe is the term, although I personally hate Yiddishisms — family. On December 23, 2011, Simon once again arranged to have pranky little Nayder visit his show with tunes selected, as Nayder put it, for "that [sic] birth on the 25th" and proceeded to treat his radio listeners with nothing less than psilanthropic delight to four or five patently offensive *anti*-Christmas carols, each one chosen to mock the feast day. It is a show served up annually for those who hate Christmas, mainly non-Christians, general curmudgeons, and religions like the Jehovah's Witnesses who not only condemn all holidays, particularly Christmas and Hallowe'en, but a long list of other Jehovah-offending entities — offenders are "disfellowshipped" — such as blood transfusions, Roman Catholics, saluting the flag, military service, the United Nations, and, among other things, the celebration of birthdays which they find sinful. I notice that Simon did not play Hot Box Comedy's "All I Want for Christmas is…Jews," an actual song, by the way, but, you see, that did not fit their brand of holiday satire. As a sop to any Christians listening, I gather, to avoid criticism, perhaps, toward the end of this silly show Simon did throw in Kenny Ellis' "Hanu-calypso" — get it, Hanukkah and calypso? — which appears on his *Hanukkah Swings* LP, an album that includes such memorable holiday favorites as, "Swingin' Dreidel," "*Maoz Tzur/* Rock of Ages" ("set here to a cool big band vibe") and — I am not making this up — "'Twas the Night Before Hanukkah." Ellis who groovily snaps his fingers as he bops, wears a Cavanaugh hat as Sinatra did, and jives about on stage with a hand-held mike, has every lounge-lizard maneuver right down pat.

> Everybody's doin' the Hanu-calypso…
> the Hanu- calypso

really is hipso
so grab a dreidel and spin
and some raisins you win…

*Jewish iPhone Magazine* compares Cavanagh's music to the "swing era legends Count Basie, Les Brown and Benny Goodman," pointing out that the swinging Ellis, an entrepreneurial rabbi from California "realized the void [of Hannukah music] and did something about it" by issuing *Hanukkah Swings!* in time for the holiday season of 2006. Get your copies, fans! Hear one of the stars of Kol Yisrael (Israel National Radio)! Look for it under "Easy Listening," Don't delay! $9.90! *Albums may sell out fast!*

You will insist that I witnessed this only in a nightmare, but Cher joins Rosie O'Donnell on an LP called *A Rosie Christmas* on which, cheek to jowl, they sing a duet of "Christmas (Baby Please Come Home)." It is not exactly Nelson Eddy and Jeanette MacDonald singing into each other's mouths in *Naughty Marietta*. Typically singing out of her mandibles, as it were, Cher sounds like a hairy lumberjack chanting through a funnel, while morose Rosie's flat, leaden accompaniment ("They're singing deck the halls/ but it doesn't sound like Christmas at all…") is doubled with a gerbil-like chorus of young girls weeing away in the background. *Asinus ad lyram* is a Latin phrase that comes to mind here — "An ass at the lyre." In an odd, mismatched way the two of them singing together recalled for me the 1934 musical *Flirtation Walk* in which Dick Powell sings several duets with Ruby Keeler and with his high reedy tenor voice he sounds like a woman — he never sang in later roles — while with her deepish voice, pitched lumberingly low and almost always flat, she sounds like a man! (I would prefer to either couple Bob Dylan and Patti Smith singing their duet of "Dark Eyes" any day of the week.) You could have had the chance to hear the host herself on the Rosie O'Donnell Show in the late 1990s (a decade or so ago she played the role of Rizzo in a revival of *Grease*) sing duets — stupid words cobbled onto famous melodies — with other C-list celebrities like Alec Baldwin, Florence Henderson, and even with the tubby comedian Roseanne Barr when the two of them, cheek to jowl, looking like Mrs. Butterworth and Sara Lee Cheesecake from the Pancake Channel swayed and vocalized together to the theme song of the Patty Duke Show:

We're Rosies
Identical Rosies all the way
One pair of chubby bookends.
It's easy both night and day…

By the way, a video of Cher singing "O Holy Night" on a TV Special — wearing a Victorian overcoat, her hands in a muff, under a streetlamp, her hair sticking up in loopy whorls like fat Mrs. Jellyby's in Charles Dickens' *Bleak House* — provides ample fodder for the brutally satirical imitation that versatile Paul Shaffer did of her on the "The David Letterman Show" a few years later. The thing is, Shaffer's crow-croaking, over-voweled, befustianed, nutzo parody of Cher's gaudy Christmas appearance in its highly distinct awfulness — "O hawly naaaa-ght,/ the laaatts were braahtly sha-niaaaen!" — wins hands down.

You have to hear the moon-yodeling of the Cher original, though. Talk about a song being butchered? We are talking charcuterie!

I still cannot believe that Cher's faux-Italian accent in *Moonstruck* (1987) in which she played Loretta Castorini — she sounded as if she learned it from a Paraguayan — won an Academy Award for Best Actress! It is exceeded in sheer torture only by Ruby Keeler with pasted-on epicanthic folds trying hopelessly to imitate a Chinese accent ("I miss you velly much a long time/I think that you love me still...") in *Footlight Parade* (1933) singing with James Cagney "Looking for My Shanghai Lil." Nicholas Cage's attempt at an Italian accent in *Captain Correlli's Mandolin* is the pits — and he is of Italian extraction. Dick Van Dyke in *Mary Poppins* sounds less like a Cockney than he is chewing chicle. If that is a Mexican accent Charlton Heston is using in *Touch of Evil*, I am Howdy Doody. Julia Roberts in *Mary Reilly* ("Sahrr, you said you had an *ailn*ess") is painfully bad. But even kings nod. Charles Laughton playing the fanatical Inspector Javert in *Les Misérables* incongruously drops into his Yorkshire accent ("Ah moost do mah duty!") more than once.

While I am complaining about Christmas and tastelessness, I have to cite Miss Peggy Lee's "Happy Holiday," the definitive version of that secular song with its references to climate, snow, dreams coming true, bells, "presents and goodies," and just about every other winter or seasonal (non-Christian) reference — the vocal equivalent of the Federated Department Stores, owners of Bloomingdale's, Macy's, etc. which starting in 2004 officially banned all of its employees from greeting customers with the words, "Merry Christmas," lest anybody, you see, be offended. Peggy's version ends with her squeaking out, almost as if daring to break a taboo, the words "Merry Christmas!" Suddenly she signs off with the salutation, "Happy Holiday." I love the woman. She was a dynamite of power and courage. She sang "Ghost Riders in the Sky" for me once at the New York Hilton — smiled into the spotlight and personally dedicated it to me — but here she seems schizophrenic. Sign of the Times: "Oh, my Lord — and Taylor" is an actual line from a blasphemous Lord and Taylor television commercial that I heard, literally will vouch for having heard, on the evening of November 16, 2011.

On this note, a sour and contentiously nonreligious acquaintance of mine once went so far as to complain of the Christian reference in the powerful opening lines of the French version of "O Canada!" which with its stirring juxtaposition (roughly, "Just as your arm knows how to wield the sword, it knows how to bear the cross!")

> *Ô Canada!*
> *Terre de nos aïeux,*
> *Ton front est ceint de fleurons glorieux!*
> *Car ton bras sait porter l'épée,*
> *Il sait porter la croix!*

I must say I have always considered more poetic than the abstract jingoism one hears in the vague and, to me, far paler English form,

> O Canada!
> Our home and native land!
> True patriot love in all thy sons command.
> With glowing hearts we see thee rise,
> The True North strong and free!

Speaking of secularism and music, the late Jeff Buckley's mystically lovely but mournful "Hallelujah," a sort of waltz/gospel hybrid — it was written by Leonard Cohen and originally released on his album, *Various Positions* (1984) — was described by Buckley as "a hallelujah to the orgasm." Belief in the modern world is both scrimp and tenuous. Cohen himself sings, "Now maybe there's a God above/ as for me all I ever learned from love/ is how to shoot at someone who outdrew you/ It's not a cry you can hear at night/ It's not somebody who has seen the light/ It's a cold and it's a broken Hallelujah." Talk about an epitaph for modern man and his discarded and bewildered self. Who is surprised that an ill-at-ease, unvital people like us now feel much safer, instead of saying "God bless you," cravenly — sheepishly, insecurely — prefer the awkward, eunuchoid, "God bless"?

What could be more pathetic or pitifully inadequate at Christmas time, by the way, than to hear over the radio some moronically doctrinaire or politically-correct disc-jockey desperate to keep his job have to say, "We've been listening to beautiful *holiday* music all through this *holiday* week, friends, all presented for your *holiday* enjoyment. Soooo, Happy *Holidays!*" — as if, to be inclusive, there are Jewish or Muslim carols that must be embraced and that all options must be covered!

One of the very worst Christmas songs appeared in a movie called *In the Good Old Summertime* (1949), a wistful song which composers Fred Spielman (music) and Janice Torre (lyrics) had the actual effrontery to call "Merry Christmas" and which, believe it or not, was sung by none other than Judy Garland — pay attention, *not* "Have Yourself a Merry Little Christmas" which she effectively sang in the movie *Meet Me in St. Louis*. I am referring to the melancholy clunker with the generic title "Merry Christmas" which Garland delivers in this movie — an undermedicated remake of *The Shop Around the Corner* (1940) — with a sullenness bordering on malignancy, a slow, moody, morbid cadence that you cannot believe until you feel an overpowering urge to jump off a bridge. Listen to the repeated motif of *insistence* in Mozart's *Requiem*, that beating, overbearing, four-note, then eight-note, drive; demanding death does not give up. I hear the same laborious, taxing, toilsome thing here, a burdensome exaction that life in its weariness wants capitulation.

It is not quite the "*Dies Irae*" or the "*Stabat Mater*," But I might put it up there in terms of a general bringdown with Giacomo Leopardi's "*A sè stesso*," probably the most depressing short poem — 16 lines — ever written:

> Or poserai per sempre,
> stanco mio cor. Perì l'inganno estremo,
> Ch'eterno io mi credei. Perì. Ben sento,
> In noi di cari inganni,
> Non che la speme, il desiderio è spento.
> Posa per sempre. Assai
> Palpitasti. Non val cosa nessuna
> I moti tuoi, né di sospiri è degna
> La terra. Amaro e noia
> La vita, altro mai nulla; e fango è il mondo.
> T'acqueta omai. Dispera
> L'ultima volta. Al gener nostro il fato
> Non donò che il morire. Omai disprezza
> Te, la natura, il brutto
> Poter che, ascoso, a comun danno impera,
> E l'infinita vanità del tutto.

> Now you shall rest forever,
> My weary heart. The last deceit is ended,
> I thought myself immortal. Worthy thoughts,

and beloved delusions,
and longings to be deluded — all have perished.
Rest thee forever! Heavily, heart,
have you beaten. There is nothing
worthy to move you more, nor does earth deserve
your sighs. For life is only
bitterness and boredom, earth is merely
a pile of sludge.
Be soothed henceforth. Despair
for the last time. Our fortune
is nothing but the gift of death. Despise
yourself, along with nature, and the brute
power that, eerily, spreads its filthy damage everywhere.
Scorn the infinite emptiness of all things.
[My translation.]

Garland was pure magic, the ultimate movie star. Words are almost too solid to express the fluid quality of her musical voice. Some of us — I refuse to damn myself directly — feel that in the end she was more hurt than helped by the gay claque that encouraged her late-stage horrors and public histrionics that, one unalterably feels, hastened her death. I still feel a tug of pain when I hear her sing what critic Michael Musto calls her "twin doormat anthems," "My Man" and "The Man That Got Away." To me she was the ultimate trouper in every way, however — MGM incarnate — a woman who carried every picture in which she appeared, from the tot in *The Big Revue* in 1929 to *I Could Go On Singing* in 1963, including her three Andy Hardy movies. I proudly enroll myself in showering Frances Ethel Gumm with unceasing praise, always, in headlines, with polychromatic inks.

The frozen smile of Andy Williams, billboarding his every LP — he couldn't stop selling — evokes the worst aspects of the 1960s for me, right up there with ceramic leaf ashtrays, bottles of Lancers Rosé, and Hai-Karate after-shave lotion. He was the master of the middle register, his phonation – the production of voice — replete with lots of throat, nasal-to-vowel transitions, moan-wailing, and a general membranous sound, as for example in his singles, "Are You Sincere," "Moon River," "Canadian Sunset," vowel-mad, echo-filled schmaltziana with gliding glissandi, waveforms, aperiodic energy. He loved voice stops, uvular trills, and an echoing acoustic delivery with dabs of Iowa moocow.

Over the course of a lifetime, Williams in his tasteful red reindeer sweater has recorded as many as eight Christmas albums — and no end of Christmas songs, including "Happy Holidays/ It's the Holiday Season," which includes the lines: "He'll be comin' down the chimney, down,/ coming down the chimney, down." He turned out Christmas albums the way Cartier did vermeil nut dishes, except they were not as elegant. It was more than an industry for him, it was his anchor to windward, and he made a killing: *Christmas with Andy Williams and The Williams Brothers* (1971); *I Still Believe in Santa Claus* (1990); *We Need A Little Christmas* (1997); *It's a Wonderful Christmas* (1997), etc. The holiday was Andy's safe-house, like the rare resident Bearded Tit or Reedling, the only English bird which, while all the others make some migration or other, never stirs from home. Although he was an especially close friend of Ethel Kennedy and all that clan, he is a lifelong Republican. On September 29, 2009, Williams was quoted by the *Daily Telegraph* as spitefully accusing President Barack Obama of "following Marxist theory" and of "wanting the country to fail." He gave permission to Rush Limbaugh to use his recording of "Born Free" to mock an "Animal Rights Update" on Limbaugh's right-wing radio show where a selection of the song is immediately followed by gunfire. The crooner smugly told Limbaugh, "Hey, it's fine with me. I love what you're doing with it." The record company later blocked Limbaugh's use of the recording.

Williams was born in Iowa but, like Dave Powers and a lot of hangers-on from the New Frontier, aped the way the Kennedys spoke. No one ever quite spoke like the Kennedys, by the way, certainly not in Boston or Massachusetts. I should know, I have lived there *mutatis mutandis* all of my life. The Kennedys actually made up — settled on — that hybrid voice, a sort of dysphonic regionalistic combination of low South Boston Irish, faux upper-class Newport, and a dash of chin-jutting cuckoo-clock. They were all quite convinced without ever asking that it sounded elegant and had panache. Senator Ted Kennedy was ridiculed by critics as the "Wizard of Ahs," and his embarrassing way of talking, a badly overweight man's gasping hoots best put somewhere between toot and klaxon, a bassoon and a bagpipe, a farce and a fart, was widely mocked — "But the, ah, policies of the, ah, pahty heah in, ah, Cawngress, ah, and the, ah, causes, the issues at hand, that we, ah, believe in. I was, ah, just comin' in heah, lemme say…" Hangers on and hacks obviously told Kennedy — hugely misinformed him — many years ago that there was a mildly distingué quality in his mis-dictional hesitation, like the Oxford stutter, and that he sounded like his brother, J.F.K. Ted with his flat-footed narcissism sadly *believed* it, except that Teddy's version was a laughable parody of Jack's and not even close to anything as intelligible, never mind stylish or cultured. He was fate's buffoon, an insipid dunderhead trampling linguistic pretexts. Who was it said that a religion dies when it tolerates truths which exclude it? Fat Ted was a walking joke, and even walking he waddled. He readapted a tongue like a badly forged check. As I say, what people outside of New England should understand right off is that nobody in Boston — *nobody* — ever sounded like that. I have had dinner, several times, with the late historian Samuel Eliot Morison, a true Boston Brahmin, the lapidary quality of whose regional accent – its grace, its firmness, cultured emollience – could only be described as what Henry James would call "the real thing."

I have to pause here on the sorry subject of overzealous popular singers who personally attempt to jive up standards or traditional songs and cite what has to be one of the classic train-wrecks in this department and that would be black rapper (and sex felon) R. Kelly's, um, let us call it the vocal *reinterpollation* of the United States' national anthem at the Jermain Taylor/ Bernard Hopkins championship middleweight boxing match in Las Vegas on December 3, 2005 when on that Saturday night his would-be hip-hop, funkadelic nightmare went plumb south in mere seconds! He was actually booed by a suddenly very nasty and very unhappy crowd in the packed auditorium. While the good folk had their hands on their hearts, he was groovily trying to get them to clap! *To hand-clap*! To put snap — *doop, wap, wap, woop, chung, chung* — into the dull thing while he is giving it the Harlem shuffle!

I mention singers and the vice of autonomously jiving up standards. Frank Loesser, the composer who wrote the words and music to *Guys and Dolls*, always locked horns with singers who cheekily improvised notes of lyrics. (His contentious verbal duels over style with Frank Sinatra left them lifelong enemies.) Susan Loesser in her 1993 portrait of her father, *A Most Remarkable Fella*, explained, "My father expected singers to perform his songs clearly, meticulously, enunciating every word — with no deviation, no extra notes, no frivolous embellishments. ('Singers love to vocalize beyond the sense of the lyric,' he'd say. 'They're always so sure you want to hear their goddamned *tones!*')"

Surprisingly enough, Mr. Rogers of *Mister Rogers' Neighborhood* was of the same mind set. When they came on his show, guests were often surprised, even occasionally irked, to find that although Rogers, a minister, was as gentle, kind, and patient in real life as he was on television, he was nevertheless a perfectionist who did not allow "shoddy" ad-libbing. He believed that children, no matter how small, were thoughtful people who deserved programming as good as anything produced for adults on television.

Don't grating singers force us to wonder whether music is in fact a medium for voice at all? That it seems more normal to be listening to Duane Eddy, or Mozart, or Jimmy Smith playing the Hammond B3, the great blues organ? I mean in the Congo, everything was once done to song — there was always a drummer in a pirogue — but at least those people were working. Caterwauling folk like Anita Bryant, Pat Benatar, Steven Tyler, Celine Dion, Barbra Streisand — truly a screeching mandrill when in high register —Frankie Valli, Yoko Ono, the Osmonds? They seem not even valid practitioners of the art of music. Of course just when you are ready to shut off every vocalist and begin to walk away, you manage to hear truly brilliant singers like Luciano Pavarotti's "*Non to scordar di me*," Sam Cooke's "A Change is Gonna Come," Ray Charles's "Night Time is the Right Time," Eddie Fisher's "Wish You Were Here," Hank Thompson's "The Wild Side of Life," the Isley Brothers' "Shout" — played real loud, it is one definition of freedom — Bobby Bare's "Detroit City," Rosie & the Originals' "Angel Baby," songs by Peggy Lee, Sarah Vaughan, Vera Lynn, and Doris Day — "Secret Love," "Windy City, "Baby It's Cold Outside," the woman could deliver a song — Ruth Brown, Leontyne Price, Ella Fitzgerald, Deanna Durbin, Judy Garland, Patsy Cline, throw in one of your own favorites.

How about young new female metal singers like The Agonist's singer, Alissa White-Gluz? Maria "Masha Scream" Arkhipova, of the Russian group, Arkona? Julie Christmas? Lilith Astaroth? Metal growls! Vocal fry! Creak! Ours is a new age. We're now talkin' glottal scrape, pulse phonation, laryngealisation, strohbass, and other unearthly vocal registers produced through a loosening of the glottal closure allowing air to bubble slowly through with a popping or rattling sound of a very low frequency!

But let us never forget Anita O'Day's "Thanks for the Buggy Ride" and "Let Me off Uptown." Barbara Lynn's "You'll Lose a Good Thing." Dido's "White Ship." Emmy Lou Harris's "One of These Days." Rebecca Lynn Howard's "Out Here in the Water." Memphis Minnie "Hoodoo Lady Blues." Donna Summer's incandescent "Love to Love You Baby" (She explained that she recorded he orgasmic groans and moans of this song by lying on her back on the studio floor with the lights out, picturing Marilyn Monroe in ecstasy) and "Hot Stuff" — two musical gems. Loretta Lynn's "You Ain't Woman Enough To Take My Man." "God's Plenty," as John Dryden said of Chaucer's *Canterbury Tales*. What about Ruth Etting singing "All of Me," Marion Harris singing, "A Good Man is Hard to Find," the driving rock-and-roll masterpieces of young Sugar Pie De Santo (born Umpeylia Marsema Balinton in Brooklyn on October 16, 1935) singing "Use What You Got," "Slip-In Mules," and "Baby What You Want Me to Do"? (Doing this same number in his 1968 concert in his black leathers, Elvis is, arguably, at his best.) Listening to Etta James's "I'd Rather Go Blind" and hearing those rare phrasal innovations — you can also hear them in Joe Tex's "Show

Me," the brilliant "Reconsider Me" by Johnny Adams who, with his swooping, beseeching vocal mannerisms and pleading falsetto, was known in New Orleans as "The Tan Canary," and Aretha Franklin's "You Lied," one of her true gems, a classic tour de force, one too often ignored — takes your breath away. Dr. Lyman Abbott, the Congregationalist theologian, after hearing Jenny Lind, the "Swedish Nightingale," sing, declared with heartfelt praise, "It is impossible to doubt the Resurrection while she was singing 'I Know That My Redeemer Liveth.'"

I have equally felt that way about the sacred anthem "Jerusalem," with music written by Sir Hubert Parry in 1916 to accompany the words of the great poet, artist, and dissenter William Blake whose magnificent poem was inspired by the apocryphal story of young Jesus who travelled to the area that is now England, accompanied by his uncle Joseph of Arimathea, and visited Glastonbury. The legend is linked to an idea in the Book of Revelation (3:12 and 21:2) describing the Second Coming.

As a medium, of course, many insist music is the nonpareil. A NASA committee was chosen to compile an audio message disc with a selection of the "Earth's greatest hits" to be sent into space for nonhuman intelligences on the *Voyager 2* spacecraft, an interstellar mission launched on August 20, 1977. The historic disc, which was made of gold-plated copper and encased in a gold-plated aluminum shield — "built to last a 1000 million years" — included 87 ½ minutes of our planet's varied music and song. (Although music was preferred over words or pictures, because it is not only based on numbers but musical harmony is easily analyzed in mathematical terms, a "Greetings to the Universe" segment in fifty-five languages was also compiled, including the less than Ciceronian "Hail" [Hittite], "How are you?" [Korean], and "Are you well?" [Burmese]). A variety of music provided the keynote. Along with a medley of natural music that included the sounds of whales, a baby crying, and waves breaking on a shore, the committee included a raga from India, Javanese gamelan music, a wedding song from Peru, panpipes from the Solomon islands, ch'in music from China, percussion from Senegal, three examples from Bach, Renaissance recorder music, arias from Mozart's *The Magic Flute*, a Bulgarian song called "*Izlel je Delyo Hagdutin*" sung by Valya Balkanska, a Pygmy girls' initiation song from Zaire recorded by Colin Turnbull, and for any and all the hipsters out there in the Far Beyond in the outer reaches of the asteroid belt past the Kuiper belt and the heliosphere blues singer Willie Johnson's "Dark Was the Night," Louis Armstrong's "Melancholy Blues," and Chuck Berry's "Johnny B. Goode."

It is an old story, often retailed by Louis himself, but back in November 1926 when they were recording "Heebie Jeebies," a song written by Boyd Atkins, a sax player in Louis Armstrong's band at the Sunset Café, "Pops" was sitting in a corner trying to finish writing out some lyrics to it before the recording light went on. He supposedly dropped the sheet of paper in haste, improvised nonsense syllables, and thereby revolutionized jazz singing just as he was transforming jazz music. It was a raw recording, and you can hear Kid Ory jumping the gun with his response, "Whatcha doin' with the Heebies?" Ricky Riccardi, the Archivist for the Louis Armstrong House Museum in Queens, N.Y. writes,

> The whole thing reeks of a first take, but, according to Armstrong, [OKeh-Odeon Records head, E. A.] Fearn was so tickled by the scat interlude that he stopped the proceedings right there, knowing they had just created something special. "Heebie Jeebies" isn't the first record to feature scat singing, and Louis Armstrong didn't invent the concept, but it did a helluva lot to make it something that people began incorporating into their vocals almost immediately (so when you see a poor amateur singer incorporate a snatch of awkward scat on "American Idol," sending the crowd into a tizzy, thank "Heebie Jeebies"). Just think: this was Louis' third full vocal on record and he already upset the world. Amazing.

But let us return to some other odd vocal presentations. Where is Elton John going with that sort of adopted yowl that, as he sings, so often seems to eat the lyrics that we can never quite discern, a kind of tragoudiphagy, with yukkish growling diner sounds like the stomach-drumbling sounds of Aiken Drum masticating chunks of steak. Singer Karen Carpenter who had a sweet voice sounded at times almost exactly like a rural Derbyshire farmer in old England, pronouncing cow "ky-ow" and care "cy-are" and cart "ky-art" when with her kind of sad, darkly-tinged voice she sang words like "cy-om," for example, in "Superstar" — "What can I do/ to make you cy-om again?" Actor Henry Fonda who came from the tall grasses of the Midwest, specifically Grand Island, Nebraska, had the same problem. You can find many examples of it. In the movie, *Mister Roberts*, he asks Ensign Pulver, "Wanna go to the ward room and get a cyup of cyoffee?" and later he confronts Captain Morton played by James Cagney with an indignant, "How'd you get in the navy, Cy-apn?" I can't explain just why, but it gives me the creeps.

Singers can be bad.

But it can get worse.

When it comes to either understanding or approving what we hear in songs, we are forced to face a whole new set of problems. The lyric, born on the music, the vehicle of the whole operation in many instances, can be converted to a simple appeal or made an entire complex of deeper emotions, telling our story, explaining our shames, classifying our frenzies. Clarifying our *vision*! Songs are of course melodies with words. How on earth was composer Richard Rodgers's soul and spirit filled so richly with such incomparable music? We will never know. To me, Richard Rodgers was the definitive genius. (After early songs of his hit for the lively Garrick Gaieties of 1925-26, he gave up his alternate career — a fact — selling children's underwear, and are we not grateful?) To be able to imagine, to compose, to translate onto paper all those poignant and haunting and lilting and soulful and profound, almost supernaturally dreamy melodies? Lerner and Loewe were brilliant. "They Call the Wind Mariah." "I Could Have Danced All Night." "Wand'rin' Star." "The Heather on the Hill." Who composed "The Folks Who Live on the Hill"? Whoever he was, he was surely a genius. "Sweet Sixteen." "Deep River." "Shenandoah" "I Ride an Old Paint." All of Gershwin. Gilbert and Sullivan. Victor Herbert. Cole Porter. Irving Berlin. Harold Arlen. The too-often overlooked Jerome Kern. The Beatles. Randy Newman. Who wrote "In the Valley Where the Sun Goes Down," the song Judy Garland opens with in *The Harvey Girls*? Superb. Too amazing. Irving Berlin's "What'll I Do?" Pure genius. "I'm Funny That Way." A masterpiece. As I have mentioned, so many songs in shows or in sermons, movies or magazines, documents or dramas, ballads or billboards, out of reasoning and perception are worthy of note. The song in pop or rock permits us to realize one way or another a certain *value* of a kind, even if it is to dismiss one lyric or another as a lie or a half-truth or a calumny or a bit of worthless propaganda.

That is if we can *understand* the lyric in question. Never mind, first off, the incomprehensibility of the Kingsmen's "Louie, Louie." No one can comprehend that, and maybe that was their point. But how about Zager and Evans' "In the Year 2525," a hodgepodge of muddled neo-science-fiction or the bombastic Harry Chapin's "The Cat's in the Cradle" or Simon and Garfunkel's "The Dangling Conversation" or Iron Butterfly's twanky "In-a-Gadda-Da-Vida"? I still haven't the remotest idea what The Tee Set were singing on their single "Ma Belle Amie" or Desmond Dekker with song "The Israelites." Was it this type of song that Morrissey had in mind (he has often been charged with racism) when he stated in 1985, "All reggae is vile"? How about the incessant nonsense of The Grateful Dead whose songs for *decades* all sounded alike, vacant, artless, and pretentious, like "Truckin,'" all fifteen long minutes of it ("Sometimes the light's all shining on me / Other times I can barely see") or the songs on talentless Lou Reed's *Metal Machine Music*, a flat-out awful LP of squawks and shrieks that has been out of print virtually from the time it was released or the entire oeuvre of every single big-hair group that swished through the 1970s?

The crudely racist, anti-Palestinian lyrics to the theme from the political song, "Exodus," written by the blatantly anti-intellectual, pro-Zionist, fundamentalist, no-longer even-listened-to Pat Boone — it was his delight to baptize new Christians in his Hollywood swimming pool — especially the mad imperialist line, "This land, this land, God gave this land to me," have always struck me as fascistic, grasping, and vile, not unlike the humble remark made by Israeli Prime Minister Benjamin Netanyahu, the morning after his 1996 post-election victory, "This proves that there's a God in heaven." Palestine was also stolen. Peter Minuit must have felt the same greedy bit of luck when on May 24, 1626 he swindled the entire island of Manhattan from gullible Native Americans for the value of 60 Dutch guilders, which was estimated to be the equivalent of a scant $24.

Dylan's lyrics are often so subjective and inaccessible and privately symbolic as to be almost totally meaningless, like the dim and unrelenting verses of Simon and Garfunkel who, having developed formidable defenses against logic at a very early age, somehow manage to mix and mingle bombast, bathos, and platitude in equal measure all at once. But whether it is "Sad-Eyed Lady of the Lowlands" or "The Sound of Silence," "I Pity the Poor Immigrant" or "Mother and Child Reunion," the irrational jabber and nonsense in such songs never fail to remind us that, while almost a moral fault, incompetence in bad lyrics almost always does far more to confuse than to provoke, more to bewilder than to intrigue, more to discombobulate than to satisfy.

What allegorical interpretation, for example, can give meaning to that hopeless concatenation of scrambled images evoking the thief, the joker, the wildcat, and the watchtower in Dylan's "All Along the Watchtower"? Or Mrs. Robinson's connection to cupcakes and Joltin' Joe? Or to Reid and Brooker's "A Whiter Shade of Pale" with its pretentious muddle of allusions to playing cards, Chaucer's "Miller's Tale," and Roman vestals? Does anyone have any idea what's going on? The winner in this category, Bathos, or the Art of Sinking is, of course, the hellishly oppressive "Elusive Butterfly," a harsh emetic from 1966 sung (!?) by Bob Lund where the flying-about melody is not only as bad as the lyrics — a perfect storm, musically speaking, that calls to mind what George Frazier, long a dapper wit at the Boston *Globe*, once wittily declared about the married couple, Steve Lawrence and Edie Gormé, two reputations disguised as singers (major balsamic reductions, respectively, of Frank Sinatra and Jo Stafford) that "the best thing about the two of them singing together was that you could ignore them both at the same time" — but the lyrics are to music what gargling is to speech:

Out on the new horizon
you may see the floating motion
of a distant pair of wings,
and if the sleep has left your ears,
you might hear footsteps
running through an open meadow,
you might have heard my footsteps
echo softly in the distance
through the canyons of your mind

A butterfly with footsteps? Footsteps run? And echo softly? Echo softly in the canyons? A mind has canyons? Is the speaker here a complete schizo? Aren't "open meadows" and "ruined canyons" contradictory images? (I am reminded of the lines in Vanessa Williams's "Save The Best For Last:" "Sometimes the snow comes down in June/ Sometimes the sun goes 'round the moon" [sic]) What song of the millions there are could possibly prove the great cynic Voltaire more correct when he made the observation, "Anything that is too stupid to be spoken is sung"? The song's crude unmusic without so much as the trace of a melody cluster is mercilessly shoved at you, relentlessly, abusively, in the way, for example, that in the dramatic movie, *High Noon,* unsuspecting film-goers are actually manipulated by the unceasing cascades of music which, loud and repetitious, actually *snatch* at you — usurping your emotions to point you in this or that direction — for two interminable hours. It is the "shock of the unintelligible," a long, stammering, lacunary text in which I see a comic contradiction of the very disclosures the film is trying to make in all seriousness. Can anyone even deny it is a shaggy-dog story? It reminds me of Orson Welles's befuddled and befuddling *The Lady of Shanghai* (1947) and Harry Cohn's despairing remark, "I'll give $1000 to anyone who can explain the plot!" (Welles's Irish accent playing the character Michael O'Hara is truly the pits.) The song repeats the same words with inartistic abandon, reminding me of the inarticulate dolt George W. Bush using the words "freedom" and "liberty" over and over again — something like forty-nine times — in his truly unmemorable Inauguration Speech on January 20, 2005 with almost incantatory stupidity, reminding me of what Sydney Greenstreet tells adman Clark Gable in the *Hucksters,* "Beautee soap, Beautee soap, Beautee soap. Repeat it until it comes out of their ears. Repeat it until they say it in their sleep. Irritate them, Mr. Norman. Irritate, irritate, irritate them." There is a lot more to "Elusive Butterfly" and far too much to despise in this beastly incantation — *de*cantation — which I hate to ruin by recapitulation or diminish by detail, but what are we to make of the reference made later when the mentally-addled speaker, or pursuer, or whatever he is — or symbolizes — becomes utterly confused and proceeds to tell the listener that the long-abandoned ruins of her dreams have been left behind? "There is no difference between music and opium," Ayatollah Khomeini notoriously once pronounced in one of his many Malvolionian moments. "Both create lethargy in different ways." Is it possible one afternoon in Iran that the Imam had actually *heard* this song and formed his pronouncement?

This skewed sort of blunder has its vulgar and hare-brained correlative in warped point-of-view or lyrics of misbegotten ingenuity, such as in absurd offerings like Jan and Dean's "Baby Talk," a song which is supposedly sung by a 5-year-old or in Neil Sedaka's neo-incestuous pop-hit of 1963, "Happy Birthday, Sweet Sixteen," a song of passionate ardor sung to a young girl by — drum roll — *her brother!* I suppose in the end it is no worse than the dubious extravagance one finds in P.G. Wodehouse's 1940 novel, *Eggs, Beans, and Crumpets*, where four of the nine stories in the collection are narrated by a *crumpet*. I will also confess here that I always get a negative frisson upon hearing George Jones sing to Tammy Wynette in "Let's Build a World Together," "I want you as much as a child wants its mother." Talk about the effects of simultaneous contrast! And juvenile maudlin on top of that! In her song, "When I'm With You," tiny Shirley Temple, quite unapologetically, sings "Marry me, I want to be your wife," to her *father*. Do you find that odd? I do not see why it should, at least to true Curleytop fans. It is an ungainsayable truth that in at least half of her movies the extremely cute, chubby little girl is sitting in some older man's lap — even old grandfather's — and pawing him or kissing him or trying to crowd into his being with clutching arms.

In the dubious odd-couple department, the King of the Cowboys Gene Autry in his western ballad, "Goldmine in the Sky," blithely apostrophizes his romantic sentiments — wait for it — to his favorite mule! You also find that strange? How about Elvis Presley in the movie *Stay Away, Joe* singing a love song. "Dominick" — crooning it — to a goddam bull, no less. Why to a bull? Why, to get him romantically interested in the cows, of course. Can't you discern the profound plots and intricacies of Elvis movies? At that point, Scotty Moore, Elvis's original lead guitar player from the early 1950s and who was playing on that "bull" session, sadly looked at Elvis and said, "Has it come to this, man?" ("Dominick" is widely considered, and not surprisingly, the most hated song in Presley's entire musical catalogue, and, although Elvis specifically requested that the song never be released commercially, did anyone ever bother to adhere to the poor guy's wishes? Not once.) There is precedent for such a thing in American literature, by the way. A late maudlin story of Mark Twain's called "A

Dog's Tale" is narrated by a dog that at one point drags the family baby away from a fire and for his pains is beaten by the father who mistakenly believes that the dog is actually hurting the baby. "I did not know what I had done," says the dog who seems far more rational and even kinder than his blundering owner, "yet I judged it was something a dog could not understand, but which was clear to a man and dreadful.") We find another talking dog, a hip, articulate, satirical, often grumbling French poodle named Pancho in cartoonist John Held, Jr.'s witty novel, *The Gods Were Promiscuous* (1937) who casually dispenses advice to anyone without the slightest hesitation: "The ass is out of the gray pants. In fact, the combined asses are worn thin in all your trousers. Sire, both pairs." A pig[10] is the protagonist in Ludwig Bemelman's novel, *Dirty Eddie*. I have to say, I must have read at least ten novels in which dogs either talk or become heroic figures. Call it the "Flush Syndrome" (See Virginia Woolf's novel of the same name.) Brian, the talking dog on television's *Family Guy*, not only dates lovely human women and eats at the table with his own special place but is frankly the only intelligent creature in the entire dysfunctional Griffin family. I have no doubt that this dubious genre reaches its logical culmination in Chapter 14, "Willard Comes Clean," in the vulgar Hollywood writer Joe Eszterhas's crude satire, *American Rhapsody*, where readers are dubiously treated in one remarkably less-than-elegant neo-Boschian encounter to a book chapter communicated by a, um, body part. The candid prose confession that is spoken, unambiguously, I might add, is by President Bill Clinton's penis! In spite of Clinton's obsequious attempts during his White House years as well as afterwards to look cool playing the saxophone on television and "getting' down," from all the accounts I have read in various books by many women he has bumblingly come on to and/or tried to seduce he is a far cry from the Way Out Willie as in "I Know a Cat Named."

On the subject of sexual eeriness, what about Al Martino, a crooner whose gender was undisputed the last time I checked, in his unrelenting song, "I Love You More and More Every Day," blithely singing,

---

10      Leo Tolstoy actually wrote a long strange story called "Yardstick," arguably the most original horse-narrative in all literary history, a Russian fable that is addressed to the human reader by a horse! A poor skewbald mistreated by people, the benighted animal proves ultimately, traumatically, to be shocked by the fact that he is owned by someone! As why shouldn't he be? I have always insisted that all the monsters who run zoos and any and all zealous and inveterate zoo-goers, than whom in terms of compassion there are no more unfeeling creatures, will be consigned to a special *bolgia* of Hell. Spanish and Mexican bull-fighting mavens, the royalty of Gehenna, at least in terms of animal rights, will, prayerfully, be pitchforking them with delight at all hours of that eternal and everlasting midnight to newscasts of Fox News's cantankerous and flannel-mouthed wingnut, Bill O'Reilly played over and over again.

...and, darling, still

it grows and grows inside me

I love you more and more every day.

Blech! Yuck! Wretch!

Jerry Vale. Al Martino. Tony Martin (who, curiously enough, happened to be, not Italian, but Jewish). These were the fervid shlockmeisters who always managed to put a bit too much *olio* into their voices — it was a '50s crooner phenomenon in popular music — and pointlessly, often farcically, over-lubricated even the simplest songs, and almost always with echo chambers and multiple tracks. I am always reminded, when having the bad luck to hear such recordings, of the late, strange, madly innovative John Cage's actual experimental orchestrations with twelve radios tuned to different stations! As I have mentioned, Ben E. King's oleaginous version of "Amor" — the word greasy, g-r-e-a-s-y, comes to mind as I hear his overpronounced licks and throaty mouthpulls and sexual grunthumps — remains for me the most definitive lounge-lizard song of them all, in spite of the fact that King was a black man and of neither Italian nor Sicilian heritage. In 1959 Chuck Berry with his single "Anthony Boy" tries (in vain) to give a St. Louis black guy's version of pushcart Italian: "Look at him he's a blush" (I myself am proudly half-Italian and must say that we have a big corner on the "*cumpari*" — the goomba — song-style.) Let it be proclaimed that greasiness did not — and does not — always adhibit to the genre of croonerdom. Sinatra rarely, if ever, showed that side of himself when singing, certainly never the way that Lou Monte or Louis Prima did. Listen to Matt Munro's version of "Walk Away," potentially a song in this sub-genre but as a matter of fact a song that, saved from such excesses, has become a pop-classic — true art, in my opinion — by Munro's amazing style and graceful delivery. If you are inclined to think a pop-singer by definition cannot pull off the coup of a beautiful recording with this type of song, listen as well to Perry Como's unadorned but soulfully splendid version — matchless — of "Then You Can Tell Me Goodbye," a small masterpiece in the soft wistful elegance of his easy and unforced presentation. Unfortunately, however, Como could not really *wail*. Catch his strained, belabored, unhip rendition of "Route 66," for example — no pickup, no swing, nothing. It is as flat and dull and depressing as a 1950's mental-patient crew-cut.

Trust me, by the way, I am not against ingenuity. Imagination is required in really good song-writing. The catchy ditty, "Sam's Song," sells the very song it celebrates. The extremely peculiar song, "I Happen to Like New York," which was written by Cole Porter for the 1930 musical, *The New Yorkers,* and of the many versions of which (Bobby Short, Caterina Valente, etc.) Judy Garland has the most notable —

> I like to go to Battery Park
> and watch those liners booming in

was intentionally written in an entire *monotone*, devised as one long insistent note. It drones. It undeviatingly drones! Meredith Willson, of *The Music Man* fame, in his pop-song, "You and I," for which he wrote both words and music, gave us a (the only?) song-lyric that is just one sentence long: "Darling, you and I know the reason why a summer sky is blue, and we know why birds in the trees sing melodies, too, and why love will grow from the first 'hello' until the last 'good-bye,' so to sweet romance there is just one answer: You and I."

It sounds less like a bad idea than an unnecessary complication to work "big words" into a lyric, but in the song, "Make Believe" from *Showboat*, Oscar Hammerstein II employs the ugly five-syllable word "technicality" and yet makes it work:

Magnolia Hawks sings:

> We only pretend,
> You do not offend
> In playing a lover's part.
> The game of just supposing
> Is the sweetest game I know.
> Our dreams are more romantic
> Than the world we see

and Gaylord Ravenal replies

> And if the things we dream about
> Don't happen to be so,
> That's just an unimportant technicality.

Very daring. Very brave.

Frank Loesser with "Adelaide's Lament" from the Broadway showstopper *Guys and Dolls* actually translates *medical* jargon into chorus girl-speech, an amazing tour de force from a talent who was able to write music and lyrics both. "It says here," sings Adelaide (Vivien Blaine)

"The average unmarried female,
Basically insecure,
Due to some long frustration, may react
With psychosomatic symptoms
Difficult to endure,
Affecting the upper respiratory tract."
In other words, just from waiting around
For that plain little band of gold,
A person can develop a cold.

What can one say about Loesser's savvy, cheeky, contagiously memorable lyrics? He also wrote complete scores for the musicals *Where's Charley?* (1948), *How To Succeed in Business Without Really Trying* (1961), and *The Most Happy Fella* (1956). He could do anything! Then throw in songs like "Once in Love with Amy," "Baby, It's Cold Outside," and "On a Slow Boat to China." I have always wondered of any great songwriter exactly how loose and how tight they have to be in the creative process, what substance imbues their wit, what genius presides over their art, that in their work they can construct not merely lyrics but such wonderful little worlds. The short answer is surely imagination.

Which reminds me of a wonderful story. One often-repeated story took place in the early 1940s, when singer Margaret Whiting was 19. Her friend, Johnny Mercer had had asked her to sing the lovely song "Moonlight in Vermont," which he had just heard and felt was ideal for her voice. "I've never been to Vermont," said a diffident Whiting. "How can I sing a song about a place I've never been to?" she asked. "What is the significance of pennies in a stream? What are ski tows?" "I don't know," Mercer replied and shrugged. "I'm from Savannah. We'll use our imagination."

Why not? I believe UFO abductee Travis Walton, missing for five days and the object of one of Arizona's biggest-ever manhunts after being zapped with a mysterious hovering craft's laser-like energy beam in full view of six fellow-loggers in a forest near the town of Snowflake, Arizona in 1975, is a good case for extra-terrestrial (and extra-intelligent) life. Walton's fellow-logger, Steven Pierce, was an eye-witness to Walton's encounter with the strange craft and its energy beam.

On Procol Harum's second album, there is a long song, actually a suite of songs, called "In Held 'Twas I." I have to confess that for twenty years I have tried in vain to figure that one out. Were they singing, "It was in held I (was) in'? If not, what in the hell were they saying? Was it a translation from Albanian? I have always been amazed that in Eric Burdon and the Animals' big hit, "The House of the Rising Sun," the opening few lines of which go,

There is a house in New Orleans
they call the Rising Sun,
and it's been the ruin
of many a poor *boy*,
and, Lord, I know I'm one."
[My italics.]

the tragic point-of-view is entirely male-centered, with no reference whatsoever to the poor girls working as prostitutes, treated as chattel, imprisoned in a bordello.

The '60s was a comparatively inarticulate decade. Gestures, images, signs, and symbols meant everything, words very little. When words were analyzed, they were usually of the insipid sort and valued by girls who ironed their hair and thin, mustachioed guys wearing Navajo headbands who wrote "Frodo Lives!" on walls and found incomprehensible nitwittery like Donovan's "There is a Mountain" with lyrics like

First there is a mountain,
Then there is no mountain,
Then there is…
Lock upon my garden gate's a snail,
That's what it is
The lock upon my garden gate's a snail,
That's what it is

to carry deep, portentous messages that spoke to them. Back then people met, courted, married, and lived together without saying much more than "Wow," "Groovy," "Don't hassle me, man" and "Outta sight." Language was suspect. Explanations meant guile, ritual hypocrisy, and words in almost any form or context were traps, snares, the politique of lying and longwindedness. During that period, any and all meaningful procedures — at least in the minds of true believers — were non-verbal. Gestures were coolspeak. It was a decade when couples related without a single meaningful conversation. People read *The Hobbit* and *The Strawberry Statement* and *Jonathan Livingston Seagull* and found them profound. The '70s, a decade that seemed to pass in a vague lemony dumbness, was even worse. Its songs were as bland as a pair of beige curtains. As I say, I cannot understand half the lines in The Tee Set's "Ma Belle Amie" (ironically, the French is much clearer than the English); or that gobbledygookish line in the Eagles' "Take It to the Limit" — "where the bright lights have faded in two" or is it "into"? — and so many songs of Elton John's, thanks to his farcical elisions and inexplicably refaned pronunciations, that it has virtually come to constitute his signature.

An irony of that inarticulate decade of the '60s — where symbols spoke for sense, words were held in suspicion, part of the "system," as it were — was that so many of the songs were verbose. I am thinking of things like "Eve of Destruction," P.F. Sloan's faux-prophetic rant of 1965. James Brown's "Say It Loud, I'm Black and I'm Proud." A lot of them were protest songs. Didactic and preachy. "I Ain't Marching Anymore" by Phil Ochs. Malvina Reynolds' "Little Boxes." Bob Dylan's "Maggie's Farm."

When I consider the rag-and-bone-shop lyrics of, say, Donovan's "There is a Mountain" or Bob Lind's "Elusive Butterfly," I cannot help but ponder with nostalgia how deftly the great prose writers made language aspire to music. One thinks of the force that James Joyce had, for example, with his lilting sense of words, his dominion over language. At the opening of the ingenious "Sirens" passage in the novel, *Ulysses*, we find a literal "overture." With repetition, incantation, inversions, music plays throughout the chapter. Words and sounds in the passages evoke the Sirens who call to tempt us and in this mock-epic establish melodies as themes which in the early paragraphs have a lyrical quality like the finger exercises of musical scales that, as leitmotifs, lilt and ring changes on the same set of words:

> Miss Kennedy sauntered sadly from bright light, twining a loose hair behind her ear. Sauntering sadly, gold no more, she twisted twined a hair. Sadly she twined in sauntering gold hair behind her curving ear

and

> Bronze by gold heard the hoofirons, steelyringing.
> Imperthnthn thnthnthn.
> Chips, picking chips off rocky thumbnail, chips.
> Horrid! And gold flushed more.
> A husky fifenote blew.
> Blew. Blue bloom is on the.
> Gold pinnacled hair.
> A jumping rose on satiny breast of satin, rose of Castile.
> Trilling, trilling: Idolores.
> Peep! Who's in the... peepofgold?

Tink cried to bronze in pity.

And a call, pure, long and throbbing. Longindying call.

Decoy. Soft word. But look! The bright stars fade. O rose! Notes chirruping answer. Castille. The morn is breaking.

Jingle jingle jaunted jingling.

Coin rang. Clock clacked.

Avowal. *Sonnez.* I could. Rebound of garter. Not leave thee. Smack. *La cloche!* Thigh smack. Avowal. Warm. Sweetheart, goodbye!

Overwriting is of course a major hobble with a good many songwriters. Is it a didactic compulsion? The need to appear intelligent? Or "committed?" What exactly is behind the temptation to get gabby or garrulous in a lyric if it is not to wax philosophical, its attendant crime, while writing a song? It is a kind of oversharing, a desperate neediness that is annoying, often downright embarrassing. Blabbiness can be ruinous, songs like Bernie Taupin's "Captain Fantastic" or Paul Simon's "Outrageous" or Stephen Sondheim's interminable "I'm Still Here." Wordy, diffuse, long-winded, prolix, a song by sheer length can have the boredom factor of a Calvinistic sermon. One thinks of Bob Dylan's overlong "Catch the Wind," Donovan's "Sunshine Superman," Joan Baez's "Diamonds and Rust." Folk music as a genre is a hot cupboard of wordiness. Phil Ochs was the Pope of Garrulity. A song often cannot bear the weight of too much imagery, never mind indulgent word-salads. The English singer, Morrissey, can be charged of having major lyrical preoccupations, with many of his songs seemingly endless and chock-full of personal keening and outré allusions. The same can be said of Pink Floyd — especially in the more pronounced aural space-rock extremes of philosophical search — the Talking Heads, and the early Led Zeppelin who songs were a potpourri of blues, folk, and narcissistic rant mixed in with lyrical fragments from different songs.

This is not a cack-handed plea for brainless simplicity, mind you. I love style and manner and have nothing whatever against the pyrotechnic and the encyclopedic. Why write at all if there is no magic? If some lazy or idle reader angrily finds a word in my work he does not like or does not know, tough biscuits. I well remember a teacher of mine, something of a Malvolio, who dogmatically insisted that the best writing is simple writing, repeatedly pointing out that Abraham Lincoln's Gettysburg Address — this was his sole template for style — had 194 words of one syllable, 53 words of two syllables, 13 words of three syllables, and seven words of four syllables. Imagine him *counting!* What about *Paradise Lost, Bleak House, War and Peace, Moby-Dick, Absalom, Absalom!, Tristram*

*Shandy, Gargantua and Pantagruel, In Search of Lost Time, Infinite Jest?* I have always thought it peculiar that the only wood that the famous London cabinetmaker, Thomas Chippendale, would use was mahogany.

Wordiness is an offense on most fronts and in virtually all instances, however. Isn't the 2011 Jeep "Grand Cherokee Laredo," for example, a tad overnamed, particularly for a compact car? The official name of Rhode Island, the "State of Rhode Island and Providence Plantations," seems a more endearing place when it goes by "Little Rhody," no? One should not forget that L.A. is a pocket term for the more fulsomely denominated "El Pueblo Nuestra Senora la Reina de Los Angeles de Porciuncula." Consider the titles that Erik Satie gave to his musical compositions — he did not approve of the word composer and referred to himself as a "phonometrician," someone who measures sounds — "Three Pieces in the Form of a Pear," "The Man Carrying Heavy Stones," "Genuine Lazy Preludes for a Dog," etc. Listen to the ornate speeches — *"magna professis purpureus,"* in Horace's words — of General Douglas MacArthur. What about the noisome prattle and cant of creations like Carl Sandburg's psychotoxically dull *Remembrance Rock,* the *Yongle Encyclopedia,* the *Book of Mormon* (insanely *unpunctuated* in its first printing)? Then there was all that merciless and unending taradiddle shoveled out for decades under the name of sex and social behavior in the *Playboy* "Forum," a veritable Alps of horseshit. I am astonished that a forum still exists for pipe-smoking Hugh Hefner, a self-aggrandizing fraud — that raised lower lip and pugnaciously extended jaw of his in "affect theory" indicates self-disgust, distress, fakery, and rage — who has been trading for more than half a century in superficialities rather than anything like substance or truth. The cranky self-indulgence in French filmmaker Claude Lanzmann obsessively editing his documentary film *Shoah* (1985), an oral history of the Holocaust, from three hundred and fifty hours of footage into the wretched excess of a nine-and-a-half hour documentary — without voice-overs, without sub-titles — seems somehow out-topped when he wrote in his autobiography that in making the film he became the "master of time." The periphrastic Mr. Wilkins Micawber in Dickens' *David Copperfield* who with all of his flim-flams and flub-dubs would have happily referred to celery as *apium graveolens* thrived on the waves of his effortless pleniloquence. ("You will pardon the monetary laceration of a wounded spirit, made senstive by a recent collision with a minion of the law — in short, with a ribald turncock attached to the waterworks. Emma, my love, our supply of water has been cut off. Hope has sunk beneath the horizon! Bring me a pint of laudanum!"), but was it bearable? I cannot enumerate how many times Cary Grant stupidly calls Joan Fontaine "Monkey Face" in the film, *Suspicion* (1941) — twenty or so? — but allow me to go on record as saying that that silly phrase, which frankly sounded foolish the first time, becomes incrementally ineffective each time he repeats it and after the third or so mention truly intolerable. One thinks of other flatulent yam-in-the-mouth broadcasters, candidates, long-winded Nestors like the late Senator Hubert Humphrey, Defense Secretary Donald Rumsfeld, Jim Kramer of TV's *Mad Money*, sportscaster Steven A. Smith — even annoyingly loquacious poets like Christopher Smart, the older William Wordsworth, Hart Crane, Algernon Swinburne, Vachel Lindsay, Sidney Lanier, John Berryman, and, among others, Amy Lowell. I remember Janet Maslin's memorable denunciation of Alexander Ripley's turgid novel *Scarlett* (1991), a faux-sequel to Margaret Mitchell's *Gone with the Wind*, as a "stunningly uneventful 823-page holding action"? Nothing worse could be said of a book. Who that saw it could ever forget the scene of the late Sir Laurence Olivier, a bald, eye-crazed, depressingly doddering old 71, being given an honorary Academy Award in Hollywood in 1978, somewhat impaired and lost, in his dotage, clutching that cheap Oscar to his bosom and cravenly falling all over himself while effervescing,

> In the great wealth, the great firmament of your nation's generosities, this particular choice may perhaps be found by future generations to be a trifle eccentric, but the mere fact of it — the prodigal, pure human kindness of it — must be seen as a beautiful star in that firmament which shines upon me at this moment, dazzling me a little but filling me with the warmth of the extraordinary elation, the euphoria that happens to so many of us at the first breath of the majestic glow of a new tomorrow.

Fustian? Too kind. Utter bullshit is more like it. After a long lifetime of trying to convince us he was the graceful nonpareil of all actors, a man of exquisite appointment and taste, a wordmaster par excellence. Olivier proved in one disastrous minute that, off-script, he was a doddering old fool, an uneducated wordy buffoon who had no sense of language whatsoever. In his memoirs, the Chairman of ABC News, Roone Arledge, gives an example of the kind of fustian that the manifestly insincere and self-aggrandizing moron, Howard Cosell, mistook for eloquence when broadcasting, impressive only to the duncical and the aboriginal: "From the desperation of your tone, the bon vivant who is Roone Pinckney Arledge is beseeching me to rescue the trifle he's devised for Monday evenings. Am I not correct?"

"What is written without effort is in general read without pleasure," said the sagacious Dr. Sam Johnson. Too much effort, or the wrong effort, on the other hand, can have the same dismal effect. An attempt to achieve new fluencies of expression and mood by renouncing traditional forms and disciplines usually end up abandoning logic. "Language is wholly cerebral: it is an artificial medium of communication," writes Lincoln Barnett in *The Treasure of Our Tongue*. "It was devised by man, it is unique to man, and it works only when men agree on what its components mean."

Da Vinci once declared that it took two artists to do a painting, one to do the painting, the other to take the brush away. If that were the case, then why did not Simon stop Garfunkel (or vice-versa) from driving us mad with those painfully embarrassing, pretentious, overwritten lyrics of theirs? I am convinced, incidentally, that in their "Dangling Conversation" can actually be found a sub-textual if unwitting self-criticism of the very kind of bad lyric they wrote — "like a poem poorly written/ we are verses out of rhythm/ couplets out of rhyme" — and that they themselves are singing!

> We are couched in our indifference
> like shells upon a shore
> you can hear the ocean's roar
> in the dangling conversation
> and the superficial sighs
> at the borders of our lives.

It is noteworthy how the abuse of language can seem not only subversive but prove to be downright corruptive, as well. he subject raised in Thomas More's Utopia, Henry James's *The Golden Bowl*, Kafka's *The Trial*, Julio Cortázar's *Hopscotch*, George Orwell's *Nineteen Eighty-Four*. It is taken to be threatening the state (in the form of poetry, thus reorienting our priorities) in Plato's *Republic*. Vladimir Nabokov in his novel, *Bend Sinister*, at one point in the narrative advances a theory of *Hamlet*, essentially stating that the true hero of the play is Fortinbras, the one legitimate heir, "a fine Nordic youth" who deserves to reign in a Denmark which had been criminally misruled not only by the dead, degenerate King Hamlet (who killed Fortinbras's father, remember) and his murderer and vile usurper, Claudius, but also the would-be king, young Prince Hamlet, characterized as an "impotent" Dane with many "chameleonic moods." What is noteworthy in the novel is that, among the worst of their crimes — the very proof of their iniquity and indeed the linchpin of their unworthiness — are their excesses of cant, flattery, and *garrulity*. Over-theorizing Hamlet, yakking Polonius, the bumbling courtiers Rosencrantz and Guildenstern with their smooth and courtly talk, foolishly summoning Osric, all of the actors and the acted upon, capsulize corruption and in a dehydrated and condensed form ("a kind of swollen collection") make manifest, by default, from decadence, all that is wrong with that diseased government. We hear Nabokov in the palimpsest scolding as he writes,

> As with all decadent democracies, everybody in the Denmark of the play suffers from a plethora of words. If the state is to be saved, if the nation desires to be worthy of a new robust government, then everything must be changed; popular commonsense must spit out the caviar of moonshine and poetry, and the simple word, *verbum sine ornatu*, intelligible to man and beast alike, and accompanied by fit action, must be restored to power.

It is part of the comforting resolution at the climax of the play, a triumph of right reason, that Fortinbras, entering with his troops and to claim his place — with the dying Hamlet's blessing — will be made the true King of Denmark.

The urge to write songs surely involves the possibility in the heat of expression to overwrite, a hazard of effervescence. It is amazing how many people have been driven to write songs, from David the Psalmist to Taylor Swift, from Solomon to sexy Jane Birkin, from King Henry VIII to Bertolt Brecht, from William Shakespeare to Eleanor Farjeon, from Moses (cf. Exodus 15:1) to fat, nutty, spontaneous Peter Griffin on TV's *Family Guy*. St. Francis who in his youth was a devotee of the troubadours — and, by the way, wandering through Tuscany, the marches, Lazio, and along the Clitunno and Corno rivers, all of his poor friars, cheerful, living on donations, but filled with the spirit of God, would often burst into godly song — wrote the magnificent and now celebrated, "*Cantico delle creature*" (a.k.a. "The Canticle of the Sun") in his native Umbrian dialect, beginning, "*Altissumu, omnipotente, bon Signore/ Tue so le laude la Gloria l'honore…*" Martin Luther wrote lyrics to what were the street songs of the day. As his father did, Ferdinand III, Leopold I (1640-1705), the Holy Roman Emperor, wrote music that is considered highly meritorious. Among his most successful compositions are the *Missa angeli custodis*, a Requiem Mass for his first wife, and *Three Lections*, composed for the burial of his second wife. William Booth and his members of the Salvation Army often injected Biblical passages into familiar secular melodies that their listeners recognized, as well. John Bunyan's beautiful "To Be a Pilgrim" ("Those who would valiant be...."), the hymn, his only one, that is indelibly associated with him, first appeared in Part II of *The Pilgrim's Progress* (1684), its words recalling Hebrews 11:13: "...and confessed that they were strangers and pilgrims on the earth." (The original version is not commonly sung in churches today, perhaps due to the references "hobgoblin" and "foul fiend." It was given a new tune by British composer Vaughan Williams using the traditional Sussex melody, "Monk's Gate.") Mary Baker Eddy, the founder of Christian Science, wrote songs and poems. (Her music box, upright grand piano, Aeolian pianola, along with her personal Victrola can be seen today at the library of the Mother Church in Boston.) Frau Alma Mahler wrote excellent *lieder* and as many as 17 of her songs for voice and piano — "*Waldseligkeit*," "*Ekstase*," "*Bei dir ist es traut*," etc. — were published during her lifetime, by husband Gustav's own publisher, Universal Edition. (Gustav, nineteen years her senior, has been roundly criticized for asking his wife to cease all of her composing as one of the conditions of their — nine-year — marriage.) The astronomer, William Herschel, who famously discovered the planet Uranus in 1781 — the first planet discovered with a telescope —wrote an impressive 24 symphonies. He was a polymath and played the cello, the oboe, the harpsichord, and the organ, later becoming organist of the Octagon Chapel, a fashionable chapel in the well-known English spa-town of Bath.

St. Francis of Assisi wrote poems and songs, notably the celebrated

Lord, make me an instrument of your peace
Where there is hatred, let me sow love.
Where there is injury, pardon, etc.

as did Thomas Aquinas, who composed, "*Panis angelicus,*" the penultimate strophe of the hymn *Sacris solemniis* for the Feast of Corpus Christi. In 1643, the Jesuit martyr St. Jean de Brébeuf, a Christian missionary among the Indians in Canada — the "Apostle of the Hurons — at Ste. Marie wrote the beautiful "Huron Carol" ("'Twas in the Moon of Wintertime"), a Christmas carol which is still used today in a modified version. Brébeuf wrote the lyrics in the native language of the Huron/ Wendat people, and the song's original Huron title is "*Jesous Ahatonhia*" ("Jesus, He is Born"). The melody of the carol is taken from the traditional French, "*Une Jeune Pucelle*" ("A Young Maid"). Martyred by the Iroquois, enemy of the Huron, at the mission of St. Ignace in 1649, he was canonized by Pope Pius XI in 1930.

In 1906, Leo Tolstoy, then an old man, played a little waltz in F for string orchestra with flute solo obbligato that he had composed in his youth to the Russian pianist and teacher Alexander Goldenweiser, who wrote it down for posterity. (*Anna Karenina* is filled with aristocratic waltzes and balls.) Friedrich Nietzsche was a composer. A great admirer of Richard Wagner, in 1871 he sent as a birthday gift to the composer's wife, Cosima, an early work for violin and piano

— a supremely beautiful piece — that bore the rather Wagnerian title "*Nachklang einer Sylvesternacht*" [Reminiscences of New Year's Eve]. He is said to have been an excellent pianist. Most of his music was written in his late teens, solo piano pieces, piano duets, songs for female and male voice, and choral works, pieces that show an influence of several masters from the early to mid-19th-century. Franz Schubert and Mendelssohn are obvious models for many compositions, while Schumann begins to exert more influence around 1862, in such piano pieces as "*Heldenklage*" and "*Klavierstuck.*"

Charlie Chaplin wrote songs. So did dapper Mayor Jimmy Walker of New York City. As did Jimmy Durante who composed, "Jimmy, the Well-Dressed Man," "I Ups to Him and He Ups to Me," and "Who'll be With You When I'm Far Away." Bert Williams, the black comedian and entertainer, wrote, "Nobody," "Dar's No Coon Warm Enough for Me," and "I May Be Crazy, but I Ain't No Fool." Truman Capote wrote the lyrics to "A Sleepin' Bee," while Harold Arlen provided the music. The earliest aspiration of the American novelist Owen Wister, author of the classic *The Virginian* (1902), the first true "cowboy" novel, was to be a composer. After graduating from Harvard College, where as a senior he wrote both the music and libretto for a comic opera performed at the Hasty Pudding Club, *Dido and Aeneas*, which toured professionally in New York and beyond, he spent two years in Paris studying music.

One rarely if ever thinks of the great Fred Astaire as a songwriter, but from his earliest days that is what he wanted to be. A matchless dancer, he was a musician all around. (He also played drums, accordion, and piano.) He wrote "You're Such a Lot" in 1924 and "Just Like Taking Candy from a Baby" in 1940, words by British lyricist Gladys Shelley who also wrote the lyrics to "Tappin' the Time." That with "If Swing Goes, I Go Too," another song Astaire wrote, he performed in the MGM movie, *Ziegfeld Follies*, although the latter number was cut from the movie before it was released. "I'm Building Up to An Awful Let-down," probably Astaire's most successful song — Johnny Mercer wrote the lyrics — which reached as high as #4 in the U.S. pop charts in 1936 appeared in the London stage show, *Rise and Shine*, and was sung by Bonnie Hale and Jack Whiting (Margaret Whiting's father). As late as 1962, at age 61, he wrote "I Love Everybody But You," with lyrics by his daughter, Ava, and himself. All in all, he had 26 songs published in his lifetime. I have inveighed earlier against actors. Among their worst faults are envy, lack of taste, and stupidity, handmaidens all to rank narcissism Fred Astaire never won an Academy award, neither did Cary Grant. Staggering, no? It is like not letting the Pope join the Knights of Columbus.

It may also be pointed out that Charles Gates Dawes, the 30th Vice President of the United States under Calvin Coolidge (1925-1929) was a self-taught but very talented pianist whose 1912 composition "Melody in A Major" became a well-known piano and violin piece in his day, often called for, that was played at many official functions as his signature tune, a tune that was so sweetly melodious that it was eventually transformed in 1951 to the popular song, "It's All in the Game," when Carl Sigman added lyrics to it. Tommy Edwards's soulful popular recording of the song remained a number one hit on the American *Billboard* record chart for six weeks in the fall of 1958. Were you aware that SS-Obergruppenführer Reinhard Heydrich, one of the highest-ranking Nazi officials of the Third Reich and hatefully known as the "Butcher of Prague," was taught both the piano and violin (on which he became a virtuoso) at the Gütchenstrasse Conservatory — his father, Richard, a composer and opera singer, founded the Halle Conservatory of Music and his mother, Elizabeth, taught piano there — and also tried his hand at musical composition as well? "Reini" also sang but had a peculiar voice which, with his bleating laugh, earned him the nickname *Hebbe* — "goat." On his deathbed, reconciled to his fate, in a phone call to the notorious Heinrich Himmler two days before expiring, he recited part of one of his father's opera, *Amen* (1895):

> *Ja, die Welt ist nur ein Leierkasten,*
> *den unser Herrgott selber dreht.*
> *Jeder muß nach dem Liede tanzen,*
> *das gerade auf der Walze steht.*

> Indeed, the world is only a barrel-organ,
> which the Lord God himself is grinding.
> Each of us has to dance to the song
> that is on the roller at the moment.
> [My translation.]

Let us not forget the erstwhile composer Charlie Manson. He was once an aspiring songwriter in L.A. whose ditty, "Cease to Exist," ended up uncredited, and much revised, as the Beach Boys' "Never Learn Not to Love" which appears on their album *20/20*. Fourteen demo tracks of Manson's were in fact recorded in Brian Wilson's home recording studio. Manson arrived at the studio with six of his female groupies and lashings of dope. The recording session which became the album *Lie* is thought to be among Manson's best compositions recorded during those three days. Among some of the songs on *Lie* are such notable titles as "The Eyes of the Dreamer," "Mechanical Man," "Look At Your Game Girl," and "Home is Where You're Happy."

Patti Davis, Ronald and Nancy Reagan's daughter, with Bernie Leadon wrote the song, "I Wish You Peace" which was recorded by the Eagles. Playwright Maxwell Anderson wrote the lyrics to "September Song" for which Kurt Weill wrote the music. Rachel Field, the American author of the bestsellers *Time Out of Mind* (1935) and *All This and Heaven Too* (1938) — a woman probably most famous for her novel for young adults, *Hitty, Her First Hundred Years* (1929) — wrote the much loved poem-turned-song "Something Told the Wild Geese," as well. It was Field, by the way, who wrote the English lyrics for the version of Franz Schubert's *Ave Maria* used in the Disney film, *Fantasia*. Novelist and playwright William Saroyan had a hit single — composed with his cousin Ross "David Seville" Bagdasarian — with "Come On-A My House," based on an Armenian folk song. Although he was never credited, Thomas Dekker, the 17th century poet, wrote the lyrics for the Beatles' song, "Golden Slumbers." (Paul McCartney changed only two words.) And I sang a hymn in church recently, "Surely It is God Who Saves Me," that was written by Thomas Merton.

I believe that St. Paul wrote hymns. A small pastime for me is trying to discern exactly where they occur — he supposedly imbedded them in various letters (Philemon 1:3-6; Ephesians 1:4-10; Galatians 3:26-28, etc.). The only literature that survives from the first Christian generation is St. Paul's letters. Remember, he not only passed on what was passed to him (1 Corinthians 11:2), material both oral and written, but the oral tradition still flourished when he wrote his epistles. One bishop of the second century, Papias, Bishop of Hierapolis in Asia, ca. AD 140, told us that he preferred "the living and abiding voice" to anything that he found in documents. One is hard-pressed to know exactly what for St. Paul constituted a hymn. I took a very demanding course in bibliography in my first year in graduate school and became familiar with foul copies and "muddy" texts, learning how various song-fragments, poems, and formulae can lurk in a work, an especially difficult problem here since the very earliest surviving Christian documents are precisely those letters, written a mere two or three decades after the death of Jesus, despite many people's mistaken notion — including Thomas Jefferson's — that they came later than the Four Gospels.

Poet Vachel Lindsay wrote lyrics, many of which were meant for music, songs like "John Brown," "The Fairy Bridal Hymn," and "General Booth Enters Heaven," of which he said, "I set [my poem] to a tune that is not a tune, but a speech, a refrain used most frequently in the Meetings of The Army on any public square to this day." He traveled across the United States singing his very American verses, an account he gives in his essay "Adventures While Singing These Songs." As to others who contributed song lyrics, another obvious one is Rudyard Kipling whose poem "Mandalay" was performed as a sung rendition in an episode of *Rumpole of the Bailey*, "Rumpole and the Show Folk," and also recorded by Frank Sinatra. What is noteworthy is that Kipling almost always had a melody in his head when he wrote poems (see the Carrington biography), or so he said. Speaking of Sinatra, were you aware that he himself sat down and wrote the lyrics for "This Love of Mine"? We know that many poems have been set to music: W.B. Yeats's "The Song of Wandering Aengus," Robert Frost's "The Road Not Taken." I once heard Edward Arlington Robinson's "Richard Cory" sung by a choir. James Fenton, a very good British poet, wrote some of the lyrics to the musical *Les Misérables,* and got very rich on the proceeds I have heard. Writing music is a singular drive, a unique means of expression, and surely subsumes all sorts of motives. "The strange thing is that all I want to do now is write a song about this," Amanda Knox innocently confided to her diary just after the grisly murder in Perugia, Italy on Nov. 2, 2007 of her fellow student, Meredith Kercher. "It would be the first song I've ever written, and it would talk about someone who died in a horrible way and for no motive. How morbid is all this?"

The witty novelist P.G. Wodehouse of course collaborated with Jerome Kern on musicals. They wrote *Miss Springtime* (1916), an early Ziegfeld show, one called *Have a Heart* (1917) which ran for five years (mostly on the road), and after that came *Oh Boy* also in 1917, a show that was a huge success. Among the songs in *Oh Boy* were "Nesting Time in Flatbush," "A Pal Like You," "An Old Fashioned Wife," and — the most memorable — "'Til The Clouds Roll By." Another hit that same year was *Leave It to Jane*, for which, again, Kern wrote all the music and Wodehouse all the lyrics. Wodehouse also wrote the song "Bill" for the 1917 musical *Oh, Lady! Lady!* for Vivienne Segal to perform, and although it was withdrawn as it was felt to be too melancholy for that show, it was later used in the musical *Show Boat* (1927) with lyricist Hammerstein giving full credit to PGW.

Collaboration is compromise. It is about concessions. Wodehouse who was also a playwright and lyricist was in his wide-ranging talent and inventiveness also part author and author of 15 plays and as many as 250 lyrics for more than thirty musical comedies, was content to work not only with Jerome Kern but with Guy Bolton, as well. He also developed a close friendship with the ingenious Ian Hay, not only collaborating with him on several movies, stage-plays, and various dramas, but socializing, for they holidayed together in Scotland. It must be said that it is not always the case that the act of collaboration is a rich bonding experience. Gilbert and Sullivan were often at loggerheads. Nelson Eddy and Jeanette McDonald longed to shine solo. Oh, forget the co-star wars! One would need volumes to document it. Even Astaire and Ginger Rogers competed in many petty ways. The immensely successful composer Richard Rodgers and lyricist Oscar Hammerstein II, the former genial, warm and outgoing, the latter considered somewhat petty and egotistical, aside from their fruitful working arrangement on Broadway musicals — together they wrote nine, as well as a movie, and one television musical — had little in common and seldom saw each other socially. One gets the distinct impression that they did not like each other very much.

We have mentioned comedian Ed Wynn. He wrote songs, as well. "I'm Going to Get Myself a Black Salomé" was one of them. He grew discouraged enough however to stop writing when young, chubby Irving Berlin wandered up from Atlantic City and scored a hit in 1911 with "Alexander's Ragtime Band." (There is some evidence, although inconclusive, that Berlin borrowed the melody from a draft of "A Real Slow Drag" by Scott Joplin that had been submitted to a publisher.) Although Wynn went into vaudeville, Sophie Tucker made his song a hit, in 1910 or so, around the time the Portland, Oregon police arrested her for singing "The Grizzly Bear and the Angle Worm Wiggle." A writer needs a singer to pitch his song. What would George Evans have been without Blanche Ring singing — and hitting with — "In the Good Old Summertime"? Or Eben Rexford and Hart Danks without the Irish contra-tenor Dick Jose singing "Silver Threads Among the Gold"? Or Saxie Dowell without lusty, busty Eva Tanguay — known as "Miss Tabasco" or "The Cyclonic Comedienne"— squeaking out, "I Don't Care" (she manages to fit as many as five vowels into the word "care"!) in 1922? (She wore a dress made entirely out of coins when performing, costing $2000 and weighing 45 pounds, and also danced wearing a pedometer which showed that she covered four miles at each performance.) Or Ed Wynn without May West (it wasn't Mae in 1918) singing "What Do I Have to Do to Get It?" while launching the Shimmy-Shake? Back then, the signature line of May or Mae — she was actually born Mary Jane West in Bushwick, Brooklyn — was not the later "Come up and see me" but actually (with the same nasal huskiness), "Stop fascinatin' me!"

That was the time of Maxwells, Lanpher furs, the 300 Club, and Lenthéric perfume, when strippers were called "peelers," songs were full of double meanings, musical asterisks, animal sounds, and ta-ra-ra-boom-de-ay, and the 1903 ballad, "Sweet Adeline," was being sung by Mlle. Irene Bordoni and not Mayor John F. "Honey Fitz" Fitzgerald, the runty, florid-faced mayor of Boston singing it to his "dearos." We're talking back when you would have found Sigmund Romberg, an unknown Hungarian composer, plunking away on the piano at Bustanoby's nightclub on 39ᵗʰ Street and 6ᵗʰ Avenue where that fellow with the patent-leather hair on the dance floor is young Rudy Valentino!

Writing songs can even be a hobby. When the highly influential historian Walter Lord, author of several classics such as *A Time to Stand*, on the fall of the Alamo and his best-seller on the sinking of the R.M.S. *Titanic, A Night to Remember*, heard from a close friend who knew David O. Selznick that the famous Hollywood director — in order to cash in on any sheet-music sales from *The Third Man* (1949) starring Orson Welles — wanted someone to write a lyric for the film score, "The Third Man Theme," a very catchy instrumental by Anton Karas prominently featuring a zither, Lord wrote down the words. "I was the only person who knew what Selznick wanted," he later told William Zinsser, "that whoever wrote the lyric, it had to have *zither* in the first line. That's how I won out over all those other lyrics that were probably infinitely better. Somebody like Yip Harburg wrote a lovely lyric, which I later saw, that was all about autumn leaves. Selznick didn't want autumn leaves. He wanted a zither." So Lord suitably obliged, writing out a lyric that went on for as long as 64 bars, "the most meandering lyric since 'Begin the Beguine,'" added Zinsser. The first stanza goes:

> When a zither starts to play
> You'll remember yesterday
> In its haunting strain
> Vienna lives again
> Free and bright and gay
> In your mind a sudden gleam
> Of a half forgotten dream
> Seems to glimmer when you hear The Third Man Theme.

Who has not written songs? Carla Bruni, the former First Lady of France, has done so. So had radio gossip Walter Winchell. George Jessel co-wrote the lyrics for a hit, "Oh How I Laugh When I Think How I Cried About You." Ho Chi Minh while in jail wrote lyrics and poems — "A Comrade's Paper Blanket," "Autumn Night," etc. — that were put to music. So did beautiful Amanda Knox who wrote lyrics to songs about freedom while serving almost four years in Capanne Prison in Perugia, Italy. During the Civil War, when the Army of the Potomac was in camp, Brig. Gen. Daniel Butterfield in July 1862 summoned to his tent young Pvt. Oliver Wilcox Norton, his brigade bugler. Tired of hearing the colorless "extinguish lights" call then in use, Butterfield whistled an original tune and asked Norton to play it. After repeated trials and changing the time of some notes which were scribbled on the back of an envelope, the haunting "Taps" was born. Novelist Paul Bowles who wrote *The Sheltering Sky* not only composed sonatas, ballets, and several concertos but studied with Aaron Copland? (Why should we be surprised that Bowles wrote music? John Philip Sousa, composer of 136 marches, also wrote five novels, all sadly o.p., including the *The Fifth String* [1902], which I have read and enjoyed — it is actually an amazingly original story about the Devil — especially the memorable line, "I never hear a pianist, however great and famous, but I see the little cream-colored hammers within the piano bobbing up and down like acrobatic brownies.") I believe that Henry David Thoreau also wrote musical notes to play on his wooden flute. He loved to sing, often for friends, songs like "Will You Come to My Mountain Home?" a big hit in those days, which is to say a lot of that sheet-music sold. His favorite tune, which he often sang — and melodiously, "far beyond all expectation," according to William Ellery Channing — was a sad song of drowning called "Poor Tom Bowling, or The Sailor's Epitaph," one of many nautical songs by the Englishman Charles Dibdin, the first stanza of which goes,

> Here, a sheer hulk, lies poor Tom Bowling
> The darling of the crew;
> No more he'll hear the tempest howling
> For death has broach'd him to.
> His form was of the manliest beauty,
> His heart was kind and soft,
> Faithful, below he did his duty,
> But now he's gone aloft.

Two or three song lyrics written at Dollarton, North Vancouver appear in the correspondence of Malcolm Lowry, who also of course wrote poetry, and he is in fact portrayed in Conrad Aiken's major prose work, *Ushant*, as "Hambo," a character who is well known for drifting around, playing his taropatch ukelele, and singing. According to accounts of Lowry's first wife, Jan Gabrial, among her husband's favorite songs to sing were "St. Louis Blues," "Jerusalem," and "The Bastard King of England."

Abe Lincoln – from all reports not particularly great at it — loved to sing. A lawyer who lived next door to him in Springfield, Milton Hay, recalled, "There were some song singers amongst us, and Lincoln was without a rival in the singing of pathetic pieces. 'Mary's Dream,' 'Lord Ullin's Daughter,' 'The Soldier's Dream,' and other pieces of this description he sang frequently with much effect. You will recollect he was just then recovering from the Ann Rutledge affair, and had not as yet gotten into the Mary Todd 'embrigglement' as Uncle Jesse Dubois would term it."

His knowledge of music was limited. "He claimed, 'I know only two tunes, one is "Old Hundred," and the other isn't,'" wrote Kenneth A. Bernard in his *Lincoln and the Music of the Civil War*, who goes on to say, "When a group of lawyers pressed him to sing a song one night, he responded to singer Lois Newhall Hillis: 'Why, Miss Newhall, if it would save my soul, I couldn't imitate a note that you would touch on that instrument. I never sang in my life, and those fellows know it. They are simply trying to make fun of me.' Instead he recited his favorite poem: 'Why Should the Spirit of Mortal Man Be Proud.'" Attorney Henry C. Whitney claimed that Lincoln "did not know when music was artistic or in bad taste. He did know, however, if it suited him, and he had a certain taste in that direction, but it was not for anything classical, but something of a style to please the rustic ear." Who that has read much about Abe Lincoln could doubt that he would treasure song lyrics?

Folks in the Midwest and frontier thrived on witty, sometimes rude and bawdy, often sentimental ballads, and of course singing at dances and recitals is an old American tradition. Pennsylvania Republican leader Alexander K. McClure wrote: "While humorous songs delighted [Lincoln] also loved to listen to patriotic airs and ballads containing sentiment. He was fond of hearing 'The Sword of Bunker Hill,' 'Ben Bolt,' and 'The Lament of the Irish Emigrant.'" Bernard explains in his splendid book that Lincoln's preference of the verses in the latter was this: "I'm lonely now, Mary/ For the poor make no new friends/ But, oh, they love the better still/ The few our Father sends!/ And you were all I had, Mary, my blessing and my pride/ There's nothing left to care for now/ Since my poor Mary died." Lincoln was also fond of Negro melodies. A favorite was "The Blue-Tailed Fly." He loved the song "Dixie" and would have known many if not all of the contemporary staples like "Lorena," "Annie Laurie," "Juanita," "Lilly Dale," "Sweet Evelina," "The Girl I Left Behind Me," and, quite surely, the Irish drinking song, "Garryowen," the favorite song of George Armstrong Custer and the regimental air of the 7th U.S Cavalry.

It may seem incongruous today but Lincoln enjoyed slave spirituals, minstrel music — we know that he loved a performance of the Rumsey and Newcomb Minstrels in Chicago in 1860 — while, oddly enough, the truly inspired Stephen Foster was bit dubious to be known as the composer of what her called "Ethiopian songs" and, impoverished much of his life, had no qualms about selling songs like "Old Folks at Home," "Old Dog Tray," and others to E.P. Christy of Christy's Minstrels for little money.

Lincoln sang from high-spirits and self-delight. Rewards have little to do with one's efforts, if upon them you depend. It is the same with recognition, if that is a person's sole ambition. The great songwriters all knew that, otherwise they would have capitulated and written rubbish. I have lived for 37 years less than a geographical mile from Cape Cod Community College and have never once been asked by the school to give a reading or so much as sign a single book there. I offer them the very same answer the museum guard at the Louvre gave to the lady who disliked the art, "The paintings are not on trial, madam — you are."

Great turgid songs full of mixed metaphors and incomprehensible allusions like "MacArthur Park," "The Windmills of Your Mind," "I am a Rock," etc. always tend to sound far worse with all their heavy-footedness than those, say, with the opposite problem, as for example, "On the Wings of Love," "People," or (raised claws) Morris Albert's "Feelings," the person or persons responsible for which — I want to *kill* when I hear it — in my opinion should instantly be dispatched to the lowest point in the nether world and forced by the devil's pitchfork to have to listen to Barry Manilow albums for the rest of eternity. (I honestly hate to inquire, but can't you still find exhaustive collections of this stuff being energetically hawked on late-night television by "trusted" Guthy Renker?) Are you aware that Morris Albert is in real life a furry-faced Brazilian singer by the name of Mauricio Alberto Kaisermann? He is a songwriter who is not only still making records, you will or will not be happy to hear, but obviously a person who felt the need to change his name so he could not be personally identified with that abortion from 1975, "Feelings." It is not merely that the song has the most insipid lyrical and musical qualities of 1970s "soft rock" music — it is a guaranteed party killer — there is no melody and what is there is beyond bad. It was such songs Johnny Mercer must have been listening to when he snapped, "I could eat alphabet soup and *shit* better lyrics."

As I have pointed out, Imelda Marcos sang "Feelings." In June of 1989 the First Lady of the Philippines who was later to be deposed in disgrace — after 21 years of brazenly stealing virtually all of the country's money and personally amassing (these are official figures) 15 mink coats, 508 gowns, 1000 handbags and 1,060 pairs of shoes, to say nothing of gutting its national treasure, while millions of poor people in that country were literally starving to death — had the effrontery to release her first record album, *Imelda Papin Featuring Songs with Mrs. Imelda Romualdez Marcos*, as a gift to her fascist dictator husband, Ferdinand, on the occasion of their 35th anniversary. At 59, Mrs. Marcos "agreed to join" pretty, talented Ms. Papin, a Filipina pop-star who had 25 gold or platinum albums, as if it were a favor to the young woman. A video of beefy bowling-ball-headed

Marcos singing soon followed, fully to complete a perfect trifecta of Just Plain Awfulness: Imelda sings four solos, "Feelings," and then three songs in Tagalog. I have listened to it all. It is enough to make a person go psychosomatically deaf. On September 14, 2010, then, that female predator, still whining, was ordered to return the sum of 12 million pesos ($280,000) in government funds that had been secretly embezzled by her late husband from the National Food Authority 27 years before. "There's something addictive about a secret," J. Edgar Hoover once famously remarked, and the Marcoses had been stealing money from the country's treasury for a quarter of a century. One thing that was not a secret: Imelda had a voice like a steam calliope with a hole in it.

A song with scrimp or negligible lyrics need not be bad. What can beat two masterpieces with little in the word department, the Falcons' "You're So Fine" ("sweet as your kiss... heart skips a beat") or the Velvets' "Tonight (Could Be the Night)" ("ring... finger... hold me tight"), two doo-wop hits — archetypal 45s — with conventional, even clichéd lyrics. Strange to say, perhaps, but the best lyrics are often the ones, it seems to me, which are the plainest or, better, simply do not try to say more than the frame of rhythm or melody that they hang on can actually support. Asked to give a statement on "The Meaning of Democracy" back in 1944, E.B. White poetically replied, "It is the line that forms on the right. It is the *don't* in Don't Shove. It is the hole in the stuffed shirt through which the sawdust slowly trickles; it is the dent in the high hat. Democracy is the recurrent suspicion that more than half the people are right more than half the time... It is an idea which hasn't been disproved yet, a song the words of which have not gone bad." I find that last as good a definition of Democracy as it is for a good lyric.

I realize that, although I have just mentioned "On the Wings of Love," Mephistopheles did not suddenly appear. A miracle — nothing happened, as in fact nothing does in the song! It is not simply a bad song. It is a truculently bad song, a poisonous, natterjacking toad of a bad song, almost diabolical in its dreadfulness. It may be the Atom Bomb of bad songs. This is the kind of insane music that SWAT teams or fully armed ATM squads play at piercingly high decibels in major standoffs to flush out lunatics barricaded in houses or gun-toting nut-jobs in rural Arkansas or Oklahoma. Composer Richard Strauss who rather eccentrically always made a point of conducting all music, including his own, while sitting down — only for Wagner would he conduct standing — but for "On the Wings of Love"? I haven't the slightest doubt that he would have conducted *that* standing upside-down with his head stuck in the ground, like a leek!

"History is irony, on the move," E.M. Cioran has told us. But could he explain the mystic ironies in Gary Puckett and the Union Gap's "Lady Will Power" when the singer urgently insists, "It's now or never,/ give your heart to me," vowing "I'll shower your heart with tenderness," while at the very same time he is urging his apparently hesitant or shy virgin lover, presumably a diffident young girl, to show will-power? So does he want her to have will-power or to give herself to him? If he is promising to shower her heart with tenderness, isn't he expecting her to show the *opposite* of will-power?

Lennon and McCartney's early lyrics, like "All My Loving," "Please Please Me," and "I Feel Fine," for example, while thin and one-dimensional, are nevertheless quite effective. The Fab Four's early musical success, in an opinion of the late great English poet Philip Larkin's that I tend to share, was, in his words, "displaced by surreal lyrics, mystic orientalia, peace messages, and anti-American outbursts. The trouble was that as surrealists, mystics, or political thinkers the Beatles were rather ordinary young men again. Their fans stayed with them, and the nuttier intelligentsia, but they lost the typists in the Cavern."

And of course they have their own doozies. In "The Long and Winding Road," we hear, "A wild and windy night/ that the rain washed away." Let me get this straight. The hammering rain ended the *storm*? I thought that wildness in weather included rain? And in "Love Me Do," I find memorable the contradiction involved when we hear,

> Somebody new, someone to hold,
> Someone like you...

If the desired girl is to be new, the singer wants someone else, and yet if he wants the new girl to be "like" the girl he is addressing, she would not be new.

Indisputably, the effect of crowding images in a lyric can play havoc with a song, giving it a weird effect, like glossolalia. ("Her half-brother never left her out of his festive raisined bread giving progresses," is one of dada-surrealistico-novelist Gertrude Stein's more memorable contributions.) You hear this sort of thing from Joni Mitchell. The prosaic Jimmy Webb. Bobby Goldsboro. Bruce Springsteen. Elton John has the added problem when singing of making lyrics sound as if they're being masticated. In far too many of the Bernie Taupin/ Elton John repertoire, the highly orchestrated songs, which initially come across as solid, seem to evaporate or dissolve in the way that, in the novels of W.G. Sebald, the railway architecture, military fortifications, train stations, and other grand edifices that seem to be his fixation, fade like a memory which loses coherence in a struggle complicated by the mind's defenses against trauma and guilt. Curiously, the handful of blabby songwriters mentioned just above also recall in their disproportionate garrulity the onslaught of Sebald's paragraphless pages. In the lyrics of "Van Dyke Parks" — in the Beach Boys' *Heroes and Villains* album — may I ask what "columniated ruins domino" is supposed to mean? Certain passages found in highly revered songs like Lennon and McCartney's "I Am a Walrus" sound like mad Hieronymo spouting nonsense in a gulf of high winds:

> Corporation teeshirt, stupid bloody Tuesday man
> You been a naughty boy you let your face grow long

or

> Semolina pilchard climbing up the Eiffel Tower
> Elementary penguin singing Hare Krishna man
> You should have seen them kicking Edgar Allan Poe

Doesn't a lyric inherently demand some comprehensibility, exact some cohesion? As the National Hockey League goalies say regarding a game, "It is not what you stop, it's what you let in." Inventive lyrics, even inexplicable lyrics, can work. But it takes style, panache, a magic having to do with point-of-view. Most great lyricists, even good lyricists, are firing on several fronts — think of Cole Porter's boundless wit and astonishing erudition, Lorenz Hart's interior rhymes, Ira Gershwin's verbal wit and word-play, Irving Berlin's whimsicalities, Johnny Mercer's homespun wisdom, George M. Cohan's unforgettable melodies, etc. — using their rich gifts, all at once, for economy, slang, and directness. These were the guys who were masters of verbs, of rhyme, of mesmerizing and bewitching turns of phrase. One need merely listen to songs like Cole Porter's "You're the Top," George Gershwin's "Fascinatin' Rhythm," Sammy Cahn's "Brooklyn Bridge," Jimmy Van Heusen and Phil Silvers' "Nancy with the Laughing Face," Sigmund Romberg's "Rose Marie," Victor Herbert's "Toyland," Duke Ellington's "Do Nothing Till You Hear From Me," "I Got It Bad and That Ain't Good," "Satin Doll," "Perdido," "Sophisticated Lady" — he wrote nearly two thousand pieces of music — Irving Berlin's "Isn't It a Lovely Day," and, hey, why not throw in the woefully neglected Walter Donaldson who just happened to have written "Maisie," "Love Me or Leave Me," "My Blue Heaven," "Little White Lies," "Carolina in the Morning," "Makin' Whoopee," "Georgia," "Yes Sir, That's My Baby," "My Mammy," "You're Driving Me Crazy," "My Baby Just Cares for Me," "How Are You Going To Keep 'Em Down on the Farm (After They've Seen Paree)?" "At Sundown" — 600 original songs in all — but the list is truly limitless. They fit the fashion and fecundity of genius. Then the rhetoric, the figures of speech they used for color — the best of them had the full tool kit — litotes, anaphora, pun, synecdoche, chiasmus, assonance, especially the creative employment of exact verbs, which Alexander Pope insisted was the singular sign of a great poet. There are roughly 8,000 verbs or more in the English language, but what does the Average Joe depend on? You got it, the same ratty old bedroom slippers, "to be" and "to have," to go scuffing through life!

As to the subjects for songs, Irving Berlin, we read in the *Atlantic Monthly* (December 2001), wrote about everything: the two world wars, of course, and most aspects of show business, but all the national holidays, billing and cooing and all sorts of courtship, then economics, FDR, Al Capone, nudist colonies, censors, airplanes, Bolsheviks, lynchings, cops — New York's "finest" — Prohibition, sex, loneliness, isolation, and insomnia. "What'll I Do," "Let's Face the Music and Dance," "Easter Parade," "There's No Business Like Show Business," "Isn't This A Lovely Day (To Be Caught in the Rain)," "How About Me?" It is measureless. The telling phrase, the wit, banter, humor, drollery, the topicality, the cheeky scenarios — that ear for the music! That ear for the words!

> I just couldn't stop her
> For dinner and supper
> Some kisses and hugs was the food.
> When she wasn't nice, it was more better twice,
> When she's bad she was better than good.

Matchless. With Irving Berlin, even the intricate or lumpish comic turns have verve. He was also unapologetically patriotic and tidily scrupulous about lyrics. As he had it, the original opening stanza of "God Bless America" — a virtual substitute for the national anthem, it was introduced by Kate Smith over the radio in 1938 —

> God bless America — land that I love;
> Stand beside her, and guide her
> To the right with the light from above

hinted too much of fascism, so he changed it to:

> Stand beside her, and guide her
> Through the night with the light from above.

Lightning can be captured in arch, extravagant lyrics. The songwriting team of Rodgers and Hart, for example, in their very first lyric, "Any Old Place With You" — it appeared in Lew Fields' show, *A Lonely Romeo* — wrote the anti-climactic and even bumpy

> I'd go to hell for ya
> Or Philadelphia

but it works. Or take the polysyllabic-studded lines in the Medallions' "The Letter"

> Let me whisper sweet words
> of dismortality and discuss
> the pompitus of love.
> Put it together and
> What do you have?
> Matrimony! Oh my darling…

It is crazy-wordy, the lyrics betray some haste, but to me it is a self-deprecating and good-natured fustian, intentionally over-the-top. Great. Odd words, when used judiciously and well, can add spice to a work. William Ellery Channing, Henry David Thoreau's closest pal, objected to his friend's use in *Walden* of several words he found queer — "drivable" and "spectatordom" were two — and he suggested they be changed or even omitted, but Thoreau, who left all of them in, surely rejoiced in their homely uniqueness.

A good lyricist, in control, puts the cookie-cutter of art into the dough of life, as it were. It takes the instinct of knowing design. He shapes his work, unencumbered by haste or circumstances or stupidity. The seasonal song "Let It Snow," for example, which was written in a room on Hollywood and Vine, incidentally, on one of the hottest days of the year, highlights — celebrates — the kind of balancing qualities necessary in a lyric. Lyricist Sammy Cahn has given us the story. "I said to Jule Styne, 'Why don't we go down to the beach and cool off?' He said, 'Why don't we stay here and write a winter song?' I went to the typewriter. 'Oh the weather outside is frightful' — architecture — 'But the fire is so delightful,/ and since we've no place to go,/ let it snow, let it snow, let it snow.' Now why three 'Let it snow's'? Why not two or four? Because three is *lyric*." Artists understand this. Does not the same point apply with the repetition of the line in Robert Frost's "On Stopping by the Woods on a Snowy Evening" "And miles to go before I sleep"? Leave it to the bitter irony of sardonic novelist (and surly detractor) Vladimir Nabokov to ridicule and belittle that hypnotic repetition in Frost's poem as a glaring example of utter pretension and fake profundity, mockingly pointing out to the reader that the meaning of the first line, taken quite literally, was quite simple, whereas the repeated line, now implying metaphorical force — and here you could hear Nabokov's scorn — is suddenly complicated and *deep*, meaning of course (just the opposite) simplistic and shallow! Touching on the Cahn and Stein composition just cited, I have always been amazed when people praise, as repeatedly they do, Irving Berlin's "White Christmas" as not simply a holiday song but something of an amazing feat in that the composer happened to be Jewish. But take a closer look. As anyone can plainly see, the lyrics of the song are pure pastiche, frankly an *imitation* of a Christmas song, the tired and hackneyed lyrics, so to speak, of someone trying to write a song in the manner of that genre and so employing virtually every winter cliché and, to me, the significant fact to be pointed out about "White Christmas," aside from that it is a perfect — or, at least, perfectly balanced — song, is not that a Jew wrote it, but rather that only a Jew could have written it. I daresay the very same observations may apply to Irving Berlin's "Easter Parade."

As Ezra Pound noted in his *ABC of Reading*, "Incompetence will show in the use of too many words." (The irony of the author of the cento-mad *Cantos* fulminating against either the pyrotechnic style or the vice of overwriting we shall have to leave to another forum.) It is my experience, however, that overwriting is one of the hazards of the amateur, the use of a shotgun, so to speak, instead of a well-aimed .22. It can be forgiven perhaps in literary criticism at Yale or in overheated Assembly of God sermons or in composers of the effervescent Bliss Carman era, that stuffed-sofa-with-antimacassars post-Civil-War period when concert orchestras thrilled Rutherford B. Hayes's America with sheet-music fustian and groups like the Fisk Jubilee Singers and performers like Emmy Destinna and Olive Fremsted and plump Nellie Melba drew big. (Were you aware that John Philip Sousa, "The March King," actually wrote words, to the "Stars and Stripes Forever"? Indeed, he did. He also in the course of his life wrote three novels!) Simplicity in writing is often the linchpin of clarity, and very few young and unseasoned energetic minds have the grit of either seeing things clearly or realizing that one good image is much more effective than, say, two or three piled on together. A popular defense of such stuff, of course, the notion commonly advanced, that it is the best way to express the disintegration of modern civilization — Lennon, Springsteen, Joni Mitchell, Joan Baez, Bob Dylan ("folk" music particularly lends itself to the disease) all have made noises in that direction — is what critic Yvor Winters calls the "fallacy of expressive form." The continuing irony of lyrical verbosity in popular music is that, more often than not, it is a kind of pedantry of the vigorous and athletic sort that usually expresses itself in a virulent form of anti-intellectualism. It is big on nature mysticism. Going out and getting grubby. Romantic solipsism. Wordsworthian trust in nature. Suspicion of ritual. The holiness of solitude. Hatred of authority. The inarticulate hero. Guitar as ikon. Spontaneity. Drugs-as-viaticum. "We learned more from a three-minute record, baby/ Than we ever learned in school," sings The Boss in "No Surrender," a song that is either a paean to education by vinyl or an indictment of the Asbury Park, NJ school system, if indeed there is one there. Am I being obtuse? Perhaps I should follow the non-confrontational response that Artur Rubenstein gave to TV's Johnny Carson when he asked him about the quality of popular and punk music, "I cannot comment on something I can't understand," but to me Bruce Springsteen's songs pullulate with illogicality, discomfiting images, melodyless prose, and the repeated kind of assbackwardness that makes one wonder about the brain coming up with it all, like the revealing remark that fat starboard-leaning radio slob Rush Limbaugh, obviously a man with no taste or education (he did not have the brains to take a college degree) and a creature with no military service (he dodged the draft because of a cyst on his ass), made on February 15, 2005 — one that surely comments on his brain as much as his belly — that "eating lobster is only an excuse to eat butter." It surely fits his form. I have to say I am ill-disposed to give credence to any creature whose lack of control is so much in evidence and whose indiscriminate eating habits resemble that of a peccary, in spite of the fact that this broadcasting capon, unlikely as it seems, remains the hero of a slavishly devoted army of like-minded robots, low-rent tardigrades, mad flag-waving fascists, beady-eyed gun-toting marginals, hateful little Bundists ("Ditto, Rush!"), and devotees with room-temperature IQs. He pours scorn on women, blacks, the working poor, schools, children, the efforts of charities, and altruism in general. His mind is full of spite and malware. I have trees on my property, single-celled life-forms, that are more diversified in their endosymbiotic relationship to people than this poltroon with his embarrassing belly baggage, shaking jowls, and EEEE shoes. Fungi show more cousinage. An über-obsessive, swollen with bile, he exhausts the language of blame, to use a phrase of the poet Karl Shapiro. Then there is the memorable lyric from Springsteen's "Born to Run"

> Just wrap your legs around these velvet rims
> And strap your hands across my engines.

Is he describing a circus act involving The Flying Wallendas or an imagined sex-scene depicting the congress of two bunnies or giving us a scene-in-part of a father taking his daughters on the Tilt-A-Whirl at Luna Park? I am reminded once again in the almost unbearably bad tabloidistic lyrics of pop-music today, especially in rap and hip-hop, of the graphic doodles, inane words, criminal illiteracy, sex-patter, and priapic grunts, more than anything, of the trashy packaging of salacious weeklies like all of those owned by the pornosleazo conglomerate American Media, Inc. (A.M.I.), the *Globe*, the *National Enquirer*, the *Weekly World News* — face it, tabloid journalism is nothing less than the modern equivalent of the 1918 flu pandemic — and, among other tabloids, the *Star*, whose profoundly in-tune-with-the-times editor Bonnie Hurowitz Fuller has made from what I read in *Vanity Fair* magazine a marked financial success regarding the nature of sales with her amazing insights and distinguished editorial wisdom that for the benefit of us all she has managed to capsulate in a mere sixteen words: "More visuals and fewer words, more celebrities and fewer serious articles, more sex and less substance." Fewer words! Less substance! Now there is an aesthetic.

The horrors proliferate. The Doors in "L.A. Woman" sing, "If they say I never loved you/ You know they are a liar." In "Run to You," Bryan Adams sings "that would change if she ever found out about you and I." "You and me could write a bad romance" sings Lady Gaga in "Bad Romance." Bobby Brown in "My Prerogative" sings "Ego trips is not my thing." Prince in "When Doves Cry" offers the gem, "Dig, if you will, a picture of you and I engaged in a kiss." The world of officialdom has no more class, so parlous are the times in which we live. In the song "I Believe," the anthem of the 2010 Olympics held in Vancouver, some propeller-head actually wrote — and it so remains — "I believe in the power of you and I." I have so frequently heard in pop music a range of phrases like "the reason is because" and "between she and I" and "I ain't never" that, I confess, they rarely register anymore. I suppose the demon-mother of all lyrical chaos is a song that was popularized a century ago by Egbert Williams, "Nobody" — with enough slang in it to drive any English teacher into a rubber room.

> Well, I ain't never done nothing to nobody.
> I ain't never got nothing from nobody, no time.
> And, until I get something from somebody sometime,
> I don't intend to do nothing for nobody, no time.

"I don't sing like nobody," young Elvis Presley proudly boasted to Marion Keisker who was working at the front desk of Sam Phillips's Sun Record company in 1953. I suppose — at least grammatically speaking — it was all downhill from there.

Speaking ungrammatically has long been embedded in the culture. "Did you finish your homework yet?" "I did good on my test." "It's the exact same thing." "He is being mis-chie-vi-ous." Bad grammar *is bad grammar* — it should be poor grammar. Actress Jamie Lee Curtis wrote a book called, *I'm Gonna Like Me* (2002). Great for kids, isn't it? Bill Cosby and Dr. Alvin Poussaint, two blubberbrains — the two of them appeared together as they often do, like their hustling forebears, the Duke and the King in *Huckleberry Finn*, on *Meet the Press* on January 11, 2009 to gasbag about it — wrote a book in 2007 titled *Come On People*, printed with no comma! (They went scurrying to correct it in the next edition.) "Of course, I am totally against racism," Cosby has also declared in passing. On the other side of his mouth, he also told his biographer, Ronald L. Smith, in *Cosby: The Life of a Comedy Legend* (1997), "As long as I am on the screen, I will never hold or kiss a white woman." I place the irony of Cosby's hypocritical but constant pose as an activist for good grammar, acting as a leader and public role model being only one of his favorite morphs — you know, taking responsibility for oneself — right up there with the adulterous affair he secretly had in the 70s with Shawn Upshaw and their illegitimate daughter, Autumn Jackson, whose existence he tried to hush up with a more than $100,000 bribe — she was also sentenced to five years for extortion — and then publishing a book entitled *Fatherhood* (1986), among the pages of which one can find the glowing sentence, "Human beings are the only creatures on earth that allow their children to come back home." Cosby won the Presidential Medal of Freedom in 2002.

"In too many English classes across America, grammar is passé; verb conjugation, a forgotten relic of the past," writes C. Edward Good in *Who's (Oops) Whose Grammar Book is This Anyway?* "Indeed, if students learn about verbs at all, they learn to conjugate them in Spanish, French or German. Today, under modern educational theory, the study of grammar is viewed by people daring to call themselves experts as a nuisance, as unnecessary dogma, as only slightly related to the skills of the writer. Students will 'get it' by reading. They will absorb grammar through 'osmosis.'"

Sad, and I am not even talking about the heavy stuff like anaphoric pronouns, glue words, the present perfect progressive tense, noun appositives, or syntactic constraints on pronoun cases in English with the goal of demonstrating how co-ordination-triggered variation relates to other known triggers of case variation!

Language today is in a state of supreme scruple. (Is it the times that are so parlous or the state of education? Michigan State cancelled Ancient Greek as a subject in the curriculum on April 29, 2011. Greek "Rush" Week began — continuing as usual, with great campus support — on September 11, 2011.) Our treat nowadays, in consequence, is to have instead of a Lennon and McCartney *jeu* or Jimmy Van Heusen gem, never mind a Cole Porter lyric or an Ira Gershwin line, that kind of inverted magic, we hear, for example, in Barry Manilow's "Ready to Take a Chance Again" like

> You get what you get when you go for it

or

> I'm feeling good but not very well

or 2-Live Crew's elegant and inspired,

> You said it yourself
> You like it like I do Put your lips on my d—k
> And suck my ass—e, too

Where are we headed? I happened to hear the other day the jingle for the Turner Classic Movie network's "One Reel Wonder," which goes in part, "You'll find a starry sky *beneath* that cloud you're under." [My italics.] Am I missing something here in the way of a logical image presented?

Rap music is another story entirely. In the "Three Dialogues" Samuel Beckett wrote with George Duthuit in 1949, he claimed to favor "the expression that there is nothing to express, nothing with which to express, nothing from which to express, no power to express, no desire to express, together with the obligation to express." Bereftness was a subject in painting as well as writing, that intrigued Beckett, in every shape and form, ideal as well as material, and in having listened to much of rap, unavoidable as it is, no matter how hard one tries to flee it, I find myself aligned with Beckett, announced in all his work, and the certitude he felt that expression is an impossible act.

Regarding rap, maybe a stand, rather than weak appeasement, just as at Munich, should have been made back in 1973, when the term "Ebonics" was coined in 1973 by Robert L. Williams, a professor at Washington University at St. Louis, for what is now referred to by the name of African-American Vernacular English but what in fact is language of mutant, lazy, defective, ungrammatical slang — "broken English" — once confined to and used by black students in

Oakland, California, but now a benison used by an entire sub-nation of free-wheeling ungrammatical Nibelungs. "So my bee-aatsh and me, ridin'd-lo and aksing shit, bust a cap on this crackaz po-lice. It be a g-thang, fa shiggidy." ("So my bitch and me, driving unnoticed, saying nothing, took a shot at a white cop. It's a gang thing. Keeping it real.") Can a more grotesque manifestation of Affirmative Action be found? Still, it did give to the world the memorable "No Hoe Remix" sung by D-Lo, which goes in part,

> D-Lo he don't giva a fuck about no hoe
> No hoe no hoe no hoe no hoe
> D-Lo he don't give a fuck about no hoe
> He'll snatch ya hoe and take her to the hoe stroll
> D-Lo you already know tho
> He don't give a fuck about no nigga or no hoe tho
> D-Lo give a fuck about ya hoe
> Put a bitch up on the track up in the rain or the snow.

This uncouth, primitive, quasi-simian rant is not so much close to, as fully defining, what the late James Thurber called "an oral culture of pure babble." Michael Eric Dyson, a graduate of Princeton University and a professor of sociology at Georgetown University breezily defends the cultural use of Ebonics, saying,

> Black English captures the beautiful cadences, sensuous tones, kinetic rhythms, forensic articulations, and idiosyncrasies of expression that form the black vernacular voice. Bad grammar does not Black English make; it is a rhetorical practice laden with complex and technical rules — for instance, the use in Black English of zero copulas, or forms of the verb "to be." To say "I am going" is one thing, suggesting a present activity; but to say "I be going" in Black English is something else, suggesting a habitual practice, a repeated action.

I confess I did miss the "forensic articulations" in "No Hoe Remix." But the zero copulas I got. Whites just have a different term for that. Dyson, who believes correctness depends upon usage, in allowing for ignorant black teenagers to "express themselves" is not only creating legions of illiterates across the land but in a blasphemy against his own people calling it the unpremeditated ecstasy of the vernacular voice. Does this contextualizing dipshit not realize the meaning of — not see the dangers in — social irresponsibility? As Christopher Hitchens in his essay "Hooked on Ebonics" points out, "There's effectively nothing in print that's written in Black English, and the nearest approximation — the "Uncle Remus" narrative of Joel Chandler Harris — was the work of a white man with a good ear,"

Dubbed the "Hip-Hop Intellectual," Dyson who would like to think that his inane permissiveness coincides with the development of an egalitarian theory of education and some kind of democratic ideal, even a standard of achievement based on compassion — he is actually a cultural vandal, a pitiful and brutish enabler of the slapdash errors of unlettered hacks — used the late Tupac Shakur's *Holler if You Hear Me* as the primary textbook for a course at the University of Pennsylvania, and he presently teaches a course at Georgetown University based on the black rapper Jay-Z, composer of songs like "Money, Cash, Hoes," "Big Pimpin'" "Do It Again (Put Ya Hands Up)," "Jigga My Nigga," "I Just Wanna Luv U (Give It 2 Me)," "Swagga Like Us," "20 Bag Shorty," "Lucifer," "Welcome to the Jungle," and, among others, with Kanye West's, "Illest Motherfucker Alive" — it is not singing, rather talking, in one long monologuous sexist, racist rant — which goes in part,

> You in line behind currency, yeah you after money
> Bullet proof condom when I'm in these hoes
> Got staples on my dick (why) fuckin' centerfolds
> And I swear to God they so cold
> Got a nigga in Miami wearing winter clothes

Before Dyson came along, J.L. Dillard in *Black English* (1972), examining ethnic slang, pidgin, Gullah, French Creole ("Gombo"), middle-class native of Detroit, Southern dialects, jazz scat, etc. contends that "eighty percent of the Black population in the United States speaks Black English." He concludes,

> It seems inescapable that the Black [sic] community has the right to make its own choice, particularly in view of the white [sic] community's poor record of accomplishment in Negro education in the past decade....It might even come about, in some areas, that white children would need to learn Black English...in order to be able to integrate themselves into Black-dominated school systems.

Pointing to the desperate paradox of the alcoholic who drinks because he feels himself a failure and then fails more dismally still because he drinks, George Orwell in his essay, "Politics and the English Language," observes, "It is rather the same thing that is happening to the English language. It becomes ugly and inaccurate because our thoughts are foolish, but the slovenliness of our language makes it easier for us to have foolish thoughts…But if thought corrupts language, language can also corrupt thought."

It is but as few short steps in the debasement of language from the silly, vulgar, anti-social, and moronic crudities of Jay Z and Biggie Smalls and Tupac Shakur to the language of torture levied by President Bush and VP Dick Cheney and that administration who engaged lawyers to define torture as narrowly as possible and to disapply prohibitions on cruel, inhuman, and degrading treatment, which, while they defended the evil practice at "black sites" (secret CIA prisons) with perverted euphemisms like "rendering," heightened interrogation norms," "enhanced coercion," their savage minions were then allowed to carry out in medieval fashion with smiling faces blithely reporting that "detainees [only] suffered rigorous information pursuit measures," "experienced imposing information integration admeasurements," "underwent magnified aquatic diagnostics," etc. Roman rhetorician and author of the *Institutes of Oratory* Quintilian once portentously declared, "One should not aim at being possible to understand, but at being impossible to misunderstand."

Dyson, who is the bridgehead — the *brückenkopf* — that both supports and defends the whole hip-hop fortification, calls Jay-Z an "incredible genius," adding that he is "one of the most remarkable artists of our time of any genre," and he goes on to say with added afflatus that "as a hip-hop artist [Jay Z] carries the weight of that art form with such splendor and grace and genius." t is strange that Dyson who considers the language of hip-hop to be the hottest thing since colored straws does not entertain the idea that such dithering might be nothing but a sad alternative to a worthwhile life. What does he make of rapper 50 Cent's remark, "If I had a chance, I would've been a college kid. I would have majored in business." He says "I admire the way in which Jay-Z carries himself and the incredible craft that he displays every time he steps up to the microphone." Mind you, Dyson is not talking about Mendelssohn or Liszt or Haydn or the "Egmont Overture" or Robert Schumann's *"Rhenish" Symphony No. 3 in E-flat major, Op. 97* or the Dresden "Amen," but rather the artless kack of a rapper — with songs like "Whatchu Want," "Ignorant Shit," "Murdergram," etc. — whose Shanghai concert in October 2006 China had to be canceled because of gross profanity, an incident that remains an international scandal and an embarrassment to the United States.

I wonder if this is what Walt Whitman had in mind when, foreseeing the possibility of language emerging from hitherto neglected places in what he saw as the fledgling United States, he wrote not without admiration that, "The nigger dialect furnishes hundreds of outré words, many of them adopted into the common speech of the mass of the people" and went on to suggest, almost prophetically — think of Gershwin's *Porgy and Bess* — that such a dialect "has hints of the future theory of the modification of all the words of the English language, for musical purposes, for a native grand opera in America." But of rap? As Raymond Chandler cogently points out, "Flip dialogue is not wit."

One recalls with melancholy reflection lines from Constantine P. Cavafy's poem from 1904, "Waiting for the Barbarians:"

> Why don't the worthy orators come as always
> to make their speeches, to have their say?
> Because the barbarians are to arrive today;
> and they get bored with eloquence and orations.
> Why all of a sudden this unrest
> and confusion. (How solemn the faces have become).
> Why are the streets and squares clearing quickly,
> and all return to their homes, so deep in thought?
> Because night is here...

Songs, like dialects, are in a sense invented languages, each with its own morphology (a structure of meaning for various words within the language), syntax (the method of combining those words into sentences), and phonology (the way those words, phrases, and sentences sound). No wonder so many imaginative writers have invented languages. Thomas More did so in *Utopia*, as did Jonathan Swift in *Gulliver's Travels*. Edgar Rice Burroughs invented one for Tarzan. Hildegard of Bingen, C.S. Lewis, George Orwell, Poul Anderson, J.R R. Tolkien, Arthur Machen, and the eccentric horror writer H.P. Lovecraft all constructed original languages — even film director James Cameron in his epic movie *Avatar* did so with his language of Na'vi, spoken by the sapient humanoid indigenous inhabitants of the fictional moon Pandora. Have you heard of Volapük? It is a constructed language, created in 1879 in the town of Baden, Germany by a Roman Catholic priest named Johann Martin Schleyer who had a dream that God had told him to create an international language. Although there has been a continuous Volapük-speaking community since Schleyer's time with an unbroken succession of *Cifals* (leaders) right up to the present, the language was largely displaced in the late 19th and early 20th centuries, specifically by Esperanto, Ido and Interlingua.

Speaking of rogue languages, are you aware of the fact that English is *not* the official language of the United States? That happens to be a true fact. No language has ever been formally so deemed. It is a dubious distinction that we also share with the United Kingdom, Pakistan, Costa Rica, Ethiopia, Somalia, Eritrea, and Bosnia-Herzegovina, which at least has the excuse of being home to three ethnic groups, or so-called "constituent peoples," a term unique for that troubled, complicated country — Bosniaks, the largest group of the three, with Serbs second, and Croats third.

I recently happened to have to listen (record shop, elevator) to R.E.M.'s "Stand," which is complete farrago of nonsense — virtually the anti-lyric record — rushed lines, hysterical enjambment, repetitive lines, dopey pretensions, etc., absolute animal crackers. But it was when I heard "Yours is No Disgrace" from *The Yes Album*

> Yesterday a morning came a smile upon your face
> Caesar's Palace morning glory silly human race
> On a sailing ship to nowhere leaving any place
> If the summer changed to winter yours is no disgrace

and their "And You and I" from *Close to the Edge*

> A man conceived a moment's answer to a dream
> Staying the flowers gaily sensing all the themes
> As a foundation left to create the spiral aim
> A moment regained and regarded both the same
> All concrete in the sight of seeds of life with you

that I desperately began to think *where is Gus Kahn, now that we need him?*

In pop-music what better proof could be given of the scrimp state of the lyric than when following bit of *haemmoragica purpurea*, wherein Bruce Springsteen, the "Boss" — a hypocorism for his first name that in the late Sixties devolved into a worshipful but obsequious euonym for him that his fans, somehow, do not find self-demeaning — proceeds to prove it in his version of "Blinded by the Light":

> Madman drummers bummers and Indians in the summer with a
> teenage diplomat
> In the dumps with the mumps as the adolescent pumps his way into
> his hat

With a boulder on my shoulder, feelin' kinda older, I tripped the merry-go-round
With this very unpleasing sneezing and wheezing, the calliope crashed to the ground
Some all-hot half-shot was headin' for the hot spot, snappin' his fingers, clappin' his hands
And some fleshpot mascot was tied into a lover's knot with a whatnot in her hand
And now young Scott with a slingshot finally found a tender spot and throws his lover in the sand
And some bloodshot forget-me-not whispers, "Daddy's within earshot, save the buckshot, turn up the band"

or

Wizard imps and sweat sock pimps, interstellar moral nymphs.

Real edjumacation, as they say.

There are places on the Nebraska album, or in songs like "Thunder Road" and "Jungleland," where Springsteen takes on in speech the quality — and randomness — of automatic writing. Word salads in his songs abound, long shotgun-blasts of crowded passages and lines, images upon images, noisemaking similes and metaphors, all mixed and matched in the most impossible of way. At times, Arthur Rimbaud in his poetry could be maddeningly obscure ("Since then the Moon has heard jackals cheeping in thyme deserts"), and do not even bring up the American poet John Ashbery who, heedless of the need for communication, writes poem after poem impossible to comprehend, surely an indefensible flaw in any artist. Ashbery of course repeatedly wins awards for it! "I don't like obscurity in poetry," declared Robert Frost. "I don't think a thing ought to be obvious before it is said, but it ought to be obvious when it is said. I like to read Eliot because it is fun seeing the way he does things, but I'm always glad it is his way and not mine." One could swot up a shortlist of incomprehensible volumes. George Meredith's *The Ordeal of Richard Feverell*, *Finnegans Wake* by James Joyce — a writer who stood for Philip Larkin as "textbook case of declension from talent to absurdity" — Immanuel Kant's *Critique of Pure Reason*, Francesco Colonna's *Hypnerotomachia Poliphili*, the Book of Revelations, Robert Musil's *The Man Without Qualities*, Joseph Conrad's *Nostromo*, Italo Calvino's *If on a Winter's Night a Traveler*, Wyndham Lewis's *The Apes of God*, Henry James's *The Bench of*

*Desolation.* Gertrude Stein's *The Making of Americans*, a "modernist novel," and *Tender Buttons*, from which I herewith extract the entire text of "A Dog:" "A little monkey goes like a donkey that means to say that means to say that more sighs last goes. Leave with it. A little monkey goes like a donkey."

Are we talking about density or just plain obfuscation? E.F. Benson explains in his memoir, *Final Edition*, that Henry James wrote an appreciation of the novelist Compton Mackenzie in the *Literary Supplement* "which ranks among the most enigmatical pieces of English prose." ("Mr. George Prothero told me that he read half of it," wrote Benson, "and then suddenly found that he did not know what it was about. He began it again and read it all through, and thought that he understood it. So, to make sure that he had grasped it, he began reading it through for the third time but the gleam had vanished, and he was completely in the dark again.") Who can fully understand James Joyce's *Finnegans Wake?* The *Cantos* of Ezra Pound? Hegel's *Phenomenology of Spirit?* Joseph Conrad's *Nostromo?* Virginia Woolf's *The Waves?* Thomas Pynchon's *Gravity's Rainbow?* Jacques Lacan's *Ecrits?* Louis Zukofsky's *"A"?* (He never referred to the long poem — it was divided into 24 sections, reflecting the hours of the day, employed medieval Italian *canzone*, sonnets, free verse, and the music of Bach, and took him an entire lifetime to write — without quotation marks.) I was going to add here Ayn Rand's turgid and pretentious *Atlas Shrugged* but then reminded myself we are confining the list to literature, not twaddle. I would also give the Twisted Palma D'Oro to Buckminster Fuller, Immanuel Kant, Martin Heidegger, as well as the authors of every single bloated production of the Federal Agency in Washington D.C. Adolf Hitler frustratedly described Alfred Rosenberg's turgid *The Myth of the Twentieth Century* as "impenetrable." (The Führer from the beginning was a very serious and discerning reader and collector of books. See Timothy W. Ryback's splendid book, *Hitler's Private Library.*)

I realize that I am putting him, rather unfairly, into heavy, indeed heady, company, but virtually none of Bruce Springsteen's many songs are hummable, his lyrics so badly written and convoluted, and his articulation is so often tortured and crudely boorish at times that you can barely understand the meaning. (So maybe we have the answer to the Cowardly Lion's question, "Who put the 'ape' in apricot?") His discernible limitations in the voice department, which occasionally mimic Walpurgis-night-like howling, only makes it worse. ("I hate Bruce Springsteen," R. Crumb yelped in a 1985 anti-Bruce cartoon. "Shlockmeister! Polluter of souls! Deceiver of the innocent! Pimp! Panderer! Sleazeball hustler!") "Was the chorus of 'Blinded by the Light'," asked John Lombardi in his article on Springsteen called "St. Boss," "really '*Wrapped up like a douche/ In the rumor of the night'"?* It is hard to imagine a more raddled song, and I mean repulsive in every way, lyrics, melody, drive, than "Blinded by the Light," and frankly I have to confess that while I am not a Springsteen fan — he has a harsh, inflexible, desperately straining, micronoetic voice and on the "Dancing in the Dark" video he dances like a bonobo chimp — I can still admire what he is "about." But I mean, when Archibald MacLeish pointed out in his insightful poem "Ars Poetica,"

> A poem should be palpable and mute
> As a globed fruit
> Dumb

he did not mean dumb in the American slang sense of stupid or idiotic.

> When you were only startin'
> To go to kindergarten,
> I'll bet you drove
> The other *childs* wild

sings Bobby Darin with his fuddled innovation in the Johnny Mercer/ Harry Warren standard "You Must Have Been A Beautiful Baby." It is so lame, so incompetently comic, that it seems almost an affront to every limbo boy and girl all around the world to ask, what was wrong with the "I'll bet you drove/ the other *kids* wild"? That it loses the assonance? The word "kids" in fact keeps the assonance. That it doesn't rhyme or juxtapose as well with the word "wild"? But that rhyme is negligible. No doubt it is one of the reasons why Otis Redding (who came from Georgia to San Francisco, remember) could not manage find a job, as he laments in his hit, "Dock of the Bay," for in his dimwittedness he sings "*two thousand miles* I roamed/ just to make this dock my home." Were he and co-writer, Stax guitarist Steve Cropper too ignorant to realize that it is *three thousand miles* from the Peach State to the City by the Bay? Which by the way, notice, rhymes just as well The use of the word "three" instead or "two" makes not a jot of difference in the song. Was this once again a case of laziness? Or does the problem go back to the year 911, when Charles the Simple allowed the Vikings to settle in Normandy, thus creating that Franco-Germanic hybrid we call the English language?

Was Louis Prima singing in Italian or half the time in a primate language? What exactly is a goomba? A *cumparo*? Can mispronunciation even among poor unschooled immigrants get that far afield? Was the word goober in old Southern songs Swahili for *ngumba*, the word for peanut? His crude "Pleaza No Squeeza Da Banana" Italian in those old novelty numbers of his was no better than Peter Griffin's on *Family Guy* in the episode when, because wearing a mustache, he feels empowered in a pasticceria to try to order in faux Italian, "*Scusi, bupi di bapa, bappoda, beebi di poopi!*" Prima's version of "*C'è La Luna Mezza Mare*" in the Sicilian dialect, with made-up interpretations — throwing in double-entendres, vocal crudities, and risqué whistles — is insane:

> *C'è la luna a mezzu 'u mare*
> *Mamà mia m'mai maritare.*
> *Figghia mia chi u da dare*
> *Mamà mia, pensaci tu.*
>
> *Se ti do nu pisciaiolo*
> *iddu va, iddu vene*
> *sempre u pisce in mano tene.*
> *Se ci pija la fantasia*
> *a pescialia a figghia mia.*
>
> *Oh mamà, me vogghiu marità*
> *Oh mamà, me vogghiu marità*
> *Oh mamà, pesce fritto e baccalà*

It is a rutting song, of course. Don't be shocked. American pop music pullulates with songs about bonking, shagging, rogering, choose whatever verb you like. The Drifters' "Under the Boardwalk," The Starland Vocal Band's "Afternoon Delight," "Carly Simon's "Nobody Does It Better," Meat Loaf's "Paradise by the Dashboard Light," Cole Porter's "Let's Do It," Tommy James and the Shondells' "Hanky Panky," The Big Bopper's "You Know What I Like," and hundreds of others.

Allow me to address some confusion about the pop hit "Que Sera, Sera"? The song written by Jay Livingston and Ray Evans in 1956 was made popular in the Alfred Hitchcock movie *The Man Who Knew too Much*. The words are indeed Spanish, but the phrase in Spanish is, as it stands, completely ungrammatical. A roughly equivalent idea can be expressed in proper Spanish in the proverb, "*Lo que ha de ser, será [o el mundo se hundirá, cf. Recopilación de Refranes y Dichos Populares]*." According to Livingston, upon seeing the film *The Barefoot Contessa* (1954), in which an Italian family has the motto "*Che sarà sarà*" carved on a stone at its ancestral castle, he wrote down the phrase as a possible song title. Later, he and Evans, who had worked together as musicians on various cruise ships to the Caribbean and South America, later re-spelled the phrase in Spanish — for money — for, as he put it, "there are so many [more] Spanish-speaking people in the world." By the way, even that phrase "*che sarà sarà*" is ungrammatical in modern standard Italian, where the apothegm would properly be rendered "*Quel che sarà sarà.*" So the long and the short of it is, the phrase, "*Que sera, sera*" remains a total solecism — utter codswollop.

But, if you want to get technical, the opening line in T.S. Eliot's poem, "The Love Song of J. Alfred Prufrock," should more properly read, "Let us go then, you and me," and is grammatically incorrect as it stands:

> Let us go then, you and I
> When the evening is spread out
> against the sky...

If it was a problem of rhyme, surely Eliot could have used the word "sea" in the second line and lost neither the effect nor the meaning. The gracelessness of inartistically putting an ungrammatical howler at the beginning of a poem that is supposedly narrated by a well-read sophisticate is nothing less than embarrassing. No doubt there are those who consider the use of correct grammar unimportant. It is less lamentable than frankly scandalous, especially in venues of public importance. It is not simply confined to bubblegum lyrics like the grating "Us girls we are so magical" in Katy Perry's "I Kissed a Girl" or "You and me could write a bad romance" from Lady Gaga's "Bad Romance." Pompous Charles Krauthammer, who is always holding forth on television programs like some kind of official supremo, on Fox News on June 13, 2012 criticized President Obama for wasting funds, saying, "He sits down and order a steak and martinis for the next thousand days and sends you and I the bill." Not even a second-grader would be making that mistake. "This reception has meant much to Mrs. Willkie and I," said the blundering candidate Wendell Willkie, an ungrammatical gaffe that cost the Indiana lawyer as many as tens of thousands of votes and, some say, even the election when he was the dark horse Republican Party nominee for the 1940 presidential contest. (Is there anyone still alive who doubts for a minute that politics is the great abattoir of language?) June Casagrande, author of *Mortal Syntax* and *Grammar Snobs are Great Big Babies,* observed on her blog post on October 3, 2008, "In last night's vice presidential debate, Senator Joe Biden used ungrammatical sentences 28 times, not counting grammar errors attributable to 'shifts and false starts.' Gov. Sarah Palin used 71 ungrammatical sentences not counting shifts and false starts." The following shows, verbatim, the kind of muddled but typical horseshit — fog-brained Biden, the King of Anacoluthon, always a bit over his skis, is speaking but it could be almost anyone one of the fat-witted political jackasses clogging up progress on Capitol Hill — that voters are subjected to in this hopeless day and age:

> We don't call a redistribution in my neighborhood Scranton, Claymont, Wilmington, the places I grew up, to give the fair to say that not giving Exxon Mobil another $4 billion tax cut this year as John calls for and giving it to middle class people to be able to pay to get their kids to college, we don't call that redistribution....The bottom line here is that we are going to, in fact, eliminate those wasteful spending that exist in the budget right now, a number of things I don't have time, because the light is blinking, that I won't be able to mention, but one of which is the $100 billion tax dodge that, in fact, allows people to take their post office box off-shore, avoid taxes.

And I am not even bringing up classics like President George W. Bush's "Rarely is the question asked: Is our children learning?" or the following memorable tweet sent by Gov. Sarah Palin: "Ground Zero Mosque supporters: doesn't it stab you in the heart, as it does ours throughout the heartland? Peaceful Muslims, pls refudiate. [sic]." I have to say it all seems part of an Annual Republican Party Variety Show. Big intro. Stand-up. Comic routines. Finish with a dance number. Kick, ball change, cross. Jazz hands.

How long gone the days of Mr. Gladstone! The Grand Old Man found much pleasure from the cares of politics in a prolonged study of Homer. In 1878, at the invitation of the admiring young George Nathaniel Curzon, later Viceroy of India, he even delivered a lecture to the Eton Literary Society on the epic poet.

I must say even the vainest of us fail. In a *Vanity Fair* piece ("The Teetotal Effect," August 2004), the at times priggish and self-regarding Christopher Hitchens, mocking the elementally thumb-tongued President George W. Bush for garbling the language, wrote, "For things like 'put food on your family' you have to be the equivalent of tone-deaf, and more or less incapable of reading for edification, let alone for pleasure," whereupon, in the same paragraph containing that rather lordly dismissal, Mr. Hitchens — unfailingly a maker of vivid sentences of which he was prone to preen — presents this noisy fender-bender: "The renowned problem of inarticulacy is not, on this analysis, the result of neural carnage or synaptic havoc caused by the sauce," almost Micawberian in its fustian.

Oddly, the author of the old ballad, "Cayce Jones" — almost always misspelled "Casey" — rhymed "Santa Fe" with the word *be*:

> The fireman said: "What can they be?"
> He said the Southern Pacific and the Santa Fe[11]

In the refrain of his song "Time in a Bottle," Jim Croce incompetently rhymes "find them" with "time with," showing the kind of laziness in writing that, to me, also bollixes up the completely confusing *olla podrida* in the same song that goes:

> If I had a box just for wishes
> And dreams that had never come true,
> The box would be empty except for the mem'ry
> Of how they were answered by you.

Talk about a passage that would give even Bertrand Russell fits! Where is the logic here? Let me see, if he loves the woman, which seems to be the premise of the

---

11      Boldness in rhyme is commendable certainly, although *be* and *Fe* is truly grotesque. Lord Byron in his long poem *Don Juan* cheekily dared to rhyme "ladies" with "Cadiz" and "intellectual" with "hen-pecked-you-all" — he did this sort of thing often — but he was being intentionally playful. Robert Browning, who had an addiction for playing with words, in "The Pied Piper of Hamelin" oddly rhymed the words "havoc" with "Vin-de-Grave, Hock" and 'fróm [his accent] mice" with "hop" but, irresistibly, with "de trop" and even "G.O.P." and "GOP"! In his rather mad poem, "Of Pacchiarotto," he rhymed "Siena's" with "hyenas" and "You Tommy-make-room-for-your-Uncle us!" with "Troop, of all you — man or homunculus" — for Browning any sacrifice would do — and
Confutation of vassal of prince meet
Wherein all the powers that convince meet
And mash my opponent to mincemeat

Swinburne in *Laus Veneris* rhymed "world to kiss" with "Semiramis." Debbie Harry in her song "Picture This" got away with rhyming the words "solid" and "wallet." In Oscar Wilde's poem *The Sphinx* he took something of a perverse delight in coming up with almost impossible rhymes for very peculiar words — offering "pedestalled" to rhyme, obliquely, with "emerald," "obelisk" with "hippogriff," and "catafalque" with "Amenalk." In Frank Loesser's "A Secretary is Not a Toy," we hear, "With a mother at home she supports/ And you'll find nothing like her/ At F.A.O. Schwartz." Toby Keith in "Whiskey Girl" moronically rhymes the line "She ain't into wine and roses" with "Beer just makes her turn up her nose and..." In the song "You Did It" from the musical *My Fair Lady* Alan Jay Lerner rhymed the words "aren't" and "foreign." Finally, the black rapper, Webbie, the pride of Baton Rouge, elegantly rhymes "drunk as a fuckin' rhino" — viva the language of hip-hop! — with "my people gon' get they shine on," which is almost as troglodytic and depressingly aboriginal as his "You my gutta bitch who I'm wit wen I'm in shit with my otha bitch" from "Gutta Bitch" and from "Thuggin," "My CD cold, my wrist fuckin' freezie/Pay for pussy, no yo, I get too many freebies"

lyric, why would the box be empty of wishes — they are clearly his wishes — if he had them? Were they not worthy enough to be included? *Did they even exist?* (He is implying either one thing or the other.) Are wishes and dreams that never come true being used as a plural subject here, so conjoined? It is hard to say and only one of a bunch of confusions. Now, one should point out that dreams that never come true, by their very nature — we are talking about a non-thing — would therefore not signify in a box that he states to be empty, right? But just for the sake of argument let is call an unfulfilled dream a commodity. So, is there one "mem'ry" or many? If one, why does he then (mistakenly?) say "they"? Beyond that, if (a) the box were empty but (b) the woman had answered his wishes and/or dreams, for those are clearly the antecedents of "they" (and with no evidence one way or another one cannot say if they were positive or negative answers), why would the memory of her answers matter if, amounting to nothing, they led to an empty box — empty, that is, except for the memory? The memory recalls the answers, the answers respond to the wishes and dreams, and the box is empty of both, like Croce's befuddled brain.

It is an endless, eternal recurrence.

Good writing is an assault on cliché, bending language in order to give it new force, an aural, a visual crank. Vitality. Originality. What is remarkable is that so many of the barbarisms and brutalities in pop music that are so obviously bad could so easily have been rectified. The poor grammar, that is. The other things, the bathos, the windy splurging, the anemia and the bombinating, the obstipation, the facile short-cuts, the duncical inability to hold the key of inspiration — all of that, sadly, is another matter entirely. For example, when Michael Jackson in the song "I'll Be There" tells his girl, "Just look over your shoulder*s*" [my italics], who is he talking to, *Rubber Woman?*

Speaking of plurality, why on earth would anyone name two songs on the same CD "Invincible" and "Unbreakable," as the so-called "King of Pop" did on his rather poor-selling 2001 *Invincible* album, Jackson's first issue of entirely new material since 1991 — and at the cost of as much as thirty million dollars? The usual and invariably hip post-modern defense of such otherwise easily correctible assbackwardness is "shit happens," which I daresay also aptly describes the album. In "Ain't Got No Home," Clarence "Frogman" Henry is a homeless boy who — as he croakingly sings with a jargogling voice that he has no sister, brother, mother, or father — feigns to be a frog! On the subject of musical incomprehension, it has taken me more than thirty years of listening to Jim Croce's "I've Got A Name" to understand the words in the last line of the refrain: "Movin', so that life won't pass me by" — and I had to hear it sung on a cover version by a woman (I can't remember the artist's name) who had a semblance of good diction, this back in the hills of northern New Mexico (everywhere in this blasted country if you shop, eat out, wherever you go, it is impossible to avoid hearing music — and almost always detestable music) where I left a large tip out of cosmic gratitude. What about the truly mind-calcifying moment in the song, "International Lover," when Prince extra-terrestrially sings, "And I expect a few turbulence along the way?" Or the ear-popping howler in rapper Ja Rule's "Loose Change" when he — for want of a better word — sings,

> I really don't care to stand
> But 50, you gon' get shot again
> By the M-U-R-E-D-R, Inc.

misspelling not only a basic word but one that happens to be the name of *his very own record label*! We have the bookend with Fergie singing "Fergielicious:"

> T, to the A, to the S-T-E-Y, girl you tasty
> T, to the A, to the S-T-E-Y, girl you tasty
> D, to the E, to the L-I-C-I-O-U-S
> To the D, to the E, to the, to the, to the
> Hit it Fergie!

Endless. Endless. Is it Mr. Prince the Innovator, by the way, we have to thank for the terrifying over-prevalence now of Text-Messager Orthography with his offering from 1985 — made a hit by Sinéad O'Connor — "Nothing Compares 2U"?

> It's been seven hours and fifteen days
> since u took your love away
> I go out every night and sleep all day
> Since u took your love away…

Or did it begin with computer-speak? Anthony Trollope in his novel *The Three Clerks* (1858) portrays a young man who "persisted in spelling blue without the final *e*" and "was therefore declared unworthy of any further public confidence." Who can forget the egregious blunder made by the not-very-bright Dan Quayle, the then-sitting Vice-President of the United States, when at an elementary school spelling bee in Trenton, New Jersey on June 15, 1992 he tried to alter — and confidently! — student William Figueroa's correct spelling of the word "potato" to "potatoe," only amplifying the ridicule he had already attracted for an official Christmas card he sent out previous year that dopily declared his nation "the beakon of hope for the world." The barbarians have long ago crashed the gates. "BFF," "TMI," "LOL" are popular phrases now. LMAO. ROLF. Shorthand, tweeterspeak, texting terms. Linguistic deviancy can now be found in more places than ever. Abbreviations are rife, creative misspellings now all the rage, along with a kind of cretinous delight in willful, playful goofs and cryptic neologisms. Go back to Walt Disney's EPCOT center, located near Orlando, Florida: am I alone in finding that the fulsome words in their acronym which stand for "Experimental Prototype Community of Tomorrow" actually cross-pollinate each other? Wouldn't you also agree, furthermore, that such a theme-park dedicated, as it is, to the "celebration of human achievement" should have and could have found a more congenial — why not start with comprehensible — name? Slick advertising with its artless misspellings ("Gene-yus") and syllable mashups ("TechnoRiffic") has helped to turn impressionable young people into semi-literate numbskulls who cannot spell for seeing words like "thru" and "e-z" and "nite" and "kwik-pix" along with products like Sunkist, Renuzit, Bud Lite, Loctite, Kwik, Cheez-its, Splenda, Gleem, Titebond Wood Glue, Vicks VapoRub, Lestoil, Everglo, Stride Rite, Gymboree, Kleenex, Wite-Out, Supr Glu, Froot Loops, Val-Pak, Blu-Ray, Ry-Krisp, Heet, Kix, Tru-Ade, and — for me, the most arseless one of them all — 'Lectric Shave, which the J. B. Williams Company, for coming up with that truly embarrassing and pointlessly bird-brained abridgement, had not the slightest rhyme or reason. For the record, this is known in advertising as "sensational spelling." Businesses are no better: Uneeda Biscuit, Toys "R" Us, Play Skool, Spam (which stands for Shoulder Pork and ham!), Compaq, Pix System, Kinect, X-Box 360, Qwest, Chew Stixx, Krispy Kreme, etc. Hashtags have now become actual words. Just like H/T, Fail Whale, FTW, and DM. Wanna tweetup, dude? Confounded by twitter twaffic, tweeheart? Having twissues with your twerminology?

During the 1960s, bands often included in their names misspelled words and/or homophones that played on double meanings of the names as spoken. The best example is the Beatles' name, of course, obviously a portmanteau of "beat" and "beetles," but it led to fugal and often credibility-straining repetitions. Led Zeppelin, in which "led" may be read as either a misspelling of "[the metallic element] lead" or a description of the aircraft as being guided in a specific direction (cf. "dirigible"). The inane misspelling of words in album or song titles, hippie in origin, in my view, took root in the late 60s with songs like Sly & The Family Stone's "Thank You (Falettinme Be Mice Elf Agin)" — an intentional mondegreen for "thank you for letting me be myself again" — Genesis' "Deep in the Motherlode" and the rock glam group Slade's "Coz I Luv You" (1971) or "Mama Weer All Crazee Now" (1972). In the 80s it became a commonplace with funk groups like Klymaxx. Con Funk Shun, Kool & the Gang, and cool funkazoids such as 2 Pak, Dr. Dre, and Prince with "U Got The Look," "Nothing Compares 2 U," "No More Candy 4U," eventually to be taken up in the rap and hip-hop genres, like Snoop Dogg's profane, chip-on-the-shoulder rants like "Paid tha Cost to Be da Boss," "From tha Chuuurch to da Palace," and "Vato Feat. B-Real," part of which goes,

> What's seen is what's sawn, Dogg is the law
> I had you niggas runnin' like a marathon
> Little Gs tryna creep on the east wit it
> Talkin' 'bout they gon get my chain
> and they gon leave wif it

with both song titles (e.g. "Kiss Me Thru the Phone," "Do Ya Thing," "Muthafucka," "Pussy Pop") and phonetic artists' names (e.g. Ludacris, Phanatik, Timbaland, Xzibit, Gorillaz) using the form. Sensational spelling was also common among "nu metal" bands of the late 1990s and early 2000s (e.g. Korn, Linkin Park and Limp Bizkit). And do you happen to remember the influential hard-rock magazine of the 1970s-80s, *Creem?*

One sign of this crisis is the Apple, Inc. slogan "Think Different.' Although Steve Jobs and his advertising team agonized over the slogan to get the phrase right, according to his biographer, Walter Isaacson, debating the grammatical issue ("If 'different' was supposed to modify the verb 'think,' it should be an adverb, as in 'think differently.'"), Jobs insisted, and from all I have read he was always insisting, that he was using the word "different" as a noun, as in, say, "die happy," "think freedom," etc. and ended up opting for the colloquial usage of the lax and repugnant phrase that has by now become fully embedded. Some will argue that it has the sanction of age, that the pedigree is distinguished — William Thackeray includes the line "[...] we drove very slow for the last two stages on the road [...]" in his novel *Vanity Fair* (1848), and even Shakespeare employed the adverbial *slow* in *A Midsummer Night's Dream*: "[...] but O, methinks, how slow / This old moon wanes!" — but I still maintain that even those examples are the language of road signs, a subalternate subordinate. So why would anyone expect Jobs not to go in for further awkward innovations — and make horrendously fashionable — iPhone and iPod and iPad and iMac and other hideous compound words with uppercase "bumps" in the middle, suggestive of a Bactrian's humps, that is called "camel case." "Jobs was someone who took other people's ideas and changed them," writes Malcolm Gladwell in "The Tweaker," an essay on Jobs's guileful ability to purloin from Xerox and Microsoft and even inventors in his own company to improve on their work, which he did successfully and with panache, but he also had no qualms about changing language, as well.

Language, because it is a living thing, is therefore a precarious one. Its life depends upon its care. After twenty-seven years of hostilities during the Peloponnesian War, which destroyed imperial Athens and ultimately Sparta as well, the historian Thucydides saw with a raw glare of grief that, along with the atrocities committed by Greek citizens on each other, in the protracted period the warring Greeks — Athenians and Spartans — could no longer understand each other. "The meaning of words has no longer the same relation to things, but was changed by men as they thought proper," he wrote. "Words had to change their ordinary meaning and to take that which was now given them."

Without man, *being* would not be. It depends upon man who, in Heideggerian terms, alone offers it an "abode," in language through which and in which and by which *thought* is made possible, even if all along in our own ignorant way we blunderingly write or speak what, more often than not, reveals us as poor stewards of the word — using what simultaneously we are confounded by — in the same dim way one complains, "If we aren't supposed to eat animals, why are they made of meat?"

A good lyric involves sharp *insight*, looking at something in a new light the way it appears in magic, innovative moments in any of the arts, like objects broken up and reassembled in an abstract form in painting (Pablo Picasso's *Les Demoiselles d'Avignon*) or the Valhalla leitmotif in music (Richard Wagner's *Die Walküre*, Act II), or the surplus-value greedily extracted by capitalists from laborers (Karl Marx, *Das Kapital*) or as a sudden flash in literature: "Everybody knows that aspens can have an unpleasant, bullying way of rustling" (Knut Hamsun's *Growth of the Soil*). To see with acuity is but to be awake. Being awake to the newly possible is all about cognition. It is ultimately self-exploration, a bold trip into one's own interiority. Wallace Stevens observed,

> I was the world in which I walked, and what I saw
> Or heard or felt came not but from myself;
> And there I found myself more truly and more strange.

Where hackery prevails, nothing is found. James Baldwin lamented, "Americans use language to cover the sleeper, not to wake him." But language is the translating, transmuting, transforming principle. *It matters.* It is the Word — we listen to hear, speak to convey, sing to express, and, even if it all takes place in the suspension of our own apostrophe, over a dark and forbidding abyss, we trust, we hope, that that intervening space will be transfigured, filled with significance, bridged, in short. We pray to ask, from gratitude, in thanks, to have a wish fulfilled. Prayer is utterance. "Hear us, O Lord, from heaven, thy dwelling place," we cry. It is as if to announce ourselves — to selve — in the smallness of our universe. "The very act of speaking announces space," declared the late, great Canadian poet Robert Kroetsch. "The apostrophe is addressed quite possibly not to God the Father but to the gap itself, the gap that separates, the speaking voice from the listener, the mouth from the ear, the spoken word from the longed-for signification." It reminds us, continually and radically, as Kroetsch points out, "that we are always in the predicament of Orpheus, listening across his shoulder, hearing first and only the silence of Eurydice who might or who might not be following, behind his uncertain head." It is all about "unreachable recovery," to use Kroetsch's bold oxymoron. "Distance is at once our vocabulary and the denial of its efficiency."

Confounding is where the word goes awry. What kind of helium were Godsmack breathing when in "Voodoo" they wrote lines like, "Never did I want to be here again" and "I'm not the one who's so far away" and what remote interplanetary language, one wonders, were they translating? It reminds me, when going to see American movies in a foreign country, of the dire perils that befall the English language when it is translated by amateurs, but that, as many people choose to say nowadays — and without irony — is a whole "nother" [sic] story. Retranslated into our language, I recall reading titles such as, "A Trolley Nominate I Desire" (*A Streetcar Named Desire* in Portuguese); "To the Wind It Satisfied" (*Gone With The Wind* in Italian); "Annie Receives Your Rifle" (*Annie Get Your Gun* in French); and "Everyone Approximately Evening" (*All About Eve* in German). You viewer the findings here of such titles are enjoyable in all cinema for the brain, yes?

Rod Stewart in his pop-song "Reason to Believe" repeatedly sings the supposedly flattering line, "Someone like you/ makes it hard to live/ without somebody else" — surely he meant the opposite? But then again with certain people either immune to irony and/or strangely depraved who can be sure? There is a line in R.E.M.'s 2004 single, "Leaving New York," that goes "Leaving was never my proud." Pop critics, such as those in the literary world, for example, who obsequiously defend poet John Ashbery's or Charles Olsen's or Gertrude Stein's most obscure lines, tend to like this sort of Cubist lunacy. But isn't that why the late Frank Zappa, who knew, once testily stated, "Rock journalism is people who can't write, interviewing people who can't talk, for people who can't read"? In his bouncy, oddly hiccuping song, "Uh-Oh, I'm Falling in Love Again," Jimmie Rodgers's line, "I met a girl with the goldenest hair," is right out of Mondo Beyondo. What about the line, "Going faster miles an hour" as heard in "Roadrunner" by the Modern Lovers. (Cop: "How many miles-an-hour were you going?" Driver: "Faster.") One lyric in the hilariously bad country yokel hit, the Marshall Tucker Band's "Heard it in A Love Song," is the musical equivalent of that dark scene in Robert Louis Stevenson's novel, *Kidnapped*, when young David Balfour visiting the House of Shaws, the home of his paranoid Uncle Ebenezer, walking up the stairs, as directed, comes to that frightening dead-end in mid-air, almost falling to his death: "I was born a wrangler and a rounder and I guess I always will." I have often cringed when listening to the lyrics in the song "It Happened in Monterey," I tried to sort out the nonsense line — what exactly is in apposition to what? — "It happened in Monterey/ without thinking twice." Even in Gene Autry's sweet version of the song something goes nuttily black. There is a line in the hit-song "Cabaret" from the musical of the same name (music by John Kander and lyrics by Fred Ebb) where Sally Bowles sings of the sorry effects of (wait for it) "too much pills and liquor:"

> The day she died the neighbors came to snicker
> Well, that's what comes from too much pills and liquor.

Fred Ebb's craft must have been ebbing that day. But it is the truly unsumptuous duet of the irrepressible Travis and Bob that wins the blue ribbon in the jerkola category hands-down, at least for me, with an almost ear-shattering atrocity committed in their hit single from 1962, "Tell Him No," that goes in part:

> And then I feel much more better
> When I hold her in my arms.

I wonder if the well-known anthropologist Claude Lévi-Strauss, when pointing out that "music unites the contrary attributes of being both intelligible and untranslatable," might just have been listening to that record?

There are more offenses against grammar in pop music than can possibly be counted, far worse than the fact that Aaron Copland, composer of *Grand Canyon Suite*, never pronounced the word rodeo as "rodéo!" (But it still fairly creeps me out when, listening to her song "Baby I'm Yours," I hear Barbara Lewis sing the word 'eter*naaa*-ty.") "I decided long ago not to walk in anyone's shadow*s* [sic]" Whitney Houston sings twice, *twice*, in her hit, "The Greatest Love of All." In her 1989 song, "Straight Up," for instance, Paula Abdul (and her songwriter) badly abuse the technique of enjambment by singing "...are you really hot for me/ Or am I just another page in your history/ Book?" — with the last insufficiently integrated word falling off the line like a smoking turd from a cart horse. Recording the classic "Birth of the Blues" in 1955, Frank Sinatra ear-splittingly — and ungrammatically, not a Sinatra trait — sang the line, "The Southland! They (!) gave birth to the blues" To me, this minor howler has its visual countergoof in the film, *Till the Clouds Roll By*. A medley of songs by Jerome Kern are dramatized in this phony re-enactment of the composer's life, when, in a memorably tasteless moment, Sinatra can be seen standing on a fluted pillar crooning "Ol' Man River" — including the line, "You and me/ we sweat and strain" — while sporting an immaculate white suit. It is the equivalent of a test-pilot imping his wings for a great flight while he is dressed in a pink tutu! (William Warfield's version of the song in the movie *Showboat* (1951) is the nonpareil. Once in a while a performance is so inimitable that it seems it will never be topped. This is one of them. Paul Robeson sings it with full power. Young Sinatra did a commendable job of it. (It was his daughter Nancy Sinatra's favorite song in her father's repertoire. In an interview with NPR on December 16, 1995 she flatly declared, "Once you hear [my father singing] 'Ol Man River,' nothing else could follow it.") Others gave strong interpretations of the song, like Judy Garland and Bing Crosby who recorded it with Paul Whiteman. But nobody, nobody at all, has ever topped Warfield's deeply felt, incandescent version of the song. If the hair doesn't stand up on the back of your neck as you listen to it, you are dead. When Marilyn McCoo and Billy Davis, Jr. sing "I don't need no superstar to be in my show" in their song "You Don't Have To Be A Star(To Be in My Show)," was it really too much of a cultural reach for them to sing, correctly, without missing a beat, notice, "I don't need *a* superstar to be in my show"? Ignorance is ugly.

Continuing, don't you just love the theological puerility in "From A Distance," when Bette (pronounced as in *wet)* Midler, she of the limited voice range and talent — incidentally, actress Bette Davis personally (and correctly) always pronounced her own name to rhyme with Jetty — sings, actually brays,

> It's the ho-pof hopes
> It's the lo-vof loves
> It's the hea-aaar-tof eee-eaaa-eeevree maaan...
> God is wutchin-gus!
> God is wutchin-gus!
> God is wutchin-gus!

I am always suitably appeased with the murderous thoughts that this song instantly invokes in me by hearkening to the comforting assurance of Emile Durkheim, French sociologist and father of criminology, who insists that crime is necessary for the progress of mankind, indeed that it serves a legitimate social function. What a lovely heresy it is, by the way, that God is watching us "from a distance," in spite of orthodox theology long having assured us for millennia that He is omnipresent and omniscient. I have to say that the idea that an anthropological God out of some evidential requirement of our own has to "watch" us is rather quaint. But then why bother to look for theological correctness in pop music, right? Or moral consistency? Or an elegant voice, for that matter? Who ever notices such things half the time? Most people, I have the distinct feeling, do not even know what brand of socks they are wearing on any given day or are even remotely alarmed that a presidential candidate is privately an immoral toad (are not 95% of them?), in spite of the fact that character is central to leadership.

Consider, for example, two consistently ignored scatological gestures, incomprehensible to Americans and in fact rarely spotted by anyone, from songs in the musical *My Fair Lady* back in the early '60s when they managed to get by the censors. Explaining how making too much money would, by corrupting him, transform him into a snob and an impossible toff, Alfred P. Doolittle (Stanley Holloway), as he ruefully laments, "And then goodbye to happiness," proceeds to flash the vulgar British hand-signal for "up yours" (or "fuck off"): two forefingers in a V thrust rudely upwards. Whereupon, lo and behold, his wayward daughter, Liza (Audrey Hepburn), then does the very same thing in her song, "Just You Wait" when she utters the line, "Will I help you?/ Don't be funny"! In a famous movie! As the old blues song goes, "It ain't what you do, it's the place that you do it."

Concision itself in a song can obfuscate meaning. In Kitty Kallen's old hit, "Little Things Mean A Lot," she sings, "Say I look nice,/ when I'm not." The logic of the lyric is saying, tell me I look good, even when *I* am not nice — morality is implied — that is, even when I am bad, please tell me the opposite. "Nice" in itself is of course a weak, neutral, and hopelessly inadequate word, like the all-purpose "interesting" — the word that people always use when they have to comment on something but crave to avoid giving an opinion — and they are words rarely if ever used by honest brokers.

In their song, "Scarborough Fair," Simon and Garfunkel clunkily sing at one point in the lyric, "Tell her to make me a cambric shirt/ (On the side of a hill in the deep forest green) Parsely, sage, rosemary and thyme/ (Tracing a sparrow on snow-crested ground) Without no seams nor needlework...Then she'll be a true love of mine." It is embarrassing, if you really want the truth, but writing

— or spouting — careless and often meaningless lyrics was the stock-in-trade of those two guys. I recall how frustrated even bright students often were back in the 1960s trying to sort through all of their garbled lyrics, mixed metaphors, mangled images, crabbed allusions, and hackneyed phrases — often saccharine enough to give you a bad toothache — of songs like "Mrs. Robinson," "The Sounds of Silence," "The Boxer," "I Am a Rock," and of course "Scarborough Fair," in which Simon and Garfunkel thoughtfully go out of their way to pass on the ingredients for stuffing used in poultry dishes — and with the lyrics, uncredited I might add, that they plagiarized from an 1889 English ballad!

I am convinced that Diana Vreeland was in her cups when she wrote, "I've known two great decades in my life, the twenties and the sixties, and I am always comparing them because of the music. Music is everything, and in those decades you got something so sharp, so new." Who was she referring to in the Sixties, The Mothers of Invention? Allan Sherman's "Hello Muddah, Hello Fadduh"? "You Were on my Mind" by the We Five? John Cage's silent *0'00"* — the directions consist of one sentence, "In a situation provided with maximum amplification, perform a disciplined action — a variation on his controversial *4'33"* which is pronounced "Four minutes, Thirty-Three Seconds"? "The Stroll" by the Diamonds? Country Joe and the Fish?

I have earlier referred to Marshall McLuhan. The idea of communication was sacred to him. Like the Viennese satirist Karl Kraus, thirty years before him, he wanted to educate his readers to an understanding of the cause of all languages written and spoken, to that height at which the written word is understood as a necessary incarnation of the thought, and not simply a shell demanded by society around an opinion. It is slovenliness in language that swindles us, seduces us, indeed enslaves us in any of a thousand ways. All of the questions of linguistic scruple that McLuhan raised in the 1960s were debated with far greater rigor and deeper insight in fact in the turn-of-the-century Vienna of Karl Kraus and Ludwig Boltzmann, Adolf Loos, and Ludwig Wittgenstein. *Dejournalizing* his readers was an important concern for Kraus, as he put it, in "a time that is thoroughly journalized, that is informed by the spirit but is deaf to the unity of form and contents". When he demanded a critique of language as the crucial instrument of reason, he did so with utter contempt for the kind of disordered logic of thought and expression that is always at loggerheads with moral truth, right reason, and individual integrity which, when missing, leaves one defenseless against the verbal deceptions and moral turpitude of duplicitous men and all of the bigotry, cant, falsity, fraud, casuistry, deceit, dissimulation, double-dealing, and imposture that they are trying to sell.

A *Sprachbesessener* — or one possessed by language — Kraus felt, like W. H. Auden, that the imperfections of a person's language mirror the imperfections of his character; in fact he actually believed with numinous conviction that the correct use of language was a "religious" matter (*"eine religiöse Angelegenheit"*). "The idea that thought cannot exist without speech was implicit in the Greek language," wrote Thomas Szasz in *The Myth of Psychiatry.* "*Phrazomai,* the Greek term for *"I meditate,* means literally *I speak to myself."* *Logos,* the Greek term for the word or speech, also means reason.

In his satirical diatribes, Kraus sought an ideal. He brought a critical eye to the infections of his time and sought to heal by way of corrosives. His repeated demand for uncompromising art is congruent, I like to think, with the accusing and allusive, mocking and satirical thrust of what you — mistakenly, I feel — may find as unkindness in the pages of this very book. "All art that is against its time is for it," wrote Kraus in *Die Fackel,* seeking moral truths in a world of fraudulent rhetoric. "Such art can make the time pass, but it cannot conquer it. The true enemy of time is language. Language lives in harmonious union with the spirit in revolt against its own time. Out of this conspiracy art is conceived. In contrast, conformity, in complicity with its time, robs language of its own vocabulary. Art can only come from denial. Only from anguished protest. Never from calm compliance. Art placed in the service of consoling man becomes a curse unto his very deathbed. True art reaches its fulfillment only through the hopeless." [translation by Thomas Szasz]

Language is in a sense the most important tell-tale for the wrongs of the world. Many great writers and thinkers, from St. John to Immanuel Kant, from Ernst Mach to Søren Kierkegaard, from Ludwig Wittgenstein to H.L. Mencken, from A.J. Ayer to Samuel Beckett, from Rudolf Carnap to George Orwell have viewed the careless treatment of language as a sign of careless treatment by the world as a whole. At its most abused, even by default, often in its most maimed form, it will still reflect to some degree the true state of the world. To the grounded thinker, language is not a means to distribute ready-made opinions, but rather the medium of thought itself. Language is the only vehicle of ideas; if it breaks down, what happens to the ideas? No, the word bears in its integrity the sanctity it does in the Joannine Gospel. As such, it therefore stands in constant need of critical and scrupulous examination, to say nothing of profitable reflection, indeed reverence.

Language is not only the church into which we are taken, but the prayer and the sermon, both. It constitutes a faith all of its own, which offers special grace and domain of comfort and growth to its loyal aspirants. At the outset of Genesis, at creation, God *said,* "Let there be light"...*said,* "Let there be an expanse between the waters," *said* "Let the water under the sky be gathered to one place." Prayer is utterance. Creation is narrated, as a punctual and verbal event. In the beginning was the Word.

Our love of what words can do, what they mean, how they feed our souls is not unrelated to the inner responses we have to music itself. As the cognitive process takes place in the mind, Thomas Aquinas taught us (*Contra Gentiles*, II, c. lxxvii and xcviii), it follows that the known objects must in some manner be present in the mind: *"Cognitio contingit secundum quod cognitum est in cognoscente."* Beyond that, it fits — is tailored to — our very own selves, what we tend to like, yearn to know, in other words. One's interests are linked to the warmth of one's desire, as it were. Whatever is received is received according to the manner of the receiver. *Quidquid recipitur ad modum recipientis recipitur.*

Great care was once taken in composition, of course, exactitude in writing held to be of paramount importance. Stephen Crane fitfully fretted, wondering whether use of the words "barbarous" and "abrupt" were wrong for characterizing waves and rendering them too anthropomorphic. When Oscar Wilde was asked what he had accomplished one day, he replied, "I was working on the proof of one of my poems all the morning and took out a comma, and in the afternoon I put it back again." Gustave Flaubert whose fiercely enduring perfectionism drove him to pursue the principle of finding *"le mot juste"* once wrote to a friend that he had spent as long as three days making two corrections and five days — always twelve-hour days for him — writing but one page. Henry James always compulsively fought to find the exact word until in decorated periods and cursive corrections he could turn the perfect phrase. "The effect was that of a tapestry of speech being audibly designed and executed," wrote E. F. Benson, an admirer. "He put what he wanted to say in a chiseled casket of words." Poring over proofs of a story for *Blackwood* magazine entitled "Youth" in 1898, Joseph Conrad and Ford Madox Ford once spent a day arguing over whether the word "azure" or "serene" best fit in several sentences, merely to settle a matter of *cadence*. "I have known writers of every degree, but never one to whom the act of composition was such a travail and an agony as it was to [Walter] Pater," critic Edmund Gosse wrote, describing that master's method of composition. So conscious was he of the modifications and additions which would supervene that he always wrote on ruled paper, leaving each alternate line blank. Consider for stylistic elegance Pater's "Conclusion" to *The Renaissance* (1893). It is neither a song lyric nor a stanza for a ballad, but just read aloud this matchless description of Da Vinci's painting of the Mona Lisa:

The presence that rose thus so strangely beside the waters, is expressive of what in the ways of a thousand years men had come to desire. Hers is the head upon which all "the ends of the world are come," and the eyelids are a little weary. It is a beauty wrought out from within upon the flesh, the deposit, little cell by cell, of strange thoughts and fantastic reveries and exquisite passions. Set it for a moment beside one of those white Greek goddesses or beautiful women of antiquity, and how would they be troubled by this beauty, into which the soul with all its maladies has passed! All the thoughts and experience of the world have etched and moulded there, in that which they have of power to refine and make expressive the outward form, the animalism of Greece, the lust of Rome, the mysticism of the middle age with its spiritual ambition and imaginative loves, the return of the Pagan world, the sins of the Borgias. She is older than the rocks among which she sits; like the vampire, she has been dead many times, and learned the secrets of the grave; and has been a diver in deep seas, and keeps their fallen day about her; and trafficked for strange webs with Eastern merchants: and, as Leda, was the mother of Helen of Troy, and, as Saint Anne, the mother of Mary; and all this has been to her but as the sound of lyres and flutes, and lives only in the delicacy with which it has moulded the changing lineaments, and tinged the eyelids and the hands. The fancy of a perpetual life, sweeping together ten thousand experiences, is an old one; and modern philosophy has conceived the idea of humanity as wrought upon by, and summing up in itself all modes of thought and life. Certainly Lady Lisa might stand as the embodiment of the old fancy, the symbol of the modern idea.

Paul Anka's fatuous and overblown composition "My Way" — he wrote the lyrics and appropriated the melody — virtually the signature song of both Frank Sinatra and Elvis Presley, each of whom presented it, by the way, as if he were singing the *"Stabat Mater,"* also has the multiple distinction, for all the solemnity it appropriates, of offering not only one of the most repulsive lines ever put down on paper ("I ate it up and spit it out") but surely one of the most fat-witted solecisms in the history of popular music:

> Regrets, I've had a few,
> But then again, too few to mention.
> I did what I had to do,
> And so it proved without exemption.

Exemption? *Exemption?* Anka, who has always seemed to me verifiable proof that the average human head needs something removed from it rather than have something inserted, means to use the word "exception," needless to say — *exemption* means immunity, but the goon badly needed a rhyme, even if he decided on a poor one, and in the Age of Shoddy anything goes. Who knows, perhaps that *was* one of the few regrets to which he alludes. One of mine is that, of the many he had, he did not have more. Yet the question poses itself: can one ascribe such incompetence merely to haste when Sammy Cahn whipped off *"Bei Mir Bist du Schön"* for the Andrews Sisters in a matter of mere minutes, Richard Rodgers wrote the melody for "Bali Hai" in a half hour, and Phil Silvers and Jimmy Van Heusen sitting around a Los Angeles swimming pool got a great idea and sat down and whipped off "Nancy with the Laughing Face" for Frank Sinatra's 2-year-old daughter in twenty minutes?

An interesting aside here is that the lyrics of the songs of a foreign group like ABBA, the most commercially successful group of the 1970s — songs like "Fernando," "SOS," "Take a Chance On Me" — are better than the kind of nocuous and pitiful orts and sorts found in such ill-considered offerings as "My Way" and "Scarborough Fair" and "Seasons in the Sun" and "If You Could Read My Mind."

But from time immemorial — even Homer nodded — gaffes and grammatical errors and tortured neo-literacy can creep into the work of experienced lyricists, even good poets. I'm not totally thrilled with poet James Russell Lowell's prosy, overly-knotted, and to my mind ultimately meaningless line, "What is so rare as a day in June/ then if ever come perfect days?" or the line from the song "My Time of Day" in *Guys and Dolls*: "And you're the only doll I've ever wanted to share it with me." Why is that "me" added? There are other songs in the same musical, such as the curious "More I Cannot Wish You," in which certain words, phrases, and even entire sentences are fully incomprehensible. Same thing in *Paint Your Wagon*. Sentences are entirely incomprehensible. Was it sheer laziness that in the musical, *Camelot*, the usually dependable Alan Jay Lerner in the title song wrote, "In Camelot/ those are the legal laws"? I respect Lerner's work, but one cannot always succeed, let's face it. Robert Louis Stevenson who wrote *Treasure Island, Dr. Jekyll and Mr. Hyde,* and *Kidnapped* also penned some rank failures, such as *Heathercat, The Great North Road,* and *The Young Chevalier.* The early plays of Eugene O'Neill are the pits. I am also convinced E.Y. Harburg should have worked a tad harder and taken a bit more time the night he wrote the lyrics for the Tin Man's song in *The Wizard of Oz*, especially the line, "I could stay young and chipper and I'd lock it with a zipper/ If I only had a heart." *Lock it with a zipper?* Crossed out with the same red pencil should have been his "I'd be clever as a gizzard" — and then of course Dorothy's rather facile

> Just then the witch, to satisfy an itch
> went flying on her broomstick
> thumbing for a hitch

No witch thumbs, least of all one on a broomstick. It is well understood that the lyrics to the songs of Dorothy's friends were supposed to be intentionally a little nutty, full of upside-down wit and comic word-play, but it was wise of the director to have cut one of the Tin Man's weaker, more unfortunate stanzas:

> Gosh, it would be pleasin'
> To reason out the reason
> To things I can't explain
> And perhaps I'll deserve ya
> And be worthy erve ya
> If I only had a brain.

By the way, no one would deny Rita Hayworth is gorgeous in the movie *Gilda*, but who doesn't find the line "That's the flame that slew Magoo" in her song "Put the Blame on Mame" not only low-rent and fairly ridiculous but nonsense?

Why should we be surprised at anomalies in music? "It Came Upon A Midnight Clear" is a Christmas carol that does not celebrate the birth of Christ or in point of fact mention the birth in Bethlehem. As I have said, Irving Berlin's "White Christmas" is strictly seasonal, if not meteorological, in intent and no more celebrates the liturgical feast of Christmas Day than does Little Richard's "Good Golly, Miss Molly." And then of course Berlin's mega-hit "Easter Parade," which has more to do with rabbits than resurrection, is in fact a hymn to the sartorial. Quirks invite queries. Noël Coward, specifically, absolutely loathed the use of the deafening split-infinitive that Alan Lerner and Frederick Loewe embarrassingly gave to Professor Henry Higgins in the musical, *My Fair Lady*, when he sings — and drops — that thudding phrase, "to ever have a woman in my life" — with Prof. Higgins being not merely a stickler of language but the supreme pedant on the subject! — and for his mispronunciation of "Dyensfor." The linguistically fastidious Higgins also asserts that anyone who speaks as his pupil Eliza Doolittle does should be taken out and "hung" as a penalty for murdering the English tongue. Excuse me, but did that pompous British academic actually use the word *hung*? The fact is that the accepted past-participle even today, when virtually anything goes, is "hanged." Incidentally, the fastidious scholar Higgins who for her linguistic infelicities mocks his poor charge as being an "insect" and "baggage" also sings, "I would never let a woman in my life," when the correct grammar should of course properly go, "I would never let a woman *into* my life."

Should good grammar in a song really be avoided when, with a deft stroke or two, it can be quite easily improved? Why for example in the lovely song, "The Brooklyn Bridge," should the line with its ugly double-negative,

> Don't let no one tell you
> I've been trying to sell you
> the Brooklyn Bridge

prevail over

> Let nobody tell you
> I've been trying to sell you
> the Brooklyn Bridge
> [my version]

although the song itself is often not in question. "The Brooklyn Bridge," for me, is a small beauty, perfect in its sublimity, a tiny jewel. Frank Sinatra, who incidentally wrote the lyrics — hard to believe, but them's the facts — delivers it in an unparalleled way, with never a maudlin moment and an ironic if devotional style that beautifully suits its cosmopolitan New York theme. Certain singers can take even a mediocre or even a very bad song and do it well, however. I'm thinking, for example, of Perry Como singing "Prisoner of Love" or Joni James singing "Purple Shades" or Connie Francis singing "My Happiness" or B.B. King singing "The Thrill is Gone" or Evan Dando and the Lemonheads singing "Waiting Around to Die." (A talented band from Boston, The Lemonheads — "The Outdoor Type,' "It's a Shame about Ray, "It's About Time," "Rockin Stroll," "The Great Big No," "Into Your Arms," etc. — are badly underrated.) An artist can by his or her art redeem the time! "Billie Holiday scarcely in her whole life ever sang a really good song," insisted Truman Capote, "but she took these perfectly mediocre songs and turned them into amazing powerhouses of style and artistry."

Although Cole Porter's song "The Tale of the Oyster" (*Fifty Million Frenchmen*, 1929) was, even if witty, undoubtedly tasteless and eventually dropped from the show — some critics, notably Gilbert Seldes, considered it "disgusting" — at least its *intention* was humor. (I love it.) The lyrics recount rather graphically the story of a "socially-climbing" oyster being eaten by a rich society dame, who, becoming seasick, then regurgitates it. Among the more offensive lines were,

> See that bi-valve social climber
> Feeding the rich Mrs. Hoggenheimer.
> Think of his joy as he gaily glides
> Down to the middle of her gilded insides.
> Proud little oyster!
> After lunch Mrs. H. complains,
> And says to her hostess, "I've got such pains,
> I came to town on my yacht today,
> But I think I'd better hurry back to Oyster Bay."
> Scared little oyster!
> Off they go through the troubled tide,
> The yacht rolling madly from side to side,
> They're tossed about till that poor young oyster
> Finds that it's time he should quit his cloister.
> Up comes the oyster!

The nonsense, however, in pop music is unceasing. Who or what is "the purple gang" in Elvis's "Jailhouse Rock"? Or the "spool that never ends" in his song "Moody Blue"? Why do the Mamas & Papas sing *pretend* to pray in "California Dreamin'"? For the alliteration? I believe they meant to write "attempt" to pray. Why not say "began"? I assume by the line, "You know the preacher likes the cold," the speaker means the church building, for if the preacher liked it warm that would explain stopping into the church under false pretenses, but the temperature of the church is the very thing the speaker is trying to escape! What does McCartney's "yesterday came suddenly" mean exactly? Who on earth can explain the peculiar spatial logistics in Question Mark and the Mysterians' "96 Tears"? In Johnny Horton's "The Battle of New Orleans" what does the word *nigh* mean in the line, "There wasn't nigh as many as there was a while ago"? Why does Diane Renay's sailor boyfriend who has shipped out to Tokyo in her song "Navy Blue" send her a "walkie-talkie windup little *China* doll"? How did the road in Eddie Rabbitt's "Rocky Mountain Music" suddenly change from an old dirt road to a gravel road in a single song? And in his "I Love a Rainy Night," how could he see the moon, as plaintively he says he does? As to moons, what is behind the incoherent reference in Anne Murray's vapid, "I Want to Sing You a Love Song," to "moon-bright days"? What are the tortured and incomprehensible lyrics in "Ma Belle Amie" by The Tee Set in aid of? What exactly is involved in getting someone to "wool the bull with you" in Domenic Samudio's (a.k.a. Sam the Sham) "Woolly Bully"? (That quiddity became a major radio debate years ago: was or was it not the name of his cat?) What exactly are the "times" of your life that are mentioned in only yet another one of Paul Anka's lugubrious songs of the same name? What precisely is a "time"? What is "scarlet brattaglia," as enigmatically alluded to in Simon and Garfunkel's "Scarborough Fair"? It is recorded in no dictionary that I ever consulted, including the matchless and supererogational *Webster's Second International*, which I have already mentioned was a favorite book of mine — one reads it like eating potato chips — and which, let me add in passing, happens to have listed every word in the English language.

Why does Pat Boone, playing a Quaker in *Friendly Persuasion*, sing "Thee is mine" to his lover and not "Thee are mine"? Isn't "you are mine" the correct phrase, and not "you is mine"? One would have thought a Columbia graduate would object to such a howler. And who exactly is that Coliarci or Coliarce alluded to in The Chordettes' 1950s hit "Mr. Sandman"? Was he perchance someone historically important that we should know about? Did he ever exist or is the name referred to merely for reasons of rhyme? I've looked up the name in books like *Lippincott's Pronouncing Gazeteer*, the *locus classicus* of names, as well as the *World's Who's Who* and found nothing. What, pray tell, is the peculiar nature of — the psychotic dramatic turmoil behind — the line, "May you find someone to love/ as much as I love you" in the McGuire Sisters', to me, schizophrenic song "May You Always"? "You're nice to me when there's no one else around," as Rosemary Clooney sings in her 1950s Hank Williams cover, "Half as Much" is surely psychologically wrong, is it not? The hypocritical and cruel lover to whom she refers would obviously be nice to her only when there *is* someone around, no? Has the man driven her crazy?

When in the Steve Miller Band' song "Jet Airliner," we hear the phrase "touching down in New England Town," precisely where are we landing? Have we somehow coasted into Allegoryville? What about the buggered time-sequence in Tom Jones's "Without Love," where he begins the song confidentially talking, "Listen please. I'd like to tell you something that happened to me *just the other day*" [my italics], and then he suddenly segues — nuttily — into song, "I awakened *this morning* [my italics], I was filled with despair...." Do you detect a minor conflict? What is the "downhearted frail" referred to in "Birth of the Blues"? Perry Como alludes in his song "Dream On" to "appleberry wine." Has a new fruit being discovered? For that matter, what exactly is a "fuzzy tree" as alluded to in Elvis Presley's "All Shook Up"? Then what sort of fuel could Bob Seger be drinking in order to be "going eight miles a minute" against the wind in his song of that title? The L.A. punk group X on their single "White Girl" (b/w "Your Phone's Off the Hook") spells the song title on the 45 r.p.m. record, "You're [sic] Phone's Off the Hook." The lyrics to Tab Hunter's "Young Love" in 1957 were copied wrong. The line "feel that it's true," should have rhymed with "you" — instead the word "me" is used. Infelicities are not confined to morons. "Smoke on your pipe and put that in," Stephen Sondheim's dopey line in *West Side Story*, is eminently forgettable.

Speaking of musicals, "On the street where you live" is, technically speaking, something of a gaffe on lyricist Alan Jay Lerner's part in the very English *My Fair Lady* — call it an Americanism, if you insist — for the British would universally say, "*In* the street where you live." And should it not be pointed out that, although we hear, "There'll be bluebirds over/ the white cliffs of Dover" in the popular World War II song "The White Cliffs of Dover," there are no bluebirds in England now and there never have been? But the 1964 musical is, among other things, a potpourri of various kinds of music, as well, as Ethan Mordden, a ruminator on popular culture, wittily points out in an *American Heritage* article — a crazy jumble of styles that range widely from Middle European operetta ("You Did It") to English music hall ("With a Little Bit of Luck," "Get me to the Church on Time") to a sort of updated Gilbert and Sullivan ("Why Can't the English?") to contemporary Broadway ("Wouldn't It Be Loverly?") while "taking in stopovers in inappropriate Latin rhythm, the habanera ("The Rain in Spain") and enraged jota ("Show Me"). Rex Harrison who plays Henry Higgins, a phoneticist, had a devil of a time at the beginning of the pre-Broadway tryouts trying literally to sing the six numbers required of him, which he frankly could not — in fact in Boston he flatly quit, walked off, but was talked out of it — until he saw, discovered happily, that he did not *need* to sing. The parlando fit his character's exasperation perfectly for the half-score built around him. "He is a leading man of a kind no musical had yet featured, cantankerous, loveless, and uninterested in anyone," notes Mordden insightfully. "He is Shaw himself."

Many of those old English music hall songs involved something like parlando — a bi' of tawk, y'know? "My Old Dutch," "Knocked 'Em in the Old Kent Road," "Two Lovely Black Eyes," "The Ratcatcher's Daughter," "A Little Bit of Cucumber," "I've Danced with a Man Who Danced with a Girl Who Danced with the Prince of Wales," "The Spaniard That Blighted My Life," "On Mother Kelly's Doorstep," and so on. Brilliant, as well as the great singers who sang them:

Marie Lloyd, Billy Merson, Charles Coburn, Ella Retford, Florrie Ford, Harry Champion, Vesta Victoria, *et alii.*

Other than quibbles, one of course has little or nothing to complain about with the masterpiece, *My Fair Lady.* I daresay, one cannot say the same thing about the state of the movie musical this last quarter decade which is in a state of musicological enantiodromia, with weak books, thin music, bad lyrics. A quick sampling of some from the recent past, *Popeye* (1980), *Yentl* (1983), *The Wiz* (1978), *Sister Act* (1992), *Hedwig and the Angry Inch* (2001), *Rent* (2005), *Mamma Mia* (2008) reflects a significant dearth of quality. Just for comparison, consider the music alone from *Rose of Washington Square* (1939). The soundtrack — of just one musical! — is an explosion of unparalleled songs: "Smiles," "My Man," "California, Here I Come," "The Vamp," "Mother Machree," "I'm Just Wild About Harry," "My Mammy," "Ja Da," "I'll See You in My Dreams," "The Japanese Sandman," "I'm Always Chasing Rainbows," "Rock-a-Bye Your Baby with a Dixie Melody," "The Curse of an Aching Heart," "Pretty Baby," "I Never Knew Home Could Speak," "Yaaka Hula Hickey Dula (Hawaiian Love Song)," "Toot Toot Tootsie, Goodbye," and "Shine On, Harvest Moon." So long ago, yet even today it sweeps away even potential opposition like a river in spate.

What about "A seasoned witch could call you from the depths of your disgrace/ and rearrange your liver to the solid mental grace" from Yes' "Close to the Edge"? And are not the lyrics to the often completely out-of-control Elton John's almost inadmissibly pathetic "Philadelphia Freedom" total gibberish? To say nothing of the lyrics to his song "Rocket Man": "Mars ain't the kind of place to raise your kids/ In fact it's cold as hell/ and there's no one there to raise them if you did"? If you did *what*? Raise kids on Mars? You mean someone planned to? Like a couple, um, who thought someone *did* live there? Whose kids are we talking about anyway? I see the song as a biune study of homosexual cowardice and impotence:

> I'm not the man they think I am at home
> Oh no, no, no, I'm a rocket man
> Rocket man burning out his fuse up here alone.

The Beach Boys sing in "Good Vibrations," "She took me there/ but I don't know where." Meaning precisely what? As to spatial half-wittedness, there is an actual album put out by the Rossington-Collins Band, an offshoot of the Lynyrd Skynyrd group, titled *Anytime, Anyplace, Anywhere.* What is the difference between "anywhere" and "anyplace"? The Who made a similar mistake in their song

"Anyway, Anyhow, Anytime." "Anytime, Anyplace, Anywhere" was a 1950 single by Joe Morris and His Orchestra, then the Monkees recorded a song by the same name, an "original" composition that debuted on *The Best of the Monkees*, and it was later a bilingual pop hit for Nena and Kim Wilde — together at last! — as well as a track by grebo band Carter the Unstoppable Sex Machine. (Lest we forget, it was also the tag-line for Martini in their 1980s advertisements.) I am sure they meant something like, "Anywhere, Anytime, Anyhow." Are you aware in the classic pop-song "Rhythm of the Rain," that in all the wooly imagery of that song the rain as an entity is not only considered to be background music but in what seems to be no end of changing morphs — good, bad, and indifferent — is called upon, consulted as an oracle, solicited as a go-between, pursued as an arbiter, and banished all at the same time? I have to say it is still a great song. Then, what image is Roy Orbison calling in "Blue Bayou" when he sings of "those fishing boats/ with their sails afloat"? Or ABBA (remember "Since many years I haven't seen a rifle in your hand"?) whose lyrics in one song actually sound like a translation from Yupik:

> The Judges will decide
> The likes of me abide
> Spectators of the show
> Always laying low[?]

Or take the atrocious Helen Reddy, who sang in the mandrill-shrill "I Am Woman," "hear me roar/ in numbers too big to ignore," a song — one of life's unbearable ones — that tried so hard to be an anthem. What a voice! "A virtusio!" [sic] as Jimmy Durante exclaimed in the 1944 film *Music for Millions*. "A musical virtusio!" Never mind why, exactly how does *one* woman roar in *numbers*? I can still recall the ugly, monochromatic, Creamsicle-colored LP that this song appeared on, one I always thought cadaverously apt, as unaesthetically part of the 1970s as lemon-colored dishwashers, shag-pile carpets, the Atari 2600, Engelbert Humperdinck, *Touch Me: The Poems of Suzanne Somers* ("I wore my green sweater today — and smiled"), pet rocks, mood rings, *The Whole Earth Catalogue*, clogs, Soul Train, or TSOP (those eyeglasses, those shoes, those fabrics, the "floods"!), a new big tidal wave of feminism, sideburns, the catlap-colored décor of psychiatrist Bob Newhart's television office (pickle-green divans, orange rugs, mustard curtains, and Bob wearing rust-dark trousers, back-belted leisure jackets with breast pockets, and wide neckties with all sorts of whorled and floral-patterns that looked like he had been eating Reuben sandwiches and been dribbling Thousand Island dressing all over them), Brut cologne, Danskin leotards, zippered jumpsuits, and (eeek!) TV's *The Carol Burnett Show*. I suspect after reading several interviews she gave to prove her sexual-political bonafides back there in the 1970s that Reddy was ready to trundle off to the blissful world of Charlotte Perkins Gilman's *Herland*, a utopian refuge inhabited only by women who reproduce parthenogenetically. (Do you find that absurd? In her hysterical polemic *Of Woman Born* (1976) Adrienne Rich's deeply aggrieved, man-hating book on mothering — one in which she notes with witchy and frankly insane regret, "I never read a child-rearing manual ... that raised the question of infanticide" — Rich more or less concludes that such a thing is distinctly possible.) Winning a Grammy Award for Best Female Pop Vocal Performance for "I Am Woman," Reddy in a conniption of bile managed to get a last savage boot in against men by famously thanking God "because *She* makes everything possible." *Così fan tutte.* Just for the record, allow me to add this: "I owe nothing to women's lib," declared serene Mrs. Margaret Thatcher, England's Prime Minister in 1982, and she never, in theory, rejected the idea that a woman's place is in the home.

Don Henley's song "The End of the Innocence," in my opinion, one rough, gritty, and abrasive monotonic quiddity, is all disordered imagery — it is made more outlandish by his voice which has this "white sound," brittle and pale. Take the bizarre line, "Lay yourself all on the ground/ Let your hair spread all around me." *Who's on top?* Or is this simply a question of someone following James Taylor's dialectically imprecise exhortation: "Shower the people you love with love/ show them the way that you feel"? Is this the kind of stuff William Congreve had in mind when he wrote the often-misquoted line, "Music hath charms to soothe the savage breast, to soften rocks or bend a knotted oak"? My savage breast is *not soothed* with this music! So show me the soft rocks! The bent oaks!

How can Grand Funk Railroad in its version of the "Locomotion" manage to sing an entire song *off key*? Were Cream hoping to be charming or anatomically precise in "Tales of Brave Ulysses" when they sang of "Carving deep blue ripples in the tissues of your mind"? In "You Belong to Me," what image are we supposed to have when Carly Simon refers to "the book of the door"? In the song "Wild is the Wind," Johnny Mathis sings the phrase "satisfy the hungriness" [sic] — not a word — instead of the "hunger." Isn't one of the many odd lines, "if the viewer cannot understand it," in Eric Burdon and the Animals' "San Franciscan Nights" totally meaningless? "You're walking along the street, or you're at a party," wrote hack-songwriter Steve Allen in "This Could Be the Start of Something Big," "Or else you're alone and then you suddenly dig." *Dig?* Come again? The implication is that you all of a sudden come to a stop, but is it too much to ask *why?* In the Mills Brothers' hit, "Paper Doll," written by Johnny S. Black, a paradox looms, for the speaker says he is "gonna buy a paper doll that I can call my own/ a doll that other fellows cannot steal," then in the third stanza he queerly confesses that he himself has been no more loyal than the girls he has loved: "I guess I had a million dolls or more/ I guess I've played the doll game o'er and o'er." (For their unrivaled harmony, I forgive the smooth Mills Brothers just about anything.) What exactly did Gordon Lightfoot mean in his caterwauling song, "The Wreck of the Edmund Fitzgerald," when he lamely wrote, "as big freighters go/ she was bigger than most"? I will concede that a bigger freighter is definitely bigger than a big freighter, but exactly how big do big freighters in fact go? I have to confess I am still bothered by the badly contrived inversion, "wondering where has some guy gone," in the song "Many A New Day" from *Oklahoma!* While we are on the subject of stupidity, in her hit, "How Much Is That Doggy in the Window?" Patti Page repeatedly sings, instead of "I do hope that doggy's for sale," "I do hope that doggy *is* for sale," utterly ruining the song's basic rhythm.

What about the neologism "lustations" as used in the Osmonds' fatuous 1973 album *The Plan*, with its apocalyptic songs condemning the vice of — or wanton, unhindered passion in — the act of divorce? "Lustations breaking family relations!" No such word exists. Needless to say, that in and of itself is not a fault if it serves originality and style, but here it indicates nothing but pointless oddity and frankly laziness. Writing "Just One of Those Things," Cole Porter spent days poring through thesauruses and dictionaries looking for the correct adjective to go with "wings" until a friend suggested a word that probably had never appeared in a popular song, "gossamer." It is the true artist who with patience waits for the correct, the exact word. Fussiness matters. Porter also self-consciously wrote as many as six versions of "Rosalie" for the 1937 film extravaganza of the same name before L.B. Mayer who, dissatisfied with all of his previous attempts, told him to forget that he was writing for the big star, Nelson Eddy, and to "go home and write a honky-tonk song." Although the final, simple version became a memorable hit, Porter for decades claimed that he disliked the song and insisted that all the previous versions that Mayer had thrown out were much better.

I have always laughed at the grotesque hyperbole of the line — surely satire was not in Andrew Lloyd Webber's mind when he wrote it — from the "Music of the Night" in *The Phantom of the Opera* when the singer pleads,

> Anywhere you go, let me go, too —
> Love me, that's all I ask of you

*All I ask*? To demand love and *a lifetime of attention* and insisting on one's company? I'd call that quite a commitment, my darling, my dear! In Pat Boone's "Moody River," the male singer laments, "Your muddy water took my baby's life," but does she drown — "I saw a lovely face/ Just looking back at me" we hear — or has she shot herself? Inexplicably, there is blood! And — get this — the corpse is also a male! Remember the 1979 solo album of Ian Hunter, of Mott the Hoople fame, *You're Never Alone with a Schizophrenic?* Is it belaboring the point to say that you are never alone when you are with *anyone*? What the obnubilated Mr. Hunter surely had in mind was the old sophomoric — and tired — joke, like "You're never alone when you are schizophrenic."

What's going on? Carly Simon in "You're So Vain" misuses the word "gavotte," a 16th century French peasant dance for groups and not at all suitable to her nemesis boyfriend in that song. It all recalls for me — the illogic, the non-sequiturs, the talking-past-the-listener, the stupid lines, the inane palaver, etc. — of the movie *Mister Buddwing* (1966), starring Katharine Ross, Suzanne Pleshette, Jean Simmons, and James Garner, the man whose head is shaped like a perfect block, one of the dumbest movies ever made.

But it has plenty of company.

In director Brian De Palma's trashy *Scarface* (1983) we find featured in Oliver Stone's screenplay a record-breaking 226 uses of the word *fuck* and its many variants — one every 1.33 minutes of the movie's 170-minute running time. "Fuck Gaspar Gomez! And fuck the fuckin' Diaz brothers! Fuck 'em all! I bury those cockroaches!" "I told you a long time ago, you fucking little monkey, not to fuck me!" "You fuck with me, you fuck with the best!" Aphex Twin's "Windowlicker" is a veritable waterfall of profanity. It is actually an instrumental track: the deliberately excessive "gangsta" dialogue at the beginning of the video — the 127 examples of cursing in the hair-raising dialogue segment includes 44 uses of the word fuck which is an average of more than one imprecation every two seconds, no small feat since it is only four minutes long — was added just in case the listener/viewer was unaware that the song is in fact a critique by Richard D. James of the brutal banality of modern hip-hop music. (It was a nominated for the Best Video award at the BRIT Awards 2000!) The f-word is repeated in Martin Scorsese's film, *Casino* (1997) in one form or another about 400 times, a figure surpassed in the film *Nil by Mouth* (1997), Gary Oldman's debut as a writer and director, where the word is used as often as 428 times — roughly about 3.75 occurrences per minute. (The title is taken from the medical instruction that a patient must not take food or water, but it obviously I does not apply to a compulsion for cursing.) But where is the art — the style? All these hipsters, incidentally. use the f-word as a verb, a noun, an adjective, standard fare. Why is it that no one ever ingeniously uses it as a conjunctive adverb? "I was determined not to confront her; fuck, I turned around and walked right back."

I have to say I almost prefer it to the priapic yammerings of the dim, sexless fuckstick in *The Rachel Papers* — the novel is worse than the film and the film sucks — in which author Martin Amis, sending his protagonist through the book on drawn-out mousehunts to get laid, chooses to discuss phlegm, spunk, smegma, etc. also serves up all sorts of gynecological twaddle ("Erections, as we all know, come to the teenager on a plate") including this loud trainwreck of a sentence: "Snatches that yo-yo between their knees, breasts so flaccid you could tie them in a knot. One would have to be literally galvanized on Spanish Fly even to consider it." *Snatches? Between their knees? Galvanized? On Spanish fly?*

Ours is a different age. The world is upside-down. Rules no longer apply. Just look around. The Olympic Games, organized to be wholly amateur in nature, with not even a façade of honor anymore is now dominated by professional athletes. PBS, utterly rotten with corruption, now runs commercials, sometimes as many as three or four in a row, while not only denying it but, while collecting those fees, also taking government money — or fiscal year 2012 its appropriation was more than $465 million — while squeezing every watcher and listener during fund-raising marathons to pony up. Taxpayer funding Big Bird! NPR salaries are way out of line, by the way, and I think if most people knew just how excessive, there might not be a revolution but contributions would stop upon the instant. It has to be the biggest scam in the nation. Among the highest paid – almost as much as the President of the United States himself ($400,000) and much more than the Vice-President, the Speaker of the House, the Chief Justice of the Supreme Court, as well as every Senator and U.S. Representative — are Robert Siegel of *All Things Considered* who receives $350,288; Renee Montagne and Steve Inskeep of *Morning Edition* who receive respectively $332,160 and $331,242, and Scott Simon of *Weekend Edition* whose annual Christmas Show we have discussed with inexpressible delight, earns a salary of $300,648 a year and defends the excess of it quite gleefully, saying, "I am grateful for the salary that I earn and feel that it is merited by the popularity of our program, the audience our show generates, the number of interviews, essays, and reported pieces that I do, and whatever value I have to NPR that may contribute to our relationship with the public."

I am neither competent to go deeply into, nor frankly interested enough to plumb, the often quaquaversal lyrics of heavy metal or thrash or punk. The Addicts, the Misfits, the Sex Pistols, the Dead Kennedys, the Ramones, the Clash, the Circlejerks, the Stooges, the Buzzcocks, Suicide, the New York Dolls, and other punk bands like Rancid and NOFX passed me by, for the most part, although I have listened a lot to the Clash. I was teaching the poetry of John Milton to students at Harvard and, in what spare time I had, trying to write my second novel, *Darconville's Cat*, during that period when the Cramps were singing "Bikini Girls with Guns" and the memorable "Queen of Pain" — "Wha choo gone do with that cane?" — and Iggy Pop and the Stooges were howling with "Tight Pants" and "Kill City" and "Your Pretty Face is Going to Hell." I confess that I'm a little too late and too old truly to "grok" contemporary rock groups like Coldplay or Linkin Park or Secret Chiefs 3 (or SC3), the instrumental rock group led by guitarist/ composer Trey Spruance (formerly of groups Mr. Bungle and Faith No More) that performs such a wide range of musical styles — usually multiple guitars wailing and manic drums beating but often with bouzoukis and sitars and such — including surf rock, film music, Persian, Arab, Indian, death metal, electronic music, and various others styles. As to punk, I can say that I have always found the Fall fairly intriguing, that British post-punk band whose music has been well described by rock critic Steve Huey as "abstract poetry filled with complicated word-play, bone-dry wit, cutting social observations, and general misanthropy." The band's enigmatic leader, Mark E. Smith, who hails from Lancashire, England but looks like a futuroidal — he often contrives to make his words impossible to hear correctly — has cut with many different members, almost 30 albums with little success beyond a handful of minor hit singles in the late 1980s, although they have maintained a strong cult following and prefigured groups like the Meat Puppets, Sonic Youth, and Captain Beefheart and the Magic Band. Back in the late 1980s and early 1990s, if we got our class business out of the way a bit early, I would engage in probing musical discussions with some of my undergraduate students at Yale, bright and engaged, dark and brooding doomsters, not quite "chop-your-white-breakfast-on-a-mirror" devotees but many of them lovers of punk, and sometimes after class, I would play them records I brought in like "The Guns of Brixton" by the Clash and the Inspiral Carpets' "Please Be Cruel" and various songs of the Fall's such as "How I Wrote Elastic Man," "Lie Dream of a Casino Soul," "The Man Whose Head Expanded," and cuts from *The Frenz Experiment* LP. The Fall are angry, punkified, and Smith can rapidly go into cuckoo snapping-turtle-like rants, but the group has always been the real thing and can really rock, with songs that have tremendous drive, with double-drums, *thump*, and are often lyrically absurd and Dadaesque — usually about drug use, unemployment, football violence, time travel, and the supernatural. You can at times hear Smith, a short, pale, chain-smoking genre-bender barking, keening crazily, simulating growls, and descending into loud incantations and recitations which make no pretense at singing at all. "Smith hocks his lyrics over the music, generally without the crutch of melody," wrote Sasha Frere-Jones in his *New Yorker* article "Plug and Play," observing that Smith's enigmatic contribution to rock lyrics "has been to liberate them from the need to make sense." To hear "Perverted by Language" (Parts 1, 2, and 3), "Totally Wired," or "Villette Sonique" — among my favorites — might give you no idea that the shy, highly literate Smith is a reader of Malcolm Lowry, Raymond Chandler, and Albert Camus, whose 1956 novel is the source of his group's name, but experiment and ass-kicking bravado is part of their genius. "To love the Fall is to love something that you can never explain, since there is rarely anything as coherent as a topic in a Fall song," adds Jones. "There's no better way to seduce someone than being impenetrable."

But no, I bailed when it came to chthonian metalspeak involving, from what I could see, guttural "death growls," high-pitched screaming, "death rasps," and aggressive vocal styles that went with down-tuned, distorted guitars and extremely fast percussion, often with rapid double-bass drumming and "wall of sound"-style blasts. At a talk in Pasadena in 1989, the prolific novelist Stephen King proudly confessed to an entire auditorium full of his fans that as a writer — "turning up the music loud" — he often listened to AC/DC and Judas Priest while he wrote. He went on to say, "I've [also] discovered new guys like Metallica and Anthrax — nobody comes near when those guys are playing." It must be a real electrical thrill to be writing serious fiction to the high decibel sounds of howling grindcore, blaring horns and drums of guys wearing corpsepaint! I still hear the whanging of my students' voices singing out incongruously across the purlieus of Jonathan Edwards and Saybrook the lyrics from "Damage, Inc," the last good song before Metallica took a distinct downturn:

> Damage jackals ripping right through you
> Sight and smell of this, it gets me goin'
> Know just how to get just what we want
> Tear it from your soul in nightly hunt

But we all know that Stephen King likes to tap into the zeitgeist. Allusions to rock and pop music — songs sung and hummed and piped in — positively fill the pages of King's many novels. I am certain any one of a number of loony Stephen King "completists" can tick off just what songs appear in *Christine* — I know that the dirge-sounding "Pledging my Love" by the late, great

Johnny Ace (suicide, Russian roulette, 1954) is one — or in *Pet Sematary*, like the nutball scene where the trucker is barreling down the road towards Gage, singing along to the Ramones' "Sheena is a Punk Rocker." I had to watch this detestable movie crossing the country by plane one day after leaving my book in the terminal. The music to the film *Stand By Me*, I recall, is a sound-track of oldies. *The Stand. The Dead Zone. Needful Things. Gerald's Game.* It is a virtual compendium of old rock 'n' roll. Isn't the last line uttered in the movie *Christine*, "God, I hate rock-and-roll"?

Songs in a sense are confessions. I have always thought that the anthem "America the Beautiful" had, as an undisclosed psychological sub-text, Katharine Lee Bates's desire to be married — and by extension to get pregnant. Bates never wed. She was a plain, unprepossessing girl growing up in Falmouth, MA, not just plump but overweight, badly near-sighted, "awkward in movement," according to the college historian at Wellesley College, where, a spinster, she taught for forty years in the English department. In 1888, seven years before the first publication of her famous poem — in *The Congregationalist* on July 4, 1895 — another Boston journal, *The Parish Choir*, published the stately melody from a hymn composed by one Samuel Augustus Ward (1847-1903) of Newark, New Jersey that was entitled "O Mother Dear Jerusalem." When somebody or other noticed that the opening lines of Bates's poem, "O beautiful for spacious skies," perfectly rhymed with the title of Ward's hymn, both words and music were immediately slapped together like ham and rye, and Professor Bates went down in musical history, getting all the glory, for the entire composition, the one thing in life that she is known for, despite the fact that she wrote six volumes of verse, travel books, and text books. It is noteworthy that Bates, having inspiredly stared out across the vast land below her from the 14,000 foot height of Pike's Peak in Colorado in the summer of 1893, always claimed that the rich lyrics of the poem — written at age 34 — "floated" into her mind. A minister's daughter, she was fatherless early and, as I say, never married. It is entirely possible we find her yearning for personal fulfillment on some level in her lyrics, although we are told she did live happily for twenty-five years with her close friend, one Katharine Coman, a history and political-economy teacher at Wellesley until Coman's death in 1915.

I believe that Bates, surveying "the sea-like expanse of this fertile country" — her words — perhaps felt a throb of maternity. The poem is a strong paean to fecundity. One hears of "spacious" skies, "waves of grain," a land where "purple mountain majesties above the fruited plain," the exordium that God "crown thy hood with brotherhood." In the original versification there are four verses to Bates's apostrophic poem with repeated images of teeming, fertility, and abundance, all hearkening to "achievement" and the attainment of "precious life," "undimmed by human tears." Wish fulfillment! (I have always taken it to be as matter of common insight to any thinking person that *Who's Afraid of Virginia Woolf?* (1966) was homosexual playwright Edward Albee's unsubtle confession not so much that all families are basically neurotic, childless or not — to my mind, the central gay subject, in whatever genre — but, defined by his own sexuality, that he himself is sterile.)

Incidentally, the first draft of "America the Beautiful" was jotted down in a notebook during the summer of 1893 rather *hastily.* "We hired a prairie wagon. Near the top we had to leave the wagon and go the rest of the way on mules," she noted on one of her pages. "I was very tired." Bates was unattended when she scribbed down the now memorable lines. A word about her sensibility, recalling for the reader, again, that she was for almost half a century a professor of English literature at a major college and surely would have taught and/or should have known *The Merchant of Venice* and admired Portia, who was characteristically insightful when she pointed out to Nerissa

> The crow doth sing as sweetly as the lark
> When neither is attended

Few people realize that the crow can sing at all. Surprisingly, it has a small musical warble which it utters when it finds itself "unattended." James Russell Lowell lends credence to this notable fact when he writes in "My Garden Acquaintance:" "Yet there are few things more melodious than his caw of a clear winter morning as it drops to you filtered through five hundred fathoms of crisp blue air." Ironically, the prolific Katharine Lee Bates at one point in life actually sat down and wrote a sonnet which she titled, "To a Crow," yet in the end she heard little but its "hoarse curses." It goes in part:

> How often, when the wild March mornings broke,
> Have I descried thee, like a demon priest,
> Heaping hoarse curses on the riotous East
> From the bare branches of some tossing oak!

Why does Al Martino idiotically flatter the lovely woman in his song "*Spanish* Eyes" by telling us she has the "prettiest eyes in *all of Mex-ee-co*" [my italics]? Isn't the line, "I need you/ like the winter needs the Spring" in America's abysmal song "I Need You," a climatological moronism? When Joan Baez in her hit "The Night They Drove Old Dixie Down" sings the lyrics, "Till *so much cavalry came/ and tore up the tracks again*," was she serious? By what privilege are such gaffes allowed to go uncriticized? In Frank Sinatra's "Love's Been Good To Me," is the line *"still and all* I'm happy" a mistranslation perhaps of some odd language other than English? Does it all matter, you may ask. Should I care? Can it matter, for instance, in a sub-genre where girls in songs have names like Be Bop A Lula, Bony Moronie, and Rama Lama Ding Dong? They are actually names of *women!* Are you surprised to know that? Do you realize that *Trout Fishing in America*, the title of one of Richard Brautigan's novels, is also a person's *name?* So is the name Sloopy the name of a girl, as in the Yardbirds's song, "Hang On, Sloopy." Such a thing in songs is not new. It goes back to the '40s or even earlier, not only with the name Poinciana — how about Ciribirribim? That indeed is someone's name. Listen closely to hear when Jeanette McDonald in her vocal of this Harry James instrumental hit passionately cries out to Ciribirribim, "Kiss me again!" Speaking of names in songs, were you aware that Frenesi is also a girl's name? (Don't doubt me. I know almost every song ever written, as Marlon Brando's mother supposedly did.) So is the floral name, Amapola ("my pretty little poppy"). I discovered that even the names of dances proved to be the names of women. Take the song "Misirlou," for example. It is a girl's name. ("Heaven will guide us/ Allah will bless our love/ ah, ah Misirlou".) Remember the song "Malagueña"? Precisely, it is the name of a woman.

> My malagueña your eyes
> shamed the purple sky...
> You were as fair as I
> dreamed you would be"
> *Malagueña ojo ne gros*
> *Malagueña de mis sue nos*

Aaaaand, believe it or not, so is the name Macarena! It was an international dance-craze during the summer of 1996, a sort of PG-13-rated Hokey Pokey or Mexican Hat Dance or Bunny Hop, a driving upbeat rhumbitita, danced with all kinds of geometric and gymnastic gyrations, a song about a love-sick temptress named — you got it — Macarena! The song was originally popularized in 1993 by Antonio Romero Monge and Rafael Ruiz, a Spanish duo from Seville called Los Del Rio. Two years later, it was popularized here by the Bayside Boys of Miami when in 1995 RCA came out with their hit single.

As to lyrical nonsense, I have always wondered why in "The Sloop John B" a young man goes fighting and drinking all night in Nassau Town with his, like, you know, *grandfather*? And do you remember that long, somber, underinspired, greeting-card-like narrative in the Righteous Brothers' "You're My Soul and My Heart's Inspiration"? The two guys in all seriousness sing, "You're my reason for laughing and for crying, for living and for dying." What was that? *You're my reason for dying?* Right, that's the way it goes. *Ipse dixit.* Now I call that real romantic, don't you? Talk about taking the gloss off the gingerbread. Whenever I hear such lyrics my desperate thoughts fly in spirit for some kind of comfort and deliverance to the Westchester Hills Cemetery in Hastings-on-Hudson, N.Y. where the Gershwin brothers are buried. Who would deny that stupidity is homely? Ugly. Disfiguring, even. I have to confess that I could never honestly take the actor John Garfield seriously again when, after Lilli Palmer in *Body and Soul* (1947) recites a poem of William Blake's, he dopily asks, "What's symmetry?" Forgive me, but how deficient can you get? That was in a *movie* — what about real life? After hearing that Gary Cooper never a read a book in his entire life, I could never watch one of his movies again without thinking of him as a footstool. I also excommunicated Diana Vreeland after reading in her autobiography, her remark, "Actually I can't stand novels — I don't care what happens to people on paper."

By the way, I believe that we have John Garfield to thank, that's right, ignorant Jacob Garfinkle from Rivington Street on Manhattan's Lower East Side, for popularizing the ugly fashion on film — was it first seen in *The Postman Always Rings Twice?* — that became the repellent anti-sartorial trend in the classless 2000s, unabashedly worn that way on television and even formal events, where men appear wearing suits with open dress shirts and no neckties, the "formal" attire of the Israeli Knesset, making even the terrorist brute, fat Ariel Sharon, look like a miniature golfer in Marco Island, Florida. A worried Vreeland once stated, "Unshined shoes are the end of civilization." What about men appearing nowadays in formal occasions wearing full suits and dress-shirts but completely tie-less?

Clear the way for the Ostrogoths.

Speaking of anti-romantic, I doubt that there will be anything but unanimous agreement that the Annual Anaphrodisiac Award should go to Jethro Tull for the ingenious and inspired lines in their aptly-named song "Thick as a Brick" that go "Let me make you a present of song as/ The wise man breaks wind and is gone while/ The tool with the hour-glass is cooking his goose." How far have we progressed these days? "I was thinking the other day if could write a nice song about the word *fuck*," confessed visionary Dave Matthews of the Dave Matthews Band in *Rolling Stone* (Jan. 22, 2004).

> It's such a great word, and such an ancient [sic] word. Ryan Adams and Liz Phair are good at putting *fuck* into songs. It's so beautiful and conversational. You need a certain kind of confidence. I don't think I have cool.

What an aesthetic insight! Matthews has obviously taken to heart, regarding "putting the word fuck into songs," what the passionate if the demonstrably less-than-literate Diana Ross left us in her hit "Don't Hurry Love" when she sings, "These precious words keeps [sic] me hanging on"!

There are of course many ironic popular lyrics, we should understand, parodies, cool commentary, often, on love-lyrics that are intentionally served up. Like the great song of paradox, "My Funny Valentine," the Rodgers and Hart classic in which a woman (gender is made clear in the song) expresses her irrational but insistent love for a poor nebbish who is all at once not only "unphotographable," a goofball with "laughable" looks, and shapeless ("is your figure less than Greek?"), but amazingly is also stupid and has a weak mouth ("when you open it to speak, are you smart?")" But "stay, little valentine, stay," her devotee begs. I guess it only goes to show that there is indeed hope for us all. The Turtles' song "Happy Together" is another good example. "So happy together/ How is the weather" is a splendidly ironic line, conjoining joy and boredom in a handful of words. A short while after that, the Turtles had a minor hit with a song, "Elenore," which had the wonderful chorus:

> Elenore, gee, I think you're swell
> And you really do me well
> You are my pride and joy *et cetera*

Those last two words could only come from people who are aware of what they are doing and spoofing the whole idea of pop lyrics. (Their later career as Flo & Eddie support this; these guys were parodying the sillier aspects of rock 'n' roll before anyone could spell parody.) And then there is that scintillating line in the Rolling Stones' "Angie," where after six verses of the singer telling Angie that he is sorry he has to leave her, he exudes, "Angie, oh Angie, ain't it great to be alive?" This, to a background of desolate minor chords. No, I'm not asking for High Seriousness. Nor am I asking for classicism, symmetry, or the Aristotelian "unities." I am simply talking about the application of thought. I open a copy of Wallace Stevens's magical *The Palm at the End of the Mind* and read:

The weather and the giant of the weather,
Say the weather, the weather, the mere air,
An abstraction blooded, as a man by thought.

*Intent* is so important — and intent involves thought being brought to a lyric, what the craft is all about. As William Gass notes in his essay "Finding a Form"

> …every mark on a page, apart from its inherent visual interest, is playing its part in the construction of a verbal consciousness, and that means commas must become concepts, pauses need to be performed, even the margins have to be sung, the lips rounded as widely as the widest vowel, round as the edges of a world. Oh as in "oral." For that's where every good idea should be found, melting like a chocolate in the curl of the tongue, against the roof of the mouth.

I look at the genius in particular songs, ponder the geometric trim of certain lyrics, and of the best of them can only marvel. A perfect example that comes immediately to mind is Jay Livingston and Ray Evans' lovely "To Each His Own" with its inspired

Two lips must insist
On two more to be kissed
Or you'll never know what love can do

or Meredith Willson's

There were bells all around
But I never heard them ringing
No, I never heard them
At all
Till there was you

or Lennon and McCartney's

I want her everywhere
And if she's beside me
I know I need never care,
but to love her is to meet her everywhere,

knowing that love is to share,
each one believing that love never dies,
watching her eyes and hoping
I'm always there

I am asking only for a workman's true art.

It may even legitimately even be asked whether popular music is in constant need of rebarbarization, as Max Lerner once said literature was. A case could be made, I suppose. It is the nature of pop music to be rebellious, and among its practitioners not only acceptable but even required. And while mistakes of the more pronounced sort do have (as Henry James once said of a musical comedy star) a certain cadaverous charm, one may also be driven to wonder if, um, exemptions repeated enough won't become the rule.

Take the matter of "agreement," the formal correspondence in grammar of one word to another, the failure of which is a constant trap-fall in popular songs, ranging all the way from the line, "I knew we *was* fallin' in love" in Manfred Mann's "Doo Wah Diddy" to the Beatles' "The long and winding road/ *They'll* never disappear" — it shows how in a lovely song pluses always fight with minuses — to Sting's "If you love *somebody*/ Set *them* free" in "Dream of the Blue Turtles." (It is a convention to mock Marilyn Monroe as a ditzoid, but in the 1969 musical comedy, *Let's Make Love*, she never fails to use correct agreement, such as "Every*one* takes *his* time," etc.) The endearing but illiterate dip in the road heard in the 1961 hit of the semi-cretinous Little Caesar and the Romans,

Those oldies but goodies
*Reminds* [sic] me of you...

is lovingly repeated — listen closely — *five times*, plus choral repetitions, during the course of a three minute song, chanted over and over again like Euripides among the folk of Abdera. "Come writers and critics," sings Bob Dylan, "who prophecie*s* [sic] with your pen." [sic] "I'm Archie Bell and the Drells," sings Archie Bell *of* the Drells in the song "Tighten Up," where he blithely proceeds to ignore in the song the very advice that he offers in the title! Frank Sinatra in his hit "Young at Heart" sings the line, "You *had* a headstart, if you *are* among the very young at heart." It should be a combination of either "have/ are" or "had/ were," however, to be correct. In Jimi Hendrix's song "Castles Made of Sand," from his 1968 album *Axis: Bold As Love*, the first verse ends, "And so castles made of sand fall into the sea, eventually," but, you got it, the second and third verses end,

And so castles made of sand
melts into the sea, eventually…
And so castles made of sand
slips into the sea, eventually

As we saw, the Beatles are not immune from this kind of mistake — which not only shows up in print, by the way, in the collection *The Compleat Beatles*, but was repeated when Procol Harum covered the song on their last album *Procul's Ninth* (1975) — where they also proceed to sing:

Eight days a week, I love you,
Eight days a week is [sic] not enough to show I care

The Beatles'' song "Night Before" refers to several different periods of time with little coherency or consistency, if any. And speaking of repetition, the thuddingly ungrammatical line

Life can never be
Exactly like we want it to be

not only appeared in the song "Dedicated to the One I Love" by the Five Royales in 1958 but was sung the same way by the Shirelles in 1961, and the error was repeated by the Mamas and the Papas in 1967. I can assure you that there is no end to these examples, they're growing by the day, but as Joyce's Molly Bloom declares, "My patience are exhausted."

There have been so many geniuses. Jack Lawrence. Sammy Kahn. Jule Styne, Hoagy Carmichael, Jimmy Van Heusen, Johnny Mercer, Hank Williams — "Your Cheatin' Heart," "I'm so Lonesome I Could Cry," "Jambalaya," "Hey, Gook Lookin'" — Harry Warren, who had more songs on the Hit Parade ("Lullaby of Broadway," "You'll Never Know," "I Found a Million Dollar Baby," and, with Mack Gordon, the sublime "There Will Never Be Another You") than Irving Berlin, Jerome Kern ("All the Things You Are," "Smoke Gets in Your Eyes," "Ol' Man River," "A Fine Romance," "The Way You Look Tonight," "Long Ago [and Far Away])," George M. Cohan ("Mary," "Over There," "Yankee Doodle Dandy," "You're a Grand Old Flag") Lennon and McCartney ("Girl," "Please Don't Wear Red Tonight," "The Long and Winding Road," "In My Life," "Here Comes the Sun," "Back in the USSR," etc., David Byrne's "I Zimbra," "Life During Wartime," and "Cities," The Smiths' "I'm So Sorry" and "Wonderful

Woman," Morrissey's "Suedehead," "Trouble Loves Me," and "I Don't Mind If You Forget Me," Roger Waters and David Gilmour of Pink Floyd's "Set the Controls for the Heart of the Sun," "Echoes," "The Happiest days of Our Lives," and "Careful with That Axe, Eugene," Randy Newman's "Louisiana" and "Rider in the Rain" and "Texas Girl at the Funeral of her Father," even Sigmund Romberg around whose life Stanley Donen made a charming film, *Deep in My Heart*, starring José Ferrer who, with a surprisingly hip Helen Traubel, does a lovely turn doing the "Leg of Mutton" dance, one of the best bits in a Hollywood musical. Go back even to the olden days of Franz Lehar, Victor Herbert, again George M. Cohan, Lorenz Hart, Gus Kahn, Charles K. Harris and Shelton Brooks, Jimmie Rodgers, Oscar Hammerstien II, Frank Loesser, Jack Norworth, and the talented Von Tilzers — Gumbinski was their surname in real life — Albert ("Take Me Out to the Ball Game," "Put Your Arms Around Me Honey") and Harry ("Wait 'till the Sun Shines Nellie," "I Want A Girl (Just Like The Girl That Married Dear Old Dad"). I think of songs like "To Each His Own," words and music by Jay Livingston and Ray Evans, that just drop together in a perfect fit:

> What good is a song if the words just don't belong
> And a dream must be a dream for two

and

> Two lips must insist on two more to be kissed
> Or they'll never know what love can do.

Pretty great stuff. As Guiseppe Ungaretti wrote in his poem, "Mattina,"

> *M'illumino*
> *d'immenso.*

> I am enlightened
> By the immenseness of immensity
> [Translated by W. G.]

In the words of the old Lefties from the 1930s those songs "*say* something." There is much fiber there. But no, no, no, this is not merely about nostalgia. I would certainly put Brian Wilson and Bob Dylan up there with Jimmie Rodgers and Bob Wills. I cannot tell you how much I enjoy Fran Landesman and Tommy Wolf's rascally ballad "Spring Can Really Hang You Up" written for the 1959 show *The Nervous Set*, a deliciously ironic look at the various moods of love: "Doctors once prescribed a tonic,/ Sulfur and molasses was the dose./ Didn't help one bit./ My condition must be chronic./ Spring can really hang you up the most." I also love Andy Razaf's "Guess Who's in Town" — sung by Bobby Short in his watershed album, *Celebrating 30 Years at the Café Carylyle* — which goes in part, "Now listen to this/ We've got a date at seven/ From her first kiss/ I'll keep her busy 'til eleven/ Speaking of bliss/ who's got the keys to heaven/ Nobody but that girl of mine."

The waters of the Pierian spring keep flowing.

Still, I fear we live in parlous times in the music and lyric department. Where has Ira Gershwin gone? It is true that he did not write the lyrics to "Summertime" — that was done by DuBose Heyward himself — but think of the magical tumbles and turns and tricks of "Someone to Watch Over Me" ("Won't you tell her/ him please to put on some speed/ Follow my lead,/ oh how I need/ someone to watch over me") and "Love Walked In" ("Love walked right in and drove the shadows away/ Love walked right in and brought my sunniest day/ One magic moment, and my heart seemed to know/ That love said 'Hello!'/ Though not a word was spoken") and "I Got Plenty of Nothin'" ("I got no lock on the door/ that's no way to be/ They can steal the rug from the floor, that's OK with me/ 'Cause the things that I prize, like the stars in the skies, are all free"). Think of Ira Gershwin at his concise, inventive best, where phrasing, intelligence, insight, drama, word-play, and wit seem all displayed together, as, for instance, in the matchless "I Can't Get Started" (1936), where we hear,

> Good grief! I'm not exactly a clod!
> *Green Pastures* wanted me to play God!
> The Siamese twins I've parted,
> But I can't get started with you.

Or take his funny "Song of the Rhineland" (1945):

> Where the wine is winier
> And the Rhine is Rhinier
> And the Heinie's Heinier
> And what's yours is minier!

Or a couplet from *Bambino* (1920),

> I'll climb to your window like in da romance
> I no give a rap if I rip-a da pants.

Or his Russian in "Katinkitschka" (1931), the first retrain of which goes:

> Popitschka, Momitschka,
> Will not sleep a winkitschka,
> Thinking of Katink, Katink,
> Katink, Katink, Katinkitschka.

He was even able to spoof love songs using no lyrics at all, as in the hilarious tour de force "Blah, Blah, Blah" (1931), part of which goes (in part), "Blah, blah, blah, blah, moon,/ Blah, blah, blah, above;/ Blah, blah, blah, croon,/ Blah, blah, blah, love," etc. — a song numbering only 90 syllables, where actual words count for only 29 of them. In 1947, Frank Loesser wrote a song titled "Bloop Beep" in which the subject is about a man tossing and turning to the music of an extremely leaky faucet. It goes in part:

> Bloop, bleep,
> Bloop, beep, bloop, bleep,
> The faucet keeps a-dripping and I can't sleep.
> Bleep, bloop,
> Bleep, bloop, bleep, bloop…

Then there was the ingenious "Yah-Ta-Ta, Yah-Ta-Ta" song from 1945 (words by Johnny Burke, music by Jimmy Van Heusen), which goes,

> They say that the art of conversation has been lost
> But under present circumstances I've been double-crossed.
> When I've got my arm around you, and we're going for a walk
> Must you yah-ta-ta, yah-ta-ta, Talk, talk, talk?

That the NBC sitcom *Seinfeld* ripped this off in the 153rd episode of that show, "The Yada Yada," which aired on April 24, 1997, was bad enough, but it was nominated for an Emmy Award — and, to top that off, the Paley Center named "Yada Yada Yada" the No. 1 funniest phrase on "TV's 50 Funniest Phrases"! The boosted phrase was never credited by the show, by the network, or by the writer of that episode, Peter Mehlman. The thing is, it was just simply appropriated wholesale, not only by the Seinfeld show but earlier by comedian Lenny Bruce, among others. What is depressing, if things like this matter to you, is that if one lets enough time pass, you can steal anything.

How about the cheekiness of Cole Porter who in his song, "Why Should I Care?" gave us the memorable lyrics, "Tra, la, la / La, la, la, la, la, la, la/ Tra, la, la / la, la, la, la, la, la, la." Unpredictably, it sparkles like jewels. John Updike described the experience of reading a book of Cole Porter's song lyrics is a little like looking at an album of photographs of delicious food. "The food looks good, but the proof is in the eating," he said. Maybe it was such flights of daring and hipness and revolutionary bravado that became part of the reason Henry Ford disgustingly called jazz "Jewish jazz" and "moron music"!

On the subject of bigotry, it should be noted that in the 1945 song "The House I Live In," made famous as sung by Frank Sinatra — a so-called musical-classic tub-thumping boomists always chauvinistically point to as the outstanding shining example of the American ideal and our altruistic values — the simple line, "My neighbors black and white" was cut as being too controversial! *God bless America*!

It should be pointed out, finally, if not out of fairness then for the sake of relief, that the lyrical mode not only can be done right, but admirably — in rock 'n' roll or pop music, as well. So many of the great lyrics of those tremendous 1940s and 1950s bird groups, mainly black, the Cardinals, The Crows, The Flamingos, The Larks, The Penguins, The Ravens, The Wrens, the Orioles, the Crows, etc., were a combination of religion and ragtime, like Vachel Lindsay's poetry, described by someone as "the Gospel preached through a hot saxophone." Contravening Igor Stravinsky's insistence that only a believer could write music in religious forms, that is, masses, hymns, spiritual songs, etc., many of those old groups coming out of some dark corners could lay down some serious spiritual stuff. Sam Cooke who was fatally shot by the manager of the Hacienda Motel in Los Angeles, California, at the age of 33 — at the time, the courts ruled that Cooke was drunk and distressed — grew up in Clarksdale, Mississippi where his father, Reverend Charles Cook [sic] was a Baptist minister. He began his career singing gospel with his siblings in a group called *The Singing Children*, first became known as lead singer with the Highway QC's as a teenager. In 1950 he replaced gospel tenor R.H. Harris as lead singer of the landmark gospel group The Soul Stirrers, a group that recorded such spiritual songs as "Peace in the Valley," "How Far Am I From Canaan?," "Jesus Paid the Debt," and "One More River," among many other gospel songs.

There is no end to great songs and brilliant lyrics. Sammy Cahn's "I've Heard That Song Before," "Come Fly With me, "All the Way." Irving Berlin's "What'll I Do?" "There's No Business Like Show Business," "Puttin' on the Ritz," "Isn't this a Lovely Day." Jerome Kern's "Ol' Man River," "The Folks Who Live on the Hill," "Smoke Gets in Your Eyes," "Make Believe." Cole Porter. Harry Warren. Harold Arlen. Nacio Herb Brown. Sammy Fain. Frank Loesser's "We're the Couple in the Castle," "A Woman in Love," "What Are You Doing New Year's," "Moon of Manakoora," and the ingeniously contrapuntal duet — a form he used many times — "Baby It's Cold Outside." Hoagy Carmichael's "Two Sleepy People," "Georgia on My Mind," "Stardust, "Old Buttermilk Sky." All the songs created by Richard Rodgers and Oscar Hammerstein II for *Oklahoma! Carousel, South Pacific, The King and I, The Sound of Music*, and *State Fair.* Are you kidding me? Lorenz Hart's "There's a Small Hotel," "This Can't Be Love," "Where or When," "My Funny Valentine." Geniuses. Pure and simple. Their great names ladder like those of the venerable Apostles, carved in stone on a transept wall. The great Johnny Mercer wrote a masterpiece for Blossom Dearie with her girlish voice, a witty, hip, sophisticated song full of *jeux d'esprit* called "My New Celebrity is You" — you can find it on Daffodil Records BMD 103 — in which, amusingly, she plays "the uke with Vernon Duke so well in Dubuque that Vladimir Dukelsky said, 'Gee!'" We delightfully hear her sing,

> I dig Modigliani, Jolson doing Swanee…
> Several Maharanee are my intimates too.
> I played with Mantovani and that's
> a lot of strings to get through.

Notice how often in truly memorable songs like those mentioned above the theme or subject is about aspiration, dreaming, reaching for something, the act of yearning or mooning. There is relatively scant attention paid to hope by psychoanalysts, which concerns itself mainly with desire and its vicissitudes. That seems to be the way of the world. Sadly, we perhaps live closer to despair. Who that has read Eric Hodgins' novel *Mr. Blandings Builds His Dream House* can ever forget the last memorable line, "He was dreaming that his house was on fire." Hope is a subject for poets, romantics, idealists, visionaries with bursting hearts filled with the yet-to-be. The debt of every songwriter is to Thales of Miletis who famously fell into a well one night while he was looking at the stars!

Yet there is no formula for lyric writing. What comes first, the method or the madness? No one can say. You need the madness to conceive the idea, but require the method to record it, to set it down. The terrible freedom, exacting your talent, is the burden as well as the blessing. You shape, shave, sharpen, tweak, touch up, transpose — Irving Berlin's original song "Smile and Show Your Dimple" became out of necessity "Easter Parade" — and of course why not borrow, even from yourself? The phrase "Who could ask for anything more?" appears in three different Gershwin songs: "I Got Rhythm," "Nice Work If You Can Get It," and "I'm About to Be a Mother" from *Of Thee I Sing*. Ira Gershwin used what he had, did what he could, had what he did, used what he could. Technique is everything. Marcel Proust wrote *Du côté de chez Swann* first and *Le Temps retrouvé*, the last volume of his masterpiece, second. He then wrote the rest of the elaborate story. When the narrator Marcel in *Le Temps* declares that he is now able to start his work, he has already written it. In a way art is always nostalgic. Yearning is at the heart of it all, no? As Schubert said, there is no happy music.

Lyricist Lorenz Hart preceded Oscar Hammerstein II as a collaborator with Richard Rodgers, but the two of them, although clearly inspired and brilliant, were as different as chalk from cheese. Both were clever, literary, and loved word-play, of course, but Hart needed a melody to provoke his lyrics, while Hammerstein tended to work quite contentedly with music that was complete or close to finished. Hart with his crazy, obstacle-ridden career — always on the run, a severe and terrible depressive filled with self-loathing, disappearing for months at a time on alcoholic binges — worked for 20 years with Rodgers and wrote the lyrics to such shows as *Babes in Arms, The Boys From Syracuse, Pal Joey*, and *On Your Toes*. Hart's lyrics for the song "Falling Love with Love" characterize his pessimism. The music, one of Rodgers' sunniest, offers the lilt of a waltz, but it is set in a minor key to match Hart's lyric which, although rich with wit and word-play, is cynical — and if you really want to push it ("learning to trust is just for children in school") — frankly quite despairing.

> Falling in Love with Love is falling for make-believe!
> Falling in Love with Love is playing the fool!
> Caring too much is such a juvenile fancy!
> Learning to trust is just for children in school.
> I fell in Love with Love one night when the moon was full
> I was unwise with eyes unable to see!
> I fell in Love with Love with love ever-lasting.
> But Love fell out, with me!

Hammerstein was relatively placid and fully dependable. Hart's lyrics were complex, knowing, urban, wistful, pragmatic, bittersweet, and often full of regret:

"Glad to be Unhappy," "I Wish I Were in Love Again," "The Lady is A Tramp," "Manhattan," "My Funny Valentine," and, among others, "Where or When." On the other hand, Hammerstein's lyrics were optimistic, carefully wrought, often dreamy, deceptively simple, romantic, at times corny: "Make Believe," "People Will Say We're in Love," "Folks Who Live on the Hill," "It's A Grand Night for Singing," Bali Hai, "Some Enchanted Evening."

Imagine how transported war-torn America was upon hearing for the first-time at the opening of *Oklahoma!* on March 31, 1943 at the St. James Theatre in New York City when the incomprehensibly beautiful but simple testament to the goodness of earth, of nature, of innocence, of fertility, of gratitude came bursting forth with Rodgers/ Hammerstein's scintillating opening song "Oh What a Beautiful Morning."

> There's a bright golden haze on the meadow,
> There's a bright golden haze on the meadow,
> The corn is as high as an elephant's eye,
> An' it looks like its climbin' clear up to the sky.
>
> Chorus:
> Oh what a beautiful morning,
> Oh what a beautiful day,
> I've got a wonderful feeling,
> Everything's going my way.
> All the cattle are standing like statues,
> All the cattle are standing like statues,
> They don't turn their heads as they see me ride by.
> But a little brown mav'rick is winking her eye.

Hammerstein said that he drew his inspiration in writing the lyrics for Rodgers's unforgettable melody from Lynn Riggs's stage directions in his 1930 play *Green Grow the Lilacs*, the work (also a musical) upon which the Broadway *Oklahoma!* is based. The words were so lovely that Hammserstein thought it a pity that the audience would not get to hear them. "It is a radiant summer morning several years ago," Riggs had written, "the kind of morning which, enveloping the shapes of the earth, men, cattle in a meadow, blades of the young corn, streams — makes them seem to exist now for the first time, their images giving off a golden emanation that is partly true and partly a trick of the imagination focusing to keep alive a loveliness that may pass away." The loveliness we know did not pass away but was captured, indeed transvalued, forever by high art. (What is it about nature? Poet E.E. Cummings claimed he needed to see a tree in order to write well!)

It is by that art we are reminded everyday of its glory A song that goes straight to the heart of any music lover is of course Hoagy Carmichael's haunting masterpiece "Skylark," for which the great Johnny Mercer, inspired in a Shelley-like way and invoking his special strain of Southern romanticism, wrote the lyrics. It is a song of profound yearning, filled with phenomenological moments of mood and feeling. An earthbound soul who aches to find love, who hungers to be transported from, to rise above, the commonplace to a pleasant valley green with spring ("where my heart can go a journeying/ over the shadows and the rain/ to a blossom covered lane"), apostrophizes a bird of the sky to inquire whether from its height, at such a distance, with its soaring perspective — a creature also lonely, he feels — can lead him to love, to a resolution, to the "wonderful music of the night," asking, "Skylark,/ have you anything to say to me?/ Won't you tell me where my love can be?/ Is there a meadow in the mist,/ where someone's waiting to be kissed?"

The genius of Carmichael and Mercer is that the song creates — to echo Gerard M. Hopkins, "fathers forth" — with its heartbreaking melody and sweet lyrics, nothing less than an intense and ravishing plea for transcendence, to surpass the ordinary, to experience the kind of moment as intense as the very music as the song he himself (or she herself) sings, "faint as a will o' the wisp, crazy as a loon,/ sad as a gypsy serenading the moon." The words are golden. Faith is belief. It is prayer as much as song:

> Oh, skylark, I don't know if you can find these things
> but my heart is riding on your wings.
> So if you see them anywhere
> won't you lead me there?

Such beauty, for its wistful reach, is almost heartbreaking. The human touch of its humility in asking help as he seeks to go beyond, to rise above, normal limits, reflects a kind of knowing in and of itself, a yearning for love that invariably precedes the finding of it, a faith or at least a full certainty ("my heart is riding on your wings") that such a place — such a meadow, such a valley, such a blossom-covered lane, such a creature waiting to be kissed — indeed exists, for where else, how else, is love, true love, ever found?

A listener may experience here what Roland Barthes call "*jouissance*," that point where, on the cusp of delight, one becomes pleasantly lost, beyond even immediate impact and free from the localized moment. In a crystal-sharp moment one enters a mystical mood, close to what the philosopher William James called the "oceanic feeling" that is at the heart of a religious experience when everything comes together, oneself, everyone else, the world, and divinity, rather like the feeling that we get when we stare out at the infinite reach of the ocean: it is a little frightening, but it also awe-inspiring and exhilarating. As human beings we seem to seek out this kind of experience. You have been sought out, seduced, as it were, by an emotion looking for *you*, convinced by the music that you are *desired*. "The text you write must prove to me that it desires me. This proof exists: it is writing. Writing is: the science of the various blisses of language, its Kama Sutra (this science has but one treatise: writing itself)," wrote Ronald Barthes in *The Pleasure of the Text*.

I must say that was why when I was a kid I so loved and admired Willie Sutton who memorably confessed, "Why did I rob banks? Because I enjoyed it. I loved it. I was more alive when I was inside a bank, robbing it, than at any other time in my life. I enjoyed everything about it so much that one or two weeks later I'd be out looking for the next job. But to me the money was the chips, that's all."

An actor and storyteller as well as a songwriter, Carmichael saw deeply into the heart and perhaps more than anyone gave perfect social cadence to that role of piano player who with a sense of knowingness, a tough, tragic, artistic intelligence, the kind of worldliness from which we all suspect we can benefit, sits tinkling the keys in the dark, smoky corner of what British film-critic David Thomson describes as "life's cabaret, cool, collected and canny if talked to, picking out some back country tune that keeps slipping closer to jazz." A night attendant, Dionysius of the dark, he provides an accompaniment to our lives as we walk from one year to the next in our own drama. He is always a realist, if occasionally a romantic, offering the type of piercing insight Hoagy does in "I Get Along Without You Very Well," "with poise shuddering at its own wound" (Thomson):

> I get along without you very well,
> Of course I do.
> Except in Spring —
> But I should never think of Spring
> For that would surely break my heart in two.

It was that spirit, those insights, this lyric, along with his "lean, taut face, the horny eyes, the suave rustic voice and the absolute aplomb of just being there, doodling, noodling, coaxing some shy cat of melody out of the keys" that epitomizes the power of a music and gives the Dapper Wolf the boldness to steal the picture in *To Have and Have Not* with his "lazy stare, the bravura deadpan teasing, the looking the girls over. It's the way he eyes Lauren Bacall in [the film] after she's asked him about the song he's playing and he comes back with: 'Did you say something?'" The man was cool. "But for Carmichael, we might not have the classic Sinatra pose of the '50s, the one more for the road," notes Thomson who goes on to observe,

> Bacall, 19, tawny and untamed. And Carmichael sitting at the upright, playing a guy named Cricket, with a match in his mouth, 45 or so, and catnip all the way home. No wonder Humphrey Bogart worried once he saw how seriously this novice was approaching the movie without ever losing his sultry cool: "Did you say something?" he asks, instead of signing away his soul, his songs and the mineral rights of Indiana just to look at her.

That was style, that was the jewelry of evocation, that was the rare and sublime completeness of lyrical mind, that was a hint of a harmony concealed, that was back at a period, to use a phrase of Ike Turner's, when "You can feel the real."

> Get in touch with that sundown fellow,
> as he tiptoes across the sand
> He's got a million kinds of stardust,
> Pick your fav'rite brand

goes the opening verse of the Johnny Mercer classic "Dream" (1944) written in the key of B-flat, it was made for the clarinet, which is how I always hear the song, but Betty Johnson had a beautiful version as of course did The Pied Pipers and Frank Sinatra

> Dream, when you're feelin' blue
> Dream, that's the thing to do
> Just watch the smoke rings rise in the air
> You'll find your share of memories there.

No wonder smoking was big in the 1940s. There is where your memories are, but there are where your memories go. It is bittersweet.

One of the most brilliant lyricists for me has always been Samuel ("Buck") Ram (an unlikely name, but the Good Lord, as the late Norman Mailer pointed out, is a great novelist) who was in real life also the manager-songwriter for The Platters. But he was a song-writer first. Ram wrote "The Magic Touch," the lyrics for "*Come Prima* (For the First Time)," "Twilight Time," "Remember When," and "Ring Telephone Ring," among others. He also wrote the lyrics to "The Great Pretender" in the washroom of the Flamingo Hotel in Las Vegas after being asked what The Platters follow-up to "Only You" would be. He was essentially a poet-musician who could put his words to music, although Nobel Prize-winning poet and essayist Joseph Brodsky thought to point out, "The poet is the last person to rejoice at his poems being set to music," explaining that the poet is "primarily concerned with linguistic meaning, and as a rule the reader does not master that all at once. When music is added on to the verse, then from the poetic standpoint, there is an additional obscuring. Generally speaking, music removes poetry to a completely different dimension." Buck who would not agree could write metaphors like nobody else, a Baroque master unique in rock literature: "When purple-colored curtains mark the end of day, I'll see you, my dear, at twilight time," and

> Deepening shadows gather splendor as day is done,
> Fingers of night will soon surrender the setting sun...

But what Buck Ram does that very few others do — Dylan Thomas in "Do Not Go Gentle" is another example that pops to mind — is to play, to pun, with the syntax of words. In Chomskian terms, he varies the deep structure of a syntactical element. In "Remember When," the title-tag introduces many of the lines:

> Remember when I first met you,
> My lips were so afraid to say, "I love you,"
> Remember when, to my surprise,
> The heaven in my heart leaped into your eyes.

However, look what happens to these words in the last stanza:

> I loved you then, and I still do,
> I can't remember when I didn't love you.

It is wonderful. The mood of the verb has changed from the imperative to indicative, further suspended by the negative of "can't" (What! After all this, there is something the speaker can't remember?) which is deliciously reversed by the second negative of "didn't." That is style with sass. Buck Ram knows how double negatives work.

He does another "deep structure shift" in his huge hit "Only You," where the title-tag is used as the grammatical subject in a number of different lines — "*Only you* can make this change in me," for example — but he brilliantly concludes by shifting the phrase, almost chiasmus-like, to a predicate nominative, as well as easing it into a cliché, thereby bringing the cliché back from the linguistic dead:

You're my dream come true, my one and *only you.*

Simple and unpretentious, yet done with artful grace and effortless magic, that is the way a song should unfold. But what about today?

One worries in this chancy age of planned obsolescence and throw-away deprecation of the state of our creative souls. "A man's obedience to his own genius is faith in its purest form," wrote Albert Camus in his brilliant essay, "Create Dangerously" in *Resistance, Rebellion, and Death.* Art is not a luxury but a necessity. That must be recognized with respect and due diligence, just as a creator must have faith in himself, the opposite of surrender — with no compromises. "This is why beauty, even today, cannot serve any party," as Camus adds. But we live in a timid, too often shoddy, frequently irresponsible, self-conscious, and unscrupulous age, where the artist, as many of these scrimp songs show, can become easily indifferent, hasty, and either ashamed of — or unfaithful to — himself and his dream. The contemporary sensibility is too often weak and indifferent which is why, laments Camus, "we have more journalists than creative writers, more boy-scouts of painting than Cézannes, and why sentimental tales or detective novels have taken the place of *War and Peace* or *The Charterhouse of Parma.*" What Camus finds even worse than weakness is, crucially, surrender — a refusal of the kind of bravery that in the face of complexity, creates. The exit is freedom of self. Is the sojourn difficult? It is. "Every wall is a door," said Emerson, however, pointing to the way out. If one has to go through that wall — and Camus prefers that to the door — do so. As he says, "Danger makes men classical, and all greatness, after all, is rooted in risk."

I realize this approach to pop music leaves me open to various charges, that I am breaking a butterfly upon a wheel, among them — that it is considered reductive to ask intelligence of, as well as snobbish to seek, altitude in popular music. That in this fallen world of ours, there can be found examples of a far richer and much more ample incompetence. I credential the truth of that as quickly as I concur. A requirement for emphatic assertion can make criticism seem harsh or caustic, furthermore. English, to be written well, declared T.S.

Eliot, needs writing with a certain *animosity*, where ideally the corrosives serve to cure, and so may it be with my criticism, for which I ask your forbearance. But there is already too much bad taste around, and from my end of things it seems definitely to be getting worse. Beyond that, as Bernard De Voto has penetratingly observed, "No manifestation of American life is trivial to the critic of culture." If we fail to see language as the crucial instrument of reason, as I have tried to show, we will only stand to inherit the many lunacies that oppose moral truth, right reason, and individual integrity which, when missing, as I say, leaves one not only defenseless against the verbal deceptions and moral turpitude of duplicitous manipulators and fools but in the end makes a ruin of our most precious dreams. Industry tampers with both nature and art — accepts *anything* — until one ends up, tragically, preferring prints to paintings, eating fast food instead of home-cooked meals, choosing chop-logic to truth, and aimlessly walking around department stores looking for something you want to need to buy rather than walking the Cape Cod dunes. If you think this is asking too much, so be it.

But since in his hunt for personal bliss I have mentioned Barthes' insistence that a given text desire *him*, let me align myself in this examination of the grammar of rock to the same kind of intense if ruthless skeptical scrutiny of art which he maintained by pointing out that this investigation is actually a kind of inverted love, a tough and demanding affection, in which one must necessarily kill what one dislikes in order to save what one idealizes. If it is true every exploration is an appropriation, every appropriation creates the deliberating requirement it be a value, not a fashion. I say it takes a concerned mind to make an analysis of the obvious, and ungrammaticalness, like the very word itself, while it is in fact grammatical, is nevertheless ugly. I promise you, mine is not a plea for the reductively doctrinal, merely an attempt to encourage a person, whenever possible, to dream, to dare, to take flight, to soar. It is to heed the wonderful final line of the Czech novelist Bohumil Hrabal's *The Little Town Where Time Stood Still*: "Up then towards that which as yet is not."

I have always loved the ancient hymn, "*Caelestis Urbs Jerusalem*" — it was originally composed by St. Ambrose, beginning "*Urbs Jerusalem beata*," then amended by Pope Urban VIII in 1629 with its present title — which describes a resplendent city built up "by living stones" where in heaven its glorious turrets shine, a place divine with iridescent walls of gold, brilliant to the eye and open to all aspirants who love Christ. The hymn reflects so perfectly the beauty of what is *made*, very like a poem. (The word poetry [*poien* in Greek] means "to make.") What I wish to note here is that the hymn stresses that the seat was built, shaped, fashioned, with each stone fitted to its purpose. Its fourth verse goes:

*Scalpri salubris ictibus, Et tunsione plurima,*
*Fabri polita malleo,*
*Hanc saxa molem construunt,*
*Aptisque iuncta nexibus*
*Locantur in fastigio*

The chisel's oft repeated stroke
urged by the mallet's pond'rous power
and fashioned, thus on high to tower,
and fitly shaped and firmly joined,
was all by skillful hands combined.

Just as the stones are selected, dressed, cut, hammered, and then polished by workmen, with each piece carefully placed in turn in its proper seat by the builder's precise calculations and then finally set in a frame and joined to be held fast forever, a song should be also so fashioned, as the Psalmist no doubt composed his music, plain in its glory, immortal in its sacredness. What we try to create may often fall short of our goal, but it is the striving that matters. What we seek we possess. The finding is in the seeking. James McNeill Whistler was right. An artist's career always begins tomorrow.

# Index

Alexander Theroux has taught at Harvard, MIT, Yale, and the University of Virginia, where he took his doctorate in 1968. A Fulbright, Gugenheim, and National Endowment of the Arts fellow, he is the author of four highly regarded novels — *Three Wogs* (1972), *Darconville's Cat* (1982), *An Adultery* (1987), and *Laura Warholic or The Sexual Intellectual* (2007) — and of several books of essays, fables, and poetry. His latest books from Fantagraphics are *The Strange Case of Edward Gorey* (2011), and *Estonia: A Ramble Through the Periphery* (2011). He lives in West Barnstable, Massachusetts with his wife, the artist Sarah Son.